Saloons, Prostitutes, and
Temperance in Alaska Territory

Saloons, Prostitutes, and Temperance in Alaska Territory

CATHERINE HOLDER SPUDE

UNIVERSITY OF OKLAHOMA PRESS : NORMAN

Also by Catherine Holder Spude
Sin and Grace: A Historical Novel of the Skagway, Alaska, Sporting Wars
   (Skagway, Alaska, 2006)
(co-ed.) *Eldorado!: The Archaeology of Gold Mining in the Far North*
   (Lincoln, Neb., 2011)
"That Fiend in Hell": Soapy Smith in Legend (Norman, Okla., 2012)

Publication of this book is made possible through the generosity of Edith Kinney Gaylord.

Library of Congress Cataloging-in-Publication Data

Spude, Catherine Holder.
   Saloons, prostitutes, and temperance in Alaska Territory / Catherine Holder
Spude.
      p.   cm.
   Includes bibliographical references and index.
   ISBN 978-0-8061-4660-7
   1. Bars (Drinking establishments)—Alaska—History. 2. Prostitutes—Alaska—
History. 3. Temperance—Alaska—History. I. Title.
   TX950.57.A4S68 2015
   647.95798—dc23

                                                                    2014028675

To Bob, whose early work in
Skagway set the standard

Contents

Contents

Illustrations

Figures

Maps

Tables

Tables

Preface

I began writing this book in 1983 when I was working as a historical archaeologist in Skagway, Alaska. My assignment was to dig a narrow trench from a National Park Service garage to the Peniel Mission, which was built in 1900 by a group of Evangelical Christian women who did not belong to any particular denomination. These missionaries placed their soup kitchen one block from the town's saloon district and two blocks from the "red light district." They entered the upstairs rooms of the saloons and dancehalls to talk to the "habitués," held daily spiritual meetings, served soup, and boasted that they occasionally saved wayward souls.

I was excavating the trench to discover if anything archaeologically significant would be destroyed by the construction of a water line, which the National Park Service (NPS) planned to install in this area. I found a trash dump dating to the gold rush days of 1897 to 1900, before the missionaries built their meeting house and residence. A layer of sheet trash generated by both the women in the mission and the occupants of a nearby house between 1901 and 1911 overlay the dump. My test excavations of this site, which we called the Mill Creek Dump, resulted in two summers' worth of further excavations that I supervised prior to the NPS replacing the old, rotting wood foundations under the Peniel Mission with sturdy, spread concrete footings.[1]

In the fall of 1983 I entered graduate school, where I obtained first my master's degree and then my PhD in anthropology with a specialty in archaeology. I chose as a dissertation topic the testing of a statistical method that would sort out mixed archaeological assemblages. This method gave me a way to estimate how much of the trash in the Mill Creek Dump came from Skagway's saloons and brothels and other businesses down the street, how much from local residences, and how much from the mission. It gave me a chance to summarize much of the archaeological work the NPS had done in Skagway over the previous decade, as well as a wealth of statistical data compiled by researchers focusing on western North America during the late nineteenth and early twentieth centuries.[2]

Thus was born my interest in prostitution, saloonism, gender, and reform. As I conducted the background research into the history of vice in Skagway, I found a traditional, but unsubstantiated, folklore, a rich collection of primary resources, and a body of secondary literature that was relevant on a broad scale but quite subjective when it came to the local area. One quickly written report had been prepared for the National Park Service by my future husband, Robert Spude.[3] He had collected a series of newspaper articles that suggested an interesting anecdotal history of female prostitutes denigrated by the newspaper editor and by the "respectable" working class people of the community. In the detailed census study I undertook for my dissertation, I was dismayed to discover that I could not find enumeration of the prostitutes, although I knew they had to have been there based on the newspaper anecdotes. Preliminary explorations of primary sources such as criminal records, deed records, and tax records did indicate that a healthy red light district thrived in Skagway, but public knowledge of it became increasingly suppressed as time passed. My statistical approach suggested that archaeological deposits above the Mill Creek Dump were generated by a mixture of both the missionaries and some prostitutes. My interest in determining exactly why the two groups mixed their trash was piqued, but in the process of finishing my doctoral dissertation, I had to put aside my quest to learn more about the interconnection between the prostitutes and the Christian missions in southeast Alaska.

In 1991, the NPS gave me the assignment of bringing together the notes of several researchers who had excavated and conducted archaeological studies at Skagway's Mascot Saloon and of integrating them with the town's well-recorded history. One missing portion of those studies was an in-depth contextual history of saloons in southeast Alaska. I began reading Skagway's newspapers published between 1897 and 1918 to fill that gap, which led to a more sophisticated study of

saloon culture between the town's founding and territorial prohibition.[4] I combined that research with a review of newspaper accounts
of the Skagway prostitutes and reform efforts, thus expanding on the
limited research I had started with my dissertation. In the process, I
discovered that the occupants of the house next door to the Peniel
Mission were indeed prostitutes. The finding vindicated my statistical study (see the discussion of Rose Arnold and Ruth Brown
in chapter 5).[5]

My initial readings soon expanded beyond the newspaper stories
into an extraordinary documentary record curated in Skagway's City
Hall and reproduced on microfilm at the Alaska State Archives. I
soon found it was possible to pull together the story of a community's
struggle with its moral conscience through the biographies of its citizens. As more and more information became available on the Internet,
through such services as Ancestry.com and GenealogyBank.com, I
discovered that it was possible to tell Skagway's vice and reform story
through the lives of the individuals who lived, worked, exploited, profited, used, benefited, or lost their fortunes in their interactions with
saloons, restricted districts, politics, and reform. I discovered that these
people were both men and women, and both middle and working
class. During the gold rush, the most powerful individuals were men.
In the end, the power structure shifted toward the women, both the
successful business entrepreneurs in the restricted district and the
determined working class social reformers of the Woman's Christian
Temperance Union (WCTU).

This book tells the story of the evolution of saloonism and prostitution in Skagway from the unregulated days of the Klondike gold rush,
when businessmen paid no fees or licenses, business-women paid
huge rents to male landlords, and men controlled the politics of Skagway, to the time of the walled-off Alaska Street restricted district,
owned by two women entrepreneurs, and the dominance of WCTU
women in the town's City Hall. Skagway once had eighty-nine saloons;
it ended its Progressive Era with four. This story comes alive through
the biographies of individual people—common prostitutes, madams,
saloonkeepers, gamblers, landlords, landladies, temperance leaders,
businessmen, politicians, and lawmen—all of whom had a deep, abiding
interest in vice, whether in its promotion or extinction, in Alaska's

First Judicial District. It is an extraordinary story because it happened
in an extraordinary place on one of America's last "frontiers," where
popular culture and mythology informs us that life was once free and
without restrictions. This was not so. But it was a place where men
and women struggled for decades to stand up for those values that
they believed were right.

———————

This book took more than thirty years to research and write. It has
evolved through more than a dozen drafts and been reviewed by twice
that many peer reviewers. There are a number of people I would like
to thank for helping me explore Skagway's underworld. Sandra Johnson at the Alaska Historical Collection of the Alaska State Library has
been extremely helpful with all of my requests for assistance. Tatyana
Stapanova of the Alaska State Archives readily hopped to when I showed
up in Juneau, dashing off at my every whim, making sure I got the
best price possible for copies of microfilm, and ensuring that I had an
exciting experience during some very dark winter hours. Likewise,
Tammy Carlisle and Susan Means at the National Archives in Anchorage rushed through my requests for file boxes and photocopies and
appeared to enjoy chatting with me about the fascinating cases I was
bringing to light. Judy Munns at the Skagway City Museum unearthed
some wonderful photographs and tidbits on city founders I had not
been able to dig up elsewhere. I thank them all.

As I neared the end of my Skagway research, I had the distinct
pleasure of working with my old mentor and friend, Ted Birkedal, and
new NPS colleagues Annaliese Jacobs Bateman and Rachel Mason,
all of whom worked on the written and oral histories connected with
the restricted district in Seward, Alaska. My new colleagues and I hit
it off immediately. They introduced me to Don Cowne, former Public
Health Investigator for the U.S. Public Health Service and the State
of Nevada. I am grateful to him for sharing some of his experiences
over thirty-one years with managing health and disease transmission
in prostitute populations in Nevada, Hawaii, and Alaska.

Bill Hunt, Frank Norris, Bob Spude, and Charlene Porsild read
varying versions of the draft manuscript. Bill, being an accomplished
author and former professor of history, taught me more than I ever

could have learned in a formal classroom setting. All four readers provided detailed comments and suggestions, not only on organization and content, but on writing style. I do not know what I would have done without them.

Doreen Cooper provided very insightful comment and corrected facts. Rogan Faith may or may not be related to one of Skagway's madams. Even if he is not, he helped when he could with enthusiasm. Karl Gurcke, as always, responded happily to my requests for photos and details about Skagway's history. Most of the other reviewers have remained anonymous, for which I am sorry, since I cannot thank them individually. Without them, I could not have pared down an unmanageable manuscript to the clean, coherent narrative I hope this book has become. I am particularly grateful to one anonymous reviewer. His or her comments were especially detailed and extremely constructive.

I am grateful to the descendants of some of the people who appear in this book, who opened their genealogy files, memories, and photograph albums to me. They include Susan Tanner Schimling, Renee Rowan, Phil Rathburn, Susan Roehr-Johnson, Marty Keller, and Rogan Faith.

I very much appreciate all the help I received from Alice Stanton, for her incredible copyediting, and Gerry Krieg, for redrafting my maps. I also extend admiration to the many staff members at the University of Oklahoma Press who do what they do so well. You all have made me look good.

Most of all, I thank my daughter Kinsey, who tolerated her mom's obsession with the work on this book and who has not once asked what a prostitute is. And my husband Bob? It goes without saying: I couldn't have done any of this without him.

Saloons, Prostitutes, and
Temperance in Alaska Territory

Introduction

"SCANT" screamed the headline. It was November 5, 1901, in Skagway, Alaska, and U.S. Marshal James M. Shoup was on his way to the federal courthouse at the east end of Seventh Avenue. The morning was cold and windy, but as he reached the corner of Broadway and Seventh Avenue, he "saw a sight that made him think he was in the South Sea Islands." The editor of the town's daily newspaper reported that "Pop Corn Kate" was taking the "Kneipp cure," a health treatment that involved wearing "only enough clothes to fill a thimble." U.S. Deputy Marshal John W. Snook and Skagway's jailer, Josias M. Tanner, managed to assist the woman into "more seasonable attire" before "giving her the box seat in an express wagon" and carting her off to jail, as Snook "blushed to his toes."[1]

According to U.S. Commissioner Charles A. Sehlbrede's journal entry for that date, a woman named Maggie Marshall was arraigned for indecent exposure, thus revealing the real name of Pop Corn Kate. He recorded that she refused to enter a plea and offered no defense for her crime.[2] She was probably drunk or under the influence of other drugs. At the time of her arrest, she stuck her hand through a windowpane, exclaiming, "My hands are aching with the cold, and if I put them through this window, the pane will be gone."[3] Her attire was perhaps another indication of her lack of sobriety, as it is difficult to believe that a Skagway morning in November could be anything but cold and windy. Pop Corn Kate's story, as elaborated in chapter 4, indicates that her habitation, arrest record, and flamboyant character typified the women who worked behind scarlet curtains in Skagway's Seventh Avenue restricted district.

Daily Alaskan editor John Troy enjoyed poking fun at Pop Corn Kate in the articles he wrote during 1900 and 1901. He portrayed her as a drunken floozy who disgraced Skagway with her presence. She did not appear in such a harsh light in the memoirs of Richard "Dixie" Anzer, who wrote about Kate more than sixty years later. Anzer recalls her as a "buxom, fun loving woman," who, like most of the harlots of the mythic West, underwent a classic transformation during that time. She became, in his telling, the golden-hearted madam.[4] All her sister prostitutes, however—with the exception of a few that went on to Dawson—were forgotten, and the significance of her life and that of those like her in Skagway faded.

Paradoxically, today's visitor to Skagway will encounter women wearing red satin dresses, black fishnet stockings, and feather boas at the Red Onion Saloon. They will hear stories about Denver's Mattie Silks, Dawson's Diamond Li'l Davenport, and Chicago's Little Egypt, all of whom visited Skagway during the gold rush. If they mention a Skagway prostitute, it will be Pop Corn Kate and none other. Why is that so? What is it about this working-class railroad town and seaport that generated such a ludicrous, brash, and yet pitiable woman of the scarlet cloth? And why were Skagway's other women of the sex industry removed from behind red curtains to be forgotten by modern storytellers? Where are Kitty Faith, Belle Schooler, Ida Freidinger, Essie Miller, Rosie Wagner, Frankie Belmont, and the more than 250 other women who inhabited Skagway's restricted district?

It is a complicated story, but it comes down to a clash between class and gender during the Progressive Era in Alaska Territory. During the first two decades of the twentieth century, vice and reform represented opposite sides of the same coin. One did not exist without the other, nor would women's suffrage have been enacted without that critical double-sided issue, morality and vice, to impel women to obtain the vote in the United States. Issues such as taxes, ownership of property, or the right to work did not drive women to seek the vote. What drove them more than anything was their passion for eliminating vice. Women were not able to convince the male electorate of America to grant them that right and privilege until the men embraced the moral issues of temperance, gambling, and prostitution. Middle-class husbands realized they could double their voting power in their political clash with unions and the working class by giving women the vote—but only if they closed down the saloons and banished the restricted districts.

In Skagway, Alaska, it appears that women's votes were bought at the cost of working men's pleasure. Can this be proven? There is a vast literature on the many interconnections between gender, class conflict, and vice. Most of it focuses on other communities, and this case study further contributes to it.[5] Not only did this conflict occur repeatedly in countless cities all over America, but, as this examination of Skagway indicates, it occurred in sparsely populated Alaska Territory, where class and gender were starkly divided. As will be shown through historical documents, the middle and working classes in southeast Alaska engaged in a class and gender war between 1897 and 1918, a war that culminated in women's suffrage, accompanied by the shutting down of gambling operations, saloons, and brothels. Middle-class married women gained political power while working-class bachelor men lost their most prized social institutions.

In addition to providing a historical account of the rise and fall of vice in Skagway, this book draws on anthropological and ethnographic findings to reveal new perspectives on class, gender, and reform in Alaska Territory. At the turn of the century, 96 percent of Skagway's population was of Euro-American heritage; more than 60 percent of the town's residents consisted of adult males, and of those men, more than 63 percent belonged to the working class. These latter two skewed statistics changed over the next twenty years, however, and the social changes that resulted are of interest not only to historians, but also to sociologists and anthropologists who study class and gender issues.

Perhaps of even greater interest is the concept of legislating morality. In the first two decades of the twentieth century, across the entire nation, middle-class women took issue with public drinking, the culture of men who gathered in saloons, and prostitution. Today, moral issues raised in political discussions include gay marriage and abortion rights. Then, like today, such issues were as much connected with beliefs about religion and morality as they were about the fundamental rights of an American. Because of the parallels between past and current conflicts over moral issues, it continues to be useful to revisit the ways that class, gender, and politics intertwined in the Progressive Era.

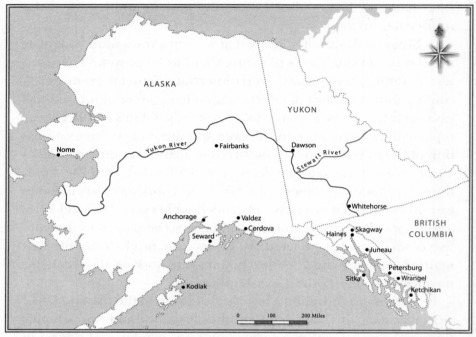

Map 1. Alaska and Yukon Territories in the early twentieth century. Map by Gerry Krieg. Copyright © 2015 by the University of Oklahoma Press.

Saloons, Prostitutes, and Temperance in Alaska Territory spotlights the case of Skagway, Alaska, to depict the struggle between married middle-class women and bachelor working-class men in a region where male-dominated boomtowns evolved into family-centered cities. Middle-class women organized to make the community a safe place for their children; working-class men organized to make the workplace safer and pay rates equitable. The two groups clashed in the arena of saloons and the restricted district, where their value systems found no common ground. The power brokers—the middle-class merchants—eventually took the side of their wives, gave them the power to vote, and, in the process, banned gambling, prostitution, and saloons from the farthest reaches of the American West, where, ironically, the traditions of popular culture and mythology boasted of personal freedoms. This book, in the process of discussing that transition, exposes the mythology of the western frontier.

Skagway lies ninety miles north of Juneau, Alaska's capital. It was settled by about two hundred merchants in August 1897 at the beginning of the Klondike gold rush as a port of entry to the headwaters of the Yukon River. These people and the laborers who worked for them decided to stay at tidewater rather than push on to Yukon Territory (map 1). It huddles at tidelands below coastal mountains that tower up to six thousand feet above the town. The Skagway River plain is only about half a mile wide at its mouth, and the city stretches more than one and a third miles away from the tidewater. A deep harbor accommodated steamships during the 1897–1901 Klondike gold rush, and today as many as four luxury cruise ships may dock at one time. The town, which came to fruition in roughly a month's time, became the headquarters of the White Pass and Yukon Route railroad (WP&YR) by the middle of 1898. This railroad was a subsidiary of a British-Canadian transportation company that also ran steamships on the Yukon River. Between 1898 and about 1985, the town consisted of two sectors: middle-class merchants who catered to the town's citizenry and to people going in and out of the Yukon, and working-class employees of the railroad and shipping companies.

In the first five years after Skagway's incorporation, middle-class businessmen and managers of the White Pass and Yukon Route railroad governed the city's largely working-class male population. This government not only tolerated, but indeed welcomed the institutions of prostitution and gambling. Paradoxically, the attitude did not change substantially until a saloon keeper named Chris Shea organized the working-class voters by forming a Labor Ticket for local elections, which succeeded in taking over City Hall. At that point, the middle-class businessmen re-evaluated their approach to Progressive-Era reforms, espoused a wider range of issues, including moral reforms, and succeeded in driving the saloon man and his working-class constituency from city government. In the process, they helped their middle-class wives achieve the moral reforms that had been the goal of the Woman's Christian Temperance Union (WCTU) as early as the gold rush days: eliminate the saloons, gambling, and prostitution. By teaming a class issue (labor) with a gender issue (moral reform), the middle-class husbands and wives of Skagway joined forces to control the social behavior of the working-class bachelors, so that the latter would not despoil their virgin daughters or influence the morals of their sons. While the motives of husbands and wives might not have been the same, the results coincided: no more saloons and no more restricted district.

Skagway, Alaska, was the largest community in the First Judicial District of Alaska in the two decades between 1897 and 1918. Although not the capital of Alaska, it hosted the district court at least once a year, sometimes twice. The *Daily Alaskan*, Skagway's newspaper, published continuously during this time period, a record that not one of the newspapers in the capital city, Juneau, can boast. Skagway's population rivaled and often exceeded Juneau's. Unlike Juneau's newspapers, the *Daily Alaskan* usually reported news about problems with vice in other cities of the First District (usually in an effort to favorably compare its city to others); unlike other cities, Skagway has retained its city's criminal, deed, and tax records, which can then serve as useful sources for comparison and contrast to newspaper reports. Vice, while not always reported in the newspapers, is well-documented in city records.

Skagway's various historical records also offer a rich trove of information about the role of social classes in a burgeoning western town. What then is class, and how is it defined for this study? Americans, as early as the 1830s, when the middle and working classes first emerged in early-industrial-era New England, defined class in terms of values instead of economics, and responded to the emerging schism by turning to religion. The middle class combated the working class's indulgence in alcohol, its spontaneous holidays, and its irregular work hours with temperance societies, Sunday schools, and church revivals. Business owners, some of whom were employers, believed that industrialization and regimentation "civilized" the barbarous working classes by imposing discipline on them.

Historian Paul E. Johnson defined emerging middle-class values in his landmark study *A Shopkeeper's Millennium*, first published in 1978. His thorough and learned use of statistics to compare class, religious affiliation, and views on temperance between 1827 and 1837 in the pre-industrial town of Rochester, New York, indicated that over the course of ten years, from 1825 to 1835, the merchants of that community began attending church twice a week, eschewed liquor, worked regular, steady hours, forced their employees to do the same (or lose their jobs), and proselytized their beliefs. Over that same decade, the citizens of Rochester transformed themselves from a kin-oriented society where employees lived with and were controlled by their craft-masters, whose families imposed moral restraint, into a more open community in which nuclear families lived in neighborhoods of similar class. This division of community reinforced shared values within each class; in the middle class, evangelical Protestantism prospered.[6]

The Progressives of the early twentieth century wished to transform the United States into a safe, wholesome, and prosperous place for all Americans, but this desire created a conflict between the middle and working classes. The middle class that grew out of the early nineteenth-century pre-industrial society sought to expand its wealth and political influence. Members of this class accumulated and displayed their increasing wealth, promoted individualism, delayed marriage, pursued education beyond primary school, kept their daughters at home or, conversely, offered them greater opportunities for education. In contrast, working-class members, with their low wages and unskilled labor and apprenticeships, valued cooperative behavior and conformism, splurged when they had the chance (often on pleasurable pursuits), and married their daughters off early or sent them off to work at a young age. What a working-class man viewed as "not being a show-off," a middle-class man saw as lack of ambition. The middle-class business-man and his wife interpreted the licentious saloons and brothels as a waste of good money that should be saved for hard times. The laborer knew them only as collective gathering places and just rewards for his mindless yet strenuous work.[7]

A number of social historians have embraced and developed this concept of class distinctions. These historians and other scholars view the middle class at the turn of the century as trying to emulate the upper class in terms of wealth acquisition but eschewing the tendency of upper-class men to ostentatiously imbibe fine liquors and keep mistresses. Bringing a double standard to their moral sensibility, the middle class held a stricter standard for its women but a somewhat looser one for its men, and defined "manliness" in terms of economic success and control of temperament.[8] They owned businesses that

employed workers or worked in white-collar jobs, management positions, professions, and in a number of occupations that required a
formal education.

The working class, on the other hand, tended to be (but were not
always) wage-laborers, factory workers, and others whose labor and
skills could be learned on the job rather than in school. Their primary strength tended to be in numbers, so they were most effective
when they worked together, not individually. They came to view communal action and community spirit as prized values, which could
take the form of devotion to a given saloon, sports team, neighborhood,
or union. Fighting for "the team" was "manly" in the working-class
value system.[9]

Social historian David Charles Beyreis specifically addresses the
notion of middle-class masculinity at the time of the Klondike gold
rush. In his thesis entitled "Middle Class Masculinity," he notes that
the seemingly contradictory ideal of a loving and nurturing bread-
winner who was also a physically fit specimen became achievable in
the perceived notion that the Klondike region was an untamed wilderness.[10] The emerging ideal of "vigorous masculinity" allowed middle
class men to unleash their "primitive" or "natural beings" and find
renewal through physical labor and "roughing it" in the wilds. When
gold was discovered in the Klondike, those men who had subscribed
to the romantic view of the vanishing frontier, as Frederick Jackson Turner would later define it in his renowned 1893 thesis, had a
renewed opportunity to prove themselves as vigorous men. Not only
that, but many believed that "those standing at the pinnacle of Anglo-
Saxon manhood" had the best opportunity at distinguishing themselves and becoming rich in the goldfields.[11] The ideal, then, for the
middle-class male, was a physically fit, patient, hardworking Anglo-
Saxon, who, incidentally, was a faithful domestic partner to his wife, as
well as a good father. Beyreis termed the combination of these ideals
"virtuous masculinity."[12]

The consequence of this dual ideal meant that while the middle-class
man did not eschew the saloons, gambling parlors, and opera houses
of the far north when he lived away from his female relatives, he most
certainly did so when his family joined him; when they arrived, he stayed
at home and avoided those places of iniquity. As the demographics

of Alaska changed, with middle-class men moving their wives and children to the north but working-class men continuing to remain bachelors, the tolerance for vice changed.

Of course, the crossover between the two classes was fluid; it was not an unbreakable boundary. The statistical data for this region in particular reveals a large middle ground with a fuzzy area at the borders. The definition, therefore, of class in this study is not the same as a modern dictionary would define the terms "middle class" and "working class," which emphasize income level more than other factors. Nineteenth- and early twentieth-century notions of class relied more heavily on social prestige and the education level required for qualification for a certain job than on the amount of pay received. Middle-class occupations included private businessmen, supervisory positions (above foremen) in corporations, clerks, professionals whose status required an advanced education, and entertainers. Working-class positions included laborers (both skilled and unskilled), farmers or farmhands, and service-industry employees. A saloon keeper, therefore, would be considered middle-class, but his bartender and gamblers, as service providers, would be working-class. According to this same definition of class, a railroad blacksmith, while a skilled craftsman, was a member of the working class, even though he might make considerably more money than his middle-class, railroad clerk neighbor. (See appendix A, which provides a sample listing of the occupations from the 1900, 1910, and 1920 censuses, and how they are categorized as middle- or working-class in the context of this book. Appendix A also provides a more detailed analysis of gender, class, and marital status during each of those time periods.)

In his book *Class and Gender Politics in Progressive-Era Seattle,* John C. Putman offers a social analysis of Seattle during the early twentieth century that is particularly relevant to the case of Skagway, given that so many people living in Skagway originally came from Seattle.[13] This becomes apparent in the answers to one of the questions asked on the 1900 census: what place do you call "home"? Ninety-three percent of people living in Skagway replied that they were from an American city, and of those, the single largest amount, 28 percent, were from Seattle, followed by Portland, Oregon, at 10 percent, and San Francisco, California, at 6 percent.

Putman observes that one of the principal arguments for women's suffrage in Seattle during the Progressive Era was the concept of "municipal housecleaning," the idea that with women's votes, the reform of vice would follow. Women were deemed to have those special traits necessary to cleanse the city of crime, filth, immorality, and political corruption. Because Seattle was thought to have one of the highest rates of "white slavery" in the country in the late 1890s, middle-class women called for the vote in order to "clean house" and save the morality of their city's daughters.[14]

Putman further demonstrates that it was "during the 1910s [that] growing class conflicts in Seattle increasingly provoked different political responses as gender and class identities were recalibrated to fit the changing social and economic environment." He states that "these complex relations and political coalitions are what define progressivism in the United States."[15]

One of the pressing political issues of this era was the growth of unions. Upper- and middle-class women could not condone organized union activity, especially when it was violent. This put a rift between another group of women, with feminist leanings, who advocated for social reforms and the rights of laborers. The tenuous alliance between unionizers and feminists that developed during the fight for suffrage was weak, however, and dissolved shortly after women were enfranchised in Seattle. When the vote for Prohibition was put before Seattle voters in 1914, feminist women and labor unionizers abandoned their temporary alliance. While middle-class women voted for Prohibition, working-class men voted against it. Women also voted against the enforcement of an eight-hour work day, and labor activists lost both measures as a result.[16]

Religious affiliation was another important aspect of class identity. Paul E. Johnson has made a substantial contribution to the understanding of how religion and politics intersected in the early American republic through his use of statistics to compare class, religious affiliation, and views on temperance between 1827 and 1837 in the preindustrial town of Rochester, New York. This study led others to conclude that religious affiliation more than social class explains political decisions. Yet according to Johnson, that was not the case. He asserted instead, "It seems unwise to treat religion and class as separate and competing categories of explanation" when attempting to understand the factors that influence political behavior. He preferred instead "to define how they made each other in history."[17] His study is particularly pertinent to the case of Skagway, in that the primary political issue of concern in both 1825–1835 Rochester and early twentieth-century Skagway was temperance.

Differing perceptions on the role of vice in society also contrasted sharply between the two classes. To understand this difference, it is necessary to understand the literature on vice, which is abundant and varied, particularly when considering the place of prostitution. While early literature focused on popular biographies of madams written by journalists who intended to titillate their audiences and who perpetuated the myth of the golden-hearted madam, scholarly studies that began in the wake of women's studies began to consider the true social role and culture of these entrepreneurs. Anne M. Butler's comprehensive description of the institution in western communities and Marion S. Goldman's sociological analysis of prostitution in Comstock Lode, Nevada, communities established important precedents for scholarly study. Ruth Rosen followed with a treatise on the effect of the women's reform movement on prostitution in the United States.[18] While southeast Alaska has been ignored in scholarly literature about vice, the more northern cities of Dawson and Fairbanks have received substantial attention from scholars in this field of study.[19]

Other important models for the understanding of gender and vice come from analyses of western communities associated with mining. Skagway, which functioned as a company town for the WP&YR, was very similar in social structure to Butte, Montana, which was a company town controlled by the Anaconda Copper Mining Company.[20] Case studies of both Butte and Helena, Montana, document the intersection between local economy, prostitutes, and politics. In Helena, prostitution changed from a major institution in the city's life and economy to a disrespectable, dingy, backwater district frequented by the working class. As prostitution became more regulated and controlled by the law, it became less controlled by the women who had formerly run their own businesses. As the institution was pushed underground, the pimps, johns, and other middlemen made more of the money, and madams faded into obscurity.[21]

Authentic biographies of prostitutes are hard to find, but the autobiography of Madeline Blaire, a middle-class madam in Montana in the 1880s and 1890s, and the edited letters of Maimie Pinzer, a young Jewish prostitute in Boston between 1910 and 1912, provide useful insight into the psychology of the working-class prostitute. Another important first-person account is that of Josie Washburn, who lived and worked for twenty years in brothels and cribs in the Nebraska cities of Omaha and Lincoln. Her autobiography helps the reader understand that prostitution was an institution with tentacles so interwoven through local economies and politics that reformers had little chance of succeeding in ending the institution on the basis of arguments about morality alone.[22]

Most of the available descriptions and analyses of prostitutes, as summarized in the previous few paragraphs, have focused on personal accounts of the women who engaged in the profession. These narratives have proved to be an effective way of communicating the social hierarchy, living conditions, and reasons that women engaged in the business of selling sex. This book mirrors that approach with a special chapter devoted to the biographies of several women who engaged in the trade in Skagway. The personal accounts in chapter 4 are arranged to display not only the social ranking of the prostitutes but also how their status changed during the important period immediately following the establishment of the restricted district. By tracing these broader developments, this chapter sets the stories of these individual women within the context of the useful body of literature that has preceded this book.

In addition to such personal accounts, the material culture—the location, architecture, and artifacts—of restricted districts in other western mining towns and brothel museums will cast light on the practices and social hierarchy of prostitution in Skagway. Literature that follows this same approach for examining prostitution in western American history includes Alexy Simmons's study of Jacksonville, Oregon (1852–1890), Silver City, Idaho (1863–1910), and Virginia City, Nevada (1859–1880). Her analysis includes a settlement model of how prostitutes were spread throughout a community.[23] Allan Bird describes details about the architecture of the "bordello" structures in the restricted districts of Silverton, Colorado.[24] Historical archaeologists examined the artifacts of prostitution in 2005 with a special publication of the journal *Historical Archaeology*, entitled *Sin City*, a compilation of seven studies on the excavations of archaeological sites of brothels and restricted districts, including one article by this author that compares the artifact assemblages of brothels to those of saloons. Scholars have applauded the growth of interest in this subject and its development from curiosity about scandalous women to a mature interest in class and gender in understudied populations.[25]

While the literature on prostitution is voluminous, the literature on liquor consumption and gambling is more scant—and less rich in content. The first efforts by historians to study these subjects seem irreverent, but they have become more sophisticated in recent years, as scholars are now placing the consumption of alcohol and its detrimental effects on society within a broader social context.[26] At the same time, other scholars have explored the effects of the Prohibition movement on social change. In particular, Jack S. Blocker defines five cycles of reform, in which the women's movement and Progressive reforms were only the third and fourth. Both Norman H. Clark and James H. Timberlake point out the relationship between middle-class women's desire to maintain the morality of the home and to legislate morality during their successful efforts to enact Prohibition. Certainly Paul E. Johnson's landmark study on the interrelationship between religious groups and politics in pre-industrial Rochester, New York, set the standard for later understanding of how class and value systems affected the legislation of vice.[27]

More recent studies of liquor consumption in American history include Perry R. Duis's *The Saloon*, which describes public drinking in the urban areas of Chicago and Boston in the four decades between 1880 and 1920. Focusing on a similar time period, Thomas J. Noel, in his *The City and the Saloon*, analyzes the drinking culture in Denver between 1858 and 1916. Together these two books provide highly useful information about saloons in urban areas before Prohibition. Yet both authors make the mistake of calculating the number of saloons per capita population instead of looking only at the number of adult males, as Johnson did in 1978. As will be noted later, Noel mistook the number of saloons in Denver, with the city's high male-to-female ratio, as being higher than that of eastern cities of the time. As women and children were not customers of saloons, overall populations should never be used in calculating how much the men of a given region patronized their saloons.[28]

The latest, and perhaps most pertinent word on the subject of saloons is that of Madelon Powers in her book, *Faces along the Bar*. She describes rituals and manners in working-class saloons of the United States between 1870 and 1920, and her observations are the source of much material relevant to saloon culture in this book. She amplifies an early and often-referenced study conducted by John M. Kingsdale entitled "The 'Poor Man's Club.'"[29]

The subject of gambling has been poorly studied in comparison to prostitution and prohibition. Political scientist James A. Morone, in *Hellfire Nation*, considered the reform of gambling as part of the larger efforts of Progressives. However, no one has addressed gambling as a vice in the same depth as have scholars studying prostitution and saloons. The biography of Malinda Jenkins, a woman who married a gambler and lived for some time in Dawson, sheds some light on the life of a gambler from an anecdotal viewpoint. Ann Fabian's *Card Sharps and Bucket Shops* describes the ploys of nineteenth-century gamblers. Jeff Smith's *Alias Soapy Smith* is a detailed account of con man and gambler Jefferson Randolph Smith, who spent a few months in Skagway, but much of his actual life has been greatly confused with the legend of his life. In my own *"That Fiend in Hell"*, I attempt to banish much of the legend, but that work is not specifically focused on the world of gambling. And despite the title of her book about community in the Klondike, Charlene Porsild's *Gamblers and Dreamers* is more about the social world of Dawson and about gambling as an aspect of mining than it is about gambling in saloons.[30]

To rectify this gap in our understanding of gambling during the Progressive and Prohibition Eras, I define gambling in these pages as a part of "saloonism." The word "saloonism" is borrowed from tracts written by Prohibitionists during the early twentieth century. In using this term, Prohibitionists were referring to the practice of going to, drinking in, socializing in, and participating in all of the activities

associated with a saloon. Besides the drinking of alcohol, these activities included gambling, the smoking of tobacco, politicking, telling
lewd jokes, and socializing in a public, male-only domain. If women
were present in such a setting, they were viewed as disrespectable,
probably harlots, and contributors to the general immorality of the
setting. By "saloonism," the Progressives simply meant the culture of
the saloon.[31]

On a broader level, the analysis of middle-class women and their
efforts at reform, especially during the Progressive Era, is the subject
of entire classes in gender study programs. One of the earliest studies
of middle-class women and reform is Ruth Bordin's landmark work
Woman and Temperance, in which she articulates how the work of the
WCTU led to the emergence of women as a political power in the
United States. Jean M. Ward and Elaine A. Maveety's compilations of
writings about Pacific Northwest women between 1815 and 1925
highlight contributions middle-class women made toward social and
political reforms in that region. Similarly, Phyllis Demuth Movius's
collection of essays on the women of Fairbanks introduces the reader
to Alaskan women who were active in the WCTU, such as Jesse Spiro
Bloom and Sarah Margaret Keenan. A particularly significant work is
Sandra Haarsager's *Organized Womanhood*, which discusses the intersection between middle-class women's club organizations and politics
in the Pacific Northwest during the Progressive Era. James Morone's
discussion in *Hellfire Nation* of women's involvement in reforming vice
of all kinds during the Progressive Era is critical to understanding
how the middle class legislated their concepts of morality.[32]

Class and gender did not constitute the only variables that accounted
for conflicting views on vice in the Progressive Era. What makes the
people of Skagway, Alaska, and its neighboring communities such an
ideal subject for the examination of class and gender is its lack of
racial and ethnic diversity during that time period. A mythic tradition of ethnic and racial equality in western North America mirrored
the myth of opportunity and equality for all in America; however, this
promise of opportunity in Alaska far exceeded its reality. Terrance
Cole, in an essay on Jim Crow laws in Alaska, demonstrates that there
were so few African Americans, Hispanics, and Asians in the territory
that the perception of racial equality could be touted, but in practice

the people of Anglo-Saxon heritage discriminated freely and with impunity against Native Alaskans. Few people of African American descent stayed in Alaska after being discharged from the military or large companies; the Chinese were so badly proscribed in the late nineteenth and early twentieth centuries that few Chinese American communities exist in Alaska even today; and the Japanese suffered extensive discrimination. Native Alaskans achieved equality under the law with the passage of the Alaska Equal Rights Act of 1945, but it took quite a bit of doing.[33] During the Klondike gold rush and Progressive Era, more than 94 percent of Skagway's citizens were Euro-American. As a result, race simply was not a significant variable in determining class.

Perhaps one factor that contributed to the lack of racial diversity in Skagway was that those traveling to the far north needed a fair amount of money even to attempt the trip. Diaries and personal correspondence indicate that undertaking the journey to Skagway was expensive; it could not be attempted by people without some cash reserves. Kirke E. Johnson, a surveyor, wrote home to his mother in Fon-du-lac, Wisconsin, in March 1898, that "it would be foolish for a man to start from home with less than $600.00, as the Mounted Police won't let a man by with less than 1100 lbs. of grub. The duty on that and the rest of his outfit will be about $35.00. Add to that and the cost of it, $100.00 for packing over or paying about $125.00 for a horse." In today's currency, that $600 would be the equivalent of more than $16,000.[34] In addition, outfitters and publishers of guidebooks written in 1897 failed to account for the fact that the Klondike was in Canada, not the United States, and did not make the costs of duty well known to the general traveler. Men who got as far as Skagway often found themselves unable to pay the duty or come up with the necessary amount of goods required by the Canadians at the border, so they ended up staying at tidewater. If middle class, they invested in real estate or started a business; if working class, they obtained jobs working for the railroad, one of the four wharf companies, or in the service sector.

During the height of the gold rush—the winter of 1897–1898—the population of Skagway was estimated at 7,000 to 8,000 people, with a thousand more ferrying their goods between tidewater and the summit of White Pass.[35] By the time the United States census was taken in the year 1900, that population of the city itself had dropped to 2,383 people. All but 4 percent were Caucasian; the remainder consisted of Tlingit, Japanese, two African Americans, and four people of mixed race. These figures confirm that the community was not racially or ethnically diverse. Indeed, three quarters of the residents in 1900 were born in the United States, less than an eighth in Western Europe, and one sixteenth in Canada. That means that only a sixteenth of Skagway's residents were not Anglo-Saxons, western Europeans, or North Americans of that western European heritage. The city's ethnic mix would remain about the same as time passed. By 1920, 93 percent of Skagwayans were Euro-American, while only 3 percent were Tlingit and 3 percent of mixed race. One Chinese, one Japanese, one Fili-pino, and one African American lived in the town. The only "ethnic" group that changed significantly during that time was the Canadians, who rose to about 10 percent. This was no doubt due to the presence of the Canadian-owned White Pass and Yukon Route railroad, the town's major employer. (A more detailed discussion of the age, gender, and ethnicity of Skagway's population appears in appendix A.)[36]

Only about a fifth of the people in Skagway in 1900 were below fifteen years of age, compared to more than a third in the country as a whole.[37] This indicates that there were not as many families with children in this Alaska port as in the rest of the United States. While the percentage of children would climb to more than a quarter of the 870 people in 1910, by 1920, it was still only at 30 percent rather than the national average of 36 percent.

In both the middle and working classes, men outnumbered women in 1900, 1910, and 1920. There were more than three men for every woman in 1900, five single men for every single woman, and almost twice as many married men as married women. By 1910, the statistics had not changed all that drastically. Men still outnumbered women two to one; single men outnumbered single women three to one; and married men and women were only just becoming even in number. Even by 1920, there would still be a preponderance of men in the community (60 percent).

As the gold rush waned at the turn of the century, about a third of the middle-class men were married and living with their wives, but only about a fifth of the working-class men were in the same domestic situation. As shown in table 1, ten years later, more than half of the middle-class men were living with their wives, and this proportion increased to two-thirds of all middle-class men by 1920. However, by that time, only a third of working-class men in Skagway lived with wives. These statistics suggest that these working-class men were less likely to marry and live with their wives. These statistics may also reflect the fact that in territorial Alaska, working-class jobs were unreliable and boom towns created unstable economic conditions. Middle-class men, whose options for obtaining stable work might have been better, were more likely to bring their families with them than were working-class men. The presence of wives is an indicator of the degree to which men engaged, or did not engage, in such masculine vices as hiring prostitutes and enjoying the camaraderie of the saloon. (See appendix A for a more detailed analysis of these data.)

Skagway evolved from a boomtown in the center of the national stage at the turn of the twentieth century to a railroad town and port city that serviced the mining and mineral hinterland of Alaska and the Yukon Territory for more than eight decades. The way its citizenry adapted to its changing social and economic conditions, particularly vis á vis the needs of its bachelor population, makes a fascinating story. When examined in the light of the typical class and gender conflicts of the Progressive Era, the story of the conflict over Skagway's prostitutes and saloons becomes a revealing case study that shows how the interaction of personality, class, and gender created a dynamic political scene during this time period.

Today, Skagway's tourism promoters downplay the town's working-class heritage in order to emphasize its gold rush history. Yet the third- and fourth-generation families who can trace their roots back to the gold rush days inevitably have railroad and wharf workers on the family tree. Most Skagwayans are extremely proud of their working-class ancestors, and rightly so. The workers of the White Pass and Yukon Route kept alive a vital northern transportation link for eighty years.

Skagway's working-class history—what happened after the gold rush boom left the city behind—has not been studied in any serious way. However, the wealth of solid historical documentation curated by a community proud of its history cannot be understated. The records of Skagway as a typical working-class railroad town struggling with

TABLE 1
Social classes of men living with wives in 1900, 1910, and 1920

	1900	1910	1920
All men who were middle class	34%	35%	45%
All men who were working class	66%	65%	55%
Middle-class men living with wives	34%	56%	68%
Working-class men living with wives	19%	31%	31%
Total men in Skagway	1,336	324	195

Source: 1900, 1910, and 1920 federal censuses for Skagway, Alaska.

many of the same issues facing all of America during the Progressive Era have been virtually ignored because of the emphasis placed by tourism promoters and historians on the nationally significant gold rush period. This study is only one of many that can address that slight.

Aside from its spectacular setting among towering peaks and a rather flamboyant start in life, Skagway's morality story is hardly different from that of most working-class towns in America during the early twentieth century. The history of saloonism, gambling, and prostitution in Skagway provides an intriguing opportunity to understand more deeply the shift in political power as an outcome of gender and class struggles in a working-class community during the Progressive Era.

CHAPTER ONE

Hell on Earth, 1897–1898

"Gold!" In late July 1897, the word shook the global economy, which was just then emerging from an economic depression. Americans, Canadians, and western Europeans flocked to the northern Canadian wilderness, where prospectors had discovered the gold. To get there, the voyagers would have to pass through a small stretch of American soil along the panhandle of Alaska, a journey that would take them well into the early winter months of 1898. Alternatively, they could wait and float up the Yukon River when the ice broke the following April or May. But who wanted to wait that long?

Gold drew men by the tens of thousands, men who wanted to move quickly and not be hampered by their womenfolk, most of whom inevitably brought along children. But men in those days had a hard time taking on a woman's role. Cooking, cleaning, sewing: those were all chores better left to women. Yes, women did go to the Klondike, not to mine the gold but to "mine the miners," by charging for services that capitalized on their familiar roles as established by the culture of the late Victorian Era. They set up restaurants, laundries, and, indeed, brothels, to cater to the needs that men looked toward women to meet.[1]

And Skagway, Alaska, although located more than five hundred miles from the goldfields, boomed along with Dawson, its sister city at the other end of the transportation network that started at tidewater and ended at the Klondike River.

Superintendent Samuel B. Steele of the Northwest Mounted Police, who described Skagway as "little better than hell on earth," had few kind words to say about Skagway in February 1898.[2] Charged with helping to regulate the sudden stream of eager migrants, he viewed his assignment to the Klondike gold rush with dismay, and Skagway met his low expectations. People from all over the world poured through Skagway's streets, up the Brackett wagon road, and over White Pass with its dead and dying packhorses littering the canyon below. The travelers were on their way to the land where, in the words of Klondike historian Pierre Berton, the gold lay "thick between the flaky slabs of rock like cheese from a sandwich."[3] These people, mostly young men in their twenties and thirties, after suffering from the silver crash of 1893, knew their luck was about to change. Yet the boisterous rowdiness of would-be miners celebrating their future wealth held little appeal for Sam Steele, the staid bastion of law and order in Canada's far northwest.

Only the latest in a long series of gold rushes that had started in 1849, this one to the Klondike began innocuously enough on August 16, 1896. George Carmacks and his Tagish brothers-in-law, Skookum Jim Mason, and Dawson Charlie,[4] acting on a tip from fellow prospector George Henderson, found rich pannings on Rabbit Creek, a tributary of the Klondike River. Within weeks, the creek was renamed Bonanza, and the nomadic prospectors, scattered across hundreds of miles of Alaskan, Yukon, and British Columbian wilderness, converged on the tributaries of the Klondike, staked their claims and began to sink their adits. Throughout the winter of 1896–1897, these furred and bearded hermits denuded the drainage slopes to stoke the fires that thawed the frozen gravels under the flickering northern lights, waiting for wash-up in the spring.

Those that decided to take their gold south the following summer arrived in San Francisco on July 14, 1897, almost eleven months after the first strike. With the spectacular docking of the S.S. *Excelsior*, the rest of the world heard of the fabulous Klondike riches. Two days later the S.S. *Portland* arrived in Seattle, with a reported "ton of gold" in its hold. The rush to the Klondike was on—regardless of the fact that almost every available claim had already been staked by people already in the North Country when the gold was first discovered.

"Gold." The very word was magic. North America was still wallowing in a depression that started with the silver collapse of 1893. Gold would pull the country out of its fiscal troubles. Gold would cure Americans of their economic woes. The Klondike was the place to go! More than a 100,000 people—mostly men[5]—borrowed the money they needed from families and friends to purchase a grubstake and ticket on anything that would float to get them at least as far as Skagway or Dyea, newly hatched Alaskan tent cities surrounding trading posts at the foot of two passes leading into the Far North. While the weather was still warm, those with more money could take a steamer all the way around the Alaska Peninsula to St. Michael and up the Yukon River to Dawson, another rough town of tents and knocked-together, unpainted buildings with false fronts. And once the river froze up in October, Skagway and Dyea were the only entrepôts to the Klondike.

Only five miles apart by sea and just a bit farther by road, these two trading posts quickly turned into staging areas for parties packing their gear for travel over the mountains. The Chilkoot Pass rose above Dyea. Used by innumerable generations of Chilkoot Indians to access trade partners in the interior, it was a well-established route but inaccessible to draft animals at the summit. People who could not afford to hire Chilkoot packers often spent weeks carrying their supplies from Dyea to Lake Bennett, a thirty-five-mile hike, before they could build a boat or raft that would take them down the lakes and streams to the Yukon River, and, finally, Dawson.

Skagway lay at tidewater, caught in a narrow valley between three-thousand-foot peaks. With a view toward building a pack trail, Captain William Moore and Tlingit Skookum Jim explored the somewhat lower White Pass, which promised an alternative to the Chilkoot Pass. Moore built a wharf in Skagway Bay in 1896, envisioning the day when gold would be found in the North. But the trail he laid out was not really built so much as trampled, and, once the rush began, so many animals died that it became known as the "Dead Horse Trail."

The first stampeders who came to the Moore's town site called it "Skaguay," a corruption of a Tlingit word meaning "wrinkled water" or "north wind," depending on the source. It is likely that the original word carried both meanings, as the notorious wind often causes rough water in Skagway's bay. The U.S. Post Office gave the town's name its modern spelling on November 13, 1897, but a number of writers, including the editor of the town's first daily newspaper, the *Skaguay News*, continued to use the older spelling until almost 1899.[6]

And how did Skagway appear to those people who first saw the town in the fall and winter of 1897? Tappan Adney, reporter for *Harper's Weekly*, described the scene he found on August 20.

> Rough frame buildings are going up as quickly as men can handle scantling, and as fast as they are finished they are turned into stores or warehouses. There are three or four hotels or restaurants; and a United States flag flying over a tent is evidence of the presence of a United States Court Commissioner—the only representative of the government here, save that organized by the miners themselves. A large painted cloth sign indicates the location of the correspondents of enterprising newspapers, and the half-dozen newspaper men here gave us a hearty welcome. Men and horses are traveling to and fro in a never-ending stream.[7]

Among the very first businesses opening in August 1897 was the Pack Train Saloon, at the tree line to the north of the original cabin and residence built by William Moore's son, Bernard. It is a good example of the earliest type of saloon: a large canvas tent with the name painted on the sides. Even those businesses that were built outside of the sheltering trees were located very close to the tree line, near what would become Sixth Avenue.

By late 1897, the people rushing to the Klondike off-loaded at Moore's Wharf, set up their tents above the high tide line indicated by the cut bank in the vicinity of Fourth or Fifth Avenue, then wandered up the trail to the Clondyke Trading Post and surrounding businesses. Particularly telling to this phenomenon was the location and name of the First and Last Chance Saloon. This tent saloon opened as early as September 1897 at the southeast corner of Broadway and Fifth Avenues; it was indeed the stampeder's first chance to get a drink as he headed into town, or his last chance as he left for the south with his full gold poke. The White Pass Trail, as it passed through the growing city, became known as Trail Street. Before the trail was re-routed to follow the city streets, it swept past the door of this southernmost saloon.

Three major newspapers agreed that there were four saloons in Skagway by August 1897.[8] Adney, of *Harper's Weekly*, named them: the

Pack Train, the Grotto, the Bonanza, and the Nugget. All were strung out along Trail Street as it entered the trees. "A glimpse inside of these, as one rides by," Adney wrote of these tent saloons, "shows a few boards set up for a bar in one corner, the other corners being filled with gambling lay-outs, around which are crowds of men playing or looking on." Unlike others who would later write about Skagway's saloons, Adney seemed not to be particularly interested in them.[9]

During the December session of the grand jury of the district court in Sitka, Alaska, eighteen people from Skagway appeared to pay fines for selling liquor without a license—despite the fact that there was no mechanism in effect for obtaining liquor licenses at the time. Seventeen saloons advertised in the *Skaguay News* in November and December of 1897. A comparison of the names of the people who paid the fines with those who advertised makes it obvious that there may have been as many as twenty-seven saloons in the burgeoning boomtown by Christmas of 1897. Four months later, in April 1898, U.S. customs agents raided the saloons, hotels, and restaurants serving liquor between tidewater and the passes. The record of the arrests shows that there were about thirty-five saloons in Skagway at the time; newspaper advertisements for that month supply the names of eight more.[10]

Between 1916 and 1930, noted northern columnist Elmer J. "Stroller" White wrote a regular column for the newspapers he owned in White-horse, Douglas, and Juneau, in which he recounted stories of the gold rush days. In these stories, he named as many as nineteen of Skagway's saloons. Between those identified by White and those advertising in newspapers of June, July, and August, at least fifty saloons can be identified by name from that summer. White claims to have observed at least seventy saloons in operation in Skagway during the spring of 1898, when he arrived to take a job with the *Skaguay News.*[11]

The number of saloons just kept growing as the White Pass and Yukon Route railroad came to town and began hiring laborers, and fewer people used the Chilkoot Trail to get to Dawson, Atlin, or other interior mining areas. When the grand jury convened in Juneau in December 1898, eighty-nine proprietors from Skagway were arrested on the charge of selling liquor without a license, and most of these were saloon owners. These merchants handed over their $100 fine, counting it simply a cost of doing business.[12]

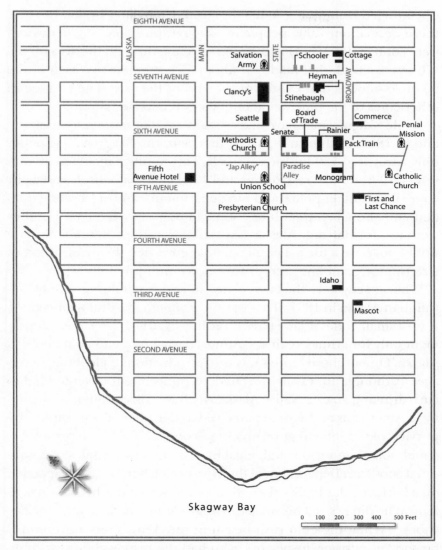

Map 2. Skagway institutions, including saloons, brothels, and churches, fall 1900. Map by Gerry Krieg. Copyright © 2015 by the University of Oklahoma Press.

By the end of 1898, most of the saloons remained clustered along Fifth or Sixth Avenue, or on Broadway between Fifth and Sixth avenues (map 2). Skagway's saloon population was largely determined by the size of its male population. Women rarely frequented Skagway's saloons, discouraged from doing so first by custom, and later by law. In 1898, there were about 7,000 people in Skagway, probably 5,000 of whom were adult males. Ignoring the men traveling through the area on the White Pass Trail, that made for about 55 customers per each of the 90 or so saloons that existed at the end of the year. The average in other cities of the time was about 80 customers per saloon.[13]

While Skagway may have had as many as 90 or more saloons at the end of 1898, in the early part of that year, the Skagway newspaper only advertised 130 businesses in all. This number included 20 out-fitters, 19 hotels, 15 restaurants and 12 of its 26 saloons. It had a city council, volunteer police and fire departments, and at least one non-denominational church. It had some loosely enforced laws, but they were not formalized. Alaska as a territory rather than a U.S. state would not have a formal civil code that governed the prosecution of vice (liquor, gambling, and prostitution) until July 1899.[14]

What exactly were the laws related to liquor, gambling, and prosti-tution in Alaska in 1897? That was the problem: hardly anyone knew. A very small code of laws passed on July 27, 1867, provided punish-ment only for crimes against customs, navigation, and commerce in Alaska. One of those crimes was the introduction of alcoholic bever-ages. Although not explicitly stated, its punishment was intended to curb drinking among Native Alaskans, whose consumption of alcohol most Americans at the time perceived as detrimental and within the purview of the federal government to control. If a saloon proprietor could obtain liquor through legal means, such as the sales of confis-cated goods at a Department of the Treasury auction—which happened on a fairly regular basis—then what he did with it was his concern, as long as he did not sell his stock to Tlingits or members of other Native tribes.[15] When the gold rush began in July 1897, there were simply far too few customs inspectors, who had the responsibility for filing complaints of trafficking in liquor, to take on the exploding commu-nities of Dyea and Skagway. Chances are that most proprietors of saloons and other establishments that sold alcoholic beverages were not even aware they were breaking the law. Everyone who knew about the law knew that prohibition for Alaska was meant to keep liquor out of the hands of Native Alaskans, not white settlers.

When the Klondike gold rush began, Alaska did not even boast the status of a United States territory. Concerned primarily with maintaining law and order, Alaska was a U.S. military district, governed by a governor, a district judge and his court clerk, marshal, deputy marshals, and commissioners, who functioned as justices of the peace. The governor, district judge and U.S. marshal were appointed by the president of the United States. The clerks, deputies, and commissioners were appointed by the district judge. There was no provision for the incorporation of cities. There were no elected positions. There was no government by representation.

Skagway, like many other Alaskan communities of the time, had ignored the fact that it had no legal code under which to incorporate. During its earliest days, a committee of about a hundred citizens knew there was more to building a community than simply maintaining law and order by means of appointed officials. This "Committee of 101" elected a city council on December 4, 1897, which in turn established voluntary taxes to pay for municipal expenses, such as street and bridge improvements; encouraged the development of public utilities; and provided a night watchman.[16] However, it relied entirely on the federal court systems to legally prosecute all crimes, both felonies and misdemeanors. For the prosecution of crimes, it had one U.S. marshal in Sitka, James Shoup. Shoup in turn appointed a U.S. deputy, H. D. McInnes, to enforce laws in both Dyea and Skagway. The U.S. commissioner assigned to administer both Dyea and Skagway was John U. Smith.

Curiously, of all the vices tempting the men of Skagway, it was gambling that the town's middle-class merchants, in the form of the Committee of 101 and the federal courts, decided to tackle first. On March 9, 1898, U.S. Deputy Marshal H. D. McInnis swore complaints against nine men on charges of gambling. City councilman J. H. Foster, saloon owners Lee Guthrie and George Rice, and the notorious "Con King," "Soapy" Smith, were among those charged.[17] This would be the only time in Skagway's history that Soapy's name would appear on a legal warrant of arrest. It was Smith and his petty form of gambling that inspired the first reform attempts in Skagway.

Born in Coweta County, Georgia, in 1860, Jefferson Randolph "Soapy" Smith spent his formative years cultivating the craft of con

People's Theater, a dance hall on Sixth Avenue that offered attractions similar to those at Clancy's Music Hall, winter 1897–1898. The woman on the far
right is probably not a customer. Courtesy Alaska State Library, William
Norton Photograph Collection, P226-842.

games, political graft, and influence-buying in Denver, Colorado. He
left that city in late 1894 when city reformers shut down gambling
places.[18] Soapy first came to Skagway in August 1897, but he stayed
only for a month before traveling to Washington, D.C., to obtain
permission to open a business on the Fort Yukon military reservation
at the mouth of the Yukon River. He did not return to Skagway until
January 21, 1898.[19]

Ten days later, after Smith's second arrival, on January 31, Ed Fay,
the bartender of the People's Theater and Klondike Saloon, killed
laborer Andy McGrath and James M. Rowan, who was acting for U.S.
Deputy Marshal McInnes while the latter was escorting a prisoner to
Sitka. The Committee of 101 took Fay into custody until U.S. Commissioner John U. Smith (not to be confused with Soapy Smith, who was
not related) could arrive from Dyea to arraign the suspect. While

there was talk of a lynching, cooler heads prevailed, and the prisoner was sent to Sitka, where he was eventually tried and sentenced to ten years for manslaughter.[20]

The Committee of 101 believed the lower class of gamblers and con men encouraged ruffians and thugs to habituate the city's saloons. Therefore, on March 8, 1898, they issued a broadside that warned "all confidence, bunco and sure-thing men to leave Skagway and the White Pass road immediately, or action would be promptly taken."[21] In response, Soapy promoted himself as a leader of Skagway's gambling sector and declared war on the town's merchants. He posted a counter broadside that claimed "the law and order society consisting of 317 citizens will see that Justice is dealt out to its full extent as no Blackmailers or Vigilantes will be tolerated."[22] At the time, the word "vigilante" did not have the negative connotation it has today; the volunteer police and city council certainly did fit the definition of a vigilance committee, but the committee was condoned by the town's law-abiding citizens. These safety committees were a traditional early American solution to frontier criminal problems, as aptly discussed by a number of social historians.[23] The town's citizens had simply decided to curb a growing sector of the community that was getting out of hand in the absence of a legal system that allowed them to pass local ordinances. The only people who had to fear the merchants' actions were those operating outside established law.[24]

Over the next few weeks, Soapy and the city founders publicly exchanged barbs: as a result, newspapers in Dyea and to the south took delight in commenting on whether or not Smith was "boss" of Skagway.[25] In the meantime, responding to all the turmoil, Alaskan governor John G. Brady sent federal troops to Skagway. They arrived on February 25, 1898, and by March 15, the Fourteenth Infantry issued orders reinforcing the Committee of 101's command that confidence men close their businesses. The bunco and confidence men had no choice but to obey orders; they could close up shop or move up the trail.[26]

All solid evidence shows that Soapy Smith lay low for the next several months. He finally opened a saloon, Jeff Smith's Parlor, on May 14, 1898, locating it at 317 Sixth Avenue in the heart of the downtown saloon district. Typical of the cheap, temporary dive of the gold rush era, this twelve-foot by forty-foot building barely had enough room for a mahogany bar and a couple of gambling tables in the back room. Knowing better than to own property in a boom town that might well go bust, Soapy rented the building from entrepreneur and city council member Frank Clancy.[27]

Skagway's two newspapers regarded Soapy with amusement until, on July 8, three members of his gang robbed miner J. D. Stewart of his gold poke containing almost $2,600 worth of dust. Sylvester Taylor, a U.S. deputy marshal known to take bribes from Smith, refused to confront the con man. Charles Sehlbrede, who had replaced John U. Smith as U.S. commissioner in May 1898, and a committee headed by J. M. "Si" Tanner demanded return of the money, but they were met with a refusal on the contention that Stewart had lost his poke in a gambling game. Convinced that word of Soapy's gang's theft would encourage stampeders to travel through Dyea and the Chilkoot Pass instead of Skagway and the White Pass, the city council called a public meeting. All hell broke loose when Soapy met members of the town's Safety Committee, including Citizen Frank Reid, on the Juneau Company Wharf. Soapy mortally wounded Reid; the committee then dispatched Smith with a few well-aimed bullets. The newly deputized Si Tanner proceeded to round up all of the characters known to be part of Smith's gang. A coroner's jury would later give credit to Reid for killing Soapy.[28]

By July 15, 1898, Skagway's *Daily Alaskan* reported that the town's vigilance committee had ordered a search for gang member Mrs. M. J. "Vi" Torpey, "charged with keeping a disorderly house." The paper further announced that the committee would "keep up the good work until all the disorderly characters have been rounded up."[29] Nationally syndicated newspaper stories announced that all criminals had been swept out of Skagway and that it was safe to openly display one's wealth on the streets. According to these reports and the legend that resulted from them, crime had been eradicated from the town with the death of Soapy and the purging of his gang. Reform had come to Skagway.[30]

The following December, a grand jury in Juneau indicted Mrs. Torpey for prostitution, and sent three of Soapy's gang members to federal prison for larceny (the robbery of J. D. Stewart) and assault of an officer of the law (J. M. Tanner).[31]

Upon reading the Skagway newspapers in the later part of 1898, one might believe that all vice truly had disappeared with the purging of the Soapy gang. The only person charged that year with keeping a house of ill fame was Vi Torpey, and that was a trumped-up charge due to her association with Soapy and his followers.

In point of fact, prostitution was thriving in Skagway during its first year. As in every mining boom town since the California gold rush in 1849, an entire industry grew up in Skagway to entertain the vast number of bachelor men who passed through on their way to the Klondike goldfields. Saloons, dance halls, gambling resorts, and the myriad forms of "bawdy houses," as houses of prostitution were called then, formed a core of what most Victorians called the "sporting world" or demimonde.

The first historic documentation of the presence of prostitutes in Skagway appears in the U.S. commissioner's journal entry of April 9, 1898. U.S. Deputy Marshal John Cudihy, assisting McInnes in Dyea, charged twenty-one women with disorderly conduct—but not prostitution. They were each fined $15, which they all paid. A prostitution charge would have demanded a much larger fine and might have driven many of the women out of business, something the authorities probably were reluctant to see happen.[32] With the exception of the indictment of Torpey and the disorderly conduct charge against the twenty-one women, there was no official recognition by governing officials that prostitution existed in Skagway during the gold rush days. As far as the historical record goes, the institution did not exist in the early days of the railroad port.

But madams besides Vi Torpey were in town. The arrest of the women for vagrancy in early April was followed by revelations of a different form of vice, when on April 22 Inspector of Customs J. C. Hartman charged fifty-four people, either as individuals or as owners of saloons, theaters, restaurants, or hotels, with the smuggling of liquor. The latter included a Mrs. Cummings, who was found to have in her possession five bottles of illicit liquor. The December 1898 raid of liquor establishments included the arrest of Belle Schooler, who would later appear as the defendant in a number of charges of keeping a house of ill fame.[33]

For the most part, though, the town's citizens tried to hide the vice in their midst. In the wake of the Soapy Smith debacle, the newspapers boasted how law-abiding and orderly the town had become. The *Daily Alaskan* published Skagway's crime statistics for the year 1899 on New Year's Day in 1900, and reported not a single case of prostitution for the entire year (ignoring the thirty-one cases of disorderly conduct as well as two cases of documented adultery).[34] In fact, other than Mrs. Torpey's case in November 1898, the next time that any woman was specifically charged with "operating a house of ill-fame" was on February 10, 1900.[35] Between May 1898 and February 1900, thirty-five women, most of whom were probably prostitutes, were arrested and paid small fines, usually less than $20. The charge was invariably drunkenness or disorderly conduct.[36] This tactic was taken, without a doubt, to keep the fines for the prostitutes low and to minimize the appearance of criminal activity. The minimum mandatory fine for prostitution in Alaska was $100, enough to drive a common prostitute out of town, and almost enough to make the madams think once or twice about whether they wanted to stay in the boom town. And the result would have been unsatisfactory for the many bachelor men who enjoyed their services.

There are few other records of the presence of vice in Skagway's early period; most of the rest of the information comes from folklore, and that is more fanciful than informative. Like Dixie Anzer's glowing depictions of Pop Corn Kate, the folktales depict the women that habituated Skagway's saloons and dance halls as humorous, drunken, golden-hearted floozies who were only out to have a good time. James Sinclair, who was a small boy in Ontario when his father, Rev. John A. Sinclair, lived in Skagway in 1898, worked his father's letters and diaries into a secondhand reminiscence more than seventy years after the reverend had died. In *Mission: Klondike*, he recounted stories about a drunken barmaid named "Dollie," whom he portrayed as hilarious: she kissed an astonished preacher on the mouth outside the Northern Light Saloon, and later interrupted church services with her coarse language. She scolded a Methodist minister for kicking her dog, something no sober-minded, "respectable" person would dream of doing (scolding the minister, that is). She interrupted his sermon when he did not include the Welsh in a list of the people for whom the good Lord had died (she was Welsh, not surprisingly). She was last heard of when she was arrested "for taking part in a rather sordid fracas in the Northern Light."[37] Because these stories were told second-hand and decades after the events supposedly occurred, their accuracy is questionable.

Despite the weaknesses of his son's account, there is no question that Rev. Sinclair was Skagway's first reformer. He had gained notoriety for being the only minister who agreed to preach a sermon at Soapy Smith's funeral. His personal papers bulge with regret for not having met and personally reformed the con man. In a sermon entitled "The Way of the Transgressor is Hard," Sinclair urged his listeners (and readers as well, for the sermon was published not only in the Skagway newspapers but also in a number of national ones) to not stop their purge of criminals with the Soapy gang. He warned that all grafters, con men, and those who "make gold from the shame of others" should be made to leave town before Skagway could be truly liberated. It was a theme he would repeat until the day he died.[38]

Sinclair was born in Lanark, Ontario, on February 27, 1863. He was well educated, having received a Master of Arts degree from Queen's University, Kingston, Ontario in 1890. The British Presbyterian ministry ordained him in Ontario in 1893, and he served as the minister at St. Andrew's Presbyterian Church in Spencerville, Ontario, until 1898. He went to Skagway on May 20 that year to relieve the Rev. Robert M. Dickey, who had been serving in Skagway prior to his service in British Columbia and the Yukon territories. Sinclair stayed in Skagway until April 1899, helping to consolidate the Presbyterian presence in the community, before moving on to Bennett, British Columbia, where he founded a church. From there he traveled to several communities in British Columbia and Yukon Territory, establishing ministries. He left the North in the fall of 1900 when he was transferred to Regina, Saskatchewan. He died there in 1905, leaving his widow, Laura, and four children.[39]

It is doubtful that the reverend himself saw vice in Skagway or any of his other parishes in the same humorous light as did his son. *Mission: Klondike* is full of errors and inaccurate transcriptions of James's father's diary and letters. The humor with which James tells the tale is probably a reflection on the son's post-sexual-revolution view of prostitutes, not that of the Presbyterian minister who encountered them.

Other humorous stories about prostitutes in Skagway come from Stroller White, who admitted embellishing the truth to make his "tales"

Fabruda Manzar, "Little Egypt," who did the "hoochy-coochy" in Skagway in 1898 before leaving for Dawson. Courtesy Alaska State Library, Wickersham State Historic Site Photographs, P277-001-188.

more interesting.[40] According to White, in the summer of 1898, Cross-eyed Liz and Gin Sling Molly had a hair-pulling match at the Palace of Delight, presumably a sporting establishment of some renown. He mentioned in passing Sweet Geraldine, who did a turn at the "hoochy-coochy"—a sort of belly dance—at Dave Blake's Palace of Delight, and noted that "Little Egypt" did her celebrated contortion act at Clancy's Music Hall. Some of the performers at the Savoy Saloon and Dance Hall included Gum Boots Kitty, the Pink 'Un, Big Bess, and Guzzling Gertie. Pierre Berton, in his landmark narrative of the gold rush, *Klondike: The Last Great Gold Rush*, repeated White's story about "Little Egypt," and added the following description: "In the dance halls that adjoined the saloons, painted women held court in caricatures of Paris fashions, with names like Sweet Marie, Babe Wallace, the Virgin, Mollie Fewclothes, Sitting Maud, Ethel the Moose and Diamond Lil Davenport."[41]

Another time, White recalled that "Little Egypt" did the hoochy-coochy on a table at the Pack Train restaurant. The "Skim Milk Queen" performed cartwheels on the tables that same night. Both were dance hall girls, though, drunk on the proceeds of a "charity" drive, and their acts may have been purely spontaneous, not meant to solicit business. White wrote jovially of Claw Finger Kitty, who sang "Just before the Battle" with an "o" instead of an "a" in the last word, to the delight of her audience. He mentioned in passing Big Bo Peep, the "lady" of Paddy the Pig's affections.[42] It is difficult to determine how many of these women were prostitutes and how many were making an "honest" living in the dance halls. At the time, some people would have it that there was no difference.

Because the early women in Skagway's demimonde were transient and of a low class compared to their chroniclers, they became subjects of ridicule. While these anecdotes add garish color to the town's mythic setting, no real information comes from these tales other than the women's pseudonyms. It is only a guess what they were really like and where they lived.

Anthropologist Alexy Simmons, in her examination of the way "sporting" women tended to settle in frontier boom towns, observed that the first prostitutes were most likely to live above the saloons or dance halls, or in one- or two-woman houses scattered about town.[43] Skagway's folklore concurs with this description. The saloons relied just as heavily as the dance halls on the practice of cutting women in on "percentages" for every drink sold. If a saloon was spacious enough to have an upstairs or back rooms, then the owner could profit even more by renting out these rooms without appearing to have knowledge of what went on in them.

Skagway's folklore concurs with Simmons's observation about where the earliest prostitution took place. One of the first gold rush–era buildings that today's tourist will encounter after exiting the cruise ship docked in the harbor is the Red Onion Saloon. A sign that reads "Skagway's Red Light District" draws in the tourist, who upon entering the building can peer at a row of four small rooms on the second story. These tiny rooms appear too small for private parties or as clubrooms. While other saloons could house their staffs of gamblers, cooks, and waiters on the second floor, the Red Onion apparently harbored prostitutes in the upstairs rooms.[44] Stroller White mentions that the Red Onion once had a "lady" bartender, who ran off with a prominent businessman.[45] This story connecting women with the Red Onion reinforces a rich folklore portraying prostitutes as working in that saloon in the summer and fall of 1898. The business was located on the southeast corner of State and Sixth Avenues, with its back entry on Paradise Alley, then one of the most notorious places for finding prostitutes in Skagway. While it is extremely unlikely that the upstairs rooms functioned as a brothel, in the sense that a madam entertained men in a parlor while they waited for their favorites, these rooms were probably available for rent by women working for percentages.[46] As far as the male owners were concerned, what went on in the women's private rooms upstairs was their business. All that the saloon owner wanted was his weekly rent and the business the upstairs activities encouraged. The rent probably brought at least $5.00 a week in the booming months of 1898.

The Red Onion went through a series of name changes from the Red Onion to the Senate in 1899 to the Totem in 1901. After the restricted district was created on Seventh Avenue in April 1901, Herman Grimm, who owned the Seattle Saloon kitty-corner from the Totem Saloon, began an expansion.[47] He rented the Red Onion-cum-Totem for a month to house his middle-class saloon. Grimm was a model of propriety. His advertisements in 1901 boasted, "Catering only to the better class of trade, Mr. Grimm never allows women within the doors of the Seattle, and this one feature has been a factor in the upbuilding [sic] of his trade."[48] While he occupied the old Red Onion, he emphatically reiterated his policy. "The saloon will be run on the same principle that characterized the old 'Seattle'—it will be 'for gentlemen only'; no gambling; no boxes; no women."[49] In view of the Red Onion's previous reputation, it is little wonder he made such a pointed statement. Grimm and the middle-class businessmen that he catered to did not condone the mixing of women with the sales of liquor. They believed that if women were in the saloon, they must be prostitutes. When he states there were no women in his saloon, he meant there were no prostitutes.[50]

Other saloon proprietors in Skagway probably had similar arrangements with their female habitués as those practiced at the Red Onion before 1901. Any place with a second story was probably a good candidate for such an arrangement. The Red Onion is the only one of these disreputable places to survive to the present day, but during the town's early years, both Fifth and Sixth Avenues between Broadway and State were crawling with these "resorts," as they were so often called. The kingpins were the Board of Trade and the Pack Train Saloons, each financed by George Rice and Company, a gaming syndicate that rivaled that of the Clancy Brothers. These resorts formed solid anchors for the Sixth Avenue business district, being located at the southwest corner of Sixth and Broadway, and in the center of the block between Broadway and State. The Grotto Hotel and Saloon, owned by Frank Clancy, had upstairs rooms, sometimes used to house "hotel" employees. This place was a neighbor to the Board of Trade. And the Red Onion was at the other end of the block (see map 2).

Just one street to the north was the Princess Hotel, owned by Emory Valentine and a Mr. Martin.[51] As White noted, the Princess "was called a number of other things that would not look well in print."[52] He included in his accounts lurid details about the Princess as he described a parade led by Soapy Smith on May 1, 1898, when the town celebrated American victories in Cuba. As the parade turned down Seventh Avenue off State, spectators were startled by excitement at the Princess:

> Babe Davenport ran out of the place and grabbed Captain
> Smith's bridle, and was followed by five or six other girls. All
> were clad in their working uniforms and the Stroller noticed,
> before he could turn his head away, that what they wore for
> uniforms was barely visible to the naked eye. The girls
> demanded that Captain Soapy Smith stop right there and then
> and organize a Ladies Auxiliary, and while this was going on
> the rear ranks kept crowding up for a look at the scenery and
> there was a lot of confusion and a great deal of advice was
> shouted up to Captain Smith as to what he should do, none of
> which he took, or at least not right then. Captain Smith finally
> shooed the girls back inside with something about "Your turn
> will come later," whatever was meant by that, and the parade
> got straightened out and started again.[53]

The Princess was not the only sporting house in Skagway. Another, identified as a cigar store and saloon on Sixth Avenue, called La Fiesta Cigar Store, went up in flames on January 31, 1900, when a fire started in the room of one of the "inmates" who lived on the second floor.[54] La Fiesta is only one more example of the types of resorts that catered to the appetites of men for pleasurable indulgences in the boom days of the gold rush. Yet this resort, along with the Red Onion, the Princess, and many others, represented the lesser establishments known to house prostitutes. The most famous resort, owned by Skagway's most powerful citizen in Skagway's first few years, was Clancy's Music Hall. To understand how Clancy gained his power, it is necessary to examine his background.

Frank William Clancy was one of six Clancy brothers who grew up in Seattle. The partnership of Clancy and Company owned saloons, gambling houses, and dance halls in Seattle, Tacoma, Skagway, Dyea, and Dawson. Frank was born in East Machias, Washington County, Maine on March 21, 1862, to Elizabeth and James Clancy. James was a laborer who later became a farmer. The couple had ten children between 1854 and 1876. Six of them were boys; Frank was the third son. By 1880, James Clancy's brother, Thomas, traveled to Seattle and purchased property along the waterfront. By 1885, James Clancy took his family to Seattle to join his brother, where they lived out the rest of their lives.[55]

In the wake of Seattle's great fire of 1889, which burned over twenty-five city blocks of the downtown area, the elder Thomas ("Tom") Clancy and a gambler from Chicago by the name of Pete Burns went into business together and opened the Mirror Saloon in Seattle on Third Avenue South and Washington. In 1915, an article in the *Seattle Daily Times* would remember this variety theater as "a type of the gilt and walnut bars of that period."[56]

By 1887, Frank and his older brother Thomas had both become saloon keepers. Burns is credited with teaching three of the Clancy brothers—Thomas, Frank, and John—the business of managing saloons, at which they became proficient. More important, Burns coached the brothers in how to engage with city politics to further their business interests by buying influence with police, councilmen, and mayoral and gubernatorial candidates. They became especially proficient at

registering voters and campaigning at election time. In return, successful political candidates passed bills in favor of the type of bawdy
house run by the elder Tom Clancy and Pete Burns at the Mirror. In
league with Burns, the Clancys as a whole took on a powerful gambling cooperative known as the M & N combination, which dominated
politics in the First Ward of Seattle. The M & N bribed the sheriff's
department, whereas Clancy and Burns favored the city police. After
the silver crash in 1893, however, the Clancys split with Burns and
opened their own dance hall, which they named the Mascot.[57]

The *Tacoma Daily News* called Tom Clancy and Burns the autocrats
of Seattle's First Ward. They accused the men of making their money
"from the Japanese women slaves to whose masters they rent the miser-
able little hovels in which the women drive their trade in obedience
to the lash of the master, and who, when they manage to make their
escape from bondage, are arrested by an accommodating police force
upon trumped-up charges of larceny, robbery and the like, thrown into
jail, convicted and imprisoned until willing to return to their old life
of submission and obedience to their master."[58] Seattle's middle-class
women would become particularly concerned about the presence of
Japanese prostitutes in places like the Mirror as they worked for
reform during the first decade of the twentieth century.[59]

Seattle vice and politics expanded greatly with the explosion of
the Klondike gold rush. In the wake of gold fever, John Considine,
Seattle's so-called Boss-Sport, opened the People's Theater, another
dance hall and gambling house in the Lava Bed, the vice district of
that city. There the women who performed in his burlesque shows
also pandered alcoholic drinks and provided sexual acts in private
box seats.[60]

In June 1897, one of Frank Clancy's brothers, John, was run over by
an excursion train that came from the Seattle suburb of Kent in Olympia. His head was injured, and his leg was so badly damaged that it
had to be amputated.[61] Upon the announcement of the discovery of
gold in late July, and perhaps to lift John's spirits during his recovery,
these two Clancy brothers decided to head north. Considering the
political influence of the Clancy brothers in Seattle, it is no coincidence that names like the Mirror, Mascot, and People's Theater all
would reappear in Skagway.

Frank Clancy was one of the first people to claim a Skagway city lot after surveyor Frank Reid began to lay out the town site on August 5, 1897. He chose lot 1 on block 6, at the southwest corner of Seventh and State Avenues on August 10, 1897.[62] This location, on Trail Street as it led to the White Pass Trail, would be where he would build Clancy's Saloon. So prominent did Frank Clancy become in the fledgling community's affairs that he was chosen to be one of its first city council members in December 1897. He survived the purging of the city council after the Soapy Smith affair in July 1898, and he was the only member to be re-elected in December 1898. When Skagway incorporated in July 1899, he was elected as one of its first official city councilmen, and he remained a powerful force in the community until he left Skagway in March 1900.[63]

Clancy's Saloon was such a local landmark that other businesses used it as a reference when giving their location in newspaper advertisements. Examples include the Skaguay Bazaar, which advertised on February 2, 1898, that it was located on "Trail [Street] just above Clancy's." Gordon, McKee, and Noyes, real estate agents, were in the office north of Clancy's. C. N. Noyes also sold tobacco from the red door above Clancy's. The Princess Hotel and Saloon was located opposite Clancy's. Eventually, Frank would also own the Mirror Saloon (named after his uncle Tom Clancy's and Pete Burns's resort in Seattle), the Grotto Hotel and Saloon, the Reception Saloon, Clancy's Café, Jeff Smith's Parlors, and the Skagway Oyster Parlors.

In a promotion piece dated January 9, 1900, the *Daily Alaskan* touted Frank Clancy as one of the city's pioneers, who had always taken an interest in "public affairs." The description of this first citizen went on to extol the popularity of his restaurant. According to the article, he had rented it out only recently so that he could devote his attention to his theater, which had "proved most acceptable to the public."[64] It was obvious that he was not one to eschew mixing politics and business; Pete Burns had taught him well. Certainly between 1898 and 1900 he was arguably one of the most influential citizens of the community.

There is no remaining physical description of Clancy's biggest and most important business, Clancy's Music Hall and Club Rooms, which was an expansion of the original saloon. However, an overview

Clancy's Saloon (and Music Hall) on Trail Street, August 1897. Courtesy Washington State Historical Society.

photograph of Skagway taken in December 1898 or January 1899 makes it clear that the building was one of the largest in the town. The first floor occupied the entire lot at the southwest corner of Seventh and State Avenues, and portions of the building rose to a second story. Standard advertisements in the newspapers for the music hall pandered liquors and cigars. A special advertisement on December 31, 1897, boasted music and dancing every evening, along with inviting club-rooms. Entertainments were too risqué to advertise in the newspaper and were probably announced with posters and broadbills. Once or twice a month, the music house would be open to "families," for which Clancy would engage famous acts, including such hits as John A. Flynn's London Gaiety Girls, who had "a worldwide reputation for the production of catchy up-to-date burlesques."[65]

In the meantime, Frank's brother John partnered with a man named Billings in Dyea to run the Potlatch Hotel. It had a dance hall and concert hall in combination, and advertised between February and

August 1898 in the *Dyea Trail* as being part of Clancy & Co. Frank also used the Clancy & Co. logo at the Clancy Music Hall, indicating the interest of all of the Clancy brothers in their combined operations. This Clancy & Co. designation implies that John, Frank, their uncle Tom, brothers James and Tom, and perhaps even two of the other brothers, Charles and George, had some financial interests in the Alaska enterprises.[66]

Clancy's Music Hall thrived during the heyday of the gold rush, but as the boom passed, the business underwent a transformation. In November 1898, a few weeks after auctioneer Frank T. Keelar opened his store next door to the Board of Trade Saloon on Sixth Avenue, he advertised an auction of the entire contents of Clancy's Music Hall. Up for auction would be the "Bed Room Suites, First Class Bedding, Stoves, Bed-Linen, Blankets, Comforts, Stools, Lamps, Chairs, Tables, Crockery, two cash registers, piano, Fire-Proof Safe, [and] Roulette Wheel."[67] These items provide a provocative glimpse into the types of entertainments provided by Clancy. Should anyone think that Clancy provided these furnishings and linens solely to his imported actors, consider the advertisements of Clancy's successor, the Simons Theatrical Company, in March 1900: "Clancy's will be run in a first class manner, devoid of any coarse or suggestive features," with "an entire change of program weekly (possibly twice a week). The admission will be 25 cents (within the reach of all) and no free list, to keep a certain element out and from intermingling with the class of patronage that the new management wish to cater to . . . everything brisk, clean and as legitimate as possible."[68] The implication was clear. The scandalous days at Clancy's no longer existed. Only clean family fare remained.

What made Clancy's Music Hall and Club Rooms so scandalous? The only conceivable answer is that prostitution was an open and active part of the dance hall entertainment. The inventory listed by Keelar calls up images of the accusations made of the Mirror in its heyday, with its "women slavery" and "courtesan bondage." Deposition from a 1902 case of prostitution at the Douglas Opera House offers a much more detailed description of how the dance halls and variety theaters in Alaska operated (see appendix B). The male customer entered through the saloon, where he purchased liquor, usually whiskey. There he was inevitably approached by a woman who expected him to buy her a drink, which seldom had much, if any, alcohol in it. The woman would receive a percentage of the proceeds from the sale of her drink and any others he might buy while in her company, somewhere between 10 and 25 percent. As long as he continued to buy her drinks throughout the evening, she would partner him on the dance floor in the next room, and provide companionship if he chose to gamble. To titillate him and other men, she would laugh at his raunchy jokes, allow him to wear his hat, swear, and smoke in her presence, and let him touch her in public, such as put his arm around her waist. This behavior was scandalous; it excited men who were accustomed to restrictive manners. A free stage show for men and these disreputable women required that the audience take seats on the dance floor. Curtained boxes on the second floor could be purchased where more privacy was available for men and their consorts during and after the show. What happened in these private boxes was beyond the ken of the proprietors of the opera house.[69]

In addition to the boxes, there were rooms above and adjacent to the dance floor and performance stage. The music hall owners rented these rooms to the women for $5.00 per week, not including board; the money was taken from the woman's percentages. At six cents per drink (the standard cost of a whiskey at the time was a quarter), a woman would have to get men to buy a dozen drinks an evening just to pay the rent.[70] Obviously, if she wanted to eat or buy clothing, she had to rely on prostitution to provide that income. If she had other family members, such as children, to support, she would have to depend even more heavily on that income.

And because the owner of the dance hall or saloon merely rented out rooms, did not act as a madam or procurer, and avowed not to know what happened in the privacy of the women's rooms, he hoped he would not be charged with keeping a house of prostitution.

Despite the fact that gambling and disreputable women offered extra entertainment, and therefore brought in extra income, at Clancy's Music Hall and Club Rooms, the sale of liquor was the primary source of income. Frank's prominence in Skagway's politics ensured he could continue to thrive in all three endeavors.

It is obvious, therefore, that Frank Clancy was the boss of vice—prostitution and saloonism—in Skagway in the first year of the city's existence. How did that translate to his role in city politics?

The contradictory facts and legend of Soapy Smith hint at the complexity of Skagway politics in the Klondike gold rush era. Soapy's legend purports that he was "con king of Skagway" in the winter of 1897–1898, but the true leaders of the town were the city council selected by the hundred or so citizens that convened on December 4, 1897. This Committee of 101 originally met on October 9, 1897, to figure out what to do about the fact that homesteader Bernard Moore had filed a claim for 160 acres of the town, including most of the lots located by the merchants who were convening. At that meeting, they hired lawyer J. C. Price and filed a lawsuit that took over a decade to settle. The committee, named after similar citizens' groups throughout the West of the time, was nothing more or less than a social-action assembly faced with organizing itself into a government in the absence of territorial law that conveyed the right to incorporate.[71]

On December 4, 1897, the Committee of 101 elected a new "city council" and charged it with "originat[ing] measures for the material and moral welfare of the town." This ad hoc "city government" claimed to be a diverse group of merchants, but almost half of them owned saloons.[72]

Mark Twain once wrote that of all the influential men in the western boom town, the saloon keeper was the most prominent and occupied the highest rank. In Twain's words, "His opinion had weight. It was his privilege to say how the elections should go. No great movement could succeed without the countenance and direction of the saloonkeepers. It was a high favor when the chief saloon-keeper consented to serve in the legislature or the board of alderman."[73] Although referring specifically to late 1860s Nevada, Twain's description applies to the conditions of most nineteenth-century mining communities. His commentary pertains to such men as Soapy Smith and Frank Clancy and members of Skagway's city council.

It follows, then, that during the Klondike gold rush, the ownership of a saloon was the first step from the working class toward middle-class respectability and political success.

While Chairman Charles Sperry was known as the owner of a warehouse on the Skagway Improvement Company Wharf (later the Alaska

Southern Wharf Company), located next to Moore's Wharf, he was less well known as the operator of an unnamed saloon. Councilman Frank Clancy owned Clancy's Music Hall and Saloon as well as the building that would later house Jeff Smith's Parlors, operated by the renowned Soapy Smith. Councilman J. Henry Foster operated the Grotto Saloon (also owned by Frank Clancy). The remaining four councilmen were staunch citizens without connections to saloons: Frank E. Burns was the agent for the Alaska Steamship Company; J. Allan Hornsby was editor of the *Daily Alaskan* and an originator of the Committee of 101; and I. D. Spencer was proprietor of an outfitters and general mercantile company.[74] Only the seventh member, merchant W. F. Lokowitz, could not be identified as to specific occupation.

In the wake of Soapy's shooting on July 8, 1898, the middle-class members of the Committee of 101 decided that the council had been lax in its duties regarding the part of its mission that specified providing for "the moral welfare of the town." The committee called for the resignation of all city council members. The council met at 10:00 A.M. on Monday morning, July 11. Former council member Allan Hornsby had been deported from Skagway due to his alleged friendship with Soapy, marking him as an undesirable citizen. The remaining members were Chairman Charles Sperry, I. D. Spencer, W. F. Lokowitz, Ed Foster, Frank E. Burns, and Frank Clancy. Spencer did not attend the meeting. All the other councilmen except Chairman Sperry immediately submitted their resignations. By the following Saturday, Spencer had resigned, as had Allan Hornsby by proxy.[75]

Although Chairman Sperry was a leader of the mass meeting that met the night of July 8 to try to find a way to retrieve J. D. Stewart's gold, the *Skaguay News* and the Committee of 101 blamed Sperry and the other city council members for letting Soapy Smith and his gang enjoy their corrupt freedom during the previous six months. For that reason, Sperry did not enjoy enough popular support to retain his seat on the city council. Only Frank Clancy was re-elected to his post in the special election that followed. Clancy was in Dawson during the robbery and shooting of Soapy and appeared immune from the happenings of the event, despite the fact that he was Smith's landlord and known to be friendly with the con man. Perhaps more important, though, Clancy owned several businesses in Skagway, and was related to the politically powerful Clancy and Burns in Seattle.[76] The committee knew it was wiser not to meddle with Clancy and Company.

Evidence of Clancy's powerful connection to Soapy's gang surfaced weeks later in a Tacoma newspaper report that claimed Frank Clancy had recovered the missing $600 belonging to J. D. Stewart from the incarcerated Soapy gang member Van Triplett in Sitka, Alaska. He then turned it over to H. E. Battin, the head of the committee who had investigated the criminals. This anecdote demonstrates Clancy's power within both the demimonde and the political network of Skagway well after Soapy's demise.[77]

When Frank Clancy's brother James died of pneumonia in March 1900, Frank left Skagway, selling his music hall to the Simons Theatrical Company. Frank and James shared four other brothers, most of whom had been involved in similar businesses in Seattle and Tacoma.[78] Apparently Skagway's waning population and the loss of his brother persuaded Frank to join the rest of his family back in Seattle. But there may have been another factor as well: by that time, Alaska had begun reforming vice, and perhaps Frank foresaw more than the loss of family. More serious reform was coming to Alaska.

Community churches often played a pivotal role in the reform efforts of early western boom towns. Skagway's first church, which supporters intended to have no denominational affiliation, was built from donated funds in late November 1897 and dedicated on December 12. Despite a fanciful legend that Soapy Smith contributed substantially to that fund, Rev. Robert M. Dickey denied this claim in a 1944 letter to the widow of his replacement, Rev. John A. Sinclair.[79] His testimony reinforces newspaper reports in 1901 and 1915 that discuss fund-raising efforts by the women of the community to build the church. Any later suggestions that Soapy Smith contributed to that effort surely must have appalled them.[80]

Although Rev. Sinclair initiated reform efforts in Skagway, a dispute between the Canadian and American branches of the Presbyterian Church led to his departure within the course of a year. At the beginning of the Klondike gold rush, both American and Canadian Presbyterians expressed some confusion as to whether it was located in Canada or the United States. Therefore, both ministries sent representatives north. As a result, clashes occurred in Skagway and Dawson about which church had jurisdiction. While the Reverend S. Hall Young of Wooster, Ohio, headed for Dawson to establish a Presbyterian Church there, Rev. Dickey of Winnipeg, Manitoba, followed by Rev. Sinclair, set up shop in Skagway. They eventually sorted it all out, and by the spring of 1899, Sinclair had moved on to British Columbia. His American replacement focused on building a church that would not be shared with other Protestants.[81]

Reform efforts then shifted to nondenominational missions under the leadership of Mabel Ulery. She was born on February 4, 1877 in St. Joseph County, Indiana, to a farming family with twelve children. She volunteered with the nondenominational Peniel Missions in Juneau, Alaska, in September 1898. ("Peniel" is a Hebrew word meaning "face of God.") Later that fall, a "Christian gentleman" with the mission, after visiting Skagway, told her of the pressing need for a mission there. She arrived before the end of 1898 and proceeded to raise money for a mission, which was built in July 1900. The Sixth Avenue Peniel Mission, located only "a block from the heart of Skagway's saloons, gambling halls, and red light district [offered] nightly meetings, Sunday services, and shelter and warmth."[82]

Few other reform efforts at the time have been documented. In her autobiography, Ulery tells of going into the upstairs rooms of Juneau's saloons to plead with prostitutes to give up their way of life and become missionaries. She claims she was rarely treated unkindly.[83] While in Skagway, she visited the jail to conduct a religious service for the prisoners. There she converted to the Peniel's type of evangelism a thirty-year-old woman who had been arrested for "vagrancy." In Ulery's words, "as they tried to take her to jail, she had used such profane and abusive language to the authorities, that instead of a light sentence, she was given a lengthy one." The prostitute was Catholic (perhaps a sin in itself), and prayed from a prayer book throughout the service. The missionary left her a hymn book. When Ulery and her fellow missionaries returned the following Sunday for a similar service, the woman had cleaned herself, dressed neatly, and appeared with a happy expression. During this second service, she sprang to her feet and declared she had been saved, saying that God had forgiven her all her sins.[84]

When this woman was released from jail, she went to live with the Peniel missionaries, where she avoided her old friends and associates,

claiming she did not want to be enticed back into her old life. Roberta
Yorba, the head of the Peniel Skagway Mission, took her to Seattle,
where she enrolled in the Seattle Seminary to study the Bible. Thereafter, she returned to her home in Ireland, where she testified to the
power of God's salvation.[85] These occasional successes made the missionaries' endeavors seem worthwhile.

———

The legendary Skagway at the height of the Klondike gold rush has
been described by its folklore as "little better than hell on earth," full
of saloons and prostitutes, and ruled by Soapy Smith, the allegorical
king of Skagway's underworld. A careful examination of the primary
documents indicates that it was, instead, a community governed by a
group of middle-class merchants willing to take the law into their own
hands in the absence of constituted authority to incorporate and
establish local ordinances. When viewed through the clear lens of
documented history rather than legend, Skagway appears to have regulated its saloons by imposing a regular fine on the proprietors and to
have confined its transient prostitute population to the upstairs
of the gambling and dance halls. The town practiced a sort of self-
regulation by appointing saloon keepers and gamblers to the city
council. The murder of Andy McGrath and James Rowan in the People's
Theater resulted in the efficient capture and extradition of bartender
suspect Ed Fay. When the notorious bunco leader Soapy Smith lost
control of his gang, the town merchants called upon their safety committee, gunned him down at the entrance to a wharf, and shipped his
gang of petty gamblers and thieves out of town.

By the end of 1898, then, saloonism, prostitution, and reform inter-
mixed freely in Skagway, with few boundaries. The prostitutes lived
above the saloons and dance halls, and gambling remained a part of
the saloon culture. There were hardly any laws addressing vice, and
reformers, what few there were, relied on their moral consciences to
drive them to action. What little action was taken against vice was done
in the name of economics: for instance, driving a con man's gang away
because it robbed a gold miner of his poke. Liquor licensing and the
fining of prostitutes took the form of casual and intermittent harassment by federal officials.

The most obvious reform effort of the year was the purging of the con men, bunco-steerers, and grafters in the form of the Soapy Smith gang, and the subsequent cleansing of city hall. This first effort at reform removed a form of petty gambling and robbery as practiced by the transients, but it did not tackle the larger problem of institutional vice. Indeed, as the owner of the largest dance hall, which housed liquor sales, gambling, and prostitution all under one roof, Frank Clancy was firmly entrenched on the city council. There seemed little likelihood that any efforts at vice reform would occur from within the town of Skagway, as Clancy assumed the mantle, if not the title, of king of Skagway.

In fact, other than the shooting of Soapy Smith and running his gang out of town, reform efforts centered around the proselytizing on a case-by-case basis by female missionaries or by Protestant ministers who wished to save the sinful from their own actions. This situation probably existed because the vast majority of people in Skagway were middle-class white males and held a consensus about the issues of vice and morality. They shared in common a reluctance to tackle problems of vice to any serious extent. That consensus would not last.

CHAPTER TWO

Saloon Reform, 1899–1901

As the Klondike rush flourished in late 1898 and Skagway entered 1899, the United States Congress finally grappled with the fact that Alaska had no formal body of laws that addressed prostitution and saloonism. The federal courts enforced only a small body of laws, which forbade the sale of alcoholic beverages to Native inhabitants. The purchase of liquor by whites rarely concerned federal officials, unless it violated customs regulations, such as the ban against importation of foreign goods without the payment of duties.[1] When the gold rush began in July 1897, proprietors of saloons and other establishments that sold alcoholic beverages understood that the liquor law was simply meant to keep alcoholic beverages out of the hands of Native peoples.

Before 1899, the federal courts in Alaska used the Oregon Code of laws to prosecute most crimes, and temperance-minded officials sometimes interpreted that law to mean that Alaska had a prohibition against the sale and distribution of all liquor. The courts periodically rounded up those selling alcohol, but because there was no legal authority to license and tax liquor sellers, all they could do was fine the perpetrators for failure to have a license. One of these round-ups occurred on December 10, 1897, when 18 men from Skagway were brought before the grand jury in Sitka, Alaska, to answer for the crime of selling liquor without a license. Included in this group were A. Bloom and George Patten, both of whom would become long-term saloon owners in the community. They joined 35 men and women from Juneau, 7 from Sitka, 10 from Douglas, 2 from Wrangel, 13 from Dyea, and a scattering of individuals from up and down the coast. That was the manner in which the courts started to enforce what little law there was against the sale of alcohol.[2]

In April 1898, Skagway and Dyea inspectors of customs finally took firmer action. At this point, it is unclear what exactly induced them to take this step. Three customs officials at Dyea had been indicted for selling impounded liquor to residents of Skagway at about this time.[3] Possibly as a result of this internal corruption, their replacements were charged with gaining control of the liquor smuggling business in Dyea and Skagway. In the wake of the arrest of 9 gamblers on March 9 and 22 prostitutes on April 9 charged with disorderly conduct,[4] records state that the Skagway inspector of customs, J. C. Hartman, filed complaints against 43 businesses in Skagway on April 22, 1898. These businesses included 30 saloons. He carried out these searches five days later, finding only a few bottles of liquor (if any) at each place of business. R. W. Bellman, the inspector at Dyea, filed complaints against 77 businesses in Dyea, including 75 saloons. It is believed that the two customs officials, with a corps of appointed deputies, attempted to inspect every saloon, restaurant, hotel, and possibly a few brothels between tidewater and the summit of the Chilkoot and White Passes. A number of the establishments inspected were actually located in Canyon City and Sheep Camp, along the Chilkoot Trail.[5]

Those saloon owners possessing even one bottle of liquor were arrested for smuggling, a federal offense. Most of the offenders pleaded not guilty, paid their $100 fines (worth the equivalent of $2,760 in today's currency)[6] and went on with their businesses. With no further arrests, it appeared that the federal government had found a way to "license" an unregulated activity. The collection of fines in lieu of requiring payments for actual licenses would continue until such time that a law was passed setting up a license system. One hundred dollars was a lot of money at that time, especially for those who were operating out of a tent with a few bottles of rot-gut whiskey. It was enough to run many of these people out of business and make competition a little easier for the serious proprietors who were ready to invest in amenities like buildings, bars, bar stock, decent whiskey, and nuisances such as these fines.

The next round of arrests was made on December 9, 1898, but the cases did not make it to the grand jury until January 16, 1899. This time, eighty-nine saloon, hotel, restaurant, and brothel proprietors marched to the courtroom in Skagway. Men who would become long-time Skagway saloonkeepers were beginning to make their first appearance, including George Rice, Charles Saake, and Lee Guthrie.[7]

By this time, the prohibition forces in Alaska began to apply pressure to enforce the antiliquor law. With the migration of thousands of bachelor men into the mining frontier of Alaska, the ban against the sale and transportation of liquor was unconscionable for economic promoters, besides being entirely impractical to enforce. Something had to be done to change the law. U.S. President William McKinley signed a new code of laws for Alaska formally based on the Oregon Code. One of the most relevant portions of the law was the provision for the licensing of saloons. Paradoxically, when he reluctantly agreed to this provision, teetotaler governor John G. Brady believed the new licensing rule was the equivalent of repealing Alaska's thirty-two years of prohibition.[8]

The law stipulated that a saloon owner must obtain the signatures of a majority of all adult white citizens living within two miles in order to apply for a license, and that the license for a city the size of Skagway would be $1,500 a year (equal to $41,400 in today's currency). Proceeds from the licenses were to be used for educational purposes. The law was a compromise with prohibitionists who wanted to ban the sale of liquor in Alaska entirely. The editor of the *Daily Alaskan* endorsed the action. He pointed out that licensing would "necessarily wipe out a class of saloons that are a menace to the welfare of any community and that make possible the breeding and nursing into life creatures as made up the Soapy Smith gang that terrorized the early days of Skagway."[9] The intent was to close down the small dives and bolster the higher-class places such as those owned by Frank Clancy, George Rice, and Lee Guthrie, men who took the time to be active in local politics, men who fit Mark Twain's definition of higher-class saloon-keeper citizens.

It was not until March 1899, when the "high license law" went into effect, that its details first became known to the saloon keepers. No license could be issued to any liquor retailer within four hundred feet of a church or school.[10] Governor Brady's report of 1899 stated that he found it amusing to watch the saloon men "out in the middle of the night with their tapelines measuring the distance from the places of business to the nearest church to see if they came within the 400-foot limit. To-day there are several such places marked 'to rent.'"[11]

In Skagway, there was still the matter of the petition to address. According to the new Alaska Code, a business wishing to obtain a liquor license must obtain the permission of the majority of the white adults within two miles. Under existing conditions, thousands of male transients traveled through Dyea and Skagway, and—if you can believe the *Skaguay News*—at least one hundred saloons wanted to do business. Therefore, Skagway needed a quicker solution to the problem than gathering a separate petition for each saloon, petitions that would be signed by people who could not be tracked down if there was a legal question at a later time. And Skagway was not the only community faced with that difficult question. There were others as well. Alaska turned to the courts for clarification.

By late May 1899, First District Judge Charles S. Johnson wrote an opinion regarding the issuance of liquor licenses. He stated that each community could decide how to implement the law in one of two ways. Instead of a separate petition for each saloon, the entire community could get up a single petition for the licensing of all the saloons to be signed by a majority of the men and women within a radius of two miles of the saloons in question. Alternatively, a town could hold a general election on the question of the local option, that is, permitting the sales of liquor to all proprietors as a group. The local option would be good for one year, at which time another election would be held. If the community did not approve the granting of all licenses, then each saloon keeper had the option of obtaining his own petition. The judge also said that each saloon would be closed on July 1, 1899, if the owner did not have a license, and the law would be strictly enforced. Costs for these special elections would be borne by the saloon keepers.[12]

Most communities in southeast Alaska quickly adopted the local option method because it was more efficient and practical. Sitka granted licenses in a 200-to-40 vote, the latter vote "drummed up by the wife of a Sitka missionary." Juneau voted for licensing with 357 for and 45 against. By May 30, the Skagway town council called for a special election, and its vote on June 14 was 468 for and 68 against. Although Judge

Johnson had classed both of the latter two communities as having more than 1,500 people (thus putting them in the $1,500 licensing category), he later judged that the voting turnout, while not 51 percent of the population, was representative of the wishes of the population.[13]

The immediate problem with Judge Johnson's solution was that no women could vote in the elections. All 563 registered voters in Skagway's 1899 special saloon license election were male.[14] The law required the women's permission on the stipulated petitions, so why could they not vote in the substituted special elections? In Wyoming and Utah, women could vote on school boards and social issues even before they obtained universal suffrage. But women were not granted the right to vote in Alaska until 1913, except in school board elections, a privilege that was granted them in 1908 with the passage of the Alaska Territorial Act. By excluding a large portion of the population that purportedly needed to grant permission for issuance of liquor licenses, Judge Johnson biased the election results for the next fourteen years. Not coincidentally, local prohibition began in the better-established Alaskan communities within two or three years of women getting the vote. It is obvious that temperance was a gender-related issue in Alaska.

It is also readily evident that no Skagway saloons closed down after the $100 fines were imposed in January 1899, except for those dives that were so impoverished they could not survive even that small of an impact on their income. As had occurred after the December 1897 and April 1898 customs raids, the fines were treated as a substitute for licensing. A liquor proprietor paid his fine, and then went back to serving whiskey and beer.

On January 16, 1899, at the same time the *Daily Alaskan* stated that "one-hundred" saloon keepers from Dyea and Skagway and all points to the summits were assessed their $100 fines for smuggling liquor, five establishments selling alcoholic beverages posted advertisements in the *Daily Alaskan:* the Coliseum, the White Navy, the Magnolia, the Skagway Brewing Company, and the Monogram. By February 3, things definitely were looking up for the saloons. Skagway's biggest saloon advertisers—the Board of Trade and the Pack Train—put their ads back in the newspaper, joining the giants of Skagway's early carousing days, Clancy's Music Hall and People's Theater. The Idaho, the First and Last

Chance, and seven other saloons participated in an advertising blitz that rivaled twenty-first century after-Christmas sales. More saloons and breweries advertised in the *Daily Alaskan* in February 1899 than during any other month between March 1898 and December 1917.

When the February sales bonanza ended, several saloons suddenly backed out of the competition. It must have become apparent there would be no getting around the $1,500 yearly license, and perhaps many owners sought to sell their businesses before they had to purchase the license. They might have been completely surprised by the stipulation that no business within four hundred feet of a church could be granted a license. Skagway's only Protestant church at the time, the interdenominational Union Church, was located on the northwest corner of Fifth and State Avenues; its Catholic church was half a block east of Broadway on Fifth. The location of most of Skagway's saloons were on Fifth and Sixth Avenues between Broadway and State, and a good many of the "hundred" saloons may have fallen within that 400-foot radius. Of the thirty-two saloons that were stable enough by the fall of 1898 to be included in the 1899 city directory, six were definitely located within this limit: the Bowery, the Red Onion (later the Senate), the Coliseum, the Merchants, the Magnolia, and the Pioneer Sample Room (see map 2).[15]

The drop in advertising shows how the saloons began to fall out of the Skagway competition in the spring of 1899. From sixteen advertisers in February, the number dropped to nine in March, then only seven in May 1899. While the names of all but four saloons would change during the next ten years, the number of advertisers in the *Daily Alaskan* would hover between seven and nine. The number being granted licenses and listed in the city directories would be only slightly higher.

Despite the seemingly bad news brought by high license requirements, there was great optimism among some Skagway saloon keepers in early 1899. Those owners who could afford the license believed that no fair government would keep them from providing a much-wanted product for their eager customers. So upbeat was the feeling, then, that Seattle restaurateur Albert Reinert went into partnership with Charles Saake, owner of the Skagway Brewing Company, one of the few who had kept advertising right through the dark days of January 1899. The two partners purchased the Northern Trading and Transportation

Company Building from Otto Wolf on June 13, 1899.[16] The northern half of this building had been leased to Charles Rohbeck, the proprietor of the Mascotte Saloon. Reinert and Saake certainly must have had no doubts about the outcome of the next day's special election, the purpose of which was to determine whether they would be able to get a liquor license. On July 1, the first day of the high license, the partners opened the Mascot Saloon, with the spelling of its name changed to accentuate the recent renovations and new ownership.

According to estimates, there were about 6,000 people in Skagway at any one time during the summer and fall of 1898.[17] If about 10 percent of these residents were women and children, then roughly 5,400 men patronized the roughly 32 to 90 saloons that operated in the winter of 1899–1900, giving the owners anywhere from 60 to 169 customers apiece. Studies of other mining communities indicate that 80 customers per saloon was closer to the average.[18] Skagway's saloon keepers did well, but they had to. Once high license went into effect, $1,500 a year was no small price to pay.

By 1899, Skagway's population had fallen considerably, and many of the men coming through were staying for a shorter period of time. They stayed in town only for a night or two as they made arrangements to get their goods on pack trains for travel over the Brackett Road or on the railroad to Bennett. At most, a waning population of 5,000 men was available to Skagway's sixteen saloons after July 1, 1899, providing each saloon keeper with an average of 312 customers. Charging 10 cents a beer and 25 cents a whiskey or stronger drink, and with most customers spending 50 cents to a dollar a day, the average saloon-keeper could bring in over $235 a day. At that rate, it would take more than eighteen weeks for the saloon man to make enough money to pay his saloon license. With the railroad getting closer by the day to Whitehorse and navigable Yukon waters, the amount of time spent in Skagway got shorter. There were simply too many saloons to support Skagway's declining male population.

It is no surprise, then, that by the fall of 1900, when the data for the 1901 city directory was collected, only ten saloons were listed in Skagway; eight were advertising on a regular basis in the *Daily Alaskan* (see map 2). Two others were mentioned prominently in news articles of September 1900, suggesting that there were about a dozen saloons left in town. The federal census enumerated 1,951 men in Skagway.[19] These dozen saloons averaged about 163 customers per saloon, half that of 1899. The clientele was declining, along with the proceeds from liquor sales.

A special election for liquor licensing was repeated in June 1900 with much the same results as in the 1899 election. Eleven saloon-keepers paid for the election, and the male voters approved the licenses by a margin of 308 to 25. The editor of the *Daily Alaskan*, John Troy, questioned the method of granting the licenses, and wryly commented that the new federal judge in Juneau, Melville C. Brown, condoned his predecessor's opinion in the matter. The tone of the story was not flattering to either the saloon keepers, whom he accused of being so complacent that many did not chose to even vote, or to the voters.[20] It is obvious that Troy wanted to stir up trouble, and he did not have to wait long.

In early July 1900, the saloon owners of Juneau, through their lawyer, presented a census to Judge Brown showing that the city's population was less than 1,500, thus qualifying them for a $500 reduction in their liquor license fees. The attorney argued that while the federal census taker had counted over 1,500 people in March, there had been a lot of people leaving town since that time. He further claimed that the federal census included transients, whom the Juneau saloon men believed should not have been counted when calculating the liquor license fee. He had more than fifteen affidavits from prominent busi-nessmen that asserted that the population of Juneau was not above 1,500.[21] This issue was critical to the city's saloon owners, because at stake was a 33 percent reduction in the license fee, the equivalent of nearly $14,000 in today's currency.

Four days later, in his editorial column for Skagway's *Daily Alaskan*, John Troy objected to the fact that the Juneau saloon keepers wanted their licenses reduced. He accused them of classifying the miners as temporary residents in order to adjust the population figures down-ward and get their license fees reduced to $1000 a year.[22] Troy, who was rarely a friend of the working class, suddenly—and hypocritically— thought it was disgraceful that Juneau's businessmen should advocate discounting the transients and laborers in their population count. Skag-way's official census number for the year 1900 had been 3,117. When the laborers working on the railroad and ships were removed, it was lowered to 2,383. Perhaps Troy and Skagway's business promoters guessed just how much these transients had swollen the size of Skagway's census. There was no talk of taking a new census of Skagway for more than two years.

As Troy was making a big fuss about the classification of Juneau's population size as a means of keeping licenses high, a powerful advocate for the saloon men, Frank Clancy, left the city council—and the city of Skagway altogether—after the death of his brother James in March 1900. Despite keen opposition from the editor of the *Daily Alaskan*, in April 1900, the voters elected another saloon man, Lee Guthrie, owner of the Board of Trade, to take Clancy's place.

Robert Lee Guthrie might have been one of Skagway's wealthiest men. When he built what is still known today as "The White House" in 1902, the *Daily Alaskan* touted Guthrie's $10,000 home as "the handsomest and most expensive residence in Alaska." The newspaper gave its readers frequent updates on the progress of the home's construction, pointing out that Guthrie needed three city lots on which to build the mansion with its twelve-foot high ceilings. When the steamships delivered the prepared eastern hardwoods for its construction, the newspaper reported on the number of pieces to be used and the length of board feet they carried.[23]

Not all of Guthrie's wealth had come from the liquor served in his saloons or the cards dealt at his gambling tables, however. Much of it came from the rents he obtained as a landlord in the restricted district.

Guthrie was born in Mississippi on January 17, 1865, to Rachel Harbour Guthrie and Shadrack R. Guthrie. As an adolescent, he worked as a farm hand in Arkansas. He came to Skagway in July 1897, after participating in the gold rush at Cripple Creek, Colorado, and was among the very first to off-load at tidewater on the Skagway flats.[24] He entered the saloon business in Alaska as a co-owner of the Board of Trade Saloon, in partnership with George Rice and Company.[25] This syndicate had been running a chain of saloons, gambling houses, and dance halls all along the West Coast, and it was now making incursions into the far north.

That Lee Guthrie and the Board of Trade were synonymous by the spring of 1898 was a given. Stroller White fondly remembers "Guthrie's

The outside of the Board of Trade Saloon with its customers, about 1900.
Lee Guthrie is second from right wearing a vest and tie. Courtesy Alaska State
Library, William Norton Photograph Collection, P226-845.

Place" as being near his favorite dining place, the Board of Trade
Restaurant, and contrasted it favorably to the Mangy Dog Saloon,
which he deemed at the opposite end of the scale of prestige.[26] As the
competition grew keener, and high licensing for the sales of liquor
drew nearer, the Board of Trade only grew in prominence in the Skagway business scene. Certainly by 1900, the Board of Trade was Skagway's
largest, fanciest, and most posh "gentlemen's resort."

   To refer to the Board of Trade simply as a saloon would do Guthrie's
establishment an injustice. Guthrie offered two English billiards tables,
two pool tables, card rooms, roulette wheels, black jack tables, and
faro tables. In later years he advertised reading rooms and a mineral
display. It is never stated—or even implied—what happened in the
rooms Guthrie rented out (the 1900 census listed twenty-four boarders[27]), but sexual commerce without a doubt occurred within those
walls, at least in the earliest days of the gold rush. The fact that Joe

Engle, Guthrie's bartender and later general manager, was accused of assaulting Hazel Henwood in July 1901 suggests that women plied their trade in connection with the business.[28] If Hazel had been a respectable woman, the matter would have been worthy of newspaper notice, but instead, the fact is recorded only in court documents.

By advertising his place as a "gentleman's resort," Guthrie was deliberately indicating that he wanted only the better class of customers and that he offered a wide range of entertainments. With this sort of service in mind, after the Clancy Brothers left Skagway in 1900, Guthrie and a new partner, Phil Snyder, bought the Clancy music hall and opera house.[29]

Like Frank Clancy, Guthrie became a city councilman long before the Alaska Code allowed for city incorporation.[30] He was elected to office every June from 1899 to 1901. The 1899 business directory featured a glowing but largely empty tribute to him, touting him as popular, successful, progressive, and liberal. What those words meant to Skagwayans is almost impossible to interpret. Twice the feature article mentioned his wide property holdings.[31] A similar feature in the *Daily Alaskan's* New Year's Special Edition for 1900 called him "liberal in most things and generous in everything else." His other accolades included his service as "an enthusiastic worker for better fire protection." The piece also praised "his billiards rooms [as among] the finest in the Pacific Northwest, and one of Skagway's show places."[32] No words were too fine, apparently, for Lee Guthrie.

The man apparently made a good impression outside of Skagway as well. On April 4, 1900, news came to town that the thirty-five-year-old bachelor had married the niece of the late U.S. senator George Hearst.[33] Hearst, the father of the more widely known William Randolph Hearst, had gone to California with the gold rush in 1850 and had done well prospecting, mining, raising stock, and farming. From these prosaic beginnings he entered politics and bought the *San Francisco Examiner* for his son, William Randolph. Although an unsuccessful candidate for governor of California in 1882, he was elected to the U.S. Senate in 1887 and served until his death in 1891.[34]

In September, Guthrie once again announced his marriage. This time he boasted that his bride, Abigail, was the daughter of a Baptist minister, Rev. A. V. Atkins of Temple, Texas. After their marriage in Texas, Guthrie briefly returned to Skagway to introduce his new wife to his friends,[35] and then the couple took an extended trip through the middle and eastern states. They did not return to live in Skagway until early May 1901.[36] Then, from the following November to May 1902, Lee treated Abigail to a six-month tour of New York State and "nearly all the important Eastern points." After leaving the East, they spent time in San Francisco, living at the Palace Hotel.[37] While in Skagway, Mrs. Lee Guthrie—the newspaper never referred to her by her Christian name, although real estate records indicate that it was Abigail—was renowned for her elegant parties, and she once won an honorable mention in a garden contest.[38]

Despite his reputation now as a respectable married man, that Guthrie ran a gambling house was without question. As early as March 9, 1898, he had been arrested for gambling (a charge that meant he was a proprietor involved in the gambling business), along with eight other men, including the notorious Soapy Smith. In that case, he successfully pleaded not guilty, and the case was dismissed for insufficient evidence. Guthrie was again arrested in November 1899 on the charge of operating a faro table. This second case was not dismissed until October 1901. The 1900 census enumerated twenty-four men employed by the Board of Trade, including seven gamblers and one faro dealer. In a wave of reform that swept southeast Alaska starting in December 1902, ten Skagway men were served warrants for gambling; all of these men worked for Guthrie at the Board of Trade Saloon.[39]

Guthrie's position as one of the wealthiest men in Skagway, the owner of a combination gambling hall and saloon, and a member of the city council, positioned him as a powerful adversary of reformers when the latter chose to take the next step in the battle to impose morality on Skagway. This happened shortly after liquor licenses were granted en masse to all of Skagway's sixteen saloons in July 1900.

Skagway viewed the liquor license fees as a financial boon due to the fact that these funds paid for the town's public schools. In September 1900, the *Daily Alaskan* announced that $12,000 had been collected from the liquor licenses, and as only half of the licenses had been approved up to this point, another $12,000 was anticipated. All of this money was to go to the public schools—or so it was believed—and the good citizens of Skagway were developing magnificent plans for their school faster than the fees could come in.[40]

It is important to remember that Skagway, in the year 1900, was still the entry point for miners transferring to and from the goldfields in the Yukon and northern Alaska. Whereas earlier these miners had used the White Pass Trail to access the north, they now traveled via the White Pass and Yukon Route railroad. The town provided needed services for travelers and freighters alike. More than 60 percent of the population consisted of working-class laborers or members of the service sector; the remaining 40 percent were merchants and professionals who served the traveling public and the people who lived in town. As shown in appendix A, however, 26 percent of the adults were women, and 34 percent of the middle-class men had their wives living with them in Skagway. This statistic stands in contrast to the only 19 percent of working-class men who had their wives living with them. Considering the studies done by social historians on middle-class women's groups in the Pacific Northwest,[41] it should come as no surprise that the middle-class women of Skagway would become alarmed at what they saw as an immorally high number of saloons. They promptly used their time-tested organizational skills to form a women's club and lobby for community morality.

On March 26, 1900, a middle-class business woman named Sarah E. Shorthill created the Skagway chapter of the Woman's Christian Temperance Union; it became the organization's first chapter in Alaska. On May 22 of that same year, members of this chapter hosted the first evangelical institute of the WCTU in Alaska. The "institute" was like a convention, with meetings and lectures held every afternoon and evening for an entire week.[42]

Sarah and Thomas Shorthill came to Skagway in the fall of 1897, when they were both in their fifties. Sarah Elizabeth Werner was born in Rockford, Illinois, on February 26, 1847. She married Thomas on October 24, 1869, in her hometown when she was twenty-two years old. She bore four children in the next twelve years, two of whom died as toddlers. The family moved to Pulaski, Ohio, in the early 1870s, then to Trego, Kansas, in the latter half of the decade.[43] By 1890, the Shorthills had settled in Tacoma, Washington, where Sarah kept a dressmaker's shop in connection with Thomas's lodging house and carpentry business.[44]

When the couple moved north to Skagway in the fall of 1897, they were accompanied by their grown son, William, their daughter, Elizabeth, and son-in-law Lloyd Harrison. Sarah and Elizabeth opened a dressmaking shop, which they called the Ladies Bazaar, at 404 Broadway. They shared space with the Skaguay News Depot, a news and stationery shop operated by Thomas Shorthill. William Shorthill opened a similar establishment in Dyea, which he called the Olympic News Company, and Lloyd Harrison operated a stenography and typewriting school in Skagway. Both younger men had been lawyers in Tacoma but apparently found their clerical skills more saleable than their lawyering skills. The five adults lived together in the rooms over the Skaguay News Depot.[45]

The Shorthills had long been involved with temperance issues. Sarah had founded a temperance organization in Wakeeny, Kansas, when she discovered that the local pharmacist was selling bitters and drugs containing alcohol to minors. She and a number of similarly minded women succeeded in making the pharmacist close down his business. The entire family was active in the Prohibition Party in Tacoma. On the Prohibition Ticket, Thomas ran for lieutenant governor of Washington State in 1896 but lost by an extremely wide margin. Sarah joined the WCTU when she moved to Tacoma.[46] Apparently she was not about to discontinue her activities after moving to the iniquitous Alaska Territory.

About six months after its founding, in September 1900, the Skagway WCTU filed a protest against the Reception, Senate, Seattle, and Fifth Avenue saloons for being located within 400 feet of the Union Church at the corner of Fifth and State. The Alaska Code clearly stipulated that the front entrance of the business and the front door of the church were to be the measuring points. The *Daily Alaskan* stated that measurements on the plat map suggested that the entrance to the Reception Saloon was 120 feet from the church, the Fifth Avenue Saloon was 335 feet, and the Seattle and Senate (originally the Red Onion) saloons were right at 400 feet. The Fifth Avenue Hotel had originally used its side entrance as the entryway for patrons to gain access to the bar but had changed the entry so that it fronted the hotel lobby during

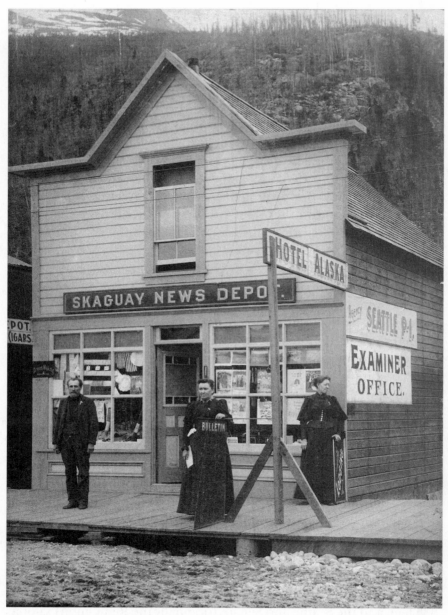

Thomas (*left*) and Sarah Shorthill (*right*), with their daughter Elizabeth
Harrison (*middle*), in front of the Shorthills' business. Courtesy Alaska State
Library, William Werner Shorthill Photograph Collection, P389-83.

a remodeling event during the current year. Apparently the protestors now considered the main entrance to the hotel to be the entrance to the bar.[47]

According to the *Daily Alaskan*, the filing angered many businessmen, who contended that the business district was so compact it was "impossible to have a saloon at all that was more than 400 feet from a church or school." This statement, however, was blatantly untrue. The reporter of this story, John Troy, added that "the Skagway saloon men have ever been most liberal contributors to the building funds of churches and schools in the city," as if their generosity should supersede the law. Troy noted in passing that First District Judge Johnson had ignored a similar protest filed the previous year.[48] Troy's charge was not true. In January 1899, Judge Johnson had determined that local elections by the male voters could replace petitions of a majority of white adults in order to determine which saloons could get their liquor licenses each year. His ruling had merely stipulated that the cities were to determine which saloons had licenses.

John Weir Troy came to Skagway with the gold rush in August 1897 from Olympia, Washington, where he had worked as a correspondent for a Seattle newspaper. He started the *Daily Alaskan* on November 11, 1898. Through his gifts as a writer, he proceeded to have considerable influence over the opinions of Skagway's citizens. As a Democrat, he espoused home rule—Alaskans for Alaskans—and was arguably Skagway's biggest booster. He never lost an opportunity to appeal to middle-class businessmen, both those existing in the community and those that might want to come and invest there.

Within days of the WCTU saloon protest, Troy called for the repeal of the law "that there shall be no saloon license issued for a business within 400 feet of a church or a school." Alternatively, he proposed, the council should remove the churches and schools from the business part of town. He did not think it was right to allow the churches to crowd the saloons out of their established places of business. The saloon men included "citizens who have done and are doing much to promote the welfare and business interest of the city." He praised the Reception Saloon for investing $40,000 in a "first-class brewery" with one of the highest payrolls in Skagway.[49] In his mind, economics far outweighed moral issues.

John Troy in 1933, when he was governor of Alaska. Courtesy Alaska State Library, John Weir Troy Photograph Collection, P523-19.

It did not take long for the owners of the Seattle and Senate saloons to ask the city engineer, J. H. Diers, to survey the distance from the church to their front doors—nor did it take long for him to do it. He found that the distance to each of their doors was 409 and one-half feet, making the WCTU's protest moot. This finding encouraged some businessmen to put pressure on the WCTU to withdraw its protest. In addition, Judge Brown declined to hear the prohibition organization's protest until after all of the other jury cases had been heard in the current session of the court.[50]

It is unclear whether all of Troy's rhetoric was fueled by sympathy for his fellow businessmen, concern over a hold-up on the license fees and the impact on school funding, or whether he was playing on the knowledge that some men did not like the idea that their favorite saloons could be shut down by a group of women. Indeed, it was probably a mixture of all three motives. And, in any case, his tactic of inciting controversy no doubt raised his newspaper sales.

Whatever the real reason for the editor's concern, Troy decided he would take the higher moral ground in his editorials and blame the "temperance people" for holding up the building of the new school and the paying of the teachers. On October 12, in what was billed as a news story, Troy told his readers that the four licenses would bring $3,000 to the city for the construction of the school, which would be sufficient "to build a very good four-room school house." The delays were enough to put off construction until the next year. Then, on his editorial page, Troy wrote that Skagway would have saloons no matter what actions the temperance people took, so the city should have the benefit of the license fees. If the saloons were crowded out of the business section of town, they would only be started in the residential section. He doubted the townspeople would like that situation any better.[51]

Although he had been reporting the other problems the city was having with the license fees, Troy chose not to highlight them at this point in time, and focused instead on the protest by the WCTU as the source for the delay in construction of the new schoolhouse. In fact, at the same time that the protest had been filed, the city's guarantee company had refused to issue a bond to the city treasurer because he did not receive a salary. For lack of this bond, the city was in danger of losing the liquor licenses funds. Rather than give the treasurer a token salary, the city tried to issue a bond on the signature of Skagway property owners. They needed a $20,000 bond in order to keep the schools open. Some teachers had not been paid for three months for lack of this bond.[52] Troy did report this situation but did so on a different day than his tirades against the women of the WCTU, making it clear that he wanted to blame the temperance movement for the lack of school funding.

Finally, on the last day of the federal court term in Skagway, Commissioner Charles Sehlbrede heard the protest against the granting of licenses to the four saloons. The city surveyor, J. H. Diers, testified that the distance from the Presbyterian Church to the Seattle Saloon was 403 feet, and on that basis, the Seattle was promised its license. The other cases were referred to the court clerk for testimony.[53] Fred Ron-kendorf and Alexander Chisholm of the Senate Saloon (once the Red Onion) and Herman Grimm of the Seattle Saloon were each granted their licenses on October 20, 1900, less than a week later.[54]

The Fifth Avenue Saloon was inside the Fifth Avenue Hotel, one of Skagway's finest establishments. It was operated by Louise A. Burke, a woman of vast business experience, respectability, and sophistication. She somehow found a way around the WCTU, for she was granted her license on November 24, 1900. She may have simply reopened the side entrance. However, the year 1900 was the last that she applied for a liquor license.[55]

Only the Reception Saloon lost its case. Curiously, the Daily Alaskan did not report the news that Judge Sehlbrede had granted the WCTU its request to shut down that saloon. Having taken the saloon owners' side against the "temperance people," Troy was probably reluctant to tout their one victory.

The collection of liquor license fees continued to be an important source of revenue for the city of Skagway in the years that followed. A new code of law for Alaska enacted on June 14, 1900, continued to provide for the collection of liquor license fees, half of which would go to the public schools in incorporated towns only. The Daily Alaskan called for rapid incorporation in order to take advantage of those taxes. A petition for incorporation with eighty-seven signatures was procured by June 16. The only protest was from the Alaska and Northwest Terri-tories Trading Company, which, in the name of Bernard Moore, claimed 160 acres in the heart of the town site. Objections were overruled, and an election for incorporation was held on June 28. The vote was over-whelmingly for incorporation. The first meeting of the newly elected city council was held July 2, only a little more than two weeks after the bill was signed into law.[56]

It did not take long for the new code to be changed again. Because Alaska had no voting representation in the U.S. Congress, the military district had to rely on other states' congressmen for legislation. In Feb-ruary 1901, former Skagwayan George L. Shoup of Idaho introduced a bill into the U.S. Senate amending Section 203 of the Alaska Code, which had provided for 50 percent of the liquor tax to be given to the public schools. The amendment allowed for the use of the funds for purposes other than the funding of schools in the local communities once the schools' needs were met. Before the ink was even dry on the new bill, Skagwayans were suggesting ways to spend the "extra moneys" from the liquor taxes. On March 2, 1901, some people in town proposed funding a public library, instead of burdening students with raising the money.[57]

But two weeks later, it became obvious that the bill would not allow indiscriminate spending of the liquor license money. The bill stipulated that municipality could not spend more than 25 percent of the revenues on purposes other than public schools, and then only if all of the public school needs were met by the remaining 25 percent (50 percent still went to the general treasury of the United States). Troy pointed out that, with the "growing population of children in Skagway," all of the liquor tax revenues would be needed to build a new school building.[58]

Four days later, Troy pressed his point about the importance of these liquor revenues when he commented on an incident that had taken place in Seattle. Two saloon owners in that city were prosecuted for violating the anti-box ordinance—taking drinks into private rooms in saloons—and were acquitted. The church people who brought the complaint grumbled that the prosecution was not made in good faith. Troy observed that without the saloon revenue, Seattle could not pay half its expenses. He suggested that if the churches wanted to put the saloons out of business, they should pay the city what the saloons currently paid in taxes. However, Troy commented, the churches "are exceedingly careful not to pay taxes."[59]

With that parting barb, Troy, the city, the saloon owners, and the temperance people seemed to settle into a sort of uneasy truce that lasted for more than a year. The only common enemy on which they all agreed to focus was the prostitutes. Periodically, throughout the following year, the U.S. deputy marshal would spend more time arresting these women than during any other period in Skagway's history. He was spurred on by the reformers who had—for the moment—given up on the saloons. They had won a small victory by closing the Reception Saloon, and had shown the community that they had some muscle. But they also realized that fighting the huge economic assets represented by the saloons was a war they could not win—at least not as long as saloon owners remained on the city council.

In the weeks before the licenses were to be granted in 1901, the saloon owners got together and hired attorney Phil Abrahams to gather a "petition for the consent of the white male and female residents of the city of Skaguay over the age of eighteen, to the barter, sale and exchange of intoxicating liquors within said city." Perhaps they believed this method would be cheaper than holding a special election, which, with the new Judge Brown in Juneau, might not be the wisest course this time around. Abrahams canvassed house to house, and then swore that a majority of said residents within two miles of the places where the liquor would be sold had consented to its barter, sale, and exchange. The petition contained 812 names.[60] Because the city issued the licenses, someone in authority must have believed that 812 was a majority of the white adult residents of the town.

By the fall of 1901, the number of saloons in Skagway had fallen from a dozen to ten. The law and order folks in Skagway and those looking for more revenues had found another way to harass the saloons. In November, the remaining saloons were fined $15 and costs each for "conducting a cigar business without a license."[61] It is curious that Troy made such a big point of this infraction. Thirty other businesses were fined during the November 1901 court session for operating without a license. Only the saloons' failures to obtain cigar licenses made news.[62]

————

With the construction of the White Pass and Yukon Route railroad through to Whitehorse, Yukon, in May 1900 and the imposition of high license fees in July 1899, Skagway went through a metamorphosis in its attitude about liquor sales. No longer would its population tolerate tent saloons, rot-gut whiskey, or small dives. The goals of the prohibitionists were to generate funds for schools and other good works, and encourage only "responsible" saloon keepers who could invest in a substantial infrastructure. As Skagway became more settled and the merchants decided that the town would not "bust" after its boom, an increasing number of middle-class wives came to live with their husbands.

These women formed clubs, prominent among them the WCTU, which grew alarmed at the number of saloons in the community. Skagway's second round of reform, therefore, was focused on the saloons and enforcement of the rule that restricted saloons from setting up business within four hundred feet of a church or school. This effort pitted the middle-class women of the WCTU against the middle-class men who operated the saloons and sought to build the first public school in Skagway.

David Charles Beyreis, in his study of masculinity and the Klondike gold rush, argues that middle-class men were conflicted by their desire to be good husbands and fathers (the "virtuous masculine") and their need to reassert their primitive or natural beings on the new frontier.[63] By bringing their families north, they were able to live up to their virtuous masculine obligations but at the cost of curtailing their self-indulgent bachelor habits: patronizing saloons and parlor houses. The merchants had first let Soapy Smith play his con games on the gullible traveling public until the bunco man made a bad name for their town. Likewise, these middle-class merchants had to bring their activity to a halt and rid the town of that class of petty gambling; however, they permitted men like Frank Clancy and Lee Guthrie with their blackjack tables and roulette wheels to stay in operation. When the middle-class wives came to town, they organized and began to curtail the more objectionable saloons, the dives run by the likes of Soapy Smith. Despite the compromises made on both sides, the clash in women's and men's values would only grow more contentious.

CHAPTER THREE

A Restricted District, 1901

The popular image of the western mining town is cluttered with dance halls and saloons. It was in these settings that pulp novelists and Hollywood filmmakers placed the western prostitute of the nineteenth century. But most of Skagway's prostitutes conducted their business on the more modest scale common to the emerging boomtowns of the turn of the century. In the early days, the average prostitute of Skagway was more likely to be found in the so-called "cribs" than in the saloons. These one-room shacks, supplied with a bed and little else in the way of comforts, brought in exorbitant rent income for their owners, and frequent, cheap customers for their tenants. The crib was a place where a woman working for the percentage of drinks she pandered—the "percentage girl"—and lacking a rented room in a saloon or dancehall, could take her customer. Or, if she just waited outside the door, the client would come to her.

As Skagway's boom turned to bust around the beginning of 1900 and the town's economy began to slide, the dance hall and resort owners such as Frank Clancy began to sell out. The value of an unimproved lot in the residential section plunged from $500 in 1898 to $100 in 1900. Due to the imposition of the high liquor license (the equivalent of $41,000 a year in today's currency), the number of saloons dropped from almost 100 in January 1899 to 16 in August of that year. By 1900, only Clancy's Theater remained to entertain the growing numbers of middle-class families, and that venue closed by the end of 1902.[1]

As the dance halls, resorts, and saloons disappeared from Skagway's landscape, so too did the prostitutes working in the upstairs of saloons. But that did not mean the disappearance of the women exchanging acts of sex in return for hard cash. The saloons and dance halls had never provided all of the living and working space for these percent-age women. The cribs in the alleys and along Seventh Avenue always served as that secondary accommodation.

Once they moved out of the dance halls and into the cribs, the prostitutes became more visible to the general public. Not surprisingly, then, they became the next target of reform efforts in Skagway. As the women solicited in front of their cribs, they could be seen by others besides the men who frequented the sporting resorts and saloons. As a result, if the authorities wished to appear to be controlling prosti-tution, they had greater success in achieving that goal if they attacked crib prostitutes rather than rounding up women who solicited in the saloons and dance halls. Therefore, Skagway's earliest efforts to enforce the laws against prostitution were directed against the prostitutes living in cribs, because that is where the reform community could witness the results.

On September 16, 1898, only a little more than a year after the gold rush began, a "Skaguay Merchant" sent a letter to the newspaper editor demanding a law to curb the solicitation of sex by "warty-nosed old prostitutes" at the "lb. shops" behind the Montana Saloon on State Street. He closed by suggesting that "a brick wall seventeen feet high be constructed across the eastern end of 'Paradise Alley.'"[2] Though the merchant was a good, solid citizen, apparently not enough of the voting citizens of town—all male, of course—agreed with him. No laws were passed because they already existed in the Oregon Code, although they were not enforced. The wall never appeared.

Two alleys held the cribs and the women who ranked lowest on the hierarchy of Skagway's sporting women: Paradise or "French" Alley, behind the saloons and resorts on Sixth Avenue between State and Broadway, and "Jap Alley," a continuation of the same lane as it ran west of State. Cribs could also be found stretched along Seventh Avenue, especially in the vicinity of dance halls such as Clancy's Music Hall, the Princess, and the Tivoli (see map 2).

Cribs were common to boomtowns throughout the West, although they could also be found in the slums and restricted districts of larger cities at the turn of the century.[3] A crib shack rented for up to $5.00 a day to the woman who used one for her place of business. At a time when the average laborer made only $3.50 a day, a landlord could make a tremendous amount of money off such a very inexpensive structure. The women solicited at the doorways of the cribs, often clothed only in nightdresses or kimonos. Their business was conducted quickly, usually for less than a dollar a visit and often for only two bits (a fourth of a dollar). The client remained clothed and wearing his boots; an oilcloth was generally placed across the foot of the bed to minimize the laundry expenses.[4] The shack had a door in front, a window on the side and back, and a stove and wash basin with few other amenities. A few of Skagway's cribs can still be seen around town.

French Alley ran behind such resorts as the Pack Train, the Board of Trade, the Louvre, and the Red Onion. The French women for whom it was named probably arrived with the earliest boatloads of stampeders. On April 9, 1898, during the first legal action taken against prostitutes, marshals charged twenty-two women with disorderly conduct. Included in the list of those who paid their token $15 fines were the fine French names of Anneta, Juliete, Josephine, Victorique, Magarite, Marie, and Louise. In a later incident, in February 1900, the U.S. Deputy Marshal arrested the French women Louise and Evan Bleur for "having kept a house of ill fame for the purpose of prostitution." Judge Sehlbrede found Evan Bleur not guilty, because she was "a guest at the house," but he fined Louise the minimum $50.[5] Then, in mid-November 1900, Marshal Snook arrested six French prostitutes because they had "often of late caused much trouble." Georgia Dubois, Jennie Brizaid, Evangeline Miller, Julia Blandast, Lillie Barge, and Susan Clark admitted to the charges believing they would receive the customary $50 fine. To their surprise, Judge Sehlbrede instead sentenced them each to three months in jail.[6]

This sentence may have frightened some of the French women into leaving Skagway altogether. That some French women moved on to Whitehorse or Dawson is evidenced by a May 1902 newspaper article about two French "sisters" who had once done business in Skagway. They took the train from Skagway to Whitehorse and engaged rooms at the White Horse Hotel. There they entertained R. E. West, a well-known Dawson news agent, and Ernest Levin, the proprietor of Whitehorse's Arctic restaurant. When the women left the room, the men threw their suitcases out of the window as a joke. They intended to use the women's clothing to dress up and surprise the drinking crowd that

A Skagway prostitute in front of her crib wearing typical "working clothes," probably on French or Paradise Alley. Courtesy John C. Sinclair, Ontario, Canada.

"One of Dawson's Favorites" in 1898 or 1899, inside her crib. Both the crib accoutrements and the woman's dress were typical of those favored by Skagway prostitutes. Courtesy Alaska State Library, P. E. Larss Photograph Collection, P41-58.

had accumulated at the hotel, but the suitcases contained valuable jewelry, and the practical jokers were charged with theft. Levin drew a jail sentence of one month and West three months of cutting wood for the constabulary (hence the northern expression "sentenced to the wood pile"). Because the men were well known and well liked, a general petition was circulated requesting a lighter sentence, which the judge obliged. These same women were later driven from Dawson for operating a house of prostitution outside the restricted district.[7] The case is instructive in that it indicates that johns were sometimes prosecuted in Canada. No similar cases appeared in Skagway's courts. As usual, the women were ridiculed by the newspapers.

Not all the French women fled Skagway, however. In July 1902, Emma Alward, "a French woman," and Lilly Berge, who occupied cribs on Seventh Avenue, were arrested for vagrancy during one of the periodic spates of arrests meant to remind the prostitutes that they would be tolerated only so long as they kept quiet and did not cause any trouble. A month later, a woman named Jennie, whose last name was either Benalt or Brizald, appeared before Judge Joseph J. Rodgers, again for vagrancy.[8]

While the newspapers branded the French women as "inmate(s) of a house of ill-repute," the criminal records inevitably charged them with vagrancy rather than prostitution. To the city of Skagway, a vagrant was, among other things, "any person not having a fixed business or employment who habitually stays in or frequents, groceries, dram-shops, drinking-saloons, houses of ill fame, gambling houses, houses of bad repute, railroad-depots, post office and street corners or fire engine houses."[9] An "inmate of a house of ill-fame" was required to pay a much larger fine than a vagrant.

Apparently the judge did not want to run the French women out of town. These lesser fines were symbolic acts to show the reform-minded that the women were being persecuted and to remind them of their places. By not imposing higher fees, the judge was allowing the institution to remain in town and not be destroyed.[10]

There can be no doubt that the six French Alley women, sent to federal prison for six months in November 1900, were indeed French, for they needed a French interpreter during their court sessions.[11] But not all the "French" prostitutes were really from France. Many prostitutes adopted the French guise because of the exotic reputation it bought them.

This enhancement to their perceived status encouraged the women of the demimonde to take on the label "French," whereas respectable women avoided it. Charlene Porsild claims that the Dawson miners preferred French women when presented with a choice, a conclusion also drawn by Mary Murphy in Butte, Montana.[12] There is little doubt that the Skagway newspapers viewed the "French" women with more respect than they did the Japanese, of which the town had quite a few. One indication of this was that the "French sisters" told to "git" to Dawson remained unnamed, perhaps out of deference to their somewhat more respectable customers.

The allure of the French women lay mostly in their race and ethnicity. The major immigrants of the late nineteenth century were Germans and Irish. These immigrants worked hard for low wages because they hoped to start anew in America. They were a threat to more established working-class Americans by keeping wages low; they threatened middle-class Americans with their differing religious and social customs. The French, on the other hand, did not comprise a large minority of cheap labor in industrial America and so never presented a threat to Americans of any class. "French" women, feigned or real, were just exotic enough to be mysterious, but not so much as to be too different. The rising middle class of the turn of the century feared nothing so much as it did anything or anybody too alien.[13]

Japanese prostitutes seemed to hit this particular nerve. As early as January 1899, the editor of the *Skaguay News* took up the cry to control the institution, and his target appeared mainly to be Japanese women. In his view, "Skagway would be entitled to a mark on the credit side of the column if every Jap woman in the town was shipped out. . . . Prostitution and mangy dogs are too common in this particular section of the broad white north. Let us have less of both evils."[14]

The editor's view was not atypical. The Japanese in general and Japanese prostitutes in particular experienced considerable prejudice at the turn of the century. The Japanese prostitutes may have seemed exotic to the hopeful miners and laborers, but they were still non-Christian, and in middle-class Skagway's racist eyes, the dark-haired women's skin was not white. In fact, in Seattle, labor advocates successfully used the presence of Japanese prostitutes in the tenderloin district to enlist middle-class women to support their efforts to obtain better working conditions for working-class women.[15]

Always subject to prejudice, the prostitutes who were not Caucasian drew particular malice and became easy targets of reform. While not subject to the same racial hatred as the Chinese at the turn of the century, Japanese women attracted the greatest public ire in Skagway. In January 1899, the editor of the *Skaguay News* announced the arrival of several Japanese women. When he urged reducing the amount of "prostitution and mangy dogs" in "the broad white north,"[16] his use of the word "white" deliberately had more than one meaning.

Reports of the Japanese women continued for the next several years. In one incident, a man named "Japanese Henry," assaulted his "former mistress" as she dreamt of "the flowery home of her inno-cent childhood."[17] Other articles reported fights on Seventh Avenue between Japanese men in which Japanese "girls" were witnesses or broke up the fight.[18] Without fail, burgeoning reform movements attacked "the denizens of Jap Alley," between Fifth and Sixth Avenues west of State.

Yuji Ichioka, an expert on Japanese prostitution in nineteenth-century America, claims there were only 985 Japanese women in the United States in the year 1900. These women seem to have first appeared in Denver in the 1860s, and were openly arriving in San Francisco in the 1880s. Japanese women were reported in Seattle by 1890. Their presence was illegal, both from the point of view of the American immigration officials and of the Japanese government, which permit-ted only merchants, students, and some laborers to leave the country, but never any women. Japanese prostitutes almost always functioned as slaves of men who had kidnapped them or who had purchased them from their poverty-stricken parents in Japan, and then smug-gled them to the United States. Occasionally, they were free women who were tricked into coming to America with promises of good jobs. The men who procured these women treated them as inden-tured servants until they could purchase their freedom with their poor profits, minus the cost of food, lodging, and clothing. If they ever did become free of the men who owned them, they were usually so humiliated by "the life" that they rarely attempted to return to their homes in Japan. Anti-Japanese sentiment in America being what it was, employment in other, more respectable occupations was next to impossible. As cooks or servants, they competed with Japanese men, who were usually offered only the poorest-paying jobs. Therefore, the women were left doing only what a man could not: continue selling sex.[19]

Japanese men usually smuggled their countrywomen to America in the holds of merchant ships. Among other commodities, there was a lively trade in lumber between Japan and the American Pacific Northwest. Most of the cooks and firemen (those who stoked the fires of the steam engines) on these ships were Japanese. The ships almost always stopped in Nagasaki, one of the principal locations from which the slave prostitutes were exported. Some of the steamships operating out of Skagway had Japanese men on their crews. As early as July 1898, the newspaper noted that an envoy from Japan visited Skagway looking into investment possibilities.[20] The resulting rise in commercial dealings between Skagway and Japanese businessmen opened the opportunity for the smuggling of prostitutes on Japanese ships.

Few of the Japanese women were able to break away from the cycle of poverty and prostitution. One notable exception was Yamada Waka, who Alaskan writer Lael Morgan suggests may have spent some time in southeast Alaska. Like many of her compatriots, she had been kidnapped from her home in Japan, a farm near Yokohama, and compelled to work as a prostitute in Seattle. She came through Skagway working for a syndicate that rotated "fresh faces" through the north. In San Francisco, she escaped to a Presbyterian mission, went to school, and married a naturalized Japanese businessman. Returning to Japan as a respectable woman, she became a leading feminist, eventually meeting Eleanor Roosevelt during her world travels.[21]

Besides their being virtual slaves, what else is known about the Japanese prostitutes in Skagway? Due to the location in town where they lived, all eight of the Japanese women enumerated in the 1900 census appear to have been prostitutes. All of them were between twenty-one and twenty-five years of age. Seven lived in a single household, listed as "Yokohomo Row." As with some of the other known prostitutes in town, the enumerator listed their occupations as "at home." Their names were Esona Eghatch, Josie Esaka, Mary Kamika, Hannah Mi, Fannie Naka, and sisters Josie and Mamie Mow. They had all moved to the United States in 1895. Two of the women had come to Alaska from San Francisco, and the others came from Seattle. They had arrived in Skagway at different times: Josie and Mamie Mow came first, arriving in May 1898, followed by Fannie Naka the following month. Hannah Mi showed up in March 1899, and the remaining women had been in Skagway only a few days before the enumeration in April 1900. None of them were on the boatload decried by the newspaper in January 1899.[22] There was likely a considerable amount of "turnover" among the occupants of Yokohama Town.

The 1900 census listed only one other Japanese woman in Skagway, and she was probably also a prostitute. Josie Elopis lived by herself on Seventh Avenue. She was enumerated right after the all-Japanese women household just described, suggesting her house was located nearby. She was twenty-four years old and came from Seattle in January 1900. She had immigrated in 1893, two years before her compatriots.[23]

One of the very first criminal actions taken by the fledgling Skagway legal system against prostitutes was a roundup of twenty-two women on April 9, 1898. Charged with disorderly conduct, all but one woman was fined $15 and court costs. Among those arrested were Katie Jap, Ida Jap, and Jopsie Jap.[24] These women's names indicate that the Japanese prostitutes were in the city as early as were the other nineteen women.

Obviously, Japanese prostitutes still lived in Skagway when the 1900 census enumerator visited "Yokohama Town"—or "Jap Alley"—on April 13, 1900. Only three weeks later, on July 7, 1900, yet another Japanese woman, Lucy Suggy (most assuredly a corruption of "Sugi," a common Japanese surname) was arrested for keeping a house of ill fame. Her attorney, John F. Dillon, asked for two continuances before her July 12 trial by jury, where she was found not guilty. Later that same day, she was charged with the same crime, this time by J. H. Sturgill, the brother of one of the jurors. This time she waived her rights, pled guilty, and paid a $100 fine.[25]

The Japanese prostitutes managed to stay out of the news for four months after this incident, until November 15, 1900, when the six French prostitutes from nearby "Paradise Alley" were hauled into court. According to the newspaper, the six-month jail sentences received by the French women "had a very wonderful effect on 'Jap Alley,' and

crib women all over town. 'Jap Alley' was dark last night and a close
watch was kept on it, but not a window was opened."[26] Yet the lights
behind the red curtains stayed dark only temporarily. There can be
little doubt that all of the prostitutes were back in business soon.

The Japanese prostitutes, like all the women living in "Jap" and
Paradise Alleys, did their business from cribs. All the crib women
ended up turning much of their earnings over to the men who owned
their place of business. Josie Washburn, a reformed Nebraska madam,
who wrote her autobiography in 1909, referred to a man who owned
a crib as the "Man Landlady" and viewed him as "the most despicable
member of the underworld." She reviled him more than the lowest
streetwalker or "crib girl" in the tenderloin. The man who owned property in the red light district, who collected enormous rents for the
squalid shelter of the cribs, earned her particular wrath because he
took but did not return. He made immense profits from women who
were already sharing their income with a pimp pretending to be a
lover. Unlike the madam, who supervised houses of prostitution, this
"man landlady" did not provide any helpful services: instruction and
guidance in sanitation and the spread of sexually transmitted diseases,
a place to rest and recuperate during illnesses, or advice on contra-
ception, abortion, or the adoption out of unwanted children. Without
the firm hand of the madam, Washburn claimed the inhabitants of
the cribs owned by men drank or drugged themselves into states of
intoxicated oblivion, further wasting what little money was left.[27]

In Washburn's world, the cribs and the saloons were inextricably
interlinked, even to the point that the saloon and restaurant owners
were also the owners of the cribs along the alleys behind the saloons.
She decried a world in which women were forced to pay daily rents of
one to five dollars in advance, then turn around and pay their man
landladies for the food or drinks they needed to sustain themselves
and serve their customers. The greatest injustice, in Washburn's mind,
was that the women inhabiting the cribs, not the man landladies,
were prosecuted by the police whenever reform movements came
along. While the madam who owned property, and preferred to call
herself a "landlady," did often suffer when the reformers thought to
"clean up" the city, the men who owned worse kinds of property
escaped untouched.[28]

Washburn's indignation may sound strident, trite, and self-serving to the modern ear. Yet her autobiography was more genuine than the many "true accounts" about prostitutes distributed by early twentieth-century reformers to advance special causes. She declaims like a Southern Baptist preacher, sincere and sure of her knowledge. She decries the injustices perpetrated upon women by a society that uses them, and then refuses to help them when they are done with them. Historian Sharon E. Wood, in writing the introduction to the 1997 version of Washburn's autobiography, assures the reader that nothing Josie wrote was concocted to advance a naïve reformer's cause. Josie Washburn was real and so was her man landlady.[29]

Not only did he exist, but his type existed outside her Nebraska city. "This same condition," Washburn wrote, "this same he-landlady, who passes as a real estate agent, the same Christian owners of land, and the same persecution of the unfortunate girls, for political and financial purposes, can be found in every city."[30] Skagway was no exception. This city's version was one of Lee Guthrie's and Frank Clancy's cohorts: Frank T. Keelar, "The Money King."

Keelar was born in New York in July 1845. In 1861, at sixteen years old, he went to California, where he "sold goods, dug for gold, and sold goods again." In San Francisco, he set himself up as a merchant and speculated on farm property. He was a salesman in 1880, he dealt in watches, jewelry and diamonds in 1884, in books and paintings in 1889, and was an auctioneer of fine art in 1892. For much of the 1890s he advertised himself as a wholesale merchant or an auctioneer in San Francisco, with a residence in Oakland, which he shared with his wife, Mattie, and his father, Truman.[31]

After moving to Skagway in March 1898, Keelar began to invest seriously in the community, grabbing up enough land to become known as one of the largest property owners in the city.[32] According to his advertisements, he bought, sold, traded, promoted, invested, and built. He claimed to own mines, sawmills, timberlands, town sites, steamboats, pack trains, stage lines, dog teams and more land than any other man in Alaska. He possessed cold storage, steam-heated warehouses, and fire- and burglar-proof vaults, all presumably for rent. He dealt in gold, silver, diamonds, clocks, watches, furs, and musical instruments: in other words, he acted as a pawnbroker. Keelar served as the town's auctioneer whenever owners went bankrupt.[33] He loaned money freely, using the borrower's real estate as collateral. Sixteen of the twenty-five deed transfers involving Frank or wife Mattie Keelar between 1897 and 1925 went for the price of $1.00, suggesting either that the land was traded for other considerations or that he did not wish to divulge the actual price of the transaction.[34]

In his role as Skagway landowner, Keelar bragged that he had fifty furnished houses to rent,[35] no doubt some of them commanding rents of $5.00 or more a week. City deed records indicate that he or his wife had at least partial interest in more than two dozen pieces of property and two mines in the vicinity of Skagway.[36] Keelar had money, and money bought power. Seven months after coming to Skagway, he hosted a meeting of the members of the Benevolent and Protective Order of Elks, and established a local lodge, one that still exists in the community today. He was elected district deputy and "Bull Elk."[37]

Hosting meetings and parties bought the Keelars much favor. "As entertainers, Mr. and Mrs. Keelar have few equals and no superiors," a columnist gushed.[38] They provided space for a social club called the Elite Clan for their semimonthly dances.[39] Mattie Keelar formed an exclusive women's organization called the Magpie Club, specializing in "sociability, the promotion of friendship among the members and general improvement."[40]

That Frank Keelar was wealthy appears undeniable. How he gained that wealth may be open to some speculation. Keelar also appears to have had considerable connections with the Japanese in Skagway. He adopted a half-Japanese man, Sangi Ikuta, as his son. Ikuta claimed to be a civil engineer in the 1900 census when he was only fourteen years old, and was the only nonwhite that the enumerator indicated could read and write. In contrast, all eight of the other Japanese men living in town were listed as cooks, and the six Japanese listed as working on board ships were men who stoked the fires of the engines.[41]

In addition, Keelar later fostered Ikuta's brother Jenjiro Ikuta. This young man worked as a watchmaker and later a clerk in Keelar's jewelry story. Jenjiro married Euro-American Lena Ostella Worth, from Barnet, Vermont, on February 11, 1909. They named their son Truman after Keelar's father. Beginning in 1911, the Keelars deeded their store

Frank Keelar and his dogs sitting in front of his Broadway store, 1904. Courtesy Alaska State Library, Clarence Leroy Andrews Photograph Collection, P45-319.

on Broadway, and, later, other Skagway property, to Jenjiro Ikuta, in return for only token amounts of money.[42]

Keelar's intimate associations with the Ikuta brothers suggests that the Money King had intimate ties with the Japanese, probably developed during his time in San Francisco, which was a Mecca of Japanese immigrants at the time. This connection, in addition to actions that Keelar would take as a city councilman, suggests that he mentored the Japanese prostitutes in town. He was probably the important middle man who not only provided the first contacts in the community, but also made it possible for them to stay there.

Frank Keelar was elected to the city council twice, the first time in company with Frank Clancy in 1899 and the second time in company with Lee Guthrie in 1900.[43] On February 26, 1901, Keelar was elected for a third time, for one of three vacancies on the town council. While his influence in local politics was once more assured, however, Keelar began to make enemies. Three months after his election he became the target of political cartoons. Besides implying that he controlled the town, these cartoons, which featured barrels of money, indicate that Keelar usually profited by his politics.[44]

In the meantime, businessmen and politicians who wanted home rule—a territorial government with an elected representative in Congress—were afraid that as long as Alaska had the *reputation* of being lawless and immoral, with such shady types as Frank Keelar setting the tone, Congress would never grant them territorial status. Therefore, the First District judge in Juneau began to respond to reformers' cries for morality-based decisions on the bench and enforcement of gambling, drinking, and prostitution laws. The middle-class women of the WCTU, which had formed a local chapter in March 1900, successfully closed down the Reception Saloon the following October.

In the wake of the WCTU's success at shutting down the Reception, *Daily Alaskan* editor John Troy decided to bring the issue of prostitution to light in Skagway. Beginning in mid-March 1901 he treated his readers to stories of the reforms in Dawson and Whitehorse. Then, on April 3, 1901, he published a heart-wrenching account of a delicate young woman led astray by an Atlin madam with promises of a flashy wardrobe. Some civic-minded Skagway women rescued the young lady from this dire fate. After the young woman repented her ill-advised

A cartoon of the Skagway City Council in 1901: Frank Keelar, the "Money King," sits to the far left; Phil Snyder is back center on the podium; Lee Guthrie stands in center front wearing the dark, droopy mustache; Frank Clancy sits with hat on the lower right. The cartoon is captioned "Our Distinguished City Council Wrestling with the important question as to 'How to Get Someone to do Something for Nothing.'" *Daily Alaskan,* June 1, 1901.

decision, her loving sister returned her to her family. Troy condemned the madam for being angry over the lost investment of the $25 fare to Atlin and $180 in clothing.[45] The court case filed by Mrs. L. C. Mitchell against Madam Edith Van Ornum on a complaint of disorderly conduct on the same date as the newspaper account was unsuccessful, although the newspaper readers would not have known it, as the madam's successful defense in court was not deemed news worth printing.[46]

On April 4, a day after he reported the news about the young woman being led astray, Troy wrote that Robert Grant, a private assigned to the U.S. Army's Company L, stationed in Skagway, was refused entrance into Marie Melgem's "bawdy house." In anger, he hurled a rock through the woman's door, earning him a three-month jail sentence in Judge Sehlbrede's court, for "defacing a building not his own."[47] What makes this story particularly noteworthy is that Company L was an African American unit. The townspeople did not need an explanation for why Private Grant was refused service. Reporting the event kept the prostitutes in the news, and primed the readers for the shocker that would follow.

After this virtual hailstorm of publicity about the problem of prostitution in the midst of Skagway, it probably came as no surprise to anyone when the subject came up at a town council meeting. A special meeting was called on April 9, 1901, to appoint a new city clerk. Before it convened, councilman Laramie Mayer announced that he had received complaints that a "sporting woman" had hiked her skirts above the tops of her hose in order to place a purse in them. While that was shocking enough by itself, she compounded the crime by doing so in front of some little girls who were "horrified at such activity." Ladies of the town complained that the prostitutes were making themselves more noticeable and ought to be moved where they would be out of the sight of those offended by their presence. The sporting women had been brought to the attention of children who "should be kept in ignorance of the existence [of prostitutes] for as long as possible." It seems that in late 1899, Skagway had opened a public school in the Union Church at State and Fifth Avenue. Incredible as it might seem, no one had noticed the presence of "Jap Alley" on the north side of the Union Church.[48]

At the April 9 meeting, the committee on health and police appointed councilman Mayer, "Money King" Frank Keelar, and John P. Laumeister, a successful butcher and respected businessman who had also held a council seat since December 1898, to investigate the "Social Evil." Laumeister and Mayer issued their preliminary report the following night, and recommended that "the most prominent of these disreputable

Public School children standing outside the Union Church as it faces State at Fifth Avenue, June 1901. Courtesy Yukon Archives, Barley Collection, H. C. Barley Fonds, YA 5046.

houses would be notified to vacate . . . to localities not so conspicuous or leave town immediately." Keelar was at odds with the other members of the committee, for upon completion of the report he expounded at great length against the inadvisability of eradicating prostitution from the town, and suggested that certain citizens were prejudiced. They simply wanted to get rid of the Japanese. Fellow councilmen and on-lookers admitted the truth of the accusation. "Jap Alley" was near the school and ought to be removed. The children played next door to the cribs, and then would ask their teachers about them. One citizen noted that "the little ones saw sights which were coarse and vulgar, from which they ought to be kept just as long as possible."[49]

Keelar was correct that people in Skagway were prejudiced against Japanese, as discussed earlier. In Alaska, the Japanese were treated only slightly better than the Chinese, who were regarded as the lowest on the social rung. Japanese proscriptions would culminate with the Immigration Act of 1924, which expelled Japanese citizens from the United States, including Jenjiro Ikuta.[50]

After observing that the townspeople did not like Japanese people, Keelar asked the council to expel only Japanese prostitutes, not the entire community of prostitutes. He suggested that some of the Japanese women were "broke" and would be moving anyway, so he asked the council to give them until June 1 to vacate. If they did not do so, he promised to swear out a warrant himself. It seems likely that Keelar did not want the council to create a special district, and he may well have thought that by targeting only this one small group of women, he could mitigate damage to himself and to other men who had invested in prostitution. The meeting ended with a charge to the committee to find a place for the prostitutes to be moved, and then to instruct the fire marshal to notify the women to vacate.

But how could Keelar be so sure that the Japanese women would vacate "Jap Alley" by June 1? A search of Skagway's deed records makes the answer obvious. Among the Keelars' plentiful real estate holdings, Frank owned lot 3 and his wife Mattie owned lot 2 of block 7.[51] The back portions of these two lots were on "Jap Alley," and contained small, crib-like structures. It was the Keelars who owned "Jap Alley."

Keelar's sympathies with prostitution in general first came to light in that town council meeting on April 9. He viewed the Social Evil as a question "which the more you stir the more it will smell." After stating that an effort to district the prostitutes in Portland had recently failed, he commented that the Skagway prostitutes were "as orderly as they are in any place on earth." He exhorted the middle-class men of town to ignore the "peculiar views" of the "ladies . . . imbued with the holy ghost," and then demonstrated his own fair-mindedness by stating, "Now as regards myself, I own a house occupied by a 'coon,'[52] and it has the 'ear-marks' of a disreputable place but I have no personal knowledge of what is carried on behind the walls in that house. If any white man can be found who will swear that that is a house of ill-fame I will guarantee to remove the tenant." The newspaper reporter who covered the meeting noted there was general laughter at the comment.[53]

Councilman Keelar argued long and hard against trying to do away with the Social Evil during the city council meeting held on the next day, April 10. In defense, Mayer made it clear that he did not want to do anything more than discuss the districting of the prostitutes, as he recognized that to do more might end his political career. As it became obvious that this argument could not be settled that evening, the council once again referred the question of districting to the Health and Police Committee, which was made up of Mayer, Keelar, and Laumeister.[54]

The timing for this matter could not have been better in some residents' minds, and was probably carefully planned by the reform-minded citizens in the community. The seven-member city council, in order to pass a vote, required a majority of four votes. In April, city council member Guthrie, owner of the Board of Trade Saloon and several other properties containing cribs on French (or Paradise) Alley (see map 2), was out of town on his honeymoon. Councilman E. O. Sylvester, another owner of many pieces of property around town, including a crib on the east end of French Alley, was also out of town. And although Laumeister was a member of the Health and Police Committee, he left town in the middle of the debate.[55] The fate of the prostitutes rested squarely on whether the remaining four councilmen could come to a consensus. Referring the matter to the Health and Police Committee meant the argument became personal between Mayer (who had presented the petition to move the prostitutes), on the one hand, and Keelar, who owned "Jap Alley," on the other.

Perhaps anticipating the direction that public opinion was taking, Deputy Marshal Snook responded to complaints by a resident of the area near Seventh and Broadway on the next night. As Troy reported in the *Daily Alaskan*, "[The marshal] went around to the several houses of ill-fame and notified the proprietresses that they must either dispense with the red curtains or stand trial for violation of law. When a reporter went down the avenue late last evening there was a remarkable scarcity of the usual abundant display of the cheap, flaming red cambric at the windows and doors of the houses. Badly tuned pianos and squeaky voices were, however, in evidence as much as ever, but the publicity of the bagnios was greatly reduced by the operators complying with the order of the marshal."[56]

The marshal denied that his actions had anything to do with the council meeting the evening before and claimed that he was just responding to a complaint. He felt sure that the women were safe from his enforcement of the law. "So far as he is now concerned," continued the article, "if the order is obeyed they will not be further molested in the plying of their nefarious vocation." As long as they kept themselves away from the attention of the children and ladies, they were safe.[57]

But editor John Troy continued his crusade. The *Daily Alaskan* took credit for bringing the matter to the notice of the community, and promised "that the removal of those operating so flagrantly in the vicinity of the city's public schools and where the mothers and daughters are forced to travel daily will soon be accomplished." He enlisted the aid of the Baptist Reverend Galon S. Clevinger and the Presbyterian Reverend Norman B. Harrison in giving testimony to the damage done by the demimonde. The latter testified, "My home for nearly two years has faced some of these alley resorts, so that their unseemly acts could not escape my notice nor be unheeded by the innocent children of the public school from their nearby playground." Both ministers claimed that prostitution was not a "necessary" evil and that it should be removed from the community entirely. They conceded, however, that such an action was unlikely and that the best that could be hoped for was that they would be moved away from the downtown business area and the vicinity of the school.[58]

The two members of the Health and Police Committee (minus Laumeister) presented their final report to the full council on April 22, 1901. Mayer and Keelar were obviously still not in agreement. Keelar disagreed with his fellow council member, opining that "the less monkeying there was with the evil the better." He observed that there were no street walkers and that ex-mayor Edgar R. Peoples did not object to "Miss Edwards" having a house near his store. Keelar believed the whole effort was aimed specifically at "Jap Alley." He did not think that this area should be an issue, as the Japanese would be gone by the first of June.[59]

This argument suggests that Keelar, with his lucrative rents in "Jap Alley," and his obvious connection with Japanese people, decided to redirect the council's discussion away from the institution of prostitution as whole, and focus instead directly on the Japanese prostitutes.[60] Paradise Alley had been cleared of the French women five months earlier. "Jap Alley" became the next target. It was obvious that few of the businessmen wanted all of the prostitutes to leave town entirely, an attitude that Marshal Snook seemed to understand well. By focusing only on the Japanese prostitutes, whose alley emerged half a block from the school, the city council could come to a reluctant agreement and appear to take action.

Councilman Keelar—district deputy of the Benevolent and Protective Order of the Elks, host of the socially prominent Elite Club's semimonthly dances, the man whose wife had formed the respectable Magpie Club for the ladies of town—was forced to capitulate. This must have grated on him, as he had tried so hard to be so respectable. The Japanese women were forced to leave their alley by the first of June. Keelar proposed that he, Mayer, and Laumeister—a trio that Troy now dubbed "The Social Evil Committee"—"thoroughly investigate these places." When they mutually agreed where the women ought to be moved, the committee members would instruct the fire warden to notify occupants to vacate.[61] That bought time for co-council members Lee Guthrie and E. O. Sylvester to return to town, as they surely had interests in the final decision. Thanks to all of Keelar's huffing and puffing, the reformers' strategy to remove the prostitutes entirely had been checked, at least for the moment.

The *Daily Alaskan* never announced the committee's final decision, nor was any decision ever reported to the city council, but as time went on, it became obvious what they had concluded. Keelar sacrificed his high rents from "Jap Alley" to mollify the women of the WCTU and the ministers. In return for the continued high regard of the voting men in town—the prostitute's customers, landlords, and other investors— the committee allowed Seventh Avenue between Broadway and State to become the official restricted district. No one but the Japanese women had to move, as Seventh Avenue had contained cribs, bagnios, and small parlor houses for some years.

It is instructive that at no time during the city council meetings of April 1901 was there any mention of the WCTU: this lack of direct participation by the women's organization had to do with the influence of John Troy and his negative reaction to them during their protest against the four saloons. He had been a citizen of Skagway since August 1897 and involved with the *Daily Alaskan* since November 1899.[62] Early twentieth-century newspapers never aspired to political neutrality, and the *Daily Alaskan* was no exception. Troy used his position as editor of the most "respectable" daily newspaper in Skagway to considerable advantage. As a Democrat, he often aimed pointed barbs at Republican appointees and continually harped on the need for territorial status. He held nothing but contempt for Republican governor John Brady during the latter's 1897–1906 appointment. Brady, who was an ordained Presbyterian minister and founder of the Sheldon Jackson mission in Sitka, drew Troy's particular ire for his sympathy for Native Alaskans and his reform measures at the expense of home rule and territorial status.

In reading Troy's editorials, it is obvious he had little patience with the reform-minded citizens in the community. Besides berating the "temperance people" for delaying the building of the school in September 1900, he wryly commented that without the saloon revenue, even such a large and prosperous a city as Seattle could not pay half its expenses. He suggested that if the churches wanted to put the saloons out of business, they should pay the city what the saloons paid in taxes. But he despaired of that ever happening.[63] Troy's continual lampooning of all reform issues were damaging to the efforts of temperance organizations in Skagway. As a powerful citizen who had unlimited access to the written word in every "respectable" person's home in Skagway, he openly belittled, criticized, and berated the early attempts at reform in the community, even while he sensationalized the prostitutes and the vice issues as they arose.

When the denizen of Paradise Alley lifted her skirts to place a purse in her garter before startled school children in April 1901, the women of the WCTU, without a doubt, embraced the saving of these innocent souls as their next great crusade. Having learned a powerful lesson the previous fall when Troy thwarted their carefully laid plans to close down the saloons through the actions of the federal courts, this time they changed their strategy. They united with the city's male clergy and reform-minded businessmen, and then approached city hall. They involved only local officials, appealing to Troy's intense belief in home rule and Skagway's ability to govern its own affairs.

Once again, to many the victory of the WCTU women seemed less than spectacular. Although they succeeded in closing down the notorious "Jap" and Paradise Alleys, the man landladies still retained their power on the city council. Convinced that prostitution was essential to Skagway's economic health, city hall chose only to restrict the demimonde to Seventh Avenue rather than obliterate the institution altogether.

Skagway's temperance ladies surely saw this decision as another defeat. It is hardly surprising that in late August 1901, the WCTU, which had hosted all of the noted Protestant speakers that had come to town for more than a year, abruptly stopped doing so. A prominent evangelist, Rev. Dr. French Earl Oliver, came to town and spoke without the WCTU sponsorship.[64] The last mention of the WCTU was shortly before his appearance. It was about this time that Sarah Shorthill ceased her activities with the WCTU in Skagway and instead became the Alaska representative to the national organization.

The Shorthills stayed in Skagway for another year and a half. When they left for Tacoma, the newspaper merely announced that the Ladies Aid Society of the Methodist Church had hosted a going-away party for Mrs. T. A. Shorthill (not Sarah E., as she liked to be called), stating that she had been a Sunday School teacher for the church. There was no mention of her activities with the WCTU.[65] It was almost as if the community was embarrassed about its involvement with the organization. She had withdrawn from activities with the local WCTU in August 1901, and the chapter disintegrated without her leadership.

Shorthill did not give up her activities with the WCTU, however. She had been a part of the national organization for twenty years, and from Tacoma, she continued her involvement with the Alaska organization. By 1915, her tireless efforts resulted in the passage of the Alaska "Bone Dry" law, a territory-wide prohibition act much stricter than the national prohibition act enacted by the Eighteenth Amendment.[66]

Starting in the fall of 1901, a number of women's clubs arose in Skagway, most of which were social rather than political in nature. Perhaps the women in Skagway were just not quite ready for Sarah Shorthill and her brand of radical reform. The wives and mothers of Skagway apparently needed to learn a lot about surviving political battles to catch up with this energetic business woman and twenty-year leader of the WCTU. It is almost certain that the male leadership of the community was not prepared for her mucking-about in what it saw as men's business.

A good part of the reason that the WCTU quit its business in Skagway in 1901 probably had to do with the pointed criticism by John Troy. Sandra Haarsager points out that many of the women who worked for the WCTU found it difficult to deal with the ridicule and denigration that they often attracted. While they could readily dismiss the jibes of saloon keepers, gamblers, and prostitutes, it was more difficult to face abrogation from "respectable" businessmen whom they wished to enlist in their cause. At the same time, the national organization was waning with the death of founder Frances Willard in 1898. Perhaps the WCTU had simply taken on too many causes, and according to Haarsager, it had lost its focus.[67] Any reform that promoted the spiritual uplifting of the family was fair game to the WCTU, and in Skagway the organization had taken on saloons, gambling, and prostitutes. These were sacrosanct institutions to the still largely male population, and "the temperance people" could not convince even such a stalwart businessman as John Troy that their causes were worthy. Sarah Short-hill probably had the thick skin it took to weather the attacks of the likes of editor Troy, and she appears to have had the support of her husband. But the other women of Skagway were probably inexperienced in political action and found his ridicule difficult to bear.

Therefore, it was the church leaders, the Presbyterian Rev. Harrison and the Baptist Rev. Clevinger, who allowed their names to be printed in the newspaper. Only one unnamed reform woman was mentioned: Anna Stinebaugh, the wife of barber J. D. Stinebaugh. As will be seen in chapter 6, it would not be until 1908 that she would reinvent the WCTU in Skagway.

Neither Harrison nor Clevinger remained in Skagway long enough to become major forces of reform, and it appears that their names in the newspaper served only to provide a masculine voice for the debate. Both ministers had arrived in the town only that year; neither would remain past 1903. In fact, the First Baptist Church would disappear from Skagway with Rev. Galon S. Clevinger's transfer in 1903. The Presbyterians enjoyed more stability in the town, but even their clergymen changed every two to three years. Only the Catholic priest Philibert S. Turnell would achieve any longevity in Skagway, and he appeared to take a hands-off attitude toward moral reforms.[68] When change in vice finally did occur, it was because of the action of the women, not the clergy.

———

James A. Morone argues that many reform struggles have been waged between the forces of morality and economics.[69] Sixth Avenue business-men in Skagway believed they knew what was good for the economic health of the community. They wished to attract men en route to or returning from the goldfields and willing to spend money at the town's saloons, hotels, restaurants, barbershops, and places of indulgence. City Hall shared this view. But Skagway's female reformers assumed that the spiritual health of the innocent children was more important than mere economics. Thus the battle began between value systems, just as it did in other American cities of the time.

A glance at the tax rolls for lots on Seventh Avenue in 1901 reveals the extent to which man landladies were involved in the city's politics. Lee Guthrie, a colleague of Frank Keelar, was on the city council in 1901 and owned five of the sixteen properties on either side of the street between Broadway and State Streets. Their friend, colleague and sometimes fellow city councilman Phil W. Snyder, who worked for Guthrie and operated one of his gambling tables, owned one lot on the north side of Seventh Avenue. In addition to the man landladies, madams Frankie Belmont and Belle Schooler were already operating houses on lots off Seventh Avenue. The total of these ownerships accounts for half of the properties on the street. There may have been other landowners who were complicit in the designation of the district.[70]

Besides the documentation of property owned by madams Schooler and Belmont, there is other evidence that Seventh Avenue had attained its unofficial tenderloin status long before the April city council debates. An April 1900 newspaper story reported a fire on the roof of a "sporting house on Seventh avenue, between Broadway and State."[71] When the six "French" prostitutes were released from their three-month jail sentences on January 28, 1901, they instigated a rumor that they "were going to open 'cribs' in the alley between Sixth and Seventh near Broadway."[72]

Marie Melgem, the woman whose door was damaged by Private Robert Grant of Company L on April 4, 1901, lived on Seventh Avenue.[73]

It is readily apparent that the Seventh Avenue tenderloin needed no official designation. It already existed as a district and was well established by April 1901. What happened during that month was a slight of hand trick on the part of the city council. It cleared out the Japanese prostitutes from behind the school, and possibly any women who still operated cribs directly off of Broadway and State avenues. These women probably did not leave town but likely just moved to hastily built cribs on Seventh Avenue or on the alley between Sixth and Seventh. In return, the city council tacitly agreed to create an openly acknowledged restricted district. As time passed, city hall "restricted" the women to Seventh Avenue by prosecuting the prostitutes who lived beyond that selected envelope and by leaving those living on Seventh Avenue alone. Eventually, people who wanted to invest in sin deduced where it would be safe to do so.

―――――――

Many middle-class men who had profited by vice in Skagway, such as Frank Clancy, left the city as the gold rush years waned. Others, such as Lee Guthrie, owner of the Board of Trade Saloon, and Frank Keelar, a man who dabbled in all sorts of real estate and property investments, chose to stay longer, making their livings by scooping up investments at dwindling prices and taking over the politics of Skagway. They obtained city council seats in these waning years of the gold rush and worked to protect their financial interests, as did most politicians of the era. These interests included renting cheap, one-room cribs to prostitutes on the alleys behind the saloons and on Seventh Avenue.

The middle-class women of Skagway were not about to allow the agents of vice to have free rein, however. After their partial success in halting the liquor license of the Reception Saloon in the fall of 1900, these women turned to the reform of prostitution, the Social Evil. John Troy first exposed the efforts that sister cities in the Yukon Territory had taken to confine their sporting women to small areas of the city, which led to a scandalous story about a madam impinging on Skagway's purity. With this heart-wrenching story of a madam procuring an innocent "white" girl, he opened the lid on the presence of vice in Skagway and then drew attention to an African American soldier who supposedly preyed on women on Seventh Avenue and to the activities of French and Japanese harlots in the city. It took only a few days before a brazen hussy did something fairly usual—exposed her stockings—thus unwittingly supplying the shocking excuse to hustle all of the iniquitous women out of sight of the reform women and children who had no reason to ever see them again. City Hall rejoiced, made a lot of noise in the process of debating the Social Evil question, and dealt with its sex trade the way every other community in America was doing at the time: restrict the women they needed so badly to a single part of town.

By removing the lower-class Japanese prostitutes and others living in cribs from the obvious view of the reformers and the members of the school board who had opened a school half a block from the sporting district (how that ever happened still baffles the mind) the middle-class men on the city council with a financial interest in the sporting world bought a stay of execution for Skagway's trade in sex.

Keeping this series of events in mind, David Charles Beyreis's discussion of middle-class masculinity at the turn of the century once again bears contemplation.[74] The duality of middle-class manliness, the conflict between their aspiration to be good husbands and fathers and their desire to be healthy, primitive men who could indulge in their natural urges, put the Skagway decision-makers in a quandary. When Frank Keelar told the city council that its members ought not to listen to the "peculiar views" of the "ladies . . . imbued with the holy ghost," he was urging them to listen to their "inner savages" and think for themselves. John Troy, on the other hand, was asking the middle-class male city council to be civilized and virtuous about the matter, and to separate the male temptations from the sensitive members of the community. The creation of the restricted district was the logical solution for just such a conundrum.

The institution of the Social Evil thereby exposed this duality of late Victorian masculinity. Male sexual needs could be accommodated in that section of the town restricted to a sullied sort of "working woman." Working-class men, who were not expected to be as restrained or civilized as middle-class married men, could slip away to the restricted district and there find release for their animal urges. If a middle-class male felt compelled to give in to his animal instincts, he could find accommodation there as well. And the middle-class woman need never see any evidence of this sordid side of human nature. It was entirely up to City Hall and the courts to see that this balance between respectability and impropriety was maintained.

CHAPTER FOUR

Behind Red Curtains, 1901–1906

Having districted the prostitutes and satisfied the temperance community, city hall and the *Daily Alaskan* settled into three years of truce regarding the restricted district. Between 1901 and 1903, the federal judge in Juneau washed his hands of regulating vice in the incorporated cities, and Skagway took over the duties of fining its own prostitutes and gamblers. The city promulgated ordinances to fine the prostitutes for keeping a disorderly house or for vagrancy, to be applied as the city magistrate saw fit. The madams gradually bought up properties in the restricted district and paid quarterly fines; troublemakers were driven out of town; saloon owners paid their high license and gambling fines; and the number of saloons increased as free lunches drew in the customers. The WCTU had dissolved as it now appeared that very little vice existed in Skagway. As a result, it was during this period that the small-time madam thrived and the man landlady began to lose his economic hold on the restricted district.

More women entrepreneurs moved onto Seventh Avenue once it became obvious where it was safe for them to invest in real estate. Some of their enterprises were one-woman businesses, such as those owned by Pop Corn Kate and Dutch Rosie Wagner with her partner, John Bonner. Others were small, two-woman brothels like that operated by Belle Schooler, Skagway's first real madam. Larger, traditional parlorhouses known as "The Cottage" and "The Lodge" required a madam such as Frankie Belmont or an absentee owner such as Dinah Heyman. True landladies, such as Kitty Faith and Ida Freidinger, established their modest bordellos. All had a place, and the man landlady fell out of power.

The following biographies of the women who worked in the Seventh Avenue restricted district during the period that followed the city council's discussion of the Social Evil in April 1901 illustrate the range of economic and social status that existed in the district. Although many of the women came to Skagway before the district was established, and some left after it was moved, all of them exemplify the kind of women who worked or owned property there. The five years that followed April 1901 could be considered the heyday of Skagway's Seventh Avenue district.

———

Pop Corn Kate, aka Maggie Marshall, whom we first met at the opening of this book, worked in a one-woman business on Seventh Avenue, a place she leased from a landlord. However, she actually resided in a home she had purchased on Thirteenth Avenue, separate from her place of business. In 1900, she told the census enumerator that she had come to Alaska in December 1898 from Pueblo, Colorado. At that time, she was twenty-eight years old, and despite the daily newspaper referring to her as "Mrs. James," she claimed to be single.[1] According to her account, she was born in Ireland in 1872, and she immigrated to the United States in 1890, but by 1900, she had not yet become naturalized. For that year's census, she listed "housekeeper" as both her current and previous occupations.[2] It was common for prostitutes to use this word to define their occupation. When Marshall identified herself as a housekeeper, she did not mean that she was a household servant in a lady's home. It was far more likely that she was referring to her management of a house of prostitution for an absent madam or landlord.

It appears that Marshall first appeared in Skagway in December 1898. There she staked a claim to half a lot on the northern edge of town, not having arrived there early enough to stake a more lucrative lot in midtown. Yet the ease with which she located, staked, and purchased property indicates that prostitutes, like other women of the time, had no trouble procuring real estate in Alaska.

Marshall seems to have acquired the nickname "Pop Corn Kate" in Skagway. It is by that name that she appears in the memoirs of Richard "Dixie" Anzer. Writing more than sixty years after the events of his Klondike adventure, he recalls her as a cheerful, high-spirited woman, in contrast to the image of the slovenly drunk that appeared in the newspaper reports of the time. Anzer claims she ran a lodging and eating establishment at Log Cabin, a packer's stop on the White Pass Trail, which led into Canada and the Klondike regions. Log Cabin was located fourteen miles north of White Pass summit and the Canadian border. While it is difficult to place exact dates in Anzer's narrative, it seems likely that this meeting with her occurred during the first few months of 1899. When he encountered her at Log Cabin, she had organized a drinking game for her male customers that took the form of a contest to see who could hold the most liquor. She charged the men a fee to join the game, as well as charging the contestants for the liquor that they drank. When a competitor fell over insensible, she helped him to her bunkhouse, where she charged for a bed while the inebriation wore off. Ironically, Anzer had nothing but praise for Kate's "generosity."[3]

The spring of 1899 witnessed a gold rush to Atlin, British Columbia, another eighty miles or so into Canada. Anzer records Pop Corn Kate buying a hotel on Dominion Road in that picturesque boomtown. Built all of logs, Kate's hotel was one of the few two-story structures in the community and, at thirty feet wide, a substantial building for the time. The lower floor was used as a saloon. A large bar placed in front of a mirror graced one wall of the saloon; the main floor also contained two small rooms of unspecified function, possibly for Kate's use in the sex trade. The upper floor constituted a single large room full of bunks. Kate claimed the glass for the front window had been hauled all the way from Skagway.[4]

Shortly after Anzer arrived in Atlin in the summer of 1899, Kate approached him with a business proposition. "I had high hopes when I came here," she said, "but now I'm so disappointed, I want to get back home. I expected to have a tavern and hotel, but the gold commissioner refuses to grant me a liquor license." The Canadians were notorious for refusing licenses to Americans, and they discouraged prostitution. She convinced Anzer to take the hotel off her hands, giving him a free and clear quit claim deed. Prior to her departure from Atlin, she said she wanted to visit friends in Bennett.[5]

Bennett was another stop for the miners on the White Pass and Chilkoot Trails into the Klondike. In the days before the White Pass and Yukon Route railroad was built—before the summer of 1899—the hopeful gold-seekers could build a boat or scow and float the lakes and streams flowing into the Yukon River, and then travel on to Dawson. The railroad reached Bennett from Skagway on July 6, 1899. The numerous laborers who received wages from the railroad company probably provided more lucrative earnings for Kate during her sojourn in Bennett rather than the Klondike-bent miners, who lived on their savings.

Anzer reported that Kate later wrote to him from Bennett, where "as soon as she finished some business" there, she planned to travel to Nome, at the mouth of the Yukon River.[6] The rush to the gold-laden sands of Nome had just begun.

Kate may well have spent a very short while in Nome, but by April 1900, the census-taker records her as being back in Skagway. It did not take long for this working-woman-turned-entrepreneur to get into legal trouble in Skagway. The firsthand newspaper accounts and criminal records are not as flattering as Anzer's memory. Her first mention in a Skagway newspaper appeared on the front page, on May 13, 1900. She had been hauled to the jailhouse in a wheelbarrow on a federal charge of drunkenness. A year and a half later she was arrested in the incident recounted at the beginning of this narrative, for "indecent exposure." These antics apparently did not amuse U.S. Commissioner Sehlbrede, who sentenced her to three months in jail.[7]

Less than two weeks after beginning her jail term, Kate was in the news again. Far from being a model prisoner, she had insisted on singing loudly, had disturbed jailer J. M. Tanner as she played games with pieces of coal on the hard wood floors, and had used her "opera cloak" as a dish towel. These offenses were nothing compared to her breaking the windows of her cell with a stove lid. U.S. Deputy Marshal Snook hauled her to court once again, this time for "willfully and maliciously defacing a building not her own." Again, Kate refused to plead, but she did retain a lawyer this time. The stiff jail sentence that the judge had given her had made an impression. Isaac Newton Wilcoxen, a prominent Skagway attorney, was unable to convince Judge Sehlbrede that Kate did not deserve further punishment for her poor behavior in the jail. He sentenced her to an additional six-month jail term, to start at the end of her current sentence.[8]

If she had served her entire sentence, Kate would not have been released from jail until August 1902. However, with time off for good behavior, she may well have been released by the middle of June. An indication of this early release is that on June 27, 1902, she sold her residential property on Thirteen Avenue to Kitty Faith, a Skagway madam, for $100.[9]

Kate's harsh sentence was unprecedented. It exceeded a six-month term in jail served by six French prostitutes in the winter of 1900–1901. Obviously the federal authorities wished to make an example of the prostitutes who made themselves visible to the community—and Pop Corn Kate certainly had made herself visible. By punishing her so harshly, they successfully drove her from Skagway.

After the sale of her Skagway property, Pop Corn Kate (aka Mrs. James, aka Maggie Marshall) disappeared from Skagway records. It seems likely that, having served at least part of her time, she simply left town. Anzer's memoirs certainly suggest that Kate moved around frequently in those days, trying several of the up-and-coming boom-towns before "settling" for a couple of years in Skagway. But after a nine-month jail sentence, she had little reason to stay in Skagway. She did not reappear as "Pop Corn Kate" until 1914. This was in Juneau, where she provided the catering services to the Sourdough Festival, a celebration also sponsored by the Malemute Bar, Candy Andy, and Killemalwin, "the famous Indian witch doctor." Kate was said to run a roadhouse at the time.[10]

While Marshall said she came from Pueblo, Colorado, in 1898, that claim appears to be pure fiction created to hide her true identity; she cannot be found in any records of that city. A Margaret "Maggie" Marshall was located in Tacoma, however, married to saloon keeper Nicholas John Marshall, the manager of the Pioneer Liquor Company. This Maggie Marshall's birth date and origin match those of Pop Corn Kate's, and the two are likely the same person. This Maggie was born to Timothy Murphy and Catherine Eustace, who had emigrated from Ireland as children. Their daughter Margaret (called Maggie) was born in Tacoma, Washington, where she married John Marshall in 1890. The couple had three children between 1889 and 1893 (two boys and a girl) and a fourth child, a boy, who died in infancy in 1905.[11]

Maggie's husband, John, died in 1907, leaving her as part owner of the Pioneer Liquor Company. She tried to run the saloon on her own for more than a year but sold it in 1909. By 1914, she was operating a roadhouse near Juneau. While she maintained an address in Tacoma until she died on January 15, 1949, it is apparent that she continued to moonlight as a madam or a tavern owner in other locations for much of her life.[12]

The fact that Marshall was enumerated in both Tacoma and Skagway in the 1900 census indicates that she traveled to the boom city from her home specifically to capitalize on the rush. Anzer's account places her in other locations than Skagway, and one newspaper article suggests she may even have gone to Montana to ply her trade.[13] Maggie Marshall, aka Pop Corn Kate, epitomizes the adventurous, transient prostitutes who moved around the North from the time of the gold rush until well into the twentieth century. Surprisingly, it turns out she was not the single, carefree, "good time girl" depicted by popular writers, but rather a mother and wife who chose to spend part of the year supplementing the family income in the northern boomtowns during their busy seasons. That her husband would not object to her occupation may not have been unusual. After all, even such a well-known figure as Wyatt Earp's brother, James, lived with a madam-wife, and he defended both his wife's career and his choice to stay with her.[14] Other couples in this account lived the same way.

———————

A more permanent occupant in Skagway was Rosie Wagner, also known as "Dutch" Rosie, because she was German (the Germans call themselves "Deutsch," a word that has been Anglicized to "Dutch"). Marshall and Wagner occupied much the same rung on the status hierarchy of the demimonde, but their lifestyles differed because of the locations of their families.

Rosie Hess Wagner was first arrested in Skagway by federal authorities for being an inmate of a house of ill fame on July 18, 1902, a charge to which she admitted her guilt. Fined $50, she stayed in jail until unspecified friends came to bail her out.[15] Two months later, Rosie, "a well known character of Seventh avenue," again occupied a cell, this time for trying to smuggle liquor into the jail for her lover, John Bonner. He had been incarcerated for vagrancy, a charge sometimes applied to those who lived off the proceeds of prostitution. It appears that Bonner had cohabited with Rosie before being arrested. Despite being warned several times that she should not be loitering at the courthouse where the jail was housed, she returned to see him, contraband liquor in hand. When the marshal put her in jail to keep her away from Bonner's cell, it was on a charge of "vagrancy by being an inmate of a house of ill-repute." Confection and tobacco merchants Nathalie and Frederick Verbauwhedes paid her $100 bail. She demanded a trial rather than simply plead guilty, and the jury suspended judgment on the condition that she move out of town within ten days. However, the judge did not feel he could let her off entirely. He fined her $20 and court costs of $26.75.[16]

This was not the first time Bonner's name had been mentioned in connection with the co-owner of the cigar store on French Alley, Frederick Verbauwhedes. Marshal Snook had suspected the "French macquereau," John Bonner, of stealing $800 from Verbauwhedes's cash register in January 1902. He was later judged to be innocent.[17] But this identification of Bonner as a "macquereau" gives a strong hint as to the relationship that emerges in the events that happened the following summer. John Bonner was regarded as Rosie Wagner's pimp.

The French term "macquereau" was widely used in the Far North to define a procurer of prostitutes. While it has been used interchangeably in the literature to mean a pimp, careful examination of the context of the words "pimp" and "macquereau" in the early twentieth century makes it clear that the two words did not carry the same meaning as they do in the twenty-first century. In the North, where prostitution was so open, a "procurer" did not have to obtain customers. Any man wanting a prostitute knew exactly where to go to find one. He did not need a male intermediary until after reform movements resulted in the closing of restricted districts and created the necessity for an intermediary. The procurer, instead, acquired prostitutes and brought them to the places where demand was high. In the North, with high transportation costs, many women needed a monetary advance to get to the often remote locations demanding the services of the prostitutes. The macquereau provided these funds. Not only would he see that she got to the North, but he would set her up in a house, sometimes with clothing and other necessary supplies, such as furniture and linens. He would continue to manage her business until she paid him back from a portion—usually a rather large portion—of the proceeds of her earnings. In Dawson, only some of the macquereaus—

"macques" for short—were actually French and procured French prostitutes, who were highly prized by the Klondikers.[18] A pimp, on the other hand, was a personal guard who obtained customers for a prostitute, and, in exchange, took a good portion of her earnings. While the two functions might overlap, they were not always the same.

In fact, the macque in Skagway seemed a rare creature indeed. Skagway was not a destination for procurers, probably because for the average prostitute it was easy to access. It was not the kind of town to which a French man would take his carefully picked *mesdames* to entertain the newly rich. It is hard to imagine Bonner as a procurer of women to serve as prostitutes in Skagway. And, as pointed out earlier, it was rare for prostitutes of the time to need men to procure clients for them. As the bartender at the Rainier Saloon—a rather seedy, working-class saloon—Bonner may well have directed a few newcomers Rosie's way. But the architecture of the cribs, the red curtains, and the landscape in which they were found were all obvious signals to anyone who was looking. Rosie would not have been hard to find working on her own. The prostitutes of Skagway needed no "pimps" in the modern sense of the word.

It is also unlikely that Rosie needed a pimp in the form of a protector. Sally Zanjani, in writing of the mining boom in Goldfield, Nevada, which took place just a few years after the Klondike rush, states that violent crime was greater against housewives than "those individuals with ruffled shirts and names like 'Billy the Wheel' who presided at the roulette wheels."[19] Likewise, violence against prostitutes in Skagway was extremely rare. Other than fights between prostitutes, there were only three recorded incidents in which men attacked prostitutes.

In April 1901, while the city council debated where to district the prostitutes, Jack Noonberg, Pearl White's macque, fractured two of her ribs in what was characterized as a "lover's quarrel." She complained to the authorities, but the perpetrator escaped to British Columbia. When he reappeared in Skagway the following June to apologize, the U.S. deputy marshal arrested him. The newspaper fell silent on his fate; no one was interested.[20]

The other case was a very different matter indeed. Instead of a reprobate like the macquereau Noonberg, this incident involved a beloved member of the town's bachelors' subculture. It was a very hush-hush affair with nary a word in the newspapers. Hazel Henwood, the woman involved, successfully took the Board of Trade's manager and extremely popular bartender, Joe Engle, to court for assault and battery, where he was fined $100.[21] In that particular case, Engle probably was serving as the bouncer and was supposed to be the one doing the protecting.

The third case—the only murder of a prostitute in Skagway ever recorded—occurred during the violent days when Soapy Smith and his gang ran amuck in Skagway. In late May 1898, Mattie Silks, one of Denver's most famous madams, passed through Skagway on her way to Dawson to check out the possibilities of opening a business. Late one evening at the Occidental Hotel, Silks overheard Soapy and his henchmen, Bill Tener and John Bowers, discuss the May 28 murder of Ella Wilson, a prostitute of mixed African American and Caucasian descent. Silks reported that Tener and Bowers had strangled Wilson, and then robbed her of cash amounting to $3,800, in compliance with orders from Soapy and U.S. Deputy Marshal Sylvester S. Taylor, who was one of Soapy's gang. When she heard Tener and Bowers begin to plot the robbery of their next victim, Silks herself, she knew it was time to leave on the next steamship south. Mattie sold her story to reporters awaiting the ships arriving from the North, and it was published in the *Seattle Times* on June 3.[22] News of the story did not come out until after Soapy's death on July 8. Police officers had found Ella Wilson dead, her hands and feet tied and her throat slit. The inquest into Ella's death appears to have been thwarted by some of Soapy's associates. City council members Frank Clancy and Allan Hornsby, both known for their friendship with Smith, were on the coroner's jury. The inquest record, dated May 31, 1898, appears on the page *after* the inquest of Frank H. Reid on July 20, 1898, who died of the wounds incurred in his July 8, 1898, shoot-out with Soapy Smith.[23]

Canadians scorned the macquereau because they viewed him as a man who did no real work, a man who lived off the earnings of women. According to author Bay Ryley, there was nothing so humorous to the Dawson newspaper subscriber than to read about a macquereau being forced to chop wood for his crime of pimping. It was only just desserts.[24] The middle-class Skagway merchant reading John Troy's newspaper would have been scornful of someone who lived entirely off the earnings of a prostitute. John Bonner did have a job—he was a bartender—at which he could make his own livelihood. While he may have shared some of Rosie's income during his slack times, it is just as likely that she shared his income during her times of unemployment. The different ways in which the working and middle classes viewed this relationship would not have been understood as a simple difference in values. Instead the fact that Bonner lived off Rosie's activity as a prostitute would have been viewed by the middle class with contempt.

In fact, it was this sort of misunderstanding of values that fueled class and gender conflict during the Progressive Era. The middle-class concept of masculinity held that a "real man" supported his wife and family; he did not rely upon them for economic means. On the other hand, working-class values commended the family members that contributed equally to the household income. Bonner, as a working-class man, probably respected Rosie, since she could bring money to the household when he could not work. He likely valued her ability to provide the partnership an income, as in return, he supported her when he could.

The real role of John Bonner in relation to Rosie Wagner was probably neither procurer nor protector, but simply lover, companion, and economic partner. Middle-class morality had no place for a man who neglected to marry the woman he loved and, at the same time, allowed her to have sex with other men. To the middle class in Skagway, the only name for a man who shared a sex partner with other men was "macque," a venomous word laden with all sorts of deleterious and moralistic undertones.

Despite the September 1902 court order that she leave town, Rosie Wagner either chose to ignore the directive or she returned to Skagway a short time later. Other prostitutes had been run out without such stiff sentences and fines. In mid-October, First Judicial District Judge Melville C. Brown instructed his newly convened grand jury that it was their duty to stop the flaunting of prostitution in the faces of decent people. The U.S. deputy marshal indicted "all the women in Skagway and it is said in other towns of Southeastern Alaska who are known to be keepers of houses of ill fame." "All of the women" turned out to number half a dozen. Four were fined $100 each, and one paid her

$250 fine after fainting before the judge's bench. Rosie Wagner, who had been expelled from Skagway just five weeks earlier, served thirty days in jail, this time with no option to buy her way out.[25]

This stiff sentencing had the desired effect. It drove Wagner out of business entirely, as it was probably meant to do. As the rest of Skagway's prostitutes gradually resigned themselves to a regular schedule of fines, albeit more modest, Rosie's name failed to show up on the city magistrate's docket. Yet the fact that she remained in Skagway despite having to give up her profession is evident in the announcement of her November 1906 marriage to John Bonner.

When Bonner married Rosie, the newspaper announced that he did so simply to save her from a charge of vagrancy.[26] At the time, the city fined all of Skagway's prostitutes on a quarterly basis for being inmates of houses of ill fame. Rosie had not been fined since city hall started enforcing its city ordinances in August 1903. Her vagrancy charge was probably related to obvious begging, loitering, or having no source of income (a crime at the time). By becoming a wife, she would be sheltered from the possibility of receiving such a charge again.

Despite Bonner's reputation as a "French" macquereau, it turns out his French-ness may have been pure affectation. The 1910 census indicates that he was Canadian English, as were both of his parents. Rose Wagner Bonner, on the other hand, was German, having immigrated to the United States in 1890, three years after John. They were both forty-four years old at the time of their marriage and probably past their "sinful" days. Rose had had a child, but he or she was no longer living. They lived in a somewhat less desirable part of town, next to the Sylvester Dock on Second Avenue.[27]

It seems that both John and Rosie had decided to settle down and become respectable. John resigned his position a bartender and obtained the more respectable job of laborer on the White Pass and Yukon Route Railroad, a position he kept until at least 1917.[28] By 1920 he had been promoted to the position of classifier for the railroad, sorting the cars for placement in the train. By 1930, John still worked for the railroad. To all appearances, he and his wife were a respectable, working-class couple. John Bonner provided for Rosie once she was no longer able to work. In middle-class manner, he had wiped both their slates clean, by marrying the woman who had once worked in partnership with him as a prostitute.

————

The woman who rented her place of business, as did Pop Corn Kate and Rosie Wagner, could make more money than the common prostitute who worked out of the upstairs of a saloon. However, the employer of prostitutes—the madam—took an even more significant step toward economic independence. If she owned her own property in addition, she had little need to share her wealth with others. Such a woman was Sarah Belle Schooler, the "Belle of Skagway."

Fred Mazulla, a Colorado collector of sporting paraphernalia and folklore, listed in his records the "Belle of Skagway" along with such memorable names as Diamondtooth Li'l, Klondike Kate, the Oregon Mare, Nellie the Pig, and Silver Heels. His collection of papers, now housed at the Colorado Historical Society, does not elaborate on her identity but does contain a photograph he took of an abandoned brothel in Skagway, indicating he spent some time talking to the old folks in that town when he was there in the 1960s.[29]

Edith Larson, the daughter of White Pass Trail packer John Feero, told author Melanie J. Mayer a story about "Skagway Belle," whom her father met in the winter of 1897–98. According to this story, Belle wanted to go over the pass when packers broke a path after a big blizzard, but most of them refused to take a woman along with them under such dangerous conditions. She convinced Feero that she would be an asset to their party by telling him, "You know what I am [a prostitute]. I can be a lady on the trail. I can help warm up your meals, and I can help you what I can." Feero agreed to those terms but stipulated "You're a lady on the trail," meaning she could not conduct her disreputable business while traveling with the men.[30]

According to Larson in her continuation of the story, the White Pass suffered another storm while the packers were on the trail. "[The packers] couldn't unload the horses 'cause the stuff would get all covered up, and they couldn't let the horses lay down. That Skagway Belle went around with the men all among them horses, they had a lot of horses up there, pattin' them, keeping them on their feet. Didn't

dare let 'em lay down. About 10 o'clock at night the storm cleared. . . .
It was so darn cold, it was a blue cold. And she walked among them
horses all that night until it stopped. And then the moon came out
and then the stars. It was the most beautiful thing that anybody could
ever picture! That snow was perfectly clear, flat, smooth as anything.
And all these horses, one by one, they put 'em on the trail and they
went up." After elaborating on how the men got the horses over the
pass, Larson concluded her story: "But that was the true story of
Skagway Belle. And she went over the trail with them and came back
and was a lady all the way."[31]

The first time Schooler's name appears in Skagway's historical records
outside of the oral history was on September 16, 1898, when the *Skaguay
News* reported that she was operating a laundry in Dawson. Her name
(without the "Sarah," which appeared only twice in court documents)
was included among a list of defendants on December 9, 1898, when
eighty-nine Skagwayans were arrested for selling liquor without a license.
The proprietors of the brothels were also rounded up in this "raid"
on the saloons. This record indicates Schooler returned to Skagway
in the late fall or early winter of 1898.[32]

In 1898, Belle was forty-six years old and probably quite experienced
in the business. Unlike the younger Pop Corn Kate and Rosie Wagner,
who chose to limit their income to the direct exchange of cash for sex,
Schooler's primary economic interest was in real estate. In January
1899, she purchased a lot at the far northern edge of town. Later, in
late April and using her full name, Sarah Belle Schooler, she bought
a lot in the middle of the residential district of town. Two months later,
Schooler sold a lot near what would eventually become the railroad
work yards at the very far north end of town. Both later transactions
were conducted with Beryl Rowan, who was Schooler's daughter and
the widow of James Mark Rowan, the man who had been killed by
bartender Ed Fay the previous year.[33] These real estate transactions
indicate that Schooler had liquid income and was able to help her
more respectable daughter prior to the designation of the restricted
district. These dealings also indicate the ease with which women were
able to conduct real estate business at the turn of the century.

By the time Schooler paid her property taxes for 1900, she had acquired
a lot and small house on the north side of Seventh Avenue across State

and two doors east of Clancy's Music Hall in the restricted district (see map 2).[34] In fact, it was probably the presence of a few madams like Schooler in 1901 that encouraged the establishment of Seventh Avenue as the restricted district when "Jap" and Paradise Alleys were closed down in September 1900. To the city council, the more responsible madams, who tended to keep their employees sober and less visible, were much preferable to those who worked out of cribs or saloons in the alleys between Fifth and Sixth avenues. The newspaper editor regarded Schooler as so "respectable," in fact, that her name was mentioned as "an extensive property owner of Skagway" when she left town on an expedition to scout out business potential in one of the newest gold rushes in the spring of 1902.[35]

This laissez-faire form of "respectability" was not to last long. Federal marshals arrested Belle Schooler and Helen Storey on June 8, 1903, for selling liquor without a license. At their hearing the following day, it was established that Storey was Schooler's employee—"only a pianist on a salary." Belle pleaded guilty and was fined $100 and costs.[36] For Schooler, the days of tax-free sin in Skagway were over.

Two months later, on August 13, 1903, the town marshal arrested Schooler and eleven other women for keeping a bawdy house, again revealing Belle's status as a madam. The court fined twelve other women twenty dollars and court costs of $6.20, considerably less than the $100 fines that the federal courts usually charged.[37] A little over a month later, on September 24, 1903, the U.S. deputy marshal arrested eleven "inmates of houses of ill-fame" on charges of vagrancy, including Storey and Schooler. The latter successfully fought the charges, the only madam who was ever able to do so.[38] Thereafter, until July 7, 1905, she appeared in the city court every three months to pay her twenty-dollar fine. Then, in October 1905, Schooler disappeared from Skagway entirely.[39] By that time, she would have been fifty-three years old. Perhaps she was ready to retire from "the life." Then, too, Skagway's economy was failing. She may have left for the Fortymile River region, or for Fairbanks, both of which were beginning to boom at the time.

Belle Schooler did not own a very large or elaborate brothel. In fact, hers was one of the more modest establishments on Seventh Avenue, as can be seen in table 2, which provides a comparison of the value of properties on both sides of the street in 1900. It is important to

TABLE 2

**Tax assessments of properties along both sides of
Seventh Avenue between Broadway and State in 1900**

Owner	Lot	Block	Portion of lot	Value of lot	Value of Improvements	Total value
Guthrie, Lee	6	3		$600.00	(none)	$600.00
Guthrie, Lee	5	3		$400.00	(none)	$400.00
Haines, Lillian	4	3		$400.00	$300.00	$700.00
Stinebaugh, J. D.	3	3		$400.00	$300.00	$700.00
Heyman, Dinah	2	3		$400.00	$300.00	$700.00
Wallace, Minnie	1	3	N 1/2, S 20 feet	$200.00	$200.00	$400.00
Ritter, A. L.	1	3	N 1/2, N 30 feet	$400.00	$100.00	$500.00
Guthrie, Lee	7	4		$600.00	$400.00	$1,000.00
Schooler, Belle	8	4		$400.00	$100.00	$500.00
Guthrie, Lee	9	4		$400.00	$100.00	$500.00
Guthrie, Lee	10	4		$400.00	(none)	$400.00
Snder, P. W.	11	4		$400.00	$500.00	$900.00
Sherpy, M. L.	12	4	S 1/2 of S 1/2	$150.00	$150.00	$300.00
Lowe and Sickenger	12	4	N 1/2 of S 1/2	$150.00	$150.00	$300.00
Belmont, Frankie	12	4	N 1/2	$300.00	$1,000.00	$1,300.00

Source: Skagway Historical Records, Taxes, Vol. 36, 1900, 47.

note that some of the landlords may have had more than one building on their lots, whereas Schooler probably just operated the one brothel. It is likely that the male landlords, in particular, erected multiple cheap cribs, each of which was meant to be occupied by one woman, instead of the brothels that held one or more women and that contained a parlor, bedrooms, and a kitchen, and exhibited a homier atmosphere. Even so, the other property-owning madams in 1900 had larger operations than Schooler's. Frankie Belmont's large place fronting Broadway was valued at $1,000, Lillian Haines's at $300, and Minnie Wallace's at $200. Schooler's brothel was worth only half of Wallace's. It is likely that Belle's place had only one or two bedrooms besides the parlor, and that she employed only one other woman. Despite Schooler's assertion that Helen Storey was her pianist, it is likely that this woman practiced other arts at Belle's place.

Considering Schooler's early interest in real estate, it is surprising that she stayed in Skagway as long as she did. After 1901, properties all over town began to lose value. Suffering with the general downturn in the town's economy, Schooler disposed of much of her Skagway property in 1904. By the time she sold her Seventh Avenue property, the value of the brothel itself was half what it had been in 1900. While there were smaller places on the street—Lee Guthrie owned a place worth $25 and another worth $10—they most assuredly had to be small cribs.

Schooler began selling her Skagway real estate in the early summer of 1904. She sold her Seventh Avenue property, two lots in the block surrounded by Ninth, Broadway, Tenth, and State, and a lot near the railroad yards, all to Grace Maloney, and all for $1000.[40] At least she seems to have gotten a good price for these holdings. She disposed of her remaining two lots by the railroad yards in September 1904, and then rented back her own brothel for another year.[41] She wisely sold at a good price, and then waited to see whether the Fortymile or Tanana districts would provide better investments.

The Belle of Skagway appears to have hit her stride during the gold rush years. But her small two-woman business could not withstand the frequent fines levied in the fall of 1903. As a shrewd business woman, she decided to leave Skagway as the bust economy that followed the boom saw a depreciation of her real estate. The last year or so that Schooler entertained Skagway's men, she did so from a rented house, but she no longer claimed primacy in Skagway's tenderloin.

One of the things that makes Belle Schooler so interesting is that ease with which she bought and sold property in Skagway. Paula Petrik notes that up to 40 percent of women owned real estate in the mining town of Helena, Montana.[42] While some of them had been prostitutes, not all were. Schooler traded properties with her daughter, Beryl Rowan, the widow of one of the town's heroes, as she determined the best part of town in which to establish her small brothel. Rowan's mother's occupation, at least at this early stage in Skagway's history, did not seem to affect the widow's social standing. In fact, Belle was touted "an extensive property owner of Skagway" in 1902; her respectability fell only as the reputation of Seventh Avenue became well known to the middle-class women who began to invade the town.

Schooler, as a property-owning madam, could be considered the first middle-class prostitute in Skagway. However, the nature of her business indicates that her customers were most assuredly working-class, and it was the fines imposed by the middle-class businessmen that ultimately drove her out of Skagway.

Skagway also had the traditional brothel, with several working prostitutes and an overseeing madam: it was called "The Cottage." The name made it sound cozy and homey, just the sort of place an aspiring gentleman would want to patronize at the end of long day of hard work. The name also evoked images of a pleasant parlor in which to sit and ladies with whom to talk. Whether he was on his way to the goldfields, or on his way out of them, or lived in town, the Cottage sounded like a pleasant place to spend an evening. Frankie Belmont, as its owner, probably worked hard to cultivate that image.

If Belle Schooler was Skagway's first madam, then Frankie Belmont was its wildest. It seems incredible that her scandals did not spawn fantastic legends that passed down by word of mouth from generation to generation; instead, all that survives of her legacy are first-hand accounts in the newspaper.

Belmont bought her choice brothel just north of Seventh Avenue on Broadway from Lizzie Adams on October 25, 1900.[43] Adams had built the Cottage into a well-known business in just over a year. This was no ordinary residence. While the quit claim deed reads like any similar transfer of lot and building, Belmont also purchased "all of the Furniture, Fixtures, Beds, and Bedding, Carpets, Kitchen and contents, and all and everything contained therein, also all of the Linen, Blankets, and other articles in use, and everything and anything contained in the [*sic*] about the premises, and known as the Cottage, situated on Broadway in said town."[44] The furniture, beds, and linens were essential to the brothel's business; any madam made sure such items were included with the sale of the property. The only items missing in this list are the red curtains: perhaps they are covered under "everything contained therein."

John Troy, as editor of the *Daily Alaskan*, was not kind to Frankie and thought little of the homi_ess_ of her place. He regarded the high liquor

The Cottage, Frankie Belmont's brothel on Seventh Avenue, decorated for the Fourth of July, about 1904. Courtesy Alaska State Library, Paul Sincic Photograph Collection, P75-206.

license as a boon to the community, one that every civic-minded citizen who sold liquor should pay with pride. While he dismissed Belmont's avocation as a "necessary evil," he thought its "necessity" was no reason to avoid paying the high license. In early August 1901, he ranted that the liquor dealers would each pay $1,500 for their licenses very soon, and then complained that "it is a well known fact that the 'Cottage' a sporting house of very questionable repute on Broadway between 7th and 8th avenues has been engaged in liquor traffic during the past year and have [sic] not taken out a license." He noted that the law required two witnesses to swear a complaint before a warrant could be issued and that therefore the Cottage proprietor carried on her business without prosecution. Marshal Snook had given her warning, but nothing had come of it.[45]

After arguing that the owner of the Cottage should be made to take out a license, Troy pointed out that the women who inhabited the place, "after a night's debauchery present themselves at the windows and doors and very frequently sally out on the street in drunken merriment. Wednesday night they were about town in an intoxicated condition making very many disturbances and themselves very objectionable."[46] Troy admitted that "people of that class are possibly a necessary evil to society, but when they roam the streets night and early in the morning they should receive official attention. The fact that they are plying an unlawful vocation makes it all the more apparent that they should be compelled to pay license and justice to saloon keepers who do pay a license to sell liquor demands it."[47]

Frankie Belmont had become a lightning rod for the *Daily Alaskan* because she had established the largest and probably the most successful brothel in Skagway, on a lot off Seventh Avenue, *before* Seventh Avenue became known as the restricted district. Ironically, the Cottage's presence on the north end of the corner lot without a doubt provided part of the impetus for the other prostitutes to move to Seventh Avenue after they were run out of Paradise and "Jap" Alleys. But the fact that Belmont's brothel faced onto Broadway irked influential middle-class citizens like Troy who would have liked to keep the scarlet women confined within a narrower prism.

At the same time, it was obvious that certain powerful men in the community really did not want to do away with the prostitutes.

In November 1901, two months after the restricted district was established, First District Judge Melville C. Brown held court. Troy reported in his newspaper that at the end of the court's session, the judge lectured his grand jury, accusing them of having "fallen all over themselves in bringing reputable business men to time in the license matter, while they overlooked many flagrant cases of open and notorious violation of the law. Cottages of ill repute flourish like the proverbial green bay tree and sell quantities of liquor without even the frame that goes around a license. When the court had finished, it appeared that the grand jury had overlooked about as many bets as a blind faro dealer."[48]

Belmont and her cohorts were safe, at least until the next appearance of the grand jury.

The madam's next brush with the law was almost a year later, on September 9, 1902, when, this time, the federal courts did indeed arrest her for selling intoxicating liquor without a license. She pled guilty and paid her one hundred dollars and $8.20 costs.[49] Curiously, Troy's newspaper did not mention the case this time. For all of the prostitutes, the occasional $100 fines were much easier to pay than were the $1,500 liquor licenses for the saloon owners. In fact, probably on the strength of the November 1901 grand jury's refusal to make the prostitutes pay liquor licenses after Troy had so pointedly brought this issue to the public's attention, no madam ever took out a liquor license in Skagway.

Because Troy had made such a fuss about Belmont, perhaps because she ran the town's largest brothel, or perhaps because it was out on Broadway where women and children could see it, she was picked out for special prosecution. On October 6, 1902, only a month after arresting her for serving liquor without a license, the U.S. attorney swore out a warrant for her arrest on the charge of "keeping a house of ill fame for the purpose of prostitution, fornication and lewdness."[50] At this time, the other prostitutes on Seventh Avenue appeared to be enjoying complete immunity from any prosecution other than regular quarterly fines of twenty dollars and costs. The *Daily Alaskan* was all aflutter because the grand jury finally had brought an indictment against Frankie Belmont for keeping a house of prostitution. Troy encouraged the jury to "keep up the work to the end."[51]

Over the course of the next ten days, Belmont and four other Skagway prostitutes—"all the women in Skagway . . . who are known to be keepers of houses of ill fame"[52] (a gross understatement) were put through the bureaucracy of the federal court system, awaiting the pleasure of the grand jury. When Judge Brown finally called Belmont to appear before him, he gave her a long, stinging rebuke, whereupon she "sank into a chair into a fainting condition." Rosie Wagner drew thirty days in jail, in lieu of a fine. Nellie Crosby and two anonymous Japanese prostitutes were fined $100 plus costs. Because Belmont alone among this group had dared to plead not guilty, she was fined $250 and costs. While the most that a prostitute could be fined under the federal statutes was a year in jail or $500, fines higher than fifty dollars were unprecedented in Skagway. No wonder she fainted.[53]

The prosecution of Skagway's most noticeable madam, Frankie Belmont, in addition to Rosie Wagner, whose name often had been in the newspapers for her drunken behavior; Nellie Crosby; and two Japanese prostitutes, who were usually easy targets, no doubt satisfied that portion of the community that really did not have a clue about the extent of Skagway's underworld. There must have been many in Skagway who naively believed these five women were indeed "all of the women . . . known to be keepers of houses of ill fame." The total was probably closer to a dozen madams and thirty or forty working prostitutes. These five highly visible cases also sent a reminder to the others to keep quiet and out of trouble or they, too, would be paying high fines or serving time in jail.

Perhaps it is only coincidental that Belmont sold a quarter interest in the Cottage to Olive Richards two weeks after these occurrences. It would have made sense if she had done so to raise money to pay the fine. However, all she got—at least according to the deed records— was one dollar for the transaction. It seems more likely that Richards had paid the $250 fine against an interest in the business (worth $6,600 in today's currency).[54]

As was the custom of many people in Skagway, Belmont decided to take a vacation south when the days grew short and the weather turned cold and ugly. On November 2, she gave a supper party for some of her friends at the Pack Train Restaurant, one of the swankier places in town. When she got home, she and her sister Ollie quarreled, resulting in "a general row at the Cottage." Ollie struck Frankie with a wine bottle, causing "an ugly gash across Frankie Belmont's forehead . . . it was some time before she regained consciousness. The wound was sewed up and the victim will recover." Ollie was fined $500 by the U.S. commissioner, comparable to more than $13,000 in today's currency.[55]

Back in town by mid-April, Frankie promptly put the Cottage up for sale, furniture and all, promising a cheap price, "as the owner desires to leave the city."[56] The heavy fines, growing respectability of the town, and her mutinous sister were becoming too great a liability as the economy began to slump. Belmont was ready to leave Skagway.

Despite her promise of a cheap price, Belmont was unable to sell the Cottage. She was still in town on August 13, 1903, when the city made its first arrest of prostitutes under the municipal code it had adopted in June of that year. However, she took her usual winter vacation in January and February.[57] In spite of her efforts to sell her brothel in April 1903, her record of fines shows that she stayed in Skagway until at least October 1904.[58]

It appears that Belmont did not return to Skagway after she left for the winter of 1904–1905, although she continued to own at least a partial interest in the Cottage for some years afterward. The 1904 taxes were late, and she paid a penalty on them.[59] Belmont eventually stopped paying her taxes, leaving that job to Lena Conrad of Seattle, Washington, who bought out Olive Richards's one-quarter interest in the business.[60] Belmont finally decided just to walk away from her failing Skagway investment. This may also mean that she had been unable to rent it out as a brothel. Troy's ranting in the newspapers may have echoed public sentiment. The Cottage was too visible, too ostentatious, and its inhabitants too loud and noisy. It could not be allowed to operate.

On January 30, 1908, Lena Conrad sold the Cottage for $550 to Fannie D. Speer, a Skagway housewife. The deed transfer specifically mentioned the two-story frame house on the lot, as if that were much more important to Speer than the lot itself. Indeed, in 1909, the middle-class Fannie Speer and her husband Lyle moved the Cottage building across Broadway to where it still stands today.[61]

Property values in the Seventh Avenue restricted district were high in 1900, soon after the height of the gold rush, but fell each year in 1901 and 1902. Then, when other buildings along Seventh Avenue continued to decline in value in 1903, Belmont's property increased in value, indicating she had made improvements that summer. In fact, it may have been these improvements that so inflamed Troy, prompting his vituperative attack against the "degraded women" at the Cottage. The combination of declining real estate values and increased scrutiny by law enforcement authorities drove Frankie's sister Ollie from Skagway entirely, along with a host of other prostitutes.[62] Belmont, tied to her investment in the Cottage, was not so free to leave, despite her efforts to sell out. What with the $250 fine in September 1903 coming after those doubtless expensive improvements to her business, it is hardly surprising she had taken up fighting with her sister and fainting before the judge.

John Troy and the respectable middle-class reformers of Skagway had won this round. They got rid of that loud, obnoxious Madam Belmont, who would not keep her employees and clients quiet and confined to their proper part of town during the wee hours of the morning. The Cottage was out of business, and the less troublesome madams were left to run businesses on Seventh Avenue. Belmont, who had over-invested in her business, could not stay in Skagway.

The first actual combined investor and madam in Skagway was Kitty Faith. She called herself a "landlady" in the 1905 liquor petition and became Skagway's longest-lasting and perhaps most influential madam. She was not one of the earliest madams, nor always the richest. But the fact that Kitty Faith ended up owning more property than any of the women entrepreneurs of Seventh Avenue indicates that she operated within the rules that the male middle-class leadership established and that she always cooperated with Skagway's men in power.

Henrietta "Kitty" Faith was born in Van Buren County, Iowa, on January 25, 1866, to farmer Josiah Faith and his wife, Elizabeth. She had at least four brothers and three sisters, including her twin, Amaretta. The family moved to Missouri sometime before 1872, then to Manzonnita, Oregon, by 1880.[63] Kitty came to Skagway in January 1898 from Grants Pass, a mining town no more than fifty miles as the crow flies from her family's farm. At the age of thirty-two, she had probably perfected her trade while living in Grants Pass.[64] The way in which she immediately began to acquire property in Skagway also indicates that she had already developed an astute business sense by the time she got to Alaska. Here was a woman who knew how to operate under the rules the men of Skagway were laying down for the prostitutes. Unlike Frankie Belmont, who insisted on being ostentatious, loud, and brassy, Faith quietly acquired real estate, kept her several businesses out of the news, and established a relatively long and prosperous career in southeast Alaska's port city.

Kitty Faith's first records, like those of Belle Schooler, had nothing to do with prostitution, but rather with her real estate purchases. In the fall and winter of 1898–99, she bought low-valued properties on the far north end of town that eventually become valuable as rentals to men working at the railroad yards.[65] Like Schooler, she was probably experimenting with location.

At the time the 1900 census was taken, Faith rented a room in the home of Ferdie J. "Doc" DeGruyter and his wife and teenage daughter, both named Jeannette.[66] Faith called herself a laundress, as did Belle Schooler in Dawson, a sly joke the prostitutes often told on themselves. The quantity of soiled towels and sheets generated by their trade turned them into laundresses until they could afford the luxury of sending the dirty linens out to a laundry service on a daily basis. At the time, Faith probably worked out of a rented establishment that was unsuitable as living quarters.

F. J. DeGruyter worked for Lee Guthrie, owner of the Board of Trade Saloon, as a gambler, running the black jack games, roulette wheels, or faro tables. By late 1903, DeGruyter was also Guthrie's head clerk, appearing in court and paying the fines for the other Board of Trade gamblers when the municipal authorities requested their quarterly fines.[67] It is possible that Faith worked for a short time as a percentage woman at the Board of Trade, at least until she could establish her own business.

Continuing her real estate investments, on September 16, 1901, Kitty Faith purchased a roughly triangular piece of land just on the east end of Seventh Avenue, to the north and east of what would become the federal courthouse.[68] She may have been using it as a place of business at the time Seventh Avenue was designated as a restricted district.

Then, on June 27, 1902, Faith bought the house Maggie Marshall (aka Pop Corn Kate) had owned at 617 Ninth Avenue, in the residential district a few blocks north of the downtown area.[69] It probably had been Marshall's home, a place to get away from the demands of the job at her place on Seventh Avenue. Faith was living in the house by September 1902, no longer needing to rent a room from the DeGruyters.[70]

Faith obviously was biding her time to see whether investing in Skagway's tenderloin was worthwhile. Perhaps the opportunity did not present itself or the prices were not right. If she indeed did business out of a rented building, it may have taken her time to amass the capital she needed. But finally the slowing Skagway economy and Faith's rising wealth afforded the balance she needed. On March 10, 1903, she bought the quarter lot at the northwest corner of Seventh and Broadway.[71] Faith's brothel, while not the largest or most noteworthy in Skagway at the time, was of average or somewhat better than average size. More important, it was the most prominently situated brothel in Skagway's red light district.

Photographs indicate that very soon after buying her corner lot, Faith added a south wing to the simple house that had fronted onto Broadway.[72] This wing allowed her to open an entrance for her customers onto Seventh Avenue, thus immediately avoiding the sort of harassment encountered by Madam Frankie Belmont, who had her main entrance on Broadway. Kitty expanded her holdings on Seventh Avenue on October 27, 1906, when she purchased J. D. Stinebaugh's three cribs from Ollie Coram.[73] She then became the largest single property owner on Seventh Avenue.

During all this time, Faith had managed to avoid arrest and stay out of the newspapers. The U.S. deputy marshal failed to notice her during his unpredictable and often costly raids. Even when Judge Brown ordered Marshal Snook to stay away from Skagway's prostitutes and leave their prosecution to the city authorities in late 1902, she and other madams employing multiple employees evaded the regular fining that the other prostitutes in town suffered. However, beginning in February 1905, the city courts began to fine all sex workers.[74] After that time, every ninety days, give or take only a few, Faith appeared before the city magistrate to pay her $20 fine plus court costs of $6.20. The fact that others besides the prostitutes and gamblers were charged court costs of $8.20 suggests that these two classes of "criminals" came to court voluntarily and without fuss, perhaps without police escort.

So even if Faith was not known to the larger community, she was known to the city marshal and the magistrate and most certainly to the people who lived on her street. That she was helpful to others of the underworld can be seen in documents such as her purchase of a worthless piece of land from Flossie Raymond, a prostitute who may have worked for her, and her witness of the marriage between John Powers and prostitute Fannie Kiger.[75]

Faith did miss three periods when she should have been fined. When other prostitutes missed paying a fine, it generally meant they were out of town on vacation (during the winter) or working a circuit (to the north in the summer and south in the winter). It did not make sense for the owner of a business to work a circuit, however. Her absences may have occurred during times when she was scouting for better places to invest.

The first missed fine was in the summer of 1906, a few months before Faith bought three cribs just to the west of a brothel owned by Dinah Heyman. She may have been in another Alaska town deciding whether to invest there or remain in Skagway. The next time she missed was in the fall of 1907, traditionally a busy time of year for the prostitutes, as the miners were making their way out of the interior. Her absence at that time is inexplicable, unless she had an illness of some sort or was investigating another port town such as Valdez or Seward, which also would have been experiencing a busy time of year. She was back in business in Skagway in January 1908, but missed appearing for her regular fine in the spring, another good time for business in the town, as the miners began to filter back into the country. By this time, Faith must have had a "housekeeper" she trusted to run her brothels. Otherwise she would not have been away from Skagway during one of the most lucrative times of year.[76]

Kitty Faith, then, epitomizes the entrepreneurial Skagway landlady from 1903 to 1909. She owned more than one property in the Seventh Avenue district, invested throughout the community, perhaps invested in other boomtowns in the north, scrupulously adhered to the rules and regulations set up by the territorial and city officials (with just a few exceptions when she missed paying fines), and kept herself and her employees out of trouble.

————

One other landlady deserves description in this chapter on Skagway's "sinful" women. In contrast to brash, ostentatious Frankie Belmont, who wore a scar on her forehead inflicted by a maddened sister armed with a broken wine bottle, Ida Freidinger exemplified the quiet, successful, middle-class madam who catered to working class men in Skagway. More like Kitty Faith, this well-established, practical businesswoman worked well with authorities, kept her name out of the newspapers, operated under the rules established by the city fathers, and increased her holdings even as the economic situation worsened.

Ida Freidinger was born in Ohio either in 1844 or 1849, depending on the source. After getting married, she bore six children, but only one survived, an estranged son who lived in Kansas City. Considering her age when she came to Skagway—either mid- or late fifties—it is likely that she had established herself as a madam in some other place before she came north.[77]

Freidinger missed the excitement of the gold rush in Skagway. Her first recorded appearance was in September 1902, when E. D. Morrison, representing R. L. Polk and Company, collected the names for the 1903 directory for Skagway. Morrison listed Freidinger at 617 Broadway, just north of the alley between Sixth and Seventh Avenues. During a criminal trial in 1905, she was called as an eyewitness to a crime that occurred outside her house on January 14, 1904. She testified that she had lived at the corner of Broadway and Seventh for about a year when the event took place. Both the directory and this testimony place her in Skagway beginning in the summer of 1902. In May 1903, she purchased a small partial lot fronting on Broadway, very near to its intersection with Seventh Avenue. This purchase allowed her to build an entrance on Seventh. Ida was then able to avoid the problem encountered by Frankie Belmont: like Kitty Faith, who had a brothel across the street, Freidinger stayed within the confines of the restricted district.[78]

Freidinger stayed out of legal trouble, except for the regular fines imposed on all prostitutes. But like Faith, Freidinger paid no fees until

January 28, 1905. Once magistrate Tanner decided that the madams as well as their employees would pay fines, Freidinger paid on an average of once every ninety-one days.[79] In fact, the regularity of her arrests suggests that she took herself in to the magistrate's office to pay her "sin tax" without being issued a warrant.

The women who lived on Seventh Avenue in the first decade of the twentieth century, then, were a diverse lot. They ranged from transients like Pop Corn Kate who rented cribs owned by man landladies to women like Dutch Rosie Wagner who struggled to run a one-woman business and who had to rely on the help of her male partner, John Bonner. Only when a woman could afford to buy her own property and house at least one employee who shared her earnings in return for food and housing was it possible to acquire some wealth. Belle Schooler was able to invest in real estate, but a fickle economy and increasing fines (to be discussed further in the next chapter) made her living dubious. The wealthier madam, as typified by Frankie Belmont, had a good chance at making some good money, but she made the mistake of operating her brothel on Broadway instead of Seventh Avenue, and then let her employees become too noticeable to John Troy and neighbors. As a result, Belmont was prosecuted until she could no longer afford to do business in Skagway.

Kitty Faith and Ida Freidinger, on the other hand, moved the entrances of their brothels from Broadway to Seventh Avenue, kept their employees quiet, obeyed the rules, and prospered. They would do so until July 1909, with the help of newspaper editors who wanted to keep home rule in Skagway, a district judge who did not want to bother with such trivialities as the Social Evil, and city councilmen who had other agendas.

CHAPTER FIVE

Nurturing Vice, 1902–1905

To understand the role of the prostitute in the years following the formation of Skagway's restricted district, it is essential to understand the town's social structure. Almost entirely Euro-American, Skagway's population was divided into a set of working-class men, most of whom were bachelors, and a growing middle class of married men and their families. These two groups of people brought to the North fixed sets of well-defined value systems, both of which embraced prostitution and the saloon as necessary elements of a well-balanced society. These two institutions were viewed, in fact, as essential components of the city's economic health and could not be completely obliterated, at least not all at once. The difficulty lay not so much in whether vice would be tolerated within the community, but in how to keep it "in its proper place" and out of the sight of those segments of society for whom vice was forbidden: middle-class women and their children.

Indeed, banishing the prostitute from the sight of the "respectable" women and children was the first and foremost goal of the reformers in Skagway. At no time, especially in the earliest days of the citizens' conflicts over the issue, did more than a very few people suggest banning the sporting women from the town entirely. Districting was the accepted cultural solution. Why that had to be can only be understood in light of Late Victorian society's expectations of the prostitutes and the men who patronized them.

"Prostitution [is] coeval with society," physician W. W. Sanger wrote in his 1897 treatise, *History of Prostitution*. Dr. Sanger spoke with unquestioned authority, and his readers believed his treatise to be the final word on the subject. He attributed the institution of prostitution to male sexual appetites for "illegitimate pleasures" and "female avarice or passion, religious superstition, or a mistaken sense of hospitality."[1] He articulated the conventional viewpoint of the middle-class American Protestant of the time. Unmarried men could not control their lust; unmarried, unwatched women were weak and catered to this uncontrolled appetite. "Ethical suasion"—conversion to a higher moral standard for both the prostitutes and the men who patronized them— perhaps combined with legislated morality, might stem the tide of moral and criminal degradation that Sanger believed was sweeping the country.

Sanger argued that the source of this ethical suasion, curiously enough, came from the married woman, whose moral superiority remained unquestioned at the turn of the century. An editorial from the *Daily Alaskan* explained this Late Victorian reasoning when it extolled women's refining characteristics over men's savage nature. While women could never compete with men in mental or physical prowess, they were "more generously endowed" with morality than men. "It is safe to assert that women possess more innate refinement, temperance, modesty and gentleness than men," the *Daily Alaskan* noted, and continued, "An ambitious woman, a woman with liberal and charitable ideas, a woman with a pure mind and a desire for the better things, can work wonders with the nature of a man who loves her."[2]

Women's suffrage must have been on the editor's mind as he continued. "Most women can either make or mar the men they have married—or love. . . . Let not women complain of a limited sphere. Men rule the destinies of the world and women rule the destinies of men—for good or evil."[3] This statement explains much about the local attitude toward prostitution at that time. If middle-class women could be viewed as equals of men when they practiced their higher morality, then immoral women were clearly inferior. As inferiors, they could be used, abused, and tossed aside when no longer needed. They had no rights unless they served some purpose to men, who after all "rule the destinies of the world."

If prostitution in Skagway during the community's first decade appears to have been an unassailable institution, in seeming violation of the ethical standard proscribed by Dr. Sanger, that picture is misleading. Skagway's religious and moral citizens waged a constant war against the Social Evil. At the same time, many others in town believed that the existence of prostitution was better left alone. In the immortal words of councilman Frank Keelar, it was something that "the more you stir the more it will smell."[4] He voiced what a good proportion of the community believed without question. To them, prostitution was an institution that was clearly needed.

The understanding of the basic "necessity" of prostitution did not need to be aired at the turn of the century. For one thing, sexual matters were something one just did not talk about. Men might do so among men. Women might do so among women—but even that rarely happened, and then in the most veiled and euphemistic terms. If people could not talk publicly about sex, they would have a hard time talking about prostitution.

In addition, Americans at the turn of the century genuinely believed that men would go insane without having sex. This innate masculine right was never discussed, of course, but was understood nonetheless. While some ministers and physicians were beginning to educate the masses that this belief was erroneous, they could not do so easily in a climate that would not allow open discussion of sexual matters.[5]

The social relationships between men and women at this point in the developing culture of western European populations—of which the North American dominant culture was a full-fledged participant— were complicated enough at the turn of the twentieth century even apart from the issue of prostitution. But we must understand that the simple nuclear family was no more a universal social grouping than it is today. In fact some maintain that in 1900 remaining unmarried— at least for men—was more popular, and that the bachelor subculture was more powerfully defined and active, than it has been in the twenty-first century.[6]

The subculture that supported bachelors in large urban areas between 1880 and 1930 had its counterpart in the mining communities of the North American West. These men slept in lodging houses or residential hotels, ate in communal dining halls or restaurants, used the services of laundries, barbers, and bathhouses, and frequented sporting establishments such as saloons, dance halls, gambling halls, and brothels.[7] While the bachelors of the western mining towns were not necessarily unmarried men by choice, they were men living a bachelor way of life. Because they needed to make a living, they eschewed chores they considered women's work, such as laundry, mending, and cooking. And, of a matter of course, most of them looked to women for sexual release. As a result, they hired others to do the work of surrogate wives so they would have time to relax at the end of the day. The proprietors fulfilling these needs knew exactly what they were doing. For instance, an advertisement in the *Daily Alaskan* announced the opening of a new laundry with the claim: "You need no wife if you send your washing to the Troy Laundry. We do mending and sewing buttons."[8]

When families began settling in Skagway, they soon realized that there were a great many of these young, single men about town. The wives knew instinctively that these men posed a threat to them. They also understood that they and their teenage daughters were safe only as long as prostitutes were available as an outlet to the unbridled passions of the bachelor men far from home. People who remember the days of World War II in Seward, Alaska, recall a town council meeting in which some of the wives begged the army not to close down the restricted district, fearing the large numbers of strange young men that would be inundating other parts of their town during these war years.[9] It is not hard to imagine a similar sentiment in the mind of the Skagway woman, whose reputation would be ruined forever if she were ravished by the rapacious stranger unable to find an outlet for his uncontrollable lust.

For the first two decades of the twentieth century, most of Skagway's men were bachelors in both the middle and working classes (see appendix A for detailed analysis). More than three-quarters of the total population of men were bachelors. In this book, the term "bachelor" is redefined as both those men who were not married and those who were married but living up north without their wives. By 1900, there were more than six of these "bachelors" for every unmarried woman in Skagway; the ratio had to have been much higher during the boom days. Most of Skagway's men in 1900, two-thirds, were occupied in working-class jobs. For the most part, these working-class men worked for the railroad and wharves and in the mines up north, and four-fifths of these lived a bachelor lifestyle. Considering the fact that thousands more of these individuals traveled through, especially in the spring and fall each year, Skagway's service economy developed around this most common denominator.

In what would ultimately become a clash of cultural values, the bachelor culture as represented by the core of the saloons and restricted district increasingly became "owned" by the working class in Skagway. As Madelon Powers has articulated so well in her treatise on the working-class saloon, *Faces along the Bar*, the realm of leisure took on a great deal of importance to working-class men, perhaps because their work was so strenuous and yet so poorly compensated. Their expression of masculinity took the form of defending their turf as these men shared interests in sports, politics, ethnic pride, or even masculinity itself. The saloon became a male sanctuary, in which any woman, if she dared enter, was taunted and discouraged with lewd language, dirty jokes, and suggestive placards on the wall.[10]

Michael McGerr, in his discussion of the Progressive Movement, defines some of the values of the working class: group loyalty, a condemnation of individuality (which could result in distain for the man who would set himself apart by trying to "better" himself), and leisure activity as an outlet for the frustrations of hard work and poor pay.[11] When confined to the working-class bachelor's domain, the saloon and the restricted district, these values did not conflict with those of the rising middle class. When the working class's "lack of ambition," apparent racism, misogyny, and drunkenness—as viewed by the middle class—spilled out of the saloons and red light districts, or took the form of labor organization, the middle-class families took notice.

David Charles Beyreis further elucidates middle-class masculine values at the turn of the century when he differentiates between what he terms "virtuous masculinity" and "vigorous masculinity." To the middle-class man entering the Progressive Era, it was highly desirable to have a family and a good job with which to support that family. He desired greatly to be able to come home in the evening to hearth and home and the love of wife and children. At the same time, he reveled in his strong body and natural impulses. As he became more "domesticated" —a better husband and father—he sought to become stronger and healthier but had to cope with his animal instincts, such as his desire for sex and stimulants.[12] That tension ultimately caused inner conflict, which eventually he worked out through his support of women's social issues.

The success of the middle-class madams in Skagway, a direct result of the dominant bachelor culture in the town's early years, coincided with increased scrutiny from reformers and resultant pressure on the federal courts. The Skagway city council had taken one step to appease the reformers by districting the prostitutes to Seventh Avenue in 1901. The federal courts used their authority to "keep them under control" by making examples of the worst offenders from time to time, especially those who made themselves most noticeable, like the Japanese prostitutes on "Jap Alley" or the French women on French Alley. However, the local authorities lusted after the fines that went into the federal coffers every time one of the local prostitutes was arrested. And the district attorney from Juneau did not always consult with the local magistrate to find out who the worst trouble-makers were. Some of the women could cause real difficulties for those in Skagway's political offices if they were not careful. And as usual, most of the argument over who should have legal authority over the prostitutes was disguised under the rhetoric of home rule.

The middle-class men in charge of Skagway's politics became determined to acquire the authority to control and fine the city's prostitutes. They wanted to choose the time when certain women were exposed to public scrutiny, air the city's own dirty laundry at the time of its (or its newspaper editor's) choosing, and keep the court revenues within the city itself. Doing so would wrestle the political grasp of the Social Evil issue from the reformers, who might complain to the federal courts, and instead would take it to the local level. As reform became a bigger issue throughout southeast Alaska, Skagway's politicians worked to bring the debate out of the federal courts and into city hall.

Part of the difficulty, at least in the minds of those who wanted local control over vice and moral reform in Skagway, lay in the fact that the government of Alaska in 1900 resembled no other government in the United States. The area did not even have the status of a territory. Its system of government by appointed officials through the courts instead of elected representatives made Alaskans feel as if they had no say in their own government, as discussed earlier in chapter 1. Lacking a legal means by which cities could incorporate, not even the voluntary city governments could act on behalf of citizens with any authority. It

Melville C. Brown. Courtesy
Alaska State Library Photograph Collection.

was not until 1901, when the 55th Congress of the United States
passed a Code of Alaska, which finally permitted municipal incorporation, that Skagway became the first Alaska city to establish its own
government legitimized by federal law. It hastily drew up a set of city
ordinances, many of which duplicated the federal misdemeanors, but
the federal courts did not permit the city to prosecute any of these
ordinances for several months. While Alaskans badly wanted to be able
to collect the fines for criminal misdemeanors, they often did not have
the jail facilities to incarcerate the prisoners who were unable to pay
the fines. At the same time, the federal judge in Juneau was anxious
to clean up Alaska's lawless reputation before letting go of what he
admitted to be burdensome and sometimes frivolous cases. The districting of the prostitutes was one of the very first actions Skagway's
city council had taken as a legally constituted government.

In the meantime, Alaska's first judicial district court judge Melville C. Brown was trying to "clean up" southeast Alaska in much the
same way that Skagway had already dealt with its own laundry. His
primary goal regarding the prostitutes was to get them out of the
saloons. Brown, a fervent Presbyterian, was not an Alaskan and had a
hard task before him. Born in Kennebec County, Maine, to Enoch and

Sarah Reed Brown on August 16, 1838, he at least had the authority of his mature sixty-two years, and he had lived in the western United States most of his adult life. He studied law in Boise, Idaho, and then followed the gold rush to California, where he dabbled in mining and merchandizing. In the 1860s, he returned to Idaho, where he served as a member of the Idaho legislature. After moving to Laramie, Wyoming, he became that city's first mayor. There he passed the bar exam and opened a law practice. On June 6, 1900, President William McKinley appointed Brown, a life-long Republican, to his seat as judge of the First Judicial District in Alaska, at a time when there were three districts.[13]

Because the federal courts initially controlled all criminal law in Skagway, what Judge Brown decided in his courtroom in Juneau had an immediate effect on how the law would be interpreted in Skagway. Moral reformers cheered when the judge empanelled a group of reformers as a grand jury in December 1902, and began a sweep to clean up the First District. In his charge to the jury on December 1, 1902, he called special attention to the open violation of gambling and prostitution laws in southeast Alaska.[14]

One of the jurors was Thomas A. Shorthill, the husband of WCTU organizer Sarah E. Shorthill and the person who had led the effort to shut down four of Skagway's saloons in September 1900. Thomas Shorthill had made his reform opinions known in October 1902, when federal district Judge Brown opened the grand jury in Skagway. The judge charged the jurors with enforcing Alaskan laws that dealt with gambling, prostitution, and the closing of saloons on Sundays. He hinted that Alaska would never have home rule as long as those laws were flaunted and the perpetrators not brought to justice. He especially pointed a finger at businessmen—presumably those on the Skagway grand jury—who would fail to bring an indictment for fear of losing business.[15] Shorthill responded with a letter to the editor. He pointed out that "saloonism, gambling and harlotry" were common not only in Alaska but also in all American cities. He shook a literary finger at the clergymen who were afraid to expose this vice "for fear some pot-bellied pew holder will fail to drop a nickel in the corn popper." Shorthill further suggested that a territorial government— so sought after by the *Daily Alaskan*—would make no difference in the way morality laws were enforced.[16]

Predictably, editor John Troy took issue with Shorthill's letter. While he knew better than to comment on the morality issue, he went on at some length about the rights of Americans to the setting of their own laws. He accused Shorthill of assuming Alaskans were "lawbreakers and moral cowards . . . unfit for self-government, and should have our laws made for us by lawbreakers and moral cowards of other localities. Because we are as bad as those of the remainder of the United States we should not have territorial government." He argued that Alaskans, along with all Americans, had the right to ignore laws that they had no role in writing themselves.[17] He turned the entire issue into his favorite topic: home rule. As usual, he sought to minimize the reformers' issues and advance his own issues.

Shorthill got his moment of power when the grand jury convened in Juneau in December 1902, at which time he became a member of Juneau's grand jury. Away from Troy's turf, it was easy for Shorthill to practice what he preached. He helped indict fifty-four gamblers and saloon owners who ran houses of prostitution in the upstairs rooms.[18]

District Judge Brown was under considerable political pressure to enforce the reform of vice. The middle class identified the working class and saloonism with the Irish, Italian, and German immigrants who liked to drink in public.[19] There were allegations that the court was in cahoots with the mine owners at Treadwell, south of Juneau, to undermine the incipient union efforts in that area. Then too, church and temperance factions were lobbying hard for stricter control of liquor and all other manner of vice; they became natural allies of the mine owners, putting their "respectable" pressure on the judge to clean up the (military) District of Alaska. In addition, newspaper editors like John Troy in Skagway constantly harped on the unfairness of the government in Alaska, which did not even have the dignity of territorial status. With Alaska's appointed officials and government by the federal courts, and not even an elected bystander in Congress, its citizens felt completely alienated by the country that claimed them. Hearkening to the cries that "we are not wild frontiersmen, but civilized Americans," Judge Brown felt it his duty to make sure that this claim was absolutely true by purging the district of the sinful.

The December 1902 grand jury session in Juneau finally took on the vice issue. The Skagway and Juneau newspapers focused primarily on gambling, although upstairs prostitution was part and parcel of the same package. A trial of two men accused of robbing the Douglas Opera House and a murder at a saloon in Juneau necessitated acknowledgment that gambling was rampant in both Juneau and Douglas.[20] The grand jury tried to indict over a hundred gamblers and slot machine owners in Juneau. But because a number of the gamblers "maintained respectable families in the city," they escaped the indictment. In the end, the grand jury sent fifty-four of the hundred cases on to the judge for judgment, and the newspaper named no names. While the result stopped gambling in Juneau for a short time, other businessmen complained that the laborers working in the mines on Douglas Island, having nothing to do in Juneau, avoided going there on their days off, and thus spent their recreational money elsewhere. The sentenced gamblers paid their $100 fines, and opened their black jack tables and roulette wheels, as normal. The fine was viewed in the same light as a license.

Skagway's gamblers received bench warrants a day after Juneau's gamblers were served theirs. The grand jury indicted the eleven men working for Lee Guthrie at the Board of Trade Saloon. Those gamblers each paid bonds of $500 and were bound over until the April session of the district court in Skagway.[21] As in Juneau, Skagway's saloon men continued to gamble.

The gamblers' hopes that the tempest would blow over were short-lived. Within about three weeks, gamblers and saloon owners keeping prostitutes in upstairs rooms in Juneau were once again arrested. Troy announced, "It has been stated that they will be arrested from day to day until their callings are stamped out of the town."[22] So determined was Judge Brown to stop the gambling and upstairs prostitution in the capital city, that he declared war on the Juneau *Record-Miner*, the community's leading daily newspaper. The *Record-Miner* had been "very severe in its criticisms of the grand jury for presuming to bring in indictments for gambling, keeping houses of ill fame and like offenses." In the process, it had attacked not only the court, but also the personality of the judge. In a lecture to the Presbyterian Church, the judge "made some stinging remarks that were supposed to be directed at the editor of the Record-Miner," thus escalating the war. Then, the judge appointed a committee to investigate whether the editor could be arrested for "contempt of court, sedition or something of the kind." According to the *Daily Alaskan*, both of the Juneau papers devoted a considerable amount of space to the issue.[23]

A perusal of the articles leading up to Judge Brown's sermons failed to find much in the *Record-Miner* that did more than state editorial opinion, albeit on the front page instead of in the editorial column. One item accused "little red-wagon moralists in Juneau, under the disguise of reform, [of] doing everything in their power to boycott the Record Miner for the alleged reason that it is against decency and reform." The editor went on to state his unambiguous position that he and his publication favored closing gambling of all kinds and the abolishment of all bawdy houses, among other evils, "provided it is enforced against ALL."[24]

The *Douglas Island News* was far more open and vitreous in its slurs against the judge. On the event of the judge giving a sermon in church to the Treadwell miners, the weekly's editor opined "Verily, verily Judge Brown came to Alaska to save the unrighteous, and has made a bold attack with his able general on the stronghold of the enemy. There is one good thing about judicial Christianity. If you can't coax 'em to come to Christ you can have the marshal lead 'em up to the mourners' bench at so much per head."[25] The editor of the *Record-Miner* called the District Court "the Tzar-Judge system."[26]

In addition to the gambling cases, three important cases involving prostitutes in the upstairs rooms were brought against the biggest dance halls in Juneau and Douglas. One case implicated Fred Rasmussen, who owned the Peerless Saloon in Juneau. Another case was brought against Sam Gius and J. J. Penglas, who operated the Douglas Opera House. A third case was tried against the Winn Brothers of the Opera House in Juneau, which advertised itself as a "Popular Club."[27] Because some of this testimony was recorded verbatim, it is a valuable record of the way dance halls and opera houses of the times operated (see appendix B).

W. E. Crews, attorney for Fred Rasmussen, apparently knew the odds were against his client, so he adopted an unusual defense strategy: he objected to the seating of a six-man jury as unconstitutional. The jury size was stipulated by Congress when it established the laws for Alaska, foreseeing that it might be difficult at times to seat a twelve-man

The Douglas Opera House in 1902, about the time that Sam Gius and J. J. Penglas were arrested for running a house of ill repute. Note the crib-like structures to the left of the dance hall. Courtesy Alaska State Library Photograph Collection, Douglas Businesses-13.

jury in the small outposts. Judge Brown overruled the objection and the trial proceeded. Rasmussen was found guilty and sentenced to a year in prison, as well as the forfeit of his liquor license.[28] Crews vowed to appeal.

The other defendants that had been brought up on both the prostitution and gambling charges applauded this defense strategy and promptly adopted it. In the next case before the court, *United States v. Gius and Penglas of the Douglas Opera House,* which charged the defendants with operating a house of ill fame, the defense attorney tried the same tactic (see appendix B). Once again, the judge overruled the objection, and the defendants got the same results from a different jury. Gius and Penglas were found guilty and each drew a six-month sentence in federal prison.[29] However, upon sentencing, Judge Brown openly commended attorney Crews's defense of Rasmussen's trial and his argument that the six-man jury was unconstitutional. He regretted that Congress had made the law stipulating the size of a jury for Alaska, and that therefore there was nothing he could do about it.[30]

A third prostitution case was prosecuted at the same time as the Rasmussen and Douglas Opera House cases, that of *United States v. James and William Winn.* The two Winn brothers owned the Opera House Saloon at the corner of Second and Seward in Juneau. Somehow the defense attorney was able to convince the six-man jury that reputable gentlemen testifying to the common fame of the establishment were in error. This testimony had come at great embarrassment to the witnesses, who admitted they had taken their wives and daughters to family night entertainments at the saloon despite the notoriety of the place as a bawdy house. The jury dismissed the charges against the Winn brothers.[31]

At the same time that the owners of the Peerless Saloon and the Douglas Opera House were being tried, other gamblers and saloon owners who were accused of having upstairs prostitutes awaited trial.[32] The next two defendants used the six-man jury defense as well, and the juries immediately found them not guilty. The district attorney then dismissed all the remaining cases. It seems obvious in retrospect that the court deliberately went after the two most iniquitous offenders, trusting that the heavy penalties would send a strong message to everyone else. The court wanted to put all of its effort into closing down these two businesses in particular. It is little wonder the *Record-Miner* wanted justice for "ALL."

As soon as Gius and Penglas received their jail sentences, District Attorney T. R. Lyons sent notices to all of the Juneau and Douglas saloons known to have female employees that the prostitutes must move away from the premises by the following Saturday. The *Daily Alaskan*, always eager to show Juneau in a lesser light than Skagway, crowed, "This order will cause a great change in the occupancy of the down town tenements of Juneau. All the rooms above the saloons will be vacated and it may for some time to come be difficult to find other use for them. Most of the women will undoubtedly move away from Juneau."[33]

At the same time, the Juneau *Record-Miner* stated that the proceedings in Juneau had had a wonderful effect on prostitution in Skagway:

"All Bawdy houses in Skagway were closed last night through fear of grand jury indictments. Some of the women have gone to White-horse, while others are taking positions as waitresses, chambermaids, typewriters, music teachers, plain sewing, cigar venders, and other respectable occupations."[34]

The story, no doubt written expressly for the benefit of the reform community, probably caused a great deal of laughter in Skagway's sporting world. The 1901 districting had chased the prostitutes out of the saloons, which remained on Sixth Avenue and areas south of Sixth on Broadway.[35] That the prostitutes would leave Juneau even if they abandoned the rooms above the saloons and dance halls was just as far-fetched. At all times, the only prostitution that the court attacked was that occurring in the rooms above the saloons, dancehalls, and gambling halls. It was a show for the benefit of the reformers. No one else was fooled.

The newspapers, court officials, and community boosters, without a doubt, whitewashed the truth whenever possible. Considering the fact that all charges were dismissed in the other cases, it appears that the Peerless Saloon and the Douglas Opera House were token sacri-fices offered to the reformers in Juneau, not a real "clean-up" at all. In its final report to Judge Brown, the December 1902 grand jury stated that "the principal [bawdy houses] are now under indictment, and therefore, we do not feel justified in going to additional expense for investigation of these places." In other words, with tongues firmly imbedded in cheeks, they had taken care of the problem of prostitu-tion in southeast Alaska by appeasing the reformers.[36]

Reports that women had vacated the bawdy houses were premature. Juneau court files indicate that women were living above the Louvre Saloon in 1909 and were far from "respectable." Two of the female residents had had a gunfight following a "hair-pulling and door-slamming contest." The rooms were so tiny that if a person had a clothing trunk in addition to the bed, the door could not open entirely. Walls were so thin that every word could be heard by the next-door neighbor, thus offering ample opportunity for testimony from eye-witnesses—or rather "ear-witnesses"—to the crime.[37] In 1910, a Juneau lawyer was sent to prison and disbarred for sending an "obscene letter" suggesting that one of the upstairs residents of the Opera House

Saloon spend an hour or a night or week with him—she was to name the length of time and the price. The file on the case indicates that judge, jury, and defendant all understood that only a prostitute would even entertain such a proposition.[38]

However, in 1902, the message that upstairs prostitution could be prosecuted was not lost on Skagway's saloon owners. If any prostitutes worked in the rooms above saloons after the 1901 districting, it was clear that they must be out before the April 1902 court session. With complete faith in Skagway's upstanding reputation, the *Daily Alaskan* was confident that all of the city's 1903 liquor licenses would be granted because—of course—there were no women in its saloons.[39]

After prosecuting the worst Juneau offenders, the Peerless Saloon and the Douglas Opera House, Judge Brown appeared to soften his stance on saloonism and prostitution. In an interview with the *Daily Alaskan* before the district court met in Skagway in April 1903, Brown indicated that he did not want anything but felonies and other serious crimes coming before the district court. He believed the municipalities could be counted upon to correctly deal with such "social evil nuisances" as gambling and houses of ill fame (along with a long list of other misdemeanors), and he did not want these trivialities "cluttering up his docket."[40] As a result, Skagway thought it could finally take control of its moral criminals.

Given that authority, Skagway began leveling the first of its misdemeanor fines. On August 3, 1903, the city arrested twelve prostitutes and fined them each $20 and court costs. All the women pleaded guilty. The $20 fines were moderate compared to the much steeper ones imposed by the federal courts. While it appears that most of the town's prostitutes had been brought to the magistrate's bench, as opposed to the token few in previous federal raids, the small, predictable fines were easier to incorporate into daily business. The prostitutes no doubt felt pleased with the new system.

The reader can imagine the demimonde's surprise, then, when U.S. Deputy Marshal Snook, headquartered in Juneau, arrived in Skagway and arrested "a dozen or more of the inmates of the houses of ill fame" on September 24, 1903. He claimed to do so on the orders of Skagway's U.S. commissioner Joseph J. Rogers. All but one of the women paid their federal fines of $20 and costs. During the districting debate of the year before, the *Daily Alaskan* had bitterly condemned the sporting women. Now the newspaper suddenly became the prostitutes' champion. "The opinion on the street is unanimous that if there is to be periodical raids on the inmates of houses of ill fame accompanied with fines, the money should go to the city treasury rather than that of the federal government instead of being shipped off to Washington." Troy had not changed his mind about reform; he was simply being consistent in his argument for home rule. He framed the debate in the context of city versus federal control of municipal concerns.[41]

In keeping with that stance, Troy followed his commentary on the marshal's action with a reiteration of his stance on home rule. He argued that if there was any proof that Skagway would not enforce the law as effectively as the federal courts, then he could understand letting the federal court keep its authority. However, the recent arrests proved that the municipal court could do its job. Two days later, Troy used the federal arrest of the prostitutes as an argument for acquiring a municipal jail.[42]

The matter finally got cleared up when Judge Brown told Skagway city attorney R. W. Jennings that he did not mean to interfere in "minor offenses, such as the regulation of the social evil" and would leave all that up to the city police. But he did think that both gambling and the sale of intoxicating liquors in houses of ill fame, without a license, remained federal concerns. He disavowed any knowledge of the recent raid on the Skagway brothels and promised there would be no further interference. His word was good. Only five prostitutes served federal jail terms for keeping a bawdy house between 1904 and 1918. In contrast, between November 1903 and September 1909, the city court fined the prostitutes 335 times.[43]

The local and federal courts were now down to their final volleys. Just to point out to the district attorney and Marshal Snook that the city police, magistrate, and jail were up to the challenge, on November 27, 1903, Skagway officials arrested and fined "all" eleven prostitutes in town.[44] The control of the Social Evil was now a local matter. There was only one very important exception, as stipulated by Judge Brown: selling liquor without a license. In a parting flex of muscle, on December 9, 1903, U.S. Commissioner Rogers fined three prostitutes $100 and court costs for that offense.[45] Despite avowals that the federal courts would retain the authority to prosecute that type of crime, no more prostitutes were arrested for liquor sales in Skagway for the next seven years.

Those that had paid dearest in this territorial spat were the women on Seventh Avenue. Some of Skagway's prostitutes had paid almost $200 each in fines and costs between September and December— the equivalent of more than $5,100 in today's currency—in this scrap between the federal and municipal authorities as to who was in really in charge.

Even though Skagway's prostitutes had suffered financially during these four months, they did realize some gains. Through the elimination of the high fines and unreliable prosecution that came from reformers' complaints, and the clearance for the madams and women who ran their one-woman businesses to deal one on one with local authorities, the Social Evil problem ceased to exist. The war with vice disappeared from the front page. Troy's newspaper stopped entertaining readers with humorous stories of Pop Corn Kate, Dutch Rosie Wagner, and other degraded women from French and Paradise Alleys. He saved his best shot for women like Frankie Belmont, whom he decided needed special prosecution. As long as the women paid their sin taxes, and stayed out of the attention of the reformers, Skagway no longer appeared to harbor any sin.

———

Between 1901 and 1905, politics in Skagway remained largely non-partisan with relatively few contentious issues. As had been the case in the unauthorized 1897, 1898, and 1899 city elections, the first autho-rized elections sanctioned under the Alaska Code in 1900 and 1901 were controlled by a group of middle-class merchants and business-men who called themselves the Citizens Party. These men were scions of the original Committee of 101. In 1901, John Troy was elected as chairman of the nominating committee of what he called the Citizens Ticket, and by 1905, this group of voters became institutionalized as a local party. As long as Troy lived in Skagway, he held the chair of the nominating committee. Because he was editor of the city's only news-paper, his nominees received free endorsement for office, and their rivals had no similar means of advertising their campaigns. In essence, John Troy controlled who sat in Skagway's city hall.

Throughout this period, Troy's writings made it clear that he did not believe the truism promulgated by Mark Twain that the saloon keeper occupied the highest level of society in western communities. He did not trust either the saloon men or the landlords in the restricted district. During the 1901 election, Troy lambasted Lee Guthrie in his capacity as saloon owner and F. M. Woodruff, who was friendly to the demimonde.

The voters in 1901 ignored Troy's dire warnings, and both men were elected to the city council. Woodruff received so many votes that he became mayor of Skagway. In the same election, Frank Keelar lost his coveted post. Due to Troy's hard campaigning in the following year, Guthrie lost his seat on the council, but Fred Ronkendorf, the owner of the Senate Saloon, succeeded him. William Boughton, who had owned the Idaho Saloon and co-chaired the Citizens Party with Troy, sat on the council from 1903 through 1905. Some representation from the vice sector remained in city hall throughout the period, despite Troy's efforts to keep it out.

In only one election did the Citizens encounter any organized opposition. In June 1903, thirty men met in the rooms over Josias M. Tanner's hardware store and formed the Taxpayers Party, putting up a slate of seven nominees. It is not clear what policies they endorsed, or how they differed from Troy on local issues, as the newspaper editor did not explain his rival party's viewpoints. This lack of newspaper coverage for the party probably contributed to the election results: none of the Taxpayers won a seat on the council. However, Tanner became the elected magistrate, the first and only time the position was filled by the voters of the city. To avoid a split party in the future, the council changed the position to one that its members could appoint, rather than leaving the selection up to the voters. The Citizens Party objective was not realized; Tanner proved so good at the job that subsequent councils chose him for the job every year until he resigned in 1909.[46]

Tanner's election as city magistrate was not entirely a popularity contest. He had served as city and county deputies in Iowa and Washington States in the 1880s and 1890s. In Skagway, he was head of the

Safety Committee that had held Ed Fay under guard in the Burkhard Hotel in February 1898, and had been appointed a special officer of the court, and then U.S. deputy marshal, leading the posse that rounded up the Soapy Smith gang in July 1898. He served as deputy marshal from that time until November 1899, at which time he resigned in order to take care of his hardware business in Skagway. Since that time, he had acted as the city jailer.[47] His opinions about law and order were widely respected.

Tanner's power as city magistrate over the demimonde was considerable, and it was to him that the prostitutes, gamblers, and saloon owners came when there was a dispute. A prime example happened in January 1905. On the 23rd of that month, seven gamblers appeared before magistrate Tanner, five of whom worked for the Board of Trade Saloon and two for the Pack Train Saloon. They all pleaded not guilty but nevertheless paid their $20 fines plus court costs. Next before Tanner's bench came the six prostitutes to pay their regular quarterly fines. The first four to appear were Madam Ida Freidinger; a Japanese prostitute, Fannie Atimo; Flossie Raymond, a regular who had appeared once before and would show up at least five more times over the next four years; and Emma Wilson, another regular. As was the custom—perhaps one of "the rules"?—all four pleaded "guilty" and paid their $20 plus costs.[48]

The remaining two women who came forward, each charged with "being an inmate of a house of ill-fame," broke the pattern. Rose Arnold and Ruth Brown, aka Ruth Chesterfield, pleaded "not guilty" and asked for a jury trial. Since the time Skagway had become incorporated, only two women had tried doing that, and one of them had spent ten days in jail for her impertinence: Minnie Wallace, who could also not pay her property taxes.[49] Arnold and Brown probably suspected that more than just their livelihood was at issue; their very right to live in Skagway was at risk.

On January 25, 1905, Arnold was tried and acquitted of being an inmate of a house of ill fame. Brown's charge of "keeping a house of ill repute in connection with Rose Arnold" occupied the court for the next several days. It resulted in two acquittals and two re-arrests before the persistent magistrate could find a jury who would convict her. Finally, on January 29, Judge Tanner was able to slap Brown with the standard

$20 fine and whopping court costs of $141.15 (equivalent to more than $4,100 in today's currency). By maintaining the pressure until gaining a conviction, the city court made its point: prostitutes like Brown would be prosecuted until found guilty. By February 16, both Brown and Arnold had left town for Juneau.[50]

It is interesting that Kitty Faith, Ida Freidinger, and the other madams began to pay $20 fines in February 1905. They had not done so before. Brown probably had argued that other owners of brothels had not been required to pay fines, so therefore why should she? To prevent that sort of defense in the future, magistrate Tanner demanded that all prostitutes, including the women who employed the working women, would pay the quarterly fines.[51]

Troy and Tanner (presumably at the request of the city council) had their reasons for harassing Arnold and Brown. Troy had identified the women as "colored" in seven of the eight newspaper reports about their trials. The real names of Rose Arnold and Ruth Brown were probably Josephine Arnold and Millie Wallace Brown; Millie was, without a doubt, the "Minnie" Wallace who had pleaded not guilty to a charge of prostitution in August 1904.[52] These sisters (Josephine and Millie) were in Dawson between 1898 and 1902, where they claimed to be laundresses, but where the Northwest Mounted Police arrested them several times for prostitution. They came from Arizona by way of Vancouver, and each had been married. Millie's husband, Charles Wallace, a bartender, probably pimped for them in Dawson.[53]

Arnold and Brown were members of Skagway's African American community, which had grown out of Company L of the 24th Infantry. As previously mentioned, this unit had been stationed in Skagway from August 1899 to May 15, 1902. Several soldiers were discharged during this period and chose to remain in town, along with their families and other dependents.

Besides protecting the Canadian border during the gold rush period and providing law and order before the days of city incorporation, Company L had provided valuable services, such as additional fire protection: Captain Hovey, the company's commander, had volunteered troops to man the hoses and bucket brigade of the local fire department. The men played weekly summer baseball games with the laborers who worked for the railroad, giving the townspeople much-enjoyed Sunday afternoon entertainment. The troops made a grand show when they marched down the street in full dress uniform on the Fourth of July. And they staved off the Canadians who wanted to push their border to the ocean, a real threat at a time when the boundary had not been surveyed to both nations' satisfaction.[54]

Until 1902, prostitutes such as Arnold and Brown provided sexual services first for Company L, then for the discharged men who chose to stay in Skagway. Recall that Robert Grant, the only soldier of Company L to have been maligned by the Skagway press, was refused service by Marie Melgem, a white habitué of Seventh Avenue. Prostitutes such as Arnold and Brown were in demand as long as Company L and its discharged soldiers were in town.

Racism among whites all over America was rampant and blatant at the time. John Troy believed one of the many reasons that Alaskans did not yet merit the status of a territory was that the number of white residents was underreported, leaving the false impression that other ethnic groups comprised a greater percentage of the population. According to his argument, Congress would never consent to the self-governance of Indians, Asians, and Africans. When Company L left in May 1902, racism was completely free to raise its previously only briefly lowered head. While the troops themselves were in town, very few negative reports about the African Americans in Skagway appeared. But shortly after they were replaced by a white regiment, stories about race riots, lynchings of African Americans in the South, and derisive comments and editorials about "coloreds" of all walks of life—Troy did not eschew the N-word—became regular features in the newspaper. The African American owner of a newspaper that published stories for the infamous temperance advocate Carry Nation was called a "coon" with no apparent embarrassment by the editor of the Skagway newspaper. Gruesome depictions of black men being lynched by white southern mobs were reported matter-of-factly, as if the alleged "outrageous insults" to white women sufficiently justified the violence. Ubiquitous reports of boxing matches, a favorite sport of the barroom crowds, always favored the white pugilist. The discharged African American troops and their families who had stayed in Skagway could not have felt comfortable with the sudden change in reporting about others of their race. Some evidence suggests that a dwindling African American community remained in Skagway for only two or three years after Company L left.[55]

Even so, white Skagway occasionally prided itself on its tolerant nature, and the city courts might not have worked so hard at bringing the women to justice had it not been for another factor. Arnold and Brown avoided the Seventh Avenue district, and instead rented the house next to the Peniel Mission, at the east end of Sixth Avenue.[56] There they were next door to the African American troops of Company L, housed in the old Occidental Hotel, and also across the street from the army barracks built in 1901. This location would have once been quite lucrative. Now, though, with the troops gone and with their living next door to the reform-minded Peniel missionaries, they may have endangered the entire institution of prostitution in Skagway.[57]

By 1905, it is likely that Arnold and Brown had simply outworn their welcome. The town was losing its general population to the Tanana gold rush near Fairbanks and to the booming Nevada silver mines. Encouraged by nothing but negative reporting about African Americans in other parts of the country, Skagway's "colored colony" began leaving along with the general population. By 1910, only one seventy-one-year-old African American widowed housekeeper remained in the town's population of 870 people.[58]

Because few middle-class businessmen (Troy's most desirable type of citizen) would consort with an African American prostitute, Arnold and Brown were fair game for official harassment. Perhaps city officials also feared the return of the Peniel missionaries, who were out of town on vacation at the time of this prosecution.

As discussed in Chapter 1, the Peniel missionaries were nondenominational Protestant evangelists, who offered food and lodging to unwed mothers, wayward women, and other wandering souls. They lived entirely off local donations, as the national organization in San Francisco did not provide financial support. All the Peniel Missions, including the one in Skagway, were staffed by women. These women held weekly and sometimes daily meetings, in which they preached morality. The missionaries counted drinking, gambling, and the use of tobacco as vices to be purged from American life.[59]

As the population of Skagway declined with the booms in Fairbanks and Nevada, more and more people took extended winter vacations south. The Peniel missionaries were no exception. For the first time since the Skagway mission's founding, it closed in November 1904, with the missionaries due back in early February 1905. Mrs. Victoria Yorba, the head of Skagway's mission, returned to Skagway on February 6, less than a week after Ruth Brown received her small fine and large costs. Yorba and three other missionaries were ready for daily meetings within the month.[60]

Along with the dwindling of the town's population—from almost 2,500 people in 1900 to only 1,085 remaining by 1905—the railroad was losing its labor force. The elected and appointed city officials— the city council, the city marshal, and the municipal judge—could not afford to upset the officials of the White Pass and Yukon Route by drawing unwanted attention to one of their working class employees' favorite forms of recreation. Arnold and Brown, living right next door to the Peniel missionaries, had crossed the line. Their usefulness to Skagway was over. There were no African American soldiers left in Skagway, and the African American community had dwindled to very few, if any unmarried discharged soldiers. The Peniel missionaries, on the other hand, had every reason, including religious zeal, to make the town's prostitutes a major issue in the upcoming April 1905 city election. Their very presence when Yorba and her associates returned from vacation would have upset the delicate balance that the middle-class gentlemen in city hall had reached with the women on Seventh Avenue.

After being targeted for arrest, Arnold and Brown (aka Millie and Minnie Wallace) stayed away from Skagway. Later, in 1905, when it came time to pay the 1904 taxes, Minnie Wallace gave up her Broadway property near Seventh Avenue.[61] There was no business for African American "laundresses" in Skagway.

The four years between 1901 and 1905 had seen a substantial change in the way prostitutes were prosecuted and fined in Skagway. The restricted district shrank from those lots bordering Broadway and State on either end of Seventh to only the cribs and brothels facing directly onto Seventh Avenue. Women like Frankie Belmont who could not keep her employees quiet and out of the news had been driven from town. The federal authorities stopped assessing fines, even for selling liquor without a license, and the prosecution of prostitutes became a strictly local responsibility, with all proceeds going to the city coffers. With the establishment of a well-defined restricted district, a woman with the wherewithal to invest in property, furnishings, dresses, medications, liquor, and food for her employees could go into business for herself. Middle-class prostitutes—madams and land-ladies—were now a part of Skagway's social structure.

The issue of licensing and taxation—how to pay for municipal services—began to surface as a component of the reform debate. While the proceeds of the high liquor license had been an obvious outgrowth of the early prohibition efforts in Skagway, the discussion about prostitutes paying for liquor licenses and then the questioning of who should receive the proceeds from the fines on prostitutes became a part of the equation. While John Troy believed the city should benefit from sin taxes, he could not and did not quite so blatantly state that the federal courts had no business licensing prostitution. He simply wanted to see that the city controlled its own vice. By that, he of course was referring to the middle-class male citizens who ruled the town.

The 1905 city election passed peaceably. The election aired no reform issues, because middle-class men in city hall had taken care of the problem before it became one when magistrate J. M. Tanner evicted Ruth Brown and Rose Arnold from their quarters next to the Peniel Mission. Indeed, the election had no issues attached to it at all. All council members, middle-class businessmen each and every one, were re-elected. Tanner was reappointed to his office, despite the fact that he had organized the Taxpayers Party in opposition to John Troy's Citizens Party. His recurring appointment by the council indicated that he and the town's citizens were in full accord on how to handle the "necessary evil." On the question of reform, he seemed to be of the same mind as the other businessmen in town: remove those who called attention to themselves and tax the others.

Politics, reform, and the question of prostitution: all seemed to be in balance by the end of 1905. But the balance of power was beginning to shift, both inside and out of the restricted district. Changes were occurring, even as Troy and City Hall achieved the peace that they had sought.

CHAPTER SIX

Saloons and the
Working Class, 1902–1908

By 1905, Skagway's population fell below one thousand. Because only about 40 percent of that population consisted of adult males and because about 60 percent of the adult male population belonged to the working class, less than two hundred customers were actively supporting the saloons in Skagway. (See appendix A for a more detailed population analysis.) By the fall of 1902, only seven saloons remained in Skagway. The high license fees and decreasing population drained resources faster than the saloon keepers could bring in customers. As a result, Skagway's saloon owners adopted a custom that had long been practiced in the nation's large cities but that had not been previously necessary in gold rush country: the free lunch. While this practice required that saloon keepers indebt themselves to big company brewers who would subsidize the lunches, these free meals could, conceivably, draw in more customers. Starting in October 1902, as the transients left town, Skagway's saloons engaged in a bitter warfare to see who could offer the swankiest free meal and yet continue to pay their high license fees.

Madelon Powers indicates that the free lunch was common in most working-class saloons throughout the United States between 1870 and 1920. However, the fact that Skagway saloons advertised free lunches only between late 1902 and early 1904 suggests that competition among saloons was particularly keen at that time. The purpose of the free lunch, of course, was to get the customer in the door. The code of behavior, well understood by both the customer and the bartender, was that at least one drink would be purchased, and that the size of the serving of the meal would be commensurate with the amount of liquor consumed. Powers suggests that this code was rarely broken and that bartenders were often employed for their skills at weeding out the freeloaders as much as for their ability to dole out drinks.[1]

A newspaper commentary of May 2, 1902, states that "Rumors of 5-cent beer, 10-cent whiskey and big free lunches, are now rife."[2] Skagway's saloon lunches ranged from the little neck clams at the Mascot Saloon to roasts and full buffets at the Seattle Saloon, the Board of Trade, and the Pack Train.[3] The quality of the lunches also varied with the occasion, depending on whether it was a special celebration or regular fare.

Not to be deterred and probably encouraged by the census taken in 1902, which reported less than 1,500 people in Skagway (resulting in a reduction in the saloon license fee to $1,000), Jacob Bloom and Emil Korach, owners of the Monogram Liquor House, were optimistic about the upcoming 1903 census in May of that year. This time, they were joined in their request for license renewal by John L. Gage of the Pack Train, W. W. Boughton and Joseph Smith of the Idaho Liquor House, Cleve Hall, manager of the Board of Trade, and Albert Reinert, owning what was now known as the Mascot, instead of Mascotte Saloon.[4] Wisely not embroiling the courts or any "foreign" attorneys from Juneau, the city council selected magistrate J. M. Tanner to take the census. Troy gave the census his qualified blessing with the stipulation that it must be "fair" in order to make the saloon men pay their "fair share" and so that the schools could retain their "fair share." He warned, "The name of every resident in the city should be on the list."[5]

When Tanner finished his census on May 28, he could only come up with 1,336 names. Troy made two efforts to rally people to add their names to the list, and then abruptly gave up reporting anything more on the census.[6] He made only cursory mention of the annual liquor censuses that were taken after that time.

In the meantime, the reformers fighting for a moral Alaska noted the reduction in license fees, and interpreting it as a victory for the saloons, they decided to stage an attack on another front, nor did they waste any time in doing so. The first hint of their newest battle strategy came in mid-July, when seventeen saloon keepers in Juneau were brought before the grand jury for violating the "blue laws," which stipulated that saloons should be closed on Sunday. The jury, however, refused to convict Tony Kengyel, proprietor of the Comet Saloon, the first case to come before the court. With that failure, the *Daily Alaskan* predicted that only one or two more proprietors would be prosecuted.[7]

It must have been somewhat of a surprise, then, when District Attorney John Boyce brought a protest against the issuance of liquor licenses to those Skagway saloons that had, in the past, operated on Sunday.[8] Five saloons promptly closed their doors on Sunday: the Seattle, the Monogram, the Pantheon, the Mascot, and the Last Chance.[9] It is possible that the other three saloons—the Board of Trade, the Pack Train, and the Idaho—had not received their licenses for other reasons and were not open anyway. It is difficult to conceive that any of these latter three saloons ordinarily closed on Sunday. All three had reputations for boisterous and rowdy clientele, unlikely to regard the Sabbath differently from any other day.

The same day all of this was happening in Skagway, the *Daily Alaskan* reported that the jury in Juneau had acquitted saloon owner Peter Carlson for doing business on Sunday. While his defense lawyer did not deny the charge, he claimed that the saloon did the community a service by giving the city's laborers a place to get out of the cold and rain on any given Sunday. There seemed to be no other place where they could go to get their stimulants. The jury was out for only fifteen minutes before exonerating the proprietor of any misdeed. Three weeks later, the Juneau court granted licenses to all Juneau and Douglas saloon men but two. These latter were rejected on account of their employment of women. The *Daily Alaskan* reported that it was the general belief that all Skagway licenses would be granted.[10] It was clear that juries were refusing to sustain the Sunday closings in Juneau, so the district attorney tried another tactic: accuse the worst offenders of employing women and take their licenses away in that manner.

Meantime, back in Skagway, District Judge Brown indicated that all applicants for liquor licenses would have to present their defense against the accusations of the district attorney. Less than a week later, after all the applicants promised to close their doors on Sunday from 9:00 A.M. until 6:00 P.M., the judge agreed to grant most of the licenses. On August 20, five saloons received their liquor licenses: the Board of Trade, the Idaho, the Monogram, the Pantheon, and the Last Chance. They had agreed to close on Sundays, "and not to allow women about the premises."[11] No mention was made of the Seattle, Mascot, or Pack Train saloons. It seems the Pack Train had already obtained its license for 1903 back in May, when John L. Gage and Company had undergone an internal shift in ownership.[12]

The Seattle Saloon was closed the entire month of August 1903 while owner Herman Grimm moved his business from the southeast corner of Sixth and State to his former location at the northwest corner of the same intersection. Fred Ronkendorf, the owner of the building on the southeast corner, once known as the Red Onion Saloon, was at the same time preparing to lease his building to a new manager, James E. Fitzpatrick, of the Totem Saloon. It is difficult to tell whether giving up the building and returning to his old location kitty-corner from the Totem was Grimm's idea or Ronkendorf's. It is obvious Grimm decided to take advantage of the general lull in business caused by none of the saloons having licenses to spruce up his old digs by adding an ice house, boiler and toilet. He also put a big electric sign on the front of the Seattle Saloon, flipping the switch on September 3, when he reopened in the location he had given up when he moved to Ronkendorf's building. It is probable that Grimm did not apply for his license until he was ready to reopen at his old location, thus shaving off a good percentage of the yearly fee.[13]

But what held up the licensing of the Mascot Saloon? Albert Reinert no doubt had difficulty with the provision that no women be allowed in his saloon. A sign indicating the location of the "Mascot Family Entrance" and pointing to the rear can be seen in a photograph as early as October 28, 1901.[14] By custom, women were allowed in the "family entrance" in order to buy liquor for home consumption. The German-born Reinert must have felt these family sales were perfectly legitimate. A common way that saloon keepers of the time circumvented these types of laws was by providing a separate room where women could come and go without interacting with the men. It would be another year before he could remodel and enlarge his space enough to accommodate another space just for women. Wrangling and negotiating with the court over how to handle the female customers may well have delayed the issuance of his license. In later years, Reinert continued to advertise to his "family" clientele, and eventually installed a telephone so that women could call and ask for home delivery.[15]

The Mascot Saloon, October 1901, during a high tide. Note the sign on the telephone pole, indicating the family entrance to the rear, through which women could enter the saloon. Courtesy Alaska State Library Photograph Collection, Skagway-Street-Scenes-8.

In the end, the Skagway saloon keepers vowed they would shut their doors on Sundays and keep women out the saloons. In return, they happily accepted the reduced $1,000 license fee. As a result, the number of saloons actually increased from seven to nine in Skagway during 1903. The Totem Saloon cut its ribbon in the location of the old Red Onion (former Senate, former Seattle) Saloon at the southeast corner of Sixth and State avenues. In addition, John F. Anderson, the proprietor of the Hot Scotch Saloon during the summer and fall of 1898, predating the high license, purchased the Brownwell Hardware Store at the southwest corner of Fourth and Broadway, and converted it to the Pantheon Saloon.[16] The opening of these two saloons suggests that the town's population had finally and indisputably fallen below

1,500 people. The lower $1,000 license fee opened up opportunities that had not been available to these proprietors before. The only thing that is curious about this rather momentous period in the history of Skagway's saloons is John Troy's complete refusal to cover the 1903 liquor election in the *Daily Alaskan*, an event that would have documented both the actual number of people in Skagway and the increase in the number of saloons.

For reasons that have not yet been determined, the saloons seem to have given up their free lunch war in the spring of 1904. While infrequent free lunches were mentioned after that time, especially during special occasions, such as at Christmas time or for a proprietor's birthday celebration, or for a grand opening, the daily free lunch disappeared from the advertisements in the *Daily Alaskan* pages—at least for a while. It is likely that the lower license fees made for higher profits so that the free lunches were no longer necessary to draw in the customers. The Skagway proprietors would then be free of their obligations to brewery sponsorship. For instance, while the Mascot would remain loyal to its Rainier Beer, and the Pack Train to its Lemps, both would add the locally brewed Red Star and ever-popular Anheuser-Busch to their menus.[17]

In June 1904, it was time to take another census of Skagway. This time the city council appointed city jailer John J. Burns to the task. It apparently went without a hitch or complaint from the *Daily Alaskan's* editor, who had by now resigned himself to the fact that there were fewer than 1,500 people in Skagway. As in 1903, no results were announced in the newspaper. The 1905 business directory, the data for which had been gathered in the fall of 1904, stated that the town had a population of 1,085 people.[18] Troy had finally realized there was no chance he could pump up the number from that low figure, even with the addition of the businessmen who lived in town only during the summer months.

It is hard to tell how Skagway's moral reformers and saloon keepers felt about the news that arrived in November 1904. Shortly after his election, President Theodore Roosevelt decided not to reappoint Judge Melville C. Brown to the bench in the First Judicial District of Alaska. According to the *Daily Alaskan*, the news was greeted with jubilation in Juneau and Douglas. "Two brass bands were brought out in full uniform . . . to give a combined concert first in one town and then in the other, and . . . more fireworks were burned than were consumed on the last Fourth of July." The assistant attorney general of the United States, William A. Day, who had investigated numerous complaints about Judge Brown the previous summer, affirmed that the unspecified charges had proven without merit. He added, however, that "the majority of the people of Southeastern Alaska are so suspicious of the court that there is not the confidence in it which the general welfare of the country demands the people should repose in the judiciary."[19] The saloon men had found him to be a hard prosecutor. But the reformers were probably often disappointed that he did not take a harder stance against gambling, prostitution, and the evil saloons. Both those interested in temperance and those who made their money from saloons had complained about the judge.

Judge Royal A. Gunnison took his oath of office as judge of Alaska's First District on January 2, 1905. The young bankruptcy lawyer and Cornell law instructor from Binghamton, New York, had a tough district to oversee. John Troy reserved judgment, but he did quote Juneau's *Daily Alaskan Dispatch* after it had stated that "Judge Gunnison has already won the admiration of the federal court spectators by the unassuming manner in which he is carrying on his official duties. With the strife and discord existing among the attorneys it was no easy task to take the reins."[20]

Thanks in part to this "unassuming" approach by the new district judge, all remained calm for the saloon men for over a year. The quiet emboldened saloon keeper Chris Shea of the Pack Train saloon. On March 30, 1906, he met with thirty men in the old Mondamin Hotel, now dubbed the Labor Hall, and formed a new opposition party to Troy's Citizens. Shea and his group endorsed three of the Citizens' candidates, one candidate being put up by a third, independent party, and proposed three candidates of their own. One of them was Shea. They called themselves the Labor Ticket and told the *Daily Alaskan* that their convention was "started up as a joke but taken up seriously." During the election on April 3, Charles Diers, endorsed by both the independent and Labor parties, defeated his Citizens rival. Troy graciously congratulated Shea for his skillful leadership of the party and his near loss by only twelve votes. Labor had cracked the veneer of the previously indomitable Citizens, who had run Skagway since politics were invented in the city.[21]

While politics had always been controlled by the middle class in Skagway, most of the potential voting population was working class. Two-thirds of the adult males were engaged in labor jobs or skilled crafts, most of them associated with the White Pass and Yukon Route railroad, Moore's Wharf, or one of the construction companies. While most of these men were bachelors, more and more of them were getting married, supporting families, and taking on the responsibilities of citizenship. While less than a fifth of the working-class men lived with their families in Skagway in 1900, now almost a third did so (see appendix A). This increased "settling down" of the working class coincided with a rise in the working class's interest in politics. As the working class in Skagway looked for spokesmen in city hall, they sought men who had similar roots, who understood their issues, and who, like themselves, were just beginning to "settle down." Perhaps that is why they chose Chris Shea as their representative.

Christopher C. Shea was born to Irish immigrants, Patrick and Bridget Shea, in New York in 1874. One of nine children, Chris moved with his parents to San Francisco, California, in the early 1880s. His father opened a grocery and liquor store, and by 1889, at age fifteen, Chris was working for his father at the liquor store on Folsom Street. He married a woman named Emma and they had a daughter, Nellie, in 1895, but by the end of that decade, he and Emma had divorced. In the late 1890s, Chris worked variously as merchant, teamster, and bartender for employers other than his father.[22]

Shea first appeared in Skagway, Alaska, in the fall of 1897 before going on to the Klondike. He returned in November 1898, where he registered for a night at the Mondamin Hotel, then one of the nicer places in the heart of the downtown business and saloon district. In good middle-class fashion, by 1899 he joined the Fraternal Order of Eagles, Aerie #25. Within three years, Shea had become "the popular night bartender of the Mascot" Saloon.[23]

When the German longshoreman Harry Schofield froze to death because he was too drunk to put wood in the stove on the night of November 26, 1903, Shea paid his funeral expenses. He did so probably because he was the person who collected all the donations of those who passed the hat.[24] This was the first of a long series of incidents that would build a firm relationship between Shea and the working-class men of Skagway, resulting in a sound base of support for him in the years to come.

During the summer of 1904, Shea began to demonstrate leadership skills among the bachelors of Skagway. He organized a baseball team called the Eccentrics, which played against the Monkey Wrenches, a team composed of men working for the White Pass and Yukon Route railroad. The rivalry was fierce, but friendly. For instance, "Sut" Cottrell, manager of the Eccentrics, challenged Shea and his "bunch of totem poles to play ball for any old thing except your reputation. We don't need that as we have a better one." Shea replied, "We will play you just for the love of the thing and to show the public that we can make monkeys out of your gang without a wrench."[25]

After leaving Albert Reinert at the Mascot, Shea worked behind the bar in a series of other saloons before he partnered with Fred Patten to purchase the famed Pack Train Saloon.[26] There, Shea threw his heart into his work. One of the saloon's attractions had always been its gaming tables, where the house gamblers dealt craps, twenty-one, and blackjack. He usually left the gambling to the hired hands, but, according to tradition, either he or Patton marched to court every ninety days to pay the $20 fine for each of the four men they usually kept on staff for that purpose. In April 1906, Shea himself appeared before the court for gambling, indicating that he also lent a hand at the tables from time to time.[27]

As Shea moved from bartender to businessman, he bought a house at the respectable corner of Ninth and Main. He left his bachelor days behind. The outgoing, gregarious manager of the Eccentrics, the man who had poured beer and whiskey for the guys at the Mascot, the Pantheon, and the Pack Train, and dealt cards at the gambling tables, married a preacher's daughter.[28]

Helen Eckert Shea was born in Illinois on July 13, 1882, and was orphaned early in childhood. Rev. and Mrs. J. E. Walters adopted her and brought her with them when they moved to Skagway during the gold rush. Helen appears to have been a shy person, entirely unlike her ambitious, energetic husband, or the outgoing, socially active wives of other political leaders in the community. Although her name appeared

The interior of the Trail Saloon in 1908, with mayor and saloon owner Chris Shea standing behind the bar. Note the large photograph of the volunteer fire department behind the bar instead of a mirror. The bar and back bar had originally been used in the Commerce Saloon. Courtesy Alaska State Library Historical Collections, Juneau, PCA 075-351.

often in the newspapers, it was always as a supportive wife, never as a woman who attended social functions outside the church. She gave up her Protestant denomination and joined her husband's Catholic Church, where she volunteered for that church's fund-raising events.[29]

In October 1906, the reform community gave Shea and the working class reason to become more serious about his candidacy in the 1907 city election than he had been the previous April. It all started when Judge James E. Wickersham of the Third District of Alaska denied the issuance of four liquor licenses in Valdez, Alaska, on charges of gambling and prostitution. The refusal obliterated the funding for the Valdez public school, because the revenues from half the liquor licenses went to support public education in the town.[30]

A week later, encouraged by Wickersham's action in the Third District, the grand jury in Ketchikan, Alaska, brought indictments against every gambler in that town. Judge Gunnison of the First District fined the proprietors of their gaming houses between $350 and $800 apiece, traditionally only $50 to $100 fees. He warned every city in southeast Alaska that no more gambling would be allowed.[31]

Two saloons in Skagway had gambling tables: Lee Guthrie's Board of Trade and Shea and Patten's Pack Train. For the first time since the gold rush, Guthrie closed his business for the winter. Skagway's city council decided the $80 of court revenues from the four tables at the Pack Train would not warrant Judge Gunnison's attention when he came to Skagway for the next court session. They voted to shut down "legalized" gambling in Skagway. They served notice to "all" the saloon keepers in Skagway—actually only the partnership of Chris Shea and Fred Patten at the Pack Train Saloon because Guthrie had left town—that the city would fully prosecute all gambling within city limits.[32]

On March 19, 1907, Judge Wickersham in the Third Judicial District pronounced that gambling was a local issue, not a federal one. Three days later John Troy broke with his tradition of waiting to attack any upstart political candidates who thought they could bypass Troy's nomination process in the Citizens Committee. Ordinarily, he would save his negative accusations against the opposition until a day or two before the election. That strategy usually cut short any action by the opposing political party. This year, however, he decided to choose a single campaign issue and spend almost a month dwelling on it exclusively. Before Shea even declared himself a candidate and three weeks before the April 2, 1907, election, Troy staged his campaign. He told his readers that the question of whether Skagway would be a "wide-open town" could become an issue in the upcoming election. He accused Shea of starting a campaign "to enthrone the god of chance."[33]

Troy deliberately played to the growing reform sentiment in the community. Ten days before the election, the editor of the *Daily Alaskan* began a series of editorials against Shea, continually attacking his supposed support of gambling and downplaying any discussion Shea tried to generate about equalizing taxes, which he maintained was his party's main focus.[34] Not until a week before the election did the Labor Party meet to approve its platform. At that time, it ignored the gambling issue. It called for lowering taxes for the middle class and working class alike by making the White Pass and Yukon Route railroad and Moore's Wharf pay their fair share.[35]

While he had denied it up until that point, it really was no surprise that Chris Shea was a candidate for city council on the Labor Party ticket. The real surprise occurred on April 2, 1907, when Skagway's working class voted out the party controlled by John Troy since 1901. All seven candidates put forth by Shea's Labor Party won the election. Troy graciously conceded, as if he, himself, had run and lost an election. Yet he explained his preference for the Citizens Party's candidates by editorializing, "The Daily Alaskan has no apology for the way in which it ran its campaign. It opposed the election of Mr. Shea, not on personal grounds at all or because he was on the Labor ticket, but for the reason that it believed that his business has been such that he should not be placed in a position of authority in municipal affairs." He then stated he would live with the choice the people had made.[36]

Troy and the Skagway city council comprised of the Citizens Party made one very important mistake during the winter of 1906–1907, but it was not their decision to abolish gambling from Skagway, nor when then discussed it as a campaign issue the following spring. While they tried to use gambling as a distraction, the issues were never about vice in Skagway's working class saloons. The issue was about organized labor.

On March 15, 1907, sixteen mechanics walked out on strike from the White Pass and Yukon Route railroad, joining a series of strikes that had been threatened up and down the southeast coast all winter. The men demanded wages comparable to those on the Puget Sound and the rest of the Pacific Northwest. Troy refused to cover progress reports of this strike during the critical days preceding the city election, when the Labor Party ran against the businessmen's Citizens Party. The day after the Labor Party took City Hall by storm, Troy finally printed a letter from Luke McGrath, chairman of the strikers' workforce, and, incidentally, one of the newly elected city council members. McGrath carefully outlined the position of the strikers, correcting a number of mistakes Troy had printed more than two weeks previous. The corrections came too late to influence the outcome of the election, and they are puzzling. Perhaps the newspaper editor decided there were more people interested in labor issues after none of his party's candidates obtained positions on the city council.[37] Troy's avoidance of the issue prior to the election had, without a doubt, alienated him from a large sector of the community, the working class.

Troy's objection to Shea, therefore, had never been about gambling in the saloons. It was about a businessman who would let the unions meet in his place of business—his saloon—and organize a political party in a place called the Labor Hall, and then bring that political party to power in the city council. It was about the working men in Skagway having a voice in their city government. It was about the management of the White Pass and Yukon Route not being able to dictate to city hall how the town would be run. Troy, with his thoroughly middle-class values, viewed the values of the saloon culture and the working man as anathema to Skagway's progress.

John Troy lost his control of Skagway with the election of the Labor Party. He discovered how little power he had in the three months that followed. No longer privy to the workings of the city hall, he was completely baffled by the council's plans to lease the Northwest Light and Water Company in April and May 1907. Despite his ability to convince the people of Skagway to vote against what he believed to be an expensive and "unbusiness-like" scheme, the way his editorials flipped from one stance one day to another the next day indicated he had very little clue about the real objectives of the council. Eventually, it became clear that the council meant to undercut the price of the power company enough to make it affordable to the city and ultimately purchase it, something Troy, as a Democrat and a Progressive, surely should have approved, had he been part of the power structure.[38]

Having lost control of his city to a saloon keeper with immigrant, working-class roots, and finally realizing it, staunch Democrat John Troy sold the *Daily Alaskan* to Republican Dr. Louis Keller and left Skagway on July 1, 1907, three months after losing his middle-class party's vote to Shea's working-class Labor Party.[39]

The new regime took office on April 8, 1907. A month later, the Reverend John W. Glenk of the Methodist Church presented the city council with a petition signed by ninety-eight men and more than thirty women asking to move the restricted district away from Seventh Avenue where school children had to pass it on their way to and from school. The school, by this time, had been built on State Street between Twelfth and Thirteenth Avenues, several blocks from Seventh, but protestors contended that the restricted district was in proximity to the residential section. They appear to have forgotten that the district was established only six years earlier when they had thought the alleys of sin were too close to the business district.[40]

The city council began to discuss tabling the petition, but real estate attorney Phil Abrahams asked to be acknowledged. He pointed out to the good reverend, who had come to town in July 1905,[41] that the district had been created "out of the alleys on Broadway and State streets, from the second stories of Broadway and Sixth avenue and from other parts of the town," implying it had been a whole lot worse once upon a time. Abrahams, a well-respected citizen about town, thought that because the women were settled on Seventh, "they should be permitted to remain, and he thought the other localities that had gotten free of them should be permitted to remain free." And then, as if it were the coup-de-grace, Abrahams pointed out that the petition "was signed largely by non-residents and non-taxpayers."[42]

Indeed it was so. Skagway was only the third ministry for Rev. Glenk, thirty-three years old at this time. Glenk was born in Fort Hunter, New York, on June 2, 1874, to Frederick and Charlotte Kaufman Glenk. He attended New York University, where he obtained a bachelor's degree in architecture in 1897 and a master's degree in history 1899; he went on to Drew Teaching Seminary in New York, where he was ordained as a Methodist minister on September 16, 1900. He took his first ministry in Grays River, Washington, and moonlighted as a professor of history at the Puget Sound University in Tacoma, Washington, in 1901. The young minister married Phydelia Rebecca Treat in Centralia, Washington, on July 11, 1901. He was made a full deacon of the Methodist Church on September 20, 1902, and he started a church in Dolomi, Alaska, shortly thereafter.[43]

The Glenks moved to Skagway on July 14, 1905, less than two years before the ladies of Skagway convinced him to present the petition to Shea's city council. In fact, the Glenks would leave Skagway before 1907 ended, move to Bellingham, Washington, and preach to a variety of churches for the next three years. By 1910, he abandoned his ministerial work and became a draftsman for a machinery manufacturer in Bellingham. Although he would present guest sermons at Methodist, Congregational, and other Protestant Churches in the Puget Sound region for the rest of his life, he did not return permanently to the ministry.[44]

There can be little doubt that Phydelia Glenk was behind her husband's involvement in the 1907 Skagway petition. Phydelia's parents, Adelbert Henry Treat and Louisa Rebecca Stone, were a New England couple that proudly traced their roots back to Revolutionary War ancestors, a fact that allowed Phydelia to join the Daughters of the American Revolution in the 1920s.[45]

Like her husband, who was also a well-educated New Englander, Phydelia prided herself on her social involvement and her patriotic duties. After leaving Skagway, she would become active in the Minister Wives Association of the Methodist Church, the Methodist Women's Home Missionary Society, the Queen Esther Society (a youth auxiliary of the Home Missionary Society), the Daughters of the American Revolution, and, most important with respect to the topic of vice and reform, the WCTU.[46]

Rev. John and Phydelia Glenk did not last long in Skagway. Having most recently come from the small mining town of Dolomi, near Ketchikan, they may have had too many expectations for their chances of doing good in the greater metropolis of Skagway. The firmly entrenched interests of Phil Abrahams and the other landlords on Seventh Avenue stymied the one major reform effort attempted by Rev. Glenk and his reform-minded wife. By December, only seven months after submitting the petition to the city council, Glenk was pastor of the Methodist Episcopal Church in LaConner, Washington.[47]

Abrahams had a vested interest in Seventh Avenue—and a very good reason for wanting to protect the rights of the property owners there. Besides being Skagway's foremost real estate attorney, in 1907, he owned the largest brothel in Skagway. Due to the way deeds were filed and taxes recorded, that fact would not be apparent, even to this author, until years into the research for this book.

The brothel in question sat in the middle of Seventh Avenue on the south side of the street. Part of the reason it was so difficult to unearth the history of this building lay in the fact that, despite its prominence on the block and its covered stairway in the back, it did not sport a name like "The Cottage," located a block away. Mysterious names appeared in the newspaper from time to time, and it appears they all applied to this brothel. In February 1901, U.S. Deputy Marshal Snook warned the madam of the Dew Drop Inn that she could not employ an underage boy. On September 4, 1902, Abrahams advertised that he was authorized to pay a $50 reward for the return of the jewelry taken from The Lodge. In December 1908, liquor was stolen from The Green Light, but the thieves missed a purse containing money and a set of diamonds.[48] This series of names suggests that a succession of madams changed the appellation of the building according to changes in management. They did not own the place.

The first mention of this building in historical records is dated May 27, 1899, when Tillie Page sold one-half, undivided interest in the property to Joseph Lang of Denver, Colorado, for $700. Page and Lang then sold the property to Dinah Heyman of New York City on August 3, 1900, for $1000. The latter quit claim deed indicated that the property included "all of the Furniture, Fixtures, Beds, Bedding, Stoves, Lamps, Linen, Blankets, and anything and everything contained in and about the said premises," language used when The Cottage changed ownership.[49] Lack of chain of title preceding Page's sale suggests that she was the one who built the building, which appears in photographs dating as early as January 1898.

Tillie Page appears to have been the daughter of an old friend of Phil Abrahams. One of the people who lived in Abrahams's childhood home was Moses Hyman, a cap maker. Hyman had a daughter named Tillie, born in 1873. She married William Page, a telegraph operator, in 1894.[50] It was probably this Tillie Page that provided the money to build the brothel on the south side of Seventh Avenue in 1898.

There is no evidence that either Dinah Heyman or Tillie Page were madams. Both owned other properties in Skagway, and neither was arrested for any crime having to do with prostitution. Between May 26, 1899, and October 5, 1900, Heyman's name appeared on nine real estate transactions in Skagway, with another one on July 16, 1904. These transactions involved ten lots: she was the buyer in seven of the transactions, most of which involved residential properties. Her most lucrative sale was of the northwest corner of Fourth and Broadway to William F. Matlock on October 17, 1899. He would build the Idaho Saloon at

The south side of Seventh Avenue in about 1908: the two-story building in the center was owned by Phil Abrahams's sister, Dinah Heyman; Ida Freidinger owned the brothel on its right, at the corner of Seventh and Broadway; the three adjoining cribs to its left were once owned by J. D. Stinebaugh and later by Kitty Faith. Courtesy Klondike Gold Rush National Historical Park, Mike Motzer Collection, 7th-4-1931.

that location. She also sold a small brothel on the north side of Seventh Avenue in late 1899; it would eventually become the property of Belle Schooler. But Heyman held onto most of her Skagway real estate for several more years, presumably for the rents they generated. In April 1905, Abrahams purchased seven lots from her, all for a dollar apiece. Two of them were on the south side of Seventh Avenue, including the two-story brothel with the shifting names.[51] She was not, therefore, a madam, but a capitalist, an investor in real estate.

Heyman, in actuality, was Phil Abrahams's sister. Isaac Abrahams, a tailor, and his wife, Polly, lived in London, England, where they raised two daughters and three sons, including Phillip and Dinah. Dinah married Isaac Heyman, a male relative of Moses Heyman, who had lived with the Abrahamses in 1861. Isaac Heyman, a German tailor, immigrated to the United States on August 7, 1860. By May 1870, Dinah and Phillip had immigrated to New York to join Heyman. Phil Abrahams did not stay in New York with his sister after immigrating to the United States. On June 30, 1870, he went on to Brenham, Texas, located 76 miles northwest of Houston and 90 miles east of Austin (he would later claim he was born in Texas instead of England), where he became a store clerk. He married Rachel Landa in about 1876, and they moved to Austin, where he became a grocer. By 1880, the couple had two sons, Solomon and Joseph. A daughter, Alice, was born sometime afterward. While in Austin, Abrahams advertised fine wines, liquors, brandies, imported delicacies, sauces, domestic fruits, nuts, and candies for sale. He was also active there in the Knights of Pythias, a prominent fraternal organization that would later open a chapter in Skagway.[52]

Abrahams came to Skagway with the rush in August 1897. After scouting out the potential of Dawson and other mining communities, he came to the conclusion that Skagway was the best place to invest. His name was mentioned prominently in newspapers around the country as the secretary of the executive committee of a group of miners who organized to improve the White Pass Trail in late August 1897. Some versions of the article referred to this committee as a "vigilance committee," but by that they meant it was a typical miners' committee.[53] It was surely the beginnings of the Committee of 101.

Abrahams filed claims on two city lots in the summer of 1898 and bought up a number of other lots. By the middle of June 1898, he set up shop at 321 Fourth Avenue as "P. Abrahams, Licensed Real Estate Dealer, Collection Agent, Notary and Public Conveyancer [sic]." In coming years, he would also advertise himself as a real estate attorney. He would be associated with real estate in Skagway as late as the 1924 business directory. During the height of the gold rush, in the winter of 1897–1898, there were eighteen real estate agents advertising in the Skagway newspapers. By 1903, only three realtors, including Abrahams, made a living in Skagway, and he became the sole real estate agent and broker for the town by 1905.[54]

Abrahams filed for bankruptcy in the Juneau court in 1899, having $12,000 worth of liabilities and no assets. It was about this time that Dinah Heyman purchased her properties in Skagway. It appears that

Abrahams's sister helped him out of his financial difficultly by buying up land and businesses he knew to be profitable. Instead of sending the money back to New York, he probably kept the proceeds, reinvested them, and built wealth for both her and himself. In 1904, when he had accumulated enough capital to pay her back, he did so by selling off "her" properties with his power of attorney, transferring the most lucrative businesses to his own name, and liquidating those that he no longer needed. With this strategy, he could afford to become one of three incorporators of the Home Power Company, Skagway's public utility in 1908. By 1909, Juneau newspapers referred to Abrahams as a wealthy real estate owner and capitalist.[55]

Phil Abrahams was active not only in real estate but also local politics. He was chosen as street commissioner by the first authorized Skagway city council in June 1900. The Skagway Democrats elected him as delegate to their Juneau convention the following June, and again in May 1904. The Juneau newspaper referred to him as a well-known Democratic warhorse in 1900 and again in 1913. In 1912 and 1913, he was elected city councilman as a member of the Taxpayers Party on the strength of his stance against the Sherman Anti-Trust Laws and the role he had played, along with other upstanding Skagway citizens such as J. M. Tanner and Dr. J. W. Brawand, in breaking up the monopoly held by the Moore Wharf Company and the White Pass and Yukon Route for transportation in the port city. He was again elected on Skagway's Independent Ticket in 1916. He was secretary of the Alaska Commercial Club when Skagway made national headlines during the debate on whether to adopt a national daylight savings time. Abrahams was quoted as saying that in the Yukon "it is necessary to blindfold the chickens so that they may go to roost," capturing a sort of rough, northern humor that brought laughs all over the country. When John A. F. Strong became governor of Alaska in 1912, he appointed fellow Democrat Abrahams a member of an Alaskan Defense Council, an organization that helped develop war preparations for the territory.[56]

Rachel Landa Abrahams, whom Phil married in Texas, never joined him in Skagway. The couple divorced sometime between 1900 and 1910. She stayed in Austin, and Phil was enumerated as living alone in the 1900, 1910, and 1920 censuses in Skagway. The couple's daughter, Alice, served as Abrahams's hostess in the years between 1908 and 1914, when she would have been of an age to help him entertain; before that he had sent her to a Catholic school in Washington State.[57]

As indicated above, Dinah Abrahams Heyman was a respectable tailor's wife in Brooklyn, seemingly not the type of woman who would manage a brothel; Tillie Hyman Page also appears to have been a middle-class housewife. Neither was a resident madam. Neither woman's name appears in the criminal records of either the city or the federal commissioner, or in the newspaper. The common link between Dinah Heyman and Tillie Page, owners of the brothel on Seventh Avenue (as well as other properties in Skagway), was Phil Abrahams, who was not only a real estate broker but shared a common history with each of the housewives who owned the brothel. It seems doubtful that either woman knew what sort of properties in which he had invested their money.

When Abrahams spoke out for himself and the other property owners on Seventh Avenue during the May 1907 city council meeting, Councilman Chris Shea moved that Rev. Glenk's petition be tabled indefinitely. The motion was seconded and the vote had only one dissention, a councilman who had wanted to refer the matter to committee. Shea and the Labor Party made their emphatic statement about the moral reform movement. They would stay the course. They had other issues in which they were interested. They had articulated the first point in March: equalize taxation. They were not interested in moral reforms. Apparently the Labor Party did not have enough opposition to fight them on this issue. Yet, once again, the loosely organized middle-class women and the clergymen of Skagway had lost a battle to City Hall.

The Labor Party, however, had made some concessions to reformers in a previous meeting. They passed an ordinance that required the women to keep their front doors closed, to keep the window blinds half down, and to wear appropriate street attire when out of their houses. A suggestion had also been made to fence off Seventh Avenue. The latter was never done: however, tall fences appeared around some of the properties.

The main reason the Labor Party wished to keep the prostitutes, other than the fact that its working-class constituency viewed prostitution as a normal indulgence, was the income generated by the fines.

Like those paid by the gamblers, these fines had been a source of revenue for the city since 1903, and the Labor Party could see no good reason to cut off this source of money, especially if it would help achieve the low taxation portion of their campaign promise. The direct taxes on sin, at the rate of $80 a year from every prostitute in town, went straight into the city coffers.

In November 1903, First District Judge Melville Brown had decided that municipalities had the right to prosecute and fine the prostitutes under misdemeanor charges. At that point, the city of Skagway began to fine each prostitute on a regular ninety-day schedule. The ideal was rarely met, but the intent was clearly there. The fines from the prostitutes, exclusive of court costs, represented a major source of income for the city (as shown in table 3),[58] relieving Skagway taxpayers of some of the burden of the costs of fixing streets and sidewalks, paying for a night watchman, and lighting the street lamps at night. The city budget for 1906, for instance, included an expenditure of $700 on streetlights. The general expenses for running the city and its courts were projected to run another $700. The sin taxes paid by the prostitutes and the gamblers in 1905 more than compensated for these good works, and also achieved a big step toward reducing the city debt of $600 besides.[59] These sin taxes kept other taxes low, taxes like those on real estate and personal property, taxes that the middle-class businessmen would have to pay if the prostitutes and gamblers, through paying their fines, did not.

The Labor Party had promised to keep taxes low, a measure that would help both the working and the middle classes at the expense of only two big businesses in town: the White Pass and Yukon Route, which owned the railroad, and the Moore Wharf Company. With John Troy gone, Shea and his supporters thought they would have little opposition. They would not be distracted by moral reformers—mostly clergymen and middle-class women—talking of reinstituting gambling fees or trying to move the restricted district.

Significantly, Shea and his supporters remained in office through the 1908 city election year, but not as members of the Labor Party. Shea was savvy enough to expand his constituency beyond the working-class laborers that came into his saloon. He joined with the men who had met over J. M. Tanner's hardware store in 1903 and reconstituted the

TABLE 3

Yearly court revenues from prostitutes, gamblers, and other sources, 1903–1909

	Fines from prostitutes	Fines from gamblers	All other fines
1903	$540	$380	$201
1904	$1,080	$1,040	$319
1905	$817	$877	$145
1906	$980	$720	$422
1907	$880	N/A	$397
1908	$1,110	N/A	$504
1909	$766	N/A	$400
Total	**$6,173**	**$3,017**	**$2,388**

Source: Skagway Magistrate Docket, Skagway Historical Records, 1903–1909.

Taxpayers Party in 1908. Campaigning on a platform supporting publicly owned utilities and lower real estate taxes—both favorite Progressive Era issues—he once again eschewed moral reforms. Troy's next three replacements as editor of the *Daily Alaskan* universally disliked Shea, some more than others, and some so much that they probably endeared the man to his more moderate, less reform-minded constituents. As a result, Shea became mayor of Skagway in 1908 and brought three of his Taxpayer party members with him into city hall. Among them was the friend of Lee Guthrie and Frank Keelar, a former gambler and restricted district landlord, Phil Snyder.[60]

And then in a move that seemed to irritate some of the moral reformists, Shea negotiated a deal with the privately owned Home Power Company (previously named the Northwest Power Company), which enabled the city to lease the company at a reduced price. Lloyd Harrison, the son-in-law of Sarah Shorthill, who had started Skagway's first WCTU, collected $5,000 in donated funds to make public improvements to the Home Power Company utility contingent on the lease to the city. To make the deal work, councilmen Charles Nye and Phil Snyder, both of the Taxpayers' Party, invested up to another $10,000. Snyder had been a gambler at the Board of Trade Saloon in the early days, and Shea and Nye promoted him to the position of general manager of the publicly leased Home Power Company. Phil Abrahams put up the third $10,000 required for the deal. When the temperance-minded Harrison discovered the identity of the major investors, he marched into the city council meeting and announced he was withdrawing all of the donated funds for capital improvements.[61] Not surprisingly, he later capitulated, in the interest of achieving something everyone in town seemed to want, but the saloon men's generosity obviously did not sit well with him. Harrison, Shea, Tanner and Snyder all ended up on the Board of Directors for the newly incorporated Home Power Company, until such time as the lease was finalized with the city, all of them keeping wary eyes on one another.[62]

———

At the same time the Labor Party took over Skagway's City Hall in April 1907, the working class organized a strike at the White Pass and Yukon Route railroad. From one of their favorite working class saloons, the Pack Train, the working men found a champion who would run their party for them, a businessman with a working class background who would win two more city elections, lower their taxes, reduce their utility bills, and orchestrate a wide variety of Progressive Era reforms for their city.

Taxes were indeed coming more and more into the consciousness of the people of Skagway. As reformers pushed for change, the traditional means of paying for reform became more difficult to achieve. With fewer working-class men to support the saloons and employ the gamblers and prostitutes, fewer proceeds from each of those activities found their way into city and federal coffers. The saloon-keeper mayor of Skagway proposed to change that by taxing the big businesses of Skagway for their inventory instead of their real estate. The solution did not go over well with those in power, but he kept his popularity among the working class.

Chris Shea, acting on the common knowledge of the nineteenth century—namely that the way to gain power in a mining community was through one's status as a saloon keeper—would start to find that the world was changing. He would ultimately discover that he would fail his working-class constituency, because the middle-class wives could not abide a mayor who owned a saloon. Unlike Skagway saloon owners Frank Clancy and Lee Guthrie, Shea would experience his Waterloo on Seventh Avenue.

CHAPTER SEVEN

The Closing of the Seventh Avenue District, 1909–1910

During Chris Shea's year as councilman in 1907 and his 1908 term as mayor, he led the Skagway city council in Progressive Era reforms that irritated the middle-class businessmen who owned many of the larger pieces of property around town. These reforms, however, satisfied the holders of average and smaller properties. Shea made good on his promises to equalize taxes by increasing personal property taxes (such as taxes on inventory and equipment) and lowering taxes on real estate. For instance, the biggest businesses in town, the White Pass and Yukon Route and its subsidiary, Moore's Wharf, saw increases of more than 500 percent for personal property, while the vast majority of Skagway's citizens had their property taxes cut almost in half.[1]

In the meantime, Skagway's reform community began to coalesce around a group of middle-class women. When John Troy left Skagway, middle-class women felt they might once again have a voice. The newspaper editor had soundly trounced the "temperance women" for delaying the acquisition of public school funds in October 1900 by protesting the licenses of four saloons; he discouraged a good many reform-minded women who had never before engaged in any sort of political action. Their next effort at social reform, the closing down of the "Jap" and French Alleys in April 1901, was done in cooperation with clergymen and other male reformers, but by September 1902, the WCTU had failed in its efforts due to lack of support from the women in Skagway. After that, the middle-class women turned to other social outlets. Moral reform continued, but women distanced themselves from political action, and they most certainly did not strive to achieve anything under the auspices of the WCTU.

That all changed about the same time that Shea became mayor of Skagway in April 1908. A new editor at the *Daily Alaskan* promised to be more sympathetic toward the views of the moral reformers. Middle-class women had learned some lessons in 1900 and 1901. And they had another leader at their helm this time, a woman whose personal experience gave her more drive than the rest of her compatriots in Skagway altogether. Anna Stinebaugh would not be stymied by a saloon keeper, nor by J. M. Tanner, the man who had rounded up the Soapy Smith gang. If she could force her husband, J. D. Stinebaugh, to sell his rental properties on Seventh Avenue, then she could rid Skagway of all similar properties. She only needed to organize like-minded women.

Anna Emma Mooney Stinebaugh was born on November 25, 1867, in Clemons, Iowa. She bore five children between 1891 and 1904, the last arriving on July 4 in Skagway, the others arriving every two or three years in Grants Pass, Oregon. The youngest child, Florence, lived a little less than three years, dying on June 15, 1907, of tonsillitis.[2]

Besides the inevitable work that raising a family and keeping a house entailed in the early twentieth century, before the advent of electric- and gas-powered appliances, the energetic Anna Stinebaugh found time to be active outside the home. After her initial work with the Skagway WCTU in 1900–1902, she organized the Little Women's Sewing Bee in April 1904, open to any who wished to join, not merely her own set of friends, as so many social clubs dictated in those days.[3] Its inclusiveness suggests the sewing bee served a larger function than did mere social gatherings. These meetings may well have been places where women shared information on reform issues and developed strategies to influence their husbands, who had the voting power in the community. In 1907, Anna was also commander of the Ladies of the Maccabees, another woman's social organization that devoted itself to charitable causes.[4]

Anna's husband, James D. Stinebaugh, was born in Tippecanoe County, Indiana, on April 9, 1862, to Isaiah and Sarah Jenkins Stinebaugh. His mother abandoned him and his father when he was three years old. J. D. married Anna Emma Mooney in Grants Pass on July 20, 1890, where he opened a barbershop. He left for Skagway in October 1897. By the following July, Stinebaugh had acquired a partner in J. J. Jensen, and the two had established the Principal Barbers on the east end of Sixth Avenue. This shop was a bit off the beaten track of saloons, restaurants, and cigar stores but close enough that the men headed for the Klondike could pause there to freshen up a bit.[5] He waited a while to bring the family north, just to make sure he could make a go of it. It was obvious he was no "rusher"—someone who came and went with the booms. The family still had not arrived in Skagway by March 14, 1900, when the census was taken.

By September 1900, Jensen had sold his portion of the business to Stinebaugh and left town. The family lived for a while at 740 Fourth Avenue, but by fall 1904, they had moved to a house near the barbershop on Sixth Avenue. At this time the Stinebaughs had three daughters and two sons, the oldest just becoming a teenager, the youngest only a few months old. By late 1906, the business district had moved over to Broadway, and so Stinebaugh moved both his barbershop and residence to Broadway between Fourth and Fifth Avenues.[6]

That the Stinebaughs were beloved members of the community is clear from the accounts of their toddler Florence's death from tonsillitis in 1907. The newspaper gave daily reports of her illness before she died. On the day of her passing, the newspaper wrote of the little girl's popularity, sweetness, and good nature. The description of the funeral consumed an entire column, with details of what flowers where contributed by whom. The list reads like a who's who of the women's social and reform scene of Skagway, from Mrs. R. L. Guthrie, renowned for her elegant parties, to Mrs. G. V. Zinkan, who would one day be the president of the WCTU, and to Mrs. Yorba and Mrs. Carnahan, who ran the Peniel Mission.[7]

When the issue of driving the prostitutes from Skagway came before the Skagway city council in April 1901, as has been noted, only four city council members were present to act. Frank Keelar, in his lone dissenting report to the council, noted that "a woman whose husband supports her with rents derived from property occupied by these people [the prostitutes]" had started "the moral wave" of the previous year.[8] This "moral wave" was the protest filed by the local chapter of the WCTU against the granting of licenses to the Reception, Senate, Fifth Avenue, and Seattle saloons. Anna Stinebaugh was the only member of the Skagway WCTU whose husband owned and derived income from property on Seventh Avenue.

Only a month after J. D. had come to Skagway, back in November 1897, he had purchased a lot on the south side of Seventh Avenue, less than a block from Clancy's Music Hall and just west of the two-story brothel that would be built by Phil Abrahams for Tillie Page. By 1900, Stinebaugh's lot held three cribs, one of which was probably rented by Pop Corn Kate. He did not sell the lot with the cribs until October 1906, at which time it was acquired by Kitty Faith, who was then Skagway's richest madam.[9] It may or may not be coincidental that Faith also came to Skagway from Grants Pass, Oregon.

The simultaneous occurrence of Anna Stinebaugh's participation in the WCTU in 1900 and 1901 and J. D.'s ownership of three cribs in the restricted district provides an excellent example of the difference between the way middle-class men and women viewed prostitution in the community. Their differences in this matter may well exemplify what Progressive Era historian Michael McGerr rather understatedly refers to as a growing dissatisfaction between men and women in the middle class.[10] As women began to realize that they could not have absolute control over what their children were exposed to outside the home, they also began to realize it was part of their role and responsibility to become more politically involved. It was a slow and difficult adjustment for both men and women to make. Women understood they must step outside their domestic realm to extend their moral influence beyond the home. They engaged in a battle for the moral health of the family. Men like barber J. D. Stinebaugh, on the other hand, invested in the economic health of the community by buying up property in a capital-rich part of town, which happened to be the restricted district. He did his part toward contributing to the economic health of the community and his family by assuring that the district had enough cribs for the prostitutes to conduct their working-class businesses.

Both James and Anna's names were on the deed to the restricted district property and Anna added her signature to her husband's on the quit claim deed. Significantly, the couple sold the lot and cribs just before the first petition to move the district was circulated, and well before the district was abandoned in favor of Alaska Street. J. D. must have been unable to convince his wife to leave well enough alone. As it turned out, by disposing of the property before the district was moved, he avoided a substantial loss. In fact, the couple received $1,000, more than any person had obtained for a property in the restricted district up until that time.[11] Most significantly, J. D. Stinebaugh had not let his wife's morals interfere with making a hefty profit on the sale of his rental properties.

Having convinced her husband to rid himself of the shameful rents, Anna Stinebaugh was now free to go back to her political activities. In September 1908, five months after Chris Shea became mayor, Ketchikan resident Lillian M. Conner (also the wife of a barber) helped the Skagway women reorganize a branch of the WCTU. Grace Zinkan was elected president; she was the wife of Gleason V. Zinkan, who was in charge of Canadian Customs and an agent for the Royal Northwest Mounted Police. Anna Stinebaugh was elected the secretary. About thirty members were enrolled.[12] Regular announcements of the WCTU meetings followed in the newspaper, indicating that the organization met on the first Friday of each month and sometimes more often if special events were planned. *Daily Alaskan* editor Samuel Wall was obviously far more supportive of the WCTU's efforts in the community than John Troy had been; Wall never wrote anything negative about the women's activities.

When John Troy left the *Daily Alaskan* in July 1907, he sold it to a local dentist, Louis S. Keller. Keller came to Skagway in January 1898 from Pocatello, Idaho, where he had also engaged in dentistry. Keller never actively took part in the editing of the newspaper, although he probably had veto power over the content of editorials. A. R. O'Brien and Walter Liggett served as interim editors, but by 1908, Keller had hired Samuel Wall, who ran the newspaper until late 1920. Wall was touted as "probably the most able newspaper man of Alaska."[13] While Keller took a keen interest in regional Republican politics, he often avowed to "sit the fence" when it came to local politics. His editors, on the other hand, usually espoused the favorite Citizens Party.

Simultaneous with its rebirth in Skagway, the WCTU spawned a Loyal Temperance Legion (LTL), the youth branch of the parent organization. The LTL often met immediately following the meetings of the WCTU, implying that the leadership of the junior league was actively

involved in the adult organization.[14] At the same time the LTL was
planning a Halloween party for its members in October 1908, the
WCTU was preparing for an election night party and setting up a
system for reporting the election results. Minnie I. Williams, wife of
a locomotive engineer, headed up the LTL, and there were twenty-
two members.[15]

The motto of the reincarnated WCTU in Skagway was "For God
and Home and Native Land." The *Daily Alaskan* explained that "their
work is to look up and lift up; to lift up the morals and eradicate sin
in all its forms, not by force or antagonism, but by loving, prayerful,
and by peaceful methods, by educating public sentiment to a higher
moral standard." Speakers at a St. Patrick's Day celebration in 1909
promoted the sentiment that women had a calling to be both religious
and moral. Women were to create a "pure and wholesome atmosphere sweet and lasting as the incense of the rose . . . [so] that the
children and youth of Skagway reared under its influence may go
out into the world morally equipped to fight the battles of life and
take their places among the men and women of worth in this great
land of ours." There was no mention of an anti-drinking message.[16]

The activities of the WCTU during this period seemed to eschew
the saloons. The members labored toward betterment of the community by "tearing down of unsightly shacks, improvement of sanitary
conditions, betterment of school grounds, and the erection of a public
drinking fountain" for horses and dogs. As was typical of women's
organizations at the time, they opened a general reading room to
encourage literacy in the community. They assisted the Grand Army
of the Republic in conducting ceremonies and a general cleanup of
the cemetery on Memorial Day.[17] The moral cleansing of the Skagway
could, apparently, only take place after a good, thorough, and more
literal kind of housecleaning.

In June 1909, the WCTU branched out into town promotion and
tourism when they "obtained the use of the Kirmse building on lower
Broadway . . . fitting up a rest room where tourists may rest and
receive information regarding Skagway and Alaska in general." According to the newspaper's account, "The WCTU has always stood for
progress and will do its share in advertising the home town." These
"rest rooms" later served as a location for their meetings.[18] As befitted

good housewives, the women of the WCTU served as the community's gracious hostesses.

Social gatherings and lectures on uplifting topics continued to form the core of the WCTU's activities. Besides the party at the Elk's Hall on election night November 1908 and the St. Patrick's Day celebration in 1909, they held a "watch meeting" on New Year's Eve, with "songs, informal talks and games." Lecturers included local ministers; Lillian Conner, the founder from Ketchikan and representative of Alaska to the national organization; and other local notables. Three guest speakers visited in July 1909. Mrs. A. M. Hill, president of the Toronto Council of Women, spoke on the International Council of Women. Mrs. Maude Muff, president of the British Women's Temperance Association, spoke on temperance work in England. Miss Williams, president of the Girls' Friendly Society of Wales, and sister of the Bishop of Bangor, Wales, "spoke along the lines of the 'White Slave' traffic, discussing protected immigration for women and girls from the standpoint of the mother-land." A week later, Mrs. J. Haines, state superintendent of the organization Christian Citizenship of Kansas, gave a talk to the WCTU.[19]

It is clear that the WCTU, during its rebirth in Skagway, tried to tone down its feminist stance, in much the same way that women's suffrage groups were doing across the entire nation after 1900 in order to distinguish themselves from feminists. Instead of being led by the female owner of a business, the Skagway reincarnation adopted a respectable housewife for its president. Although still primarily female in membership, the organization actively involved businessmen in its projects, enlisting them to give lectures and donate space for their projects. And the WCTU members apparently knew better than to take on the issue of prohibition, at least at first. Instead, they scrubbed and cleaned the town just as they did their homes. Apparently they took the advice of the Georgia organization president, who counseled her audience in a speech to the Illinois WCTU, "You must not sit across the table from your husband and say to him 'Honey you must do this,' but instead you should sit on his lap and say to him, 'Honey, won't you do this for me?' Husbands are human, and can be won to a good many things that you would not ordinarily think." This plea was directed toward getting husbands to vote for moral reforms, rather than getting them to stop drinking, as she also seemed to indicate: "When the fight was started for temperance, we women just began to pray . . . for men—real men—who would not be afraid to stand up for the truth."[20]

Indeed, by working with their husbands and the businessmen this time around, the Skagway WCTU members would be successful. The announcement of their motto at the St. Patrick's Day parade in 1909 ("to lift up the morals and eradicate sin in all its forms") had come only three months before yet another petition was presented to the city council demanding that the prostitutes be moved from Seventh Avenue "to a less conspicuous location."[21] The complaint, coming on the heels of the organization's declaration of purpose as stated in their motto, makes it clear that their first target of reform would not be the saloons but rather the prostitutes.

The heyday of the Seventh Avenue restricted district came to an end as the middle class reform movement flexed its political muscles in the spring of 1909, with the April city election drawing near. Enlisting the help of the *Daily Alaskan*, the reform women of Skagway saw an opportunity to curry the support of the middle-class businessmen in loosening the grip of the licentious working class. By drawing attention to the sinful women in their midst before the 1909 city election, the reformers ensured that yet another effort to move the district would become an issue that saloon keeper and mayor Chris Shea could not avoid.

The need for political and tax reforms had continued even as the WCTU gathered strength, and that is where Shea devoted his energies. He made a big mistake, however, when he took on the character of the town site trustee, William Boughton, who had been appointed at the request of the White Pass and Yukon Route railroad, the outgrowth of the Pacific & Arctic Railway & Navigation Company (P&AR&N). The latter company had been sued, along with Bernard Moore, in 1898, by the merchants of Skagway in a dispute over the ownership of the core of the city. In 1901, the U.S. Department of the Interior finally settled in favor of Moore and P&AR&N, the company that backed Moore, awarding them a quarter of the value of the lots in sixty acres of the downtown area of Skagway. Boughton's job was to oversee the assessment of those lots and the distribution of the funds. As the lot assessments also affected the taxes collected by the city, the city council expressed an interest in the appointment of the trustee and demanded annual reports.[22]

Shea chose to question Boughton about his 1909 report on March 15, about three weeks before the April city election. What the mayor and his Taxpayers Party council did not know is that Esther Mitchell, "a member of the local demi-monde," had been arrested for "lugging a larger 'load' than was allowed by law" that very evening. Chief of Police George W. Dillon and "several volunteer assistants" had carted her off to jail in a wheelbarrow. Due to the proximity of her cell to the council meeting chamber, she could be heard demanding "a drink of water or something."

In reporting the proceeds of the council meeting, the reporter from the *Daily Alaskan* chose to detail each of Shea's questions of Boughton, complete with each of Esther's disruptions as she cursed at her jailers. As was common at the time, the newspaper riddled the story with clever editorial commentary. For instance, after issuing a string of curse words that the newspaper phrased as "blankety-blank-blank-blank," the *Alaskan* noted that "this succinct statement silenced mayor Christopher Columbus Shea." The "statement" actually referred to a comment made by fellow councilman Shaw—"the people of Skagway have been kicking for five years to get a trustee appointed, and now one is appointed, and if the people of Skagway have any further kicking to do, they should kick to the town council"—but the newspaper made the comment only after describing Esther's interruption.[23]

Such rich detail in a story had not been seen in the *Daily Alaskan* since the days when Pop Corn Kate had been hauled to jail in a similar conveyance. It had been almost two and a half years since the newspaper had last mentioned a prostitute by name, and eight years since any newspaper man had had such fun writing about a prostitute in Skagway. During all this time, the women of the restricted district and the men at city hall had cooperated in keeping a low profile regarding the district, to each other's benefit. Mitchell's disruptions of the city council meeting brought that era to an end.

Sam Wall was not the articulate campaigner that John Troy had been. When the April 1909 city election began, Wall sank to slinging repeated, stinging barbs at Shea. Most of them seemed silly and harmless, childish jokes at the mayor's expense. The same paper that had insisted on referring to him as "Christopher Columbus Shea" in every article during the previous election now chose to print what started out as a human interest story about a man who had drowned in Paducah, Kentucky. The lamented deceased had seventeen middle names, one each for a famous preacher. "Skagway can boast of a name almost as long—that of Christopher Columbus Peter Patrick Lawrence Bartholomew Shea."[24] With no real negative news to report about Shea, the paper resorted to cheap personal shots.

That being the worst it could do, the respectable *Daily Alaskan* was mild in its criticism of Shea's politics compared to an individual flier published the day before the April 6, 1909, election. The entire two-page, homespun, plain-talking, mud-slinging, slanderous, libelous, "spasmodic publication" (given that it was in its "first spasm") was meant to show that every member of the Taxpayer's Ticket, including J. D. Stinebaugh, J. M. Tanner, but most especially "Christopher Columbus Peter Lawrence Bartholomew John Paul Jones O'Brien O'Shea," was out to get the taxpayer's money to spend on such worthy projects as cutting the grass growing on the sidewalks and rubbing the moss off the doorknobs of the business section at the city's expense—among other such nefarious shenanigans.[25]

During the April 1909 city election, the *Daily Alaskan* pulled out all the stops to try to get Shea off the city council, but to no avail. With the paper confidently predicting his sound defeat the morning of the election, he still won by more than enough votes to keep him on the council, although not enough to remain mayor. With him, he brought J. M. "Si" Tanner as a co-councilman. However, the Citizens took the remaining five seats.[26]

On May 4, a month after the city election, the newspaper reported that U.S. Immigration Inspector Kazias Krauczunas had deported Martha Peraux and Jennie Brown, two "French habitués of the [Skagway] Row." The *Daily Alaskan* recounted that they had come into the United States from Canada and that they "swore they were married"—presumably each to husbands—"when they first arrived." It later "devolved that they were engaged in an immoral occupation and were not married." They were deported to Vancouver.[27] The story was meant to shock the respectable people of Skagway.

Two weeks later, Esther Mitchell accused Josie Smith, "a member of the local demi-monde," of assault. The latter was arrested by the local police for being "involved in an altercation with another woman on Seventh Avenue." The magistrate booked Smith for drunk and disorderly conduct and fined her $15.[28] These petty complaints had been common in the years since 1902 but were only now being reported. For instance, in 1903, when E. O. Caswell, the owner and manager of the local telephone company, assaulted prostitute Eva Lambert and tore up some of her clothing with a knife (the record is silent about whether she was wearing the clothes), the only newspaper coverage of the case was a notice of the grand jury investigation and the bonds offered by Caswell and the complaining witness. No juicy details were discussed outside of the court documents.[29]

With the newspaper suddenly paying attention to the prostitutes, their blight in Skagway was sure to come to the attention of the reactivated WCTU. On June 7, two weeks after the drunken altercation between Mitchell and Smith, Councilman C. E. Shelley presented another petition to the city council, this one containing 123 names. The petitioners once again were objecting to the prostitutes in their midst. Given all the publicity about the women in the district over the past few weeks, the orderly system of quiet fines and avoidance of publicity practiced over the past eight years appeared to be breaking down.

It was the same old complaint. The petitioners claimed that little boys and girls were "compelled" to pass by the houses of ill fame on their way to and from school, while young girls and women from the north end of town who walked to the business district were "compelled to pass in close proximity to the 'red light' district." The signatories of the petition asked that the district be moved to a less conspicuous location.[30]

Chris Shea and J. M. Tanner, the two Taxpayers Party members, objected to consideration of the petition. According to the *Daily Alaskan*, "Councilman Shea said that he knew that certain men were trying to make money off the fallen women by having the location changed, but when asked to substantiate his allegations he could not do so. He put himself on record, however, as objecting to the present location." The petition was referred to the health and police committee, with promises to report at the next meeting.[31]

After the petition was presented to the June 1909 council meeting, Shea asked for time to substantiate his claims that the request for removal of the restricted district on Seventh Avenue "was the result of pre-election promises made by members of the Citizens ticket and that certain men were 'attempting to make money off fallen women.'" He and Tanner then eavesdropped on a conversation between Kitty Faith and W. Lyle Speer of the Horse Shoe Saloon. In the newspaper exposé that appeared the next day, Faith was identified as the owner of a house of prostitution. Ida Freidinger also provided an affidavit of what was said during the conversation, although only those readers who knew her to be a madam would understand the importance of her name in the article. The substance of the conversation dealt with the possibility of moving Faith's and Freidinger's businesses to Third Avenue. Speer purported to act as a middleman between the madams and the property owners. The article criticized "Sherlock Shea and Hawkshaw Tanner" but did not accuse them of having special interests in the decision.[32]

This article was the first time the wealthiest landladies on Seventh Avenue, Kitty Faith and Ida Freidinger, had seen their names in print in Skagway's newspaper. Tying their names to those of Chris Shea and J. M. Tanner was a deliberate strategy to wrench control of Skagway's politics back into the hands of the middle-class businessmen, who could manage the city for the good of the merchants and of the White Pass and Yukon Route, not for labor and the working class.

After enduring a dirty re-election campaign, then suffering as the *Daily Alaskan* gloated over the vision of him and Si Tanner sneaking around the backrooms of parlor houses, Shea had had enough of Skagway politics. Three weeks after exposing the negotiations between Speer and Kitty Faith, Shea left Skagway. In the middle of July, the *Daily Alaskan* formally announced that outgoing territorial governor Wilford B. Hoggatt had appointed Shea to the newly created position of game warden for western Alaska, headquartered in Seward.[33]

Why would the successful champion of the working men, a saloon keeper who had transitioned into the middle class, but who managed to keep his constituency of bachelor laborers and wharfingers content, suddenly abandon Skagway for a political appointment in another Alaskan port? It seems likely that Shea had found the transition from working to middle class compromised his own values. He could not continue to support his friends associated with the demimonde and, at the same time, cultivate the types of business relationships that would make him politically successful in an age of reform. His family consisted of a wife who had been a preacher's daughter, a teenage daughter, and an elderly, widowed mother, all of whom aspired to middle-class respectability. Although they frequented the Catholic Church, where Shea's sinful lapses could be forgiven in the confessional, the new community of Seward, on Resurrection Bay, no doubt offered an opportunity for the entire family to reinvent itself.

And Shea's family promptly did just that. In Seward, Shea renounced his working-class friends, associated with government agents and merchants, and became thoroughly middle class. While he knew many of the Skagwayans who had also moved to this burgeoning port, he stayed away from the saloons, he founded the city's Commercial Club to advertise it as the latest Gateway to Alaska, and he avoided partisan politics. He courted upper-class businessmen who came to hunt big game on the Kenai Peninsula, and became a favorite of Seward's newspaper. It never revealed the scandal that had caused him to leave Skagway.[34]

Shea had abruptly departed Skagway but probably not because he reportedly eavesdropped on a conversation between two madams and an agent trying to arrange a real estate deal. The act in and of itself would not have constituted political suicide. In fact, J. M. Tanner, who participated in the spy activity with Shea and was every bit his compatriot, stayed in Skagway and remained a respected merchant, lawman, and politician in the city for the rest of his life. How was Tanner different?

Josias M. "Si" Tanner, born in Oakland County, Michigan, on February 22, 1850, had followed the gold rush to Central City, Colorado, in the 1870s. He was a deputy sheriff in Iowa and Washington before heading north in 1896 to Juneau, where he assisted his brother-in-law, Emory Valentine, with his general store. When the Klondike gold rush began, Tanner took a small steamboat to Skagway, and with teams of horses, lightered goods from the ships. He eventually set up business in Skagway as one of its earliest pioneers. Active in the Safety Committee that first proscribed, and then disposed of Soapy Smith, he served the community as a U.S. deputy marshal from July 1898, when he led the group that rousted out the Soapy Smith gang. He resigned in

November 1899, but continued to run the jail, which he had built for the city. Tanner was elected city magistrate in 1903, and the council continued to appoint him to that position until his election to city council in 1909. He stayed in office until April 1913, serving as mayor from 1910 through 1912 as well. He became a territorial senator on the first territorial legislature in 1912, and was then re-elected in 1914. In 1917, he was appointed as U.S. marshal for the First District, a position he held for four years.[35]

Tanner had long been active in Skagway's local politics. He had orchestrated the first real opposition to the Citizens Ticket in 1903, hosting the organizational meeting of the Taxpayers Party in the rooms above his hardware store and running for magistrate. He was the only nominee from his ticket to win office until the 1908 election, despite his efforts to keep his party alive.[36]

The act that cost Chris Shea his job caused no immediate political harm to Tanner. He saved his political career by immediately suggesting that the district be shut down entirely and no that further prostitution be permitted. While the council responded with silence to the suggestion, no one forgot that he had made it. In April 1910, Sam Wall's *Daily Alaskan* reiterated the events of the previous summer on Seventh Avenue. The editor reminded Skagwayans that Tanner had tried to eliminate the district entirely but that no one would second the motion.[37]

Another factor that saved Tanner's political career was the fact that he was a businessman and solidly of the middle class. He had never owned a saloon or a piece of property on Seventh Avenue. There was no suspicion of his mixing in with the working class.

Tanner, the last of the "old guard" on the council, knew that he was fighting a losing battle when it came to Seventh Avenue. By the time the council heard the report of the Health and Police Committee in late June, Shea had already left town for Juneau, seeking a political favor from the governor. In his absence, the council unanimously decided to move the district from Seventh Avenue to an undisclosed "secluded location where they [the prostitutes] will be less conspicuous." Any prostitutes found conducting business on Seventh Avenue after August 15 would be prosecuted to the full extent of the law "as often as they may be found occupying said houses of ill-fame."[38] What

Josias M. Tanner as territorial senator, 1913. Courtesy Alaska State Library, Henry Roden Photograph Collection P461-24.

the newspaper did not report is that the city officials also agreed to stop fining the prostitutes once they moved from Seventh Avenue.[39] No citations for prostitution appeared in the magistrate's docket after September 20, 1909. In a tacit agreement to the continuation of the conspiracy of silence, City Hall behaved as if prostitution suddenly ceased to exist in Skagway.

Madams Kitty Faith and Ida Freidinger decided to fight the ruling and hired attorney Phil Abrahams to represent them. On July 19, Abrahams presented a petition to the city council asking for a delay of further prosecution by sixty to ninety days. Tanner made a motion that the two landladies be given until September 15 instead of August 15 to remove themselves from Seventh Avenue. The motion was seconded and carried.[40]

Faith was the most obstinate member of the entire Skagway demimonde, probably because she had the greatest personal investment in the properties on Seventh Avenue. Starting July 1, 1909, the magistrate began to fine the prostitutes on a monthly rather than a quarterly schedule. As they moved out of Seventh Avenue, their monthly fines ceased. By the time the September 15 deadline arrived, only one prostitute remained in the old restricted district: Kitty Faith. When arrested because she refused to leave Seventh Avenue, she hired a lawyer, probably Abrahams, and once again fought City Hall. Her defiance made headline news, not only in Skagway but also in Juneau. The jury that heard her case, composed of local businessmen, agreed with Faith. She owned property on Seventh Avenue and should not be forced to leave her own home. But the *Daily Alaskan* made sure the local people knew exactly who was on that jury.[41] This disclosure was at odds with the newspaper's longtime habit of preserving anonymity when it came to even the slightest suggestion of impropriety among the "respectable" people about town.

What was further extraordinary about the articles in the Skagway and Juneau newspapers was the tone of defense concerning Madam Faith. Until this time, her name had not appeared in a newspaper. Yet examination of Tanner's magistrate's docket and other records makes it clear that she was well established and of considerable wealth. In fact, Kitty Faith was, at this point, Skagway's wealthiest madam.

Obviously Alaskans had no problem with women acquiring and managing real estate. Land ownership was one of America's most sacred rights. The protection of property rights was an inspiration for the American Revolution and was guaranteed by the Fourth Amendment to the Constitution. But by 1910, some of the guarantees about property ownership were being eroded by the Progressives as they passed moral reform laws. In particular, the Mann Act had the effect of impinging on the rights of property owners.

By the first decade of the twentieth century, middle-class white Americans had developed a fear of immigrants, who in their minds brought foreign, non-Protestant, non-Puritan ethics with them. According to social historian James Morone, these prejudices culminated in the 1910 Mann Act. Also called the "White Slavery Act," this law prohibited the interstate commerce of any "innocent" woman or girl for the purpose of prostitution. Proponents used massive propaganda campaigns to scare middle-class white voters into believing that their virgin daughters were fodder for ruthless Jewish, black, Asian, and southern European pimps and procuring madams. While originally meant to be narrowly applied to prostitution and true cases of "slavery," in application the law quickly broadened to include other more loosely defined "immoral acts." Fornication, adultery, and the transportation of willing prostitutes were only some of the criminal acts eventually prosecuted under this federal law. One political scientist remarks that the Mann Act was "captured" by the reformers to be used for their own purposes, not the limited purpose of those who passed the legislation.[42]

Federal officers throughout the nation posted Mann Act notices in the red light districts. Beginning with Iowa in 1909, states began passing their own "red-light abatement" acts that relegated property rights to a less important status. With passage of the Mann Act, property owners could be thrown out of their own buildings and their doors sealed against them. By 1917, thirty-one states had such laws.[43] That Skagway's city council still respected Kitty Faith's right to stay in the building she owned showed that middle-class Alaskans still held deeply seated and time-honored American values about property rights. Skagway's jury of middle-class businessmen was more traditional than many of the more "progressive" thinkers in the big cities and did not force her, a businesswoman, out of her "home."

Despite the fact that Faith won her trial and was allowed to continue living on Seventh Avenue, she, Freidinger, and the madams who leased businesses on Seventh Avenue surely must have been trying to figure out where they would move their businesses. That Lyle Speer should be interested in acting as a mediator between landlords on Third Avenue and the madams made little sense. The only interest Speer had on Third Avenue was the Horse Shoe Saloon that he and Albert Reinert owned at the corner of Third and Broadway. At that time, the saloons and brothels had a reputation as competitors for liquor-consuming customers, rather than as allies.

Wallace Lyle Speer, who preferred to go by his middle name, had come to Skagway in February of 1898 from Everett, Washington. He had been a railroad clerk there, and by April 1900, he had obtained a job as a railroad clerk in Skagway. He was born in Pennsylvania in September 1859, which meant he was thirty-eight years old when he joined the stampede north. His wife, Fannie, born in March 1861, came to Alaska in May 1898 from Chicago but did not marry Lyle until 1900. At that time, Lyle and Fannie lived in their own place east of Broadway, either on Sixth or Seventh Avenue, in a not-very-nice part of town. By September 1902, Lyle quit working for the railroad and went to work for Albert Bloom and Emil Korach at the Monogram Liquor House as a bartender, where he stayed until at least 1904.[44] It is difficult to tell if this was a step up or down in life, but it probably gave him the experience he needed when he acquired his own saloon.

In a way, more is known about Fannie R. Speer than about her husband, Lyle. She excelled at gardening and won many prizes in the local gardening shows. The Speers ordered a small windmill from Sears, Roebuck and Company in order to pump water from their shallow well to irrigate their garden. Sears informed them that the company did not engage in "export trade" and could not deliver to Alaska, which caused some indignation on the part of the *Daily Alaskan*. One year, Fannie Speer's strawberries were so large the newspaper office put them on display in their front window. They were reputed to have been six inches in circumference. Fannie Speer held 4,499 shares of the capital stock of the Alaska General Electric Company as surety for a loan. This stock ended up in litigation in the estate of E. O. Caswell, the manager of the company, when he died at the age of about thirty-seven.[45]

Fannie Speer appeared to have considerable real estate holdings as well, including seven of the twelve lots along Eighth Avenue east of Broadway. She had purchased three of her most strategic properties from Frank and Mattie Keelar and Phil and Mary Snyder.[46] That Fannie should be such a capitalist in twentieth century Skagway was no great feat. Plenty of women owned property at this time. It was not uncommon for much of the family real estate to reside in the woman's name alone in order to protect the wife from a husband's debts when he died. As mentioned earlier, Anna Stinebaugh owned some real estate in Skagway, although her husband James had power of attorney to conduct all business concerning that property.

In late 1906, Lyle went into partnership with Albert Reinert of the Mascot Saloon, and together they purchased the Idaho Saloon at the northwest corner of Broadway and Third Avenues. They reopened the saloon as the Horse Shoe Liquor Company, with Speer running the business. That partnership lasted until June 30, 1909, a month after Speer had been caught trying to set himself up as a middleman between

Kitty Faith, Ida Freidinger, and some unnamed private landlords. A newspaper announcement advised that all outstanding bills and all bills due the firm should be paid to Reinert.[47] Speer was out of the saloon business.

It was not until August 1909 that Speer's true motives became known. That month, the city council received two petitions to prohibit the prostitutes from moving onto Eighth Avenue east of Broadway, a location only a block north and a block east of the Seventh Avenue location. One of them came from a landowner on the street in question. The council tabled both petitions. Then, on November 1, Lyle Speer asked the council for permission to move the Cottage.[48] Lyle's wife, Fannie, owned both the Cottage, located on the west side of Broadway between Seventh and Eighth, and the lot at the southeast corner of Eighth and Broadway, on which the Cottage sits today. The council granted this request, and the Speers moved the old brothel across the street to its present location.

The Speers had other interests on Eighth Avenue. Besides owning the corner lot at Eighth and Broadway, which now contained Frankie Belmont's once fabulous brothel, Fannie owned six of the remaining eleven lots on the street. Most of them held small rental homes, which could easily be adapted into the small brothels so prized by the women who rented from the landladies and man landladies. It appears that by fall 1909, Lyle and Fannie Speer had positioned themselves to become the new landlords of the restricted district and to profit by selling properties to Faith and Freidinger. Not surprisingly, their neighbors near Eighth Avenue did not want the restricted district to be moved to their street, which prompted the signing of two petitions in August.

It was at the same city council meeting in which Speer received permission to move the Cottage that councilman Henry C. Bowman reported that the prostitutes had vacated the Seventh Avenue district. Then, in a seeming non sequitur, he pointed out that "local representatives of the US Govt. had stated that the Government would strongly object to Seventh St. [*sic*] being used for this purpose, as it was impossible to go to or from the court House without passing this part of Seventh St."[49] The debate over the Seventh Avenue district had long since ended. Was he suggesting that the madams had put pressure on the council to move back to Seventh Avenue? This is possible. In fact, a day before the 1910 election, the *Daily Alaskan* published a cartoon that depicted young boys peering through peepholes in a high board fence in front of buildings labeled "Seventh St. Stockade." The caption read "Do YOU want this?", indicating that the issue had not been put to rest.

After April 4, 1910, the subject of prostitution in the restricted district was not broached in the newspaper again; it was all handled behind the scenes. Despite the fact that the city council ignored the petitions of citizens begging to have Eighth Avenue east of Broadway declared off limits to the prostitutes, and despite the fact that the majority landowners were obviously very willing to rent or sell to the madams, Eighth Avenue did not become the new restricted district. Everything seemed staged to make it happen. What interfered with the new designation?

There is no substantial evidence to provide an answer to this question, but a good guess is that Kitty Faith and Ida Freidinger were not about to be manipulated into any deal cooked up by the likes of Fannie and Lyle Speer. This couple probably wanted far too much money for what property—if any—they were willing to sell. And Faith and Freidinger were not the kind of women who would pay dearly or rent from a landlord. No, they would wait out the Speers or search for another part of town that the city council would find more to their liking. After all, the east end of Eighth Avenue was still very close to the federal courthouse, to the middle-class neighborhoods, and to downtown Skagway.

———

The middle-class landlords of Seventh Avenue—Lee Guthrie, Phil Snyder, and Frank Keelar—had, by no coincidence, left Skagway by the end of 1910. All four landlords registered to vote in the 1909 election, but only Snyder cast his vote in 1910. Even he had left Skagway by the time the registration had started for the 1911 election.[50] Coincidence? Perhaps. Skagway's economy had slumped. The capitalists did not do well as land values decreased. Obviously the vested interests of the man landladies no longer had anything to do with political decisions in Skagway.

As long as middle-class businessmen such as J. D. Stinebaugh maintained an economic interest in the restricted district, the middle-class women interested in moral reform, but yielding no voting power, had very little chance of accomplishing their goal of eradicating sin in all its forms, but most especially the sin of selling sex to men. Influential landlords owned property in the district; the quarterly fines paid for necessary municipal services; and the city council refused to act on any measures that would change the agreement worked out in 1901 when the prostitutes were first districted to Seventh Avenue.

Once Stinebaugh rid himself of his shameful property in 1906, his wife became free to pursue her earlier work with her more politically active woman's club. In 1908 and 1909, the less feminist and more "domestic" WCTU devoted itself to "housecleaning" and positioned itself to force popular working class politician Chris Shea out of town, thus restoring the middle class to political power. Whether they planned it or not, the middle class women of Skagway and their businessmen husbands suddenly found themselves a common enemy in the person of the saloon-keeper mayor. The working-class bachelor was no longer just a moral threat to the home but now a political threat to community. Those who could vote—the men—would indeed do something about this working-class revolution. In the spring of 1909, the middle-class businessmen of Skagway overcame the champion of the working class, Chris Shea, a man who believed that all men had equal access to the law, not just those who owned businesses and employed others. The middle-class wives and clergymen enlisted the services of Sam Wall, the editor of the newspaper, who broke the covenant of silence about the restricted district. In the wake of this publicity, the reform community brought yet another petition to move the restricted district to City Hall. Shea and Tanner made the mistake of going into a brothel to gather information about the dealings of real estate investors Fannie and Lyle Speer, who were seeking to move the district to their own properties. To avoid lasting embarrassment to his family, Shea accepted a political appointment on the Kenai Peninsula, one that did not require repeated elections or dealings with landlords of the restricted district, while councilman J. M. Tanner recommended disbanding the place altogether.

Then, as the value of their properties dropped to practically nothing, the man landladies simply slipped away into the mist of the Southeast. And almost as if she had done her duty by her active involvement in

The Presbyterian Ladies' Aid farewell celebration for Anna Stinebaugh, October 2, 1910, Skagway, Alaska, in front of the Presbyterian Church at the southwest corner of Fifth and Main. Stinebaugh is in the front row, ninth from the left. She has graying hair and wears a dark dress with a large corsage. Courtesy City of Skagway Museum, Draper and Co. Photographers, PC #92-02-5.

the WCTU and by forcing Shea out of town, Anna left Skagway in 1910 as well. Despite the absence of these male capitalists and the efforts of Stinebaugh's organization, however, investment in the restricted district did not completely die out. There was still money to be made from sin in Skagway. As long as that was the case, and women could not vote, vice would continue.

CHAPTER EIGHT

The Alaska Street District, 1910–1914

The women of Skagway's WCTU—Grace Zinkan, Anna Stinebaugh, and Sarah Shorthill's daughter, Elizabeth Harrison—may have finally won enough support from the men to overpower the man landladies and chase out one of the prostitute's last champions on the city council, Chris Shea. But it is doubtful they had counted on the savvy business sense of Skagway's two most successful madams. Kitty Faith and Ida Freidinger were still forces to reckon with. If Shea had misjudged the power of the WCTU, then the WCTU had misjudged the endurance of the landladies. It would not be long before the two women found a new place to do business in Skagway, and this time, there would be no landlords.

What happened to the prostitutes in the months immediately following the closing of Seventh Avenue is not entirely clear. It is readily evident that the city council did not presume to designate a new restricted district after they disbanded the old one. As Shea and J. M. Tanner had stated would happen, the prostitutes scattered throughout the residential district of the town. While the middle class dithered, hoping the prostitutes would simply disappear, the landladies took matters into their own hands.

Only four of Skagway's prostitute households appeared in the January 1910 census, suggesting that the disbanding of the district did what it was intended to do, at least temporarily. It was winter, which had always been a slow time for these working women. The magistrate's docket indicates that an average of only ten prostitutes had wintered over each year since 1903, and only three known prostitutes can be found in the 1910 census taken in January: Ida Freidinger, Mary Masada, and Evelyn Nelson. The low number of women could possibly be

explained by the fact that the census enumerator was city marshal
Charles T. Moore. Unless the marshal was willing to pay for the time
spent answering his questions, the prostitutes were probably not much
interested in wasting their time undergoing this interview, even if they
did answer the door to a marshal without a warrant in his hand. Somehow he appears to have bullied the Japanese woman Masada into
answering his questions. He could have gotten prostitute Nelson's
information from the man she was living with at the time, John Patter-
son, a Swedish bartender.[1]

It is likely that madam Ida Freidinger, who did answer Moore's
questions, was too old and experienced to care about her privacy any
more. In fact, she may have delighted in shocking the other prostitutes
by flaunting their conventions and answering his probing inquiries.

The placement of Freidinger's name in the census appears right
after that of the widow Cassidy and her two children on Second Avenue.
The Cassidys had lived at 524 Second Avenue since 1903.[2] The 500
block was on the far west end of town, between Main and Alaska.

The widow Cassidy may not have cared much for the downturn in
her neighborhood's status by 1910. Besides a madam living in near
proximity, ex-pimp John Bonner and ex-prostitute Rose Bonner lived
two doors away. Mrs. Cassidy had lived in town long enough to remember the days when the couple's reputation was not quite so unsullied.
Between the Bonners and Freidinger lived John Secrest, who lived
with cook Jane Coy. Secrest had been arrested on August 11, 1909,
for failure to open the door to an officer serving a warrant. The only
other arrest on that day had been that of Essie Miller, a well-established
prostitute, and the eventual heir of Freidinger's estate.[3] Miller's arrest
record indicates that she usually left Skagway during the winter. Because
the 1910 census was taken in late January 1910, she was not enumerated in Skagway, but rather in Seattle, where she kept a winter home.[4]
A photograph of a woman who was probably Essie Miller in front of
the U.S. Hotel, on Second Avenue in Skagway, was taken about this
time. She, Secrest, and Coy probably rented the hotel and entertained
customers there.

It appears that Second Avenue, near the wharves and some of the
shops of the White Pass and Yukon Route railroad, was becoming an

A woman who is probably Essie Miller, with a large dog (Tuck Flaharty's?) outside the U.S. Hotel on Second Avenue, about 1910. Courtesy Klondike Gold Rush National Historical Park, George and Edna Rapuzzi Collection, Rasmusen Foundation, no. 00219.

unofficial gathering place of the demimonde, at least until the madams could find new property to buy.

Because Kitty Faith's livelihood was not tied entirely to the Seventh Avenue district, she had more options than did Freidinger and Miller. Instead of slinking off to Skagway's version of Skid Row on Second Avenue, Faith and Josie Smith left Skagway for Petersburg, a small fishing village of 125 men and 15 women. There she invested in a two-woman brothel on the waterfront.[5] Indeed, she may have purchased this property some time before.

With Masada living on Fifth Avenue, Nelson up on Eleventh, and Freidinger and possibly Miller starting a "colony" down on Second, the city council was forced to make a decision about what to do with the prostitutes who would not leave Skagway. Despite Tanner's suggestion, the city council did not do what most of the reformers in town most fervently hoped they would do: start enforcing the law and drive them out of town entirely.

No record exists of the establishment of the new red light district, but at the city council meeting on May 2, 1910, newly elected Mayor Si Tanner acknowledged its existence when he announced that the madams were willing to pay their fair share for a night watchman in order that police protection could be extended as far west as Alaska Street. It seemed only right that they should pitch in when the businessmen on Broadway were paying half the costs of the night watchman.[6]

It seems Kitty Faith had decided that Petersburg, with its low-wage-earning fishermen, was not the kind of town where she wanted to do business. Less than two weeks after Tanner's announcement, Faith purchased two of the four lots on Alaska Street that would become the new restricted district (map 3).[7] It was she, not Fannie and Lyle Speer, who decided where the district would be. One of her new properties was located on the southeast corner of Fifth Avenue and Alaska Street. The other was on the northwest corner of Fourth Avenue and Alaska Street. She promptly moved her Seventh Avenue brothels to Alaska Street. By 1912, her new properties appraised higher than anything she had owned on Seventh Avenue.[8]

The other madam in Kitty Faith's parlor discussing a possible deal with Lyle Speer in June 1909 was Ida Freidinger. She followed Faith's lead in October 1910, buying up the lot on the northwest corner of

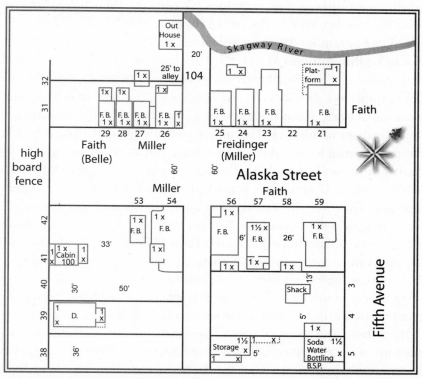

Map 3. The Alaska Street restricted district in 1914 as depicted in a Sanborn Fire Insurance map. Redrawn by Gerry Krieg. Copyright © 2015 by the University of Oklahoma Press.

Alaska and Fifth. It must have been with some relief that she was able to sell her Seventh Avenue properties on October 9, 1911. She had stopped paying taxes on them as soon as that district was closed down.[9] Unlike Faith, who owned several properties around town, Freidinger's investments were limited to the restricted district.

Essie Miller was the last madam to buy on Alaska Street. In December 1910, she purchased the lot just south of Faith's, with its existing family-sized home.[10] Skagway's prostitutes had squeezed out the man landladies. Only landladies owned the properties in the new restricted district.

When they returned to Skagway and established the new restricted district, the landladies negotiated a new deal with City Hall. There would be no fines and no penalties for running their businesses. No prostitute was arrested by the city of Skagway after Kitty Faith asked for a trial in September 1909. In replying to a letter from the mayor of Pasco, Washington, on March 27, 1915, the mayor of Skagway wrote that his fair city had dealt with the women of the underworld by confining them to a district only one block long on the extreme western outskirts of town. It was screened by a "highboard" fence, shutting off the view from neighbors. The police patrolled the district at regular intervals. Using a logic that escapes legal minds today to explain the dearth of prosecutions, J. M. Tanner's replacement, Mayor Howard Ashley, wrote, "Up until five years ago, fines were collected at regular intervals. However this custom has been abandoned, for the reason that it is against the laws of the Territory to allow prostitution, it would therefore be unlawfull [*sic*] to collect fines."[11] Given that it was unlawful to collect fines for a criminal activity, the city of Skagway chose to let that crime continue in a district restricted to a single city block, screened off from the residential district with a fence. By this logic, restricting crime to one area of town somehow made it no longer a crime.

If anything, the move to Alaska Street seemed a financial boon to the madams of Skagway. It certainly did not harm them. They no longer had any competition from the "man landladies" so hated by Josie Washburn.

Madam Ida Freidinger died on February 10, 1912, as the Alaska Street district entered its Golden Age.[12] The townspeople bowed their heads in respect for the old-timer, but, because Ida's "beloved friend" and heir, Essie Miller, was in Seattle at the time of her death, magistrate Henry B. LeFevre filed a petition to be appointed the special administrator of Freidinger's estate until such time that Miller returned to Skagway on February 26, 1912. LeFevre ordered an inventory of Ida's property and personal effects for probate purposes.[13] The result is a detailed description of two very typical working-class brothels.

The inventory of Freidinger's property reveals the material culture of working-class prostitution and the function of the madam within the demimonde. It lists the contents of both of Freidinger's Alaska Street brothels (numbers 23 and 24–25 on map 3) and demonstrates what these typical houses contained. Each house probably had only two or three prostitutes working in it. The houses were small and narrow, appraising on the lower end of the scale for restricted district properties in Skagway.

On March 12, 1912, J. M. Tanner, Edward Foreman, and G. W. Barnett conducted the inventory.[14] The first brothel they entered was actually two buildings connected by a short passageway (numbers 24 and 25 on map 3). The parlor contained a lounge, a rocking chair, a straight-backed chair, and a stand, which probably held the phonograph player that appeared on the list of possessions. This relatively new invention provided music to entertain and relax the customer. A stove warmed the room, and two rugs lay on the floor. Lace curtains framed the two windows, and two pictures and a mirror hung on the wall.

A portiere—a curtain hanging across a doorway[15]—separated the parlor from a short hallway that gave access to two bedrooms. The bedroom on the right included a bedstead with a mattress and springs, three quilts, one pair of blankets, two bedspreads, two pillows, seven sheets, and an unnumbered quantity of towels and tablecloths. A rug covered the floor. A washstand held a toilet set. A dresser no doubt sufficed to hold the clothing and personal effects of the room's occupant. A shade covered the apparently single window in the room. A stove with its utensils heated the room. This room also contained a taboret (a cylindrical stool), a small portable stand, or a small cabinet on casters used for making supplies readily available in a working area.[16] It probably permitted the prostitute to have cleansing and lubricating materials at hand.

The other bedroom contained a bedstead with a mattress and bedsprings, as well as a lounge. This bed held four pillows, three comforters, three bedspreads, seven sheets, and unnumbered towels and stand covers. Besides three rugs on the floor, the room was furnished with a dresser worth more than twice that in the first bedroom, a secretary bookcase, and a commode. It also had the obligatory toilet set and a "coles stove" (probably a coal stove). Two sets of curtains, one with shades, suggest that the room had two windows. Clearly the occupant of this room rated more comfortable accommodations than the occupant of the first bedroom. It may have been Freidinger's own room.

Returning to the parlor, the appraisers passed through another portiere into the passageway between the two small buildings. At the back of this passageway was probably an outside window, for here they inventoried a window shade and a "chieftionier." This latter word is probably a misspelling of chiffonier, which the 1897 Montgomery Ward's catalog described as a "high and narrow chest of drawers."[17] All of the chiffoniers in this popular mail-order catalog of the time were over five feet tall; all of the dressers were under four feet tall.[18] While the inventory listed three dressers—one for each bedroom—the chiffonier was probably used to store the linens, of which the numerous sheets, comforters, and unnumbered towels and washcloths were probably only the most conspicuous.

The third bedroom contained a bed with a mattress and springs, three comforters, five soft pillows, and two regular pillows. It also contained a wardrobe, something the others were missing, unless they had built-in closets. A carpet covered the floor, and a toilet set was provided. A dresser, stool, washstand, sewing table, and some other type of stand completed the furnishings. A "roman glass" (possibly a piece of decoration or a mirror) supplemented the inventory of the room's contents. No rug or stove warmed this room, and no towels or set of sheets suggested active use by a prostitute. Its location right off the kitchen implies it was used by a cook.

The inventory of the kitchen starts with two portieres, suggesting that perhaps the cook's bedroom was screened only with a curtain and most of the time benefited from the warmth of the stove in the kitchen. Besides the cook stove and pipe (worth $2.00), it contained a workstand, table, and four chairs, a rug, an "ice chest" (worth $6.00), $5.00 worth of dishes, knives and forks, and $6.00 worth of cord wood.

Freidinger's other brothel (number 23 on map 3) boasted a larger parlor, which probably spanned the entire front of the house. This sitting room featured a piano and stool instead of a phonograph, and a great "horn arm chair." Two lounges, a rocker, and four chairs afforded seating. A secretary perhaps provided a place for the madam to do her accounting during off-business hours. Eight shades and curtains blocked the view of curious eyes at the many windows at night. Four pictures and a $5.00 mirror graced the walls. A rug kept drafts from leaking through the floorboards; a stove warmed the room.

It appears that the hall was set up as an additional seating area. It contained a rug with two tables, a mirror, a rocker, a chair, a cuspidor, and lamps. Curtains suggest there might have been a window at the end of the hall.

The kitchen in this house was equipped with a stove, a kitchen table, a "center table," and a sink. Three shades, utensils, sundries, one chair, and linoleum indicate that the kitchen had few other amenities.

Because beds, bedroom furniture, and linens are not mentioned for this house, it seems likely that it was leased to another madam, who provided the missing furniture, linens, and other accoutrements. Therefore it is not known how many bedrooms were in this smaller parlor house.

Stored in the woodshed behind the two brothels was a wardrobe that seemed to contain Ida's personal effects. The wardrobe was probably moved to the shed—contents undisturbed—when Ida went to the hospital; it was noticeably missing from the main bedroom in the first house. Her possessions included a 50-cent jewelry box, a locket worth $1.50, "paste and cheap jewelry" worth $3.00, a nugget hat pin worth $1.00, a Mexican doily, a parasol, two long coats worth $15, an electric seal sack worth $10, a boa and "muii" worth $4.00, books worth $4.00, a grip, a large quantity of sheets and towels, worth $5.00, and a diamond ring worth $200 (almost $4,800 in today's currency).

There are obviously items missing from the inventory: most glaring is the stock of liquor and the glassware with which to serve it. Two of the three men conducting the inventory were on the city council. J. M. Tanner, currently the mayor, had been the city magistrate for seven years, the city jailer for four years, and a U.S. deputy marshal for two years before that. Because these men had the legal authority to order municipal arrests and alert federal authorities that liquor sales may have been conducted in the house, starting all sorts of unwanted problems best left alone, it was simpler for everyone concerned to pretend that no liquor was served at the place. Indeed, Tanner no doubt insisted on being the leader of the probate team for that very reason.

Surely the perfumes, cosmetics, personal hygiene items, medicines, and birth control devices would have been evident at the time the inventory was being taken. As they were not inventoried, they were probably considered the personal possessions of the women living in the individual rooms, rather than belonging to Freidinger. The probate inventory is therefore instructive about what the landlady supplied and what she expected the women who worked for her to provide for themselves. Those items would be similar to those found in the wardrobe in the shed.

In concluding the inventory, Tanner, Foreman, and Barnett appraised the real estate, comprised of lot 1, block 16, with three buildings on it, at $450. They placed the total value of Freidinger's estate at $1085.75, worth almost $26,000 in today's currency. The year 1912 was not one of the most prosperous for Skagway, but the city was far from the economic depths to which it would later plunge. Freidinger's estate was obviously not large, but she had acquitted herself well for an aging widow.

When Freidinger passed away, her reputation and financial standing in Skagway were similar to those of many middle-class madams in working-class communities of the time. She was not well-to-do, but comfortable enough, and not despised. She filled a niche. She met the needs of her employees, provided a service to the bachelor men of Skagway, and did so in such a manner that did not draw unwanted publicity to herself or to the women she employed. The importance of her probate shows that she continued to be successful two years after the district in Skagway was moved to Alaska Street.

Freidinger's heir differed from her substantially, however.

Essie Miller was born to Rebecca Miller in Ceredo, West Virginia. Her name at birth was Augusta Jane. Located on the Ohio River near Cattletsburg, Kentucky, Ceredo was a main terminus of the Norfolk and Western Railroad. The principal employers of the area were the railroad and coal mines.[19] Essie was raised in a large household headed by her widowed grandmother, Elizabeth Miller. This family included her single mother, Rebecca, uncles John and William, and an unmarried aunt, Nancy Jane Miller, who had two daughters, Virginia Emily and Georgiana. She would later refer to her Uncle John W. Miller as her father, and refer to her cousin John H., one of John's sons, as her brother.[20]

When Augusta was fifteen years old in 1895, she gave birth to a daughter out of wedlock. Her cousin, Virginia Emily Miller Perdue, gave birth to a child one week after Augusta had her baby. Virginia and her husband, Dewitt Clinton Perdue, adopted Augusta's daughter, named her Roma Margaret Perdue, and raised her along with their ten other children. Rejecting the life of a farmer's wife, Augusta moved west. She first appeared in Skagway in 1903, at the age of twenty-three, where she changed her name to Essie.[21]

Miller appears to have started her career in Skagway as the sort of working-class prostitute who leased a crib from a landlord or madam. She may have worked for Madam Ida Freidinger. On December 3, 1903, she was one of three "proprietors of bawdy houses" who were arrested and fined $100 apiece for selling liquor without a license.[22] As such, she was one of the women who were triple-fined in the fall of 1903 by the municipal and federal courts as they quarreled about who had jurisdiction over the prostitutes and thus the right to the proceeds from their fines.

In her early years in Skagway, Miller seems to have been one of the more problematic prostitutes in Skagway. She did not stay out of trouble in the way that Kitty Faith and Ida Freidinger did. In May 1906, she was brought before city judge Si Tanner on a charge of indecent exposure. He fined her $10 and $8.20 in court costs. In April 1907, the city marshal brought her in for being drunk and disorderly, for which she received the same fine.[23]

Miller was not arrested on the regular quarterly schedule usually sought by the city police. Between 1903 and 1907, she did not stay in Skagway year round. She paid her fines in the fall and spring, indicating she followed a regular circuit that took her to the goldfields in the summer and Seattle in the winter. She came to Skagway when the miners were there, during the "shoulder seasons," as they entered and then left the Far North.[24]

In fact, in spite of her identification by the court as a "proprietor of a bawdy house," this evidence of her transience, combined with her somewhat irresponsible acts of drunkenness and indecent exposure, suggests that she was not a madam in the sense of a woman owning a business. No madam at the time could rotate between locations or risk her business by foolishly drawing attention to herself in such a way. If she was a "proprietor of a bawdy house" in 1903, she probably operated independently as a one-woman business that leased a crib so that she would not be burdened by owning real estate.

It was not until 1908 that Miller decided to stay in Skagway for the entire year. She paid regular quarterly fines in both 1908 and 1909 right up until the time that the restricted district was moved from Seventh

Avenue and the fines were discontinued. In an extremely unusual circumstance, Madam Freidinger appeared in January 1908 to pay Miller's $20 fine. Although in Skagway saloon keepers or their managers customarily paid the fines for the gamblers, the prostitutes paid their own fines with only this one exception. Freidinger's action on behalf of Miller suggests an unusual relationship between the two women. Perhaps Miller ran Freidinger's second house as a "housekeeper."[25]

Miller became a full-fledged landlady in 1910, when she purchased her first brothel in the new Alaska Street district. When the elderly Freidinger died in February 1912, she named Miller as her heir and executrix in place of her only living son. Freidinger's probate did not release the deed to the Alaska Street brothels until December 18, 1912. Once she gained the inheritance, Miller owned half the restricted district. After paying the taxes for the lots, her buildings were worth as much as those of Kitty Faith. By 1914, Miller had moved a one-story house onto the northwest corner of Fifth and Alaska. She now owned five brothels: Freidinger's original two cottages, a small crib, and two larger parlor houses that competed with those on Faith's lots.[26]

How Miller managed five brothels is difficult to judge from the available evidence. Millie Clark Cusey, who owned four brothels on one street in Silver City, New Mexico, starting in the 1920s, tried to manage her houses herself but eventually ended up hiring "house-keepers" to assist her. Without them, she found that the prostitutes who worked for her were dishonest about their earnings, snuck in lovers or pimps, and drank or used drugs instead of attending to business.[27] It is probable that Miller hired "housekeepers" to manage her other four brothels in the same way that Cusey did. Or Miller may have simply rented out the brothels to other madams and not concerned herself with the day-to-day business inside the houses that she herself did not occupy.

———————

By 1914, the restricted district was owned in its entirety by two entrepreneurial landladies, Kitty Faith and Essie Miller. Between them, they owned a total of eleven brothels, three of which were rented out as one-woman cribs and three of which were parlor houses with as many as four boarders each. However, if earlier fining records are any indication, it is unlikely that more than a dozen women worked in the restricted district for half a dozen madams at any one time.

In the meantime, the middle-class temperance community probably felt that it had accomplished one of its goals by banning the restricted district to the far western edge of town. They had hidden the "problem" of the Necessary Evil from the probing eyes of innocent children and young adults who might be misled by its allures. Incidentally, the increasingly important business of tourism also demanded that the all-too-recognizable landscape of the restricted district be removed from mainstream traffic. As tourism increased from 5,000 visitors per year in 1900 to four or five times that number ten years later, it was recognized as an increasingly important source of income. Tourists belonged to the middle and upper classes, and they did not want to see vice districts. Skagway advertised itself as Alaska's Garden City, not as a place to taste the flavor of the Old West. And its "clean" middle-class values, which it sought to promote to the rest of the world, were a key part of its image.[28] As long as the demimonde lived up to the appearance of abiding by those values, they would be tolerated a little while longer. With the restricted district under the control of middle-class landladies Kitty Faith and Essie Miller, the WCTU left it alone. For a while.

Instead, the women's organization turned its next efforts to temperance. To do so, it must first obtain women's suffrage.

CHAPTER NINE

Women's Suffrage and the
End of Vice, 1910–1917

When the middle-class women of Skagway succeeded in moving the restricted district away from the center of town, they disassociated the man landladies from any financial interest in its continuation. Their political success rested on the removal of the Progressive politician Chris Shea, champion of the working-class men, a saloon keeper who had lowered real estate taxes while raising personal property taxes, thus hurting the businessmen at the very top of the tier. He promoted the public funding and the municipal ownership of public services, and relied on the sin taxes to fund some of those projects. Whether ejection of Shea was a deliberate effort to destroy Skagway's champion of vice—Shea would have denied he was any such thing— his disappearance from town spelled the beginning of the end of the traditional sanctuaries of the working-class bachelors in Skagway: the saloons and the brothels.

As the WCTU moved on to accomplish additional reforms, it enlisted yet another political strategy. By espousing women's suffrage, these middle-class women hoped to directly engage in changing the attitudes of the men making, interpreting, and enforcing the vice laws of Alaska. Why should a woman sit on her husband's lap and beg him to do what was right when she could go to the voting booth and do it herself? Therefore, upon closing down the Seventh Avenue restricted district, Skagway's middle-class women set aside their work against the evil of brothels and saloons and devoted themselves to obtaining a ballot.

This realization grew out of the way the saloons in Alaska Territory could renew their licenses each year only through the approval of the electorate. As discussed in chapter 2, the 1899 Alaska Code, as interpreted by Judge Melville Brown, required a yearly election to approve all of the liquor licenses in any given community. This requirement had been a concession to the Prohibition interests in 1899, and its purpose was reiterated in the Alaska Territorial Act of 1908. As the women in Skagway had discovered when they protested the issuance of licenses to four saloons in 1900, the issue was not a simple matter of wanting or not wanting saloons. The money realized from the high license fees went to fund public schools in Alaska. By virtue of the 1908 revisions to the law, once the schools were well established, then the communities could use a portion of the liquor license money for municipal improvements. As with all the sin taxes, these bad moneys designed to do good things put a serious dent in any case the reformers tried to make when advocating the closing of saloons. A classic example was the manner in which John Troy portrayed the "temperance women" as impeders of progress during their protest of September 1901.[1]

The 1908 territorial law did away with an earlier option that permitted the issuance of licenses by petition and instead stipulated that a community must vote on the matter. Every year, when the liquor vote was taken, Skagway's saloons received their licenses. Between 1908 and 1913, only men could vote, as the saloon was one of those seemingly unassailable male institutions of the late nineteenth and early twentieth centuries. Few of the working-class men in Skagway wished to do away with this institution. As Madelon Powers has so convincingly shown, the saloon was the center of socialization and relaxation for the working-class man. No reputable woman entered its doors. The saloon was the working man's social club, the place where he could escape family life and be with other men. There he could discuss politics, tell off-color jokes, and gamble in a friendly game of poker, all safe from the eyes of his mother, sister, wife, or sweetheart. Within the walls of the saloon, he could simply be a man, without having to aspire to the high standards of morality set by the women in his life.[2]

In the view of the middle-class woman, the saloon was most definitely anti-family. Because of all the cash a man would squander in the saloon, it took money from the home; it impoverished the working-class wife and child, and it encouraged drunkenness. The saloon was the epitome of what the morally superior middle-class ladies of Skagway knew they must abolish before they rid themselves, once and for all, of all other evils. The death of the saloon was the ultimate goal of the WCTU and similar reform institutions.[3]

After Troy left in July 1907, the editorial shift at the *Daily Alaskan* was readily apparent. Criticism of prohibitionists and other reformers was less biting, and the stories become bland. As discussed in chapter 7, the man who eventually came to edit the newspaper, Samuel Wall, while a Republican, was much like his employer, the dentist Louis Keller, who "liked to sit the fence." Both Wall and Keller vehemently disliked the current governor, Wilford B. Hoggatt, so that political issues rather than social issues—especially those dealing with home rule and territorial status for Alaska—dominated editorials. In fact, Wall's obsession with these two issues made for tiresome reading. As time went on, the *Daily Alaskan* increasingly evaded the reporting any but the most newsworthy stories of local vice, even to the point of not mentioning arrests of prostitutes, a sure-fire story full of humorous details during Troy's administration.

As late as February 1908, Wall, like Troy, continued to harp on the unfair burden placed on local wholesalers by the $2,000 license fee, but little happened on that front. Then Governor Hoggatt convinced Congress to consider a new liquor bill for Alaska, which would set a flat $1,000 yearly fee for all liquor licenses. The only exceptions would be to those saloons that allowed gambling or women on the premises. As part of an almost continual barrage of complaints against Hoggatt, the *Daily Alaskan* found fault with this proposal. Unlike Troy, who had argued for higher licenses to help the schools, Wall took the side of the small roadhouse owners who only paid $500 due to low populations within two miles of their locations. The new law would double their license fees and drive them out of business.[4] The argument appeared to arise simply from a desire to find fault with any issue Hoggatt favored.

But Sam Wall was not entirely happy with the old law, either. He liked the idea of eliminating the yearly census that determined the size of a community's population, which in turn dictated the amount of the license fee. In February 1908, he complained that the old high license law made the saloon men pay for the census and that the men they hired to conduct the census always managed somehow to make the population appear too low.[5] In June 1909, the chief of police circulated an annual petition for the granting of saloon licenses, receiving the signatures of 563 men and women over the age of twenty-one. Wall used this statistic to generate his own idea of the town's population. "At the usual accepted ratio of adults to minors in a community this would give Skagway a population of close to 1,200."[6] Actually, according to the federal census taken just a year later, Skagway only had 870 residents, 804 of whom were white, and 613 of whom were twenty-one years of age or older. Of these latter, 64 percent were men.[7] Skagway still had a disproportionately high male-to-female—and therefore male-to-child—ratio in 1910, so it was improper for the *Daily Alaskan* to use "the usual accepted ratio of adults to minors in a community."

And as the population of Skagway's men continued to fall, the number of its saloons fell also. By the fall of 1906, the Totem, the Last Chance, and the Idaho saloons had closed. Albert Reinert had acquired the Idaho Saloon and renamed it the Horse Shoe. The Board of Trade and the Pack Train moved away from their old Sixth Avenue addresses, on to Broadway and closer to the south end of town. The downtown was coalescing farther south, and the saloons were still struggling.

By the fall of 1908, only six saloons remained. Herman Grimm, long-time owner of the Seattle Saloon, the most respectable middle-class saloon in town, abandoned his once lucrative location at Sixth and State and purchased the old Last Chance Saloon. The previous owners had renamed it "The Pack Train," in honor of one of Skagway's first saloons. Grimm decided to keep the venerable name. Only the Trail Saloon, inside the Trail Hotel built by Chris Shea, was new to town, and the bar was simply ancillary to the lodging business. The 1908 Alaska Code, when finally passed, removed the option of a census for the granting of liquor licenses and mandated a yearly election. For the next seven years, Skagway voted for local option. Sometime during those seven years, the Monogram Liquor House closed its doors for the last time.

And Grimm's Pack Train Saloon, now occupying the location of the Last Chance Saloon, became one of the last saloons on the north end of town instead of the last one on the south end of town. After 1908, it would take only a few short years for the WCTU to close the five remaining saloons in Skagway. The saloon era in Skagway would be gone forever.

Clearly, Skagway's declining saloon population mirrored its declining population. After the swan dive caused by the rise in license fees in

1899, Skagway's eighty-nine saloons in January 1899 fell to sixteen by August of that same year. By 1902, only seven saloons remained to pay the high $1,500 license fee. When the town's saloon keepers could prove to everyone's satisfaction that the population had fallen well below 1,500 and was going to stay there, the license was finally lowered to $1,000 a year, allowing two new saloons to open in 1903. They didn't last long. By 1906, Skagway was down to only six saloons.[8]

As a further sign of these changing times, as discussed in chapter 7, the WCTU spent much of the time during its re-emergence in Skagway, from September 1908 to March 1914, enlisting the support of middle-class businessmen in its various activities to transform Skagway into a moral—and more welcoming—community by sponsoring temperance parties and dances, providing public restrooms, tearing down unsightly buildings, and building public drinking fountains. They sponsored guest lectures on a wide variety of subjects, all oriented toward bettering the mind and moral constitution. These subjects appealed to the values of middle-class men, who increasingly espoused the concept of "virtuous masculinity," as defined by scholars David Charles Beyreis, Stephen Frank, and Margaret Marsh.[9]

By the spring of 1912, the main political issue on most male voters' minds was not what the women were doing to better their community but the fact that Alaska was about to become a full-fledged territory, with the right to representation in the U.S. Congress and the ability to tax itself. This "home rule" issue had been of paramount concern to Alaska citizens since the gold rush days and figured strongly in the vast majority of newspaper editorials, especially during local election times. Previous acts passed in 1899, 1901, and 1908 had gradually meted out laws and rights granting to Alaska partial representation and taxation abilities, but the 1912 act would make Alaska a territory on par with others awaiting statehood: New Mexico, Arizona, and Hawaii.

In April 1912, as the U.S. Congress met to craft the Alaska Territorial Act, Representative Frank W. Mondell of Wyoming added an amendment to give Alaska's legislature the ability to enfranchise women. This amendment passed Congress with no objection. In the states of Colorado, Idaho, Utah, and Wyoming, women had enjoyed the voting franchise since before the turn of the century. Washington, California, and Arizona had granted women the right to vote in the previous three years; Oregon, Montana, and Nevada would follow suit before the end of 1914. Adding Alaska to the western contingent of voting women seemed the logical thing to do.[10]

Upon receiving the directive from congress to enfranchise women, Territorial Senator Arthur G. Shoup of Sitka asked the president of the National American Woman Suffrage Association (NAWSA) for literature on the women's movement. She enthusiastically accommodated his request. NAWSA sent him a sufficient quantity of literature so that each legislator in the new territorial body received his own copy of the specially printed circular "Five Reasons Why Alaska Should Adopt Woman Suffrage." Shoup introduced a bill to give women the vote on March 1, 1913. It was the first bill to pass the new territorial legislature on March 14, with only one senator, Charles E. Ingersoll from Ketchikan, refusing to vote on the grounds that he did not know the wishes of his constituents on the matter. All others legislators passed the bill without comment.[11]

Newspaper commentary presented no reason to counteract the bill. In the words of Juneau's *Daily Alaska Dispatch*, "Every state in the Union that has not passed woman's suffrage is going to pass it and if 'everybody's doin' it,' Alaska should fall in line."[12] For years the newspapers of Alaska had been supportive of women's suffrage. As early as 1908 some jokes had surfaced that mocked women who took part in suffrage marches, but those sorts of jibes had long since disappeared from the Alaska press. It was hard to find any politician in Alaska who would take a stance against suffrage. The newspapers depicted the men who did so as Catholic priests who wished to keep women confined to their homes.[13] This portrayal may have arisen from anti-Catholic sentiment rather than reflecting a true characterization of how Catholics felt about women voting.

In fact, the Republican *Daily Alaska Dispatch* actively supported the vote for women. Editor Edward Russell attempted to soothe last-minute concerns expressed by the liquor men that women might form "a class of voters opposed to saloons." Using convoluted reasoning, he stated that counting the number of women in a town would not change population figures because women had always been counted for census purposes. This argument, however, was a red herring, as it had nothing to do with the issue. Women had never been allowed to vote in the

Governor Walter Clark signing the Woman Suffrage Bill, March 21, 1913. William W. Shorthill, secretary to the governor, stands to the far right. Courtesy Alaska State Library, William Norton Photograph Collection, P226-171.

license elections. He went on to state: "Any time [the women] may determine in sufficient numbers, they can stop the granting of a saloon license but there has never been any such sentiment among Alaskan women. Should there be, the granting or withholding of suffrage would not have the slightest effect."[14] No doubt his male readers spent the next several years trying to puzzle out what he was really trying to say. The argument made no sense, and, indeed, he would be proven absolutely wrong.

When Governor Walter C. Clark signed the Alaska Woman Suffrage Bill of 1913 on March 21, 1913, it became the first act of the newly organized Territory. NAWSA touted it as a signal victory for the national women's organization. It also claimed that there had been no organization in the territory before they sent their brochures. They completely ignored the fact that the Petersburg Woman's Club had actively worked for women's suffrage for over a year and that women's groups such as the Skagway WCTU had promoted community activities since 1908. Alaska's middle-class businessmen, who controlled the territory's politics, had every reason to want to double their votes by enabling their middle-class wives to vote with them.[15]

After working to obtain the vote for women, the WCTU then began to renew its attack on the saloons in Skagway. As a whole, the business district continued to move south—and with it the saloons. On March 1914, saloon owner Frederick Coleman "Tuck" Flaharty purchased the Trail Building at the corner of Fourth and Broadway and moved his Board of Trade Saloon, at Fifth and Broadway, on to those premises. The WCTU protested the issuance of his liquor license. In a crowded court room, Flaharty's character was put on trial. After testimony by such notables as the Catholic priest Father Philibert S. Turnell, U.S. Commissioner H. B. LeFevre decided that Tuck was a trustworthy old-timer in the community and should be allowed to continue his business under his old license. LeFevre said Flaharty could petition for a new license in July when all of the other saloon keepers reapplied.[16]

Without a doubt, the middle-class women of the WCTU intended merely to flex their newly won electoral muscles by taking on Flaharty. Surely they could not have thought they could win, as Tuck was one of the most beloved, and, at the same time, most embattled saloon owners in the city. The WCTU could not have chosen a more seasoned target. Perhaps they chose this very popular personality in order to test their own strength.

Born on May 15, 1874, to Adoniram J. and Sarah N. Flaharty in Nevada, Ohio, Tuck and his brother, Harry Burton "Flick" Flaharty, had followed the pack of hopeful Klondikers over the Chilkoot Trail and up the Yukon River to Dawson in the spring of 1898. They helped dig out the bodies and survivors from the April 3, 1898, avalanche on the Chilkoot Pass. In the Yukon, Tuck regularly attended church in a log cabin and gamely withstood the jibes of his brother and friends who called him "a pillar of the church." Finding no claims left to stake in Dawson, they worked mines near Chicken and Eagle, Alaska, finally returning to Skagway in about 1902 and getting jobs with the White Pass and Yukon Route railroad.[17]

Tuck had been one of those boisterous and likeable young men who entertained the entire bachelor set at handball, baseball games, and bowling tournaments, often playing on the same team as the equally charismatic Chris Shea. Until 1908, his name filled the newspapers due to his exploits in these sporting events, in which he often beat all challengers. In late 1902, he was a laborer for the railroad, and by October 1904 he was a baggage man in the depot.[18] Then, in the fall of 1906, he went into partnership with George Woodburn and purchased the Board of Trade Saloon from Lee Guthrie, then located at the corner of Fifth and Broadway.[19] He was a working man made good, an up-and-coming good ol' boy become middle class.

Within six months of purchasing his license, the moral reform community brought its first protest against Flaharty's saloon license, claiming it was located within four hundred feet of the Catholic Church on Fifth between Spring and Broadway. Woodburn and Flaharty solved their problem by closing the front door, extending the back of the saloon all the way to the alley in the rear (once Paradise Alley), and opening up an alley entrance, which they called Limerick Alley.[20]

What most Skagwayans did not know about Flaharty was his relationship with landlady Essie Miller: the two were married. In the winter, Essie usually went to Seattle, and in 1915, she went by the name Mrs. F. C. Flaharty. In September 1918 Miller and Flaharty sold adjoining lots on State Avenue, just north of Seventh. They had bought them separately in 1912 but sold them jointly as "F. C. and Essie Flaharty nee Miller of Seattle, Washington." When Miller sold her Alaska Street properties in the 1920s, she signed herself "Essie Flaharty nee Miller."[21]

Tuck was obviously a likeable fellow, and the men of the town would not condemn him. The fact that the highly respectable Father Turnell had testified to Tuck's good character during the hearing for the liquor license for the Board of Trade Saloon probably allowed Judge LeFevre to save face with the townspeople and put off the decision about Tuck's license. The women probably should have chosen someone less charismatic to take on.

Father Turnell was a formidable ally for Flaharty. He was born Filiberto Tornielli in Venice, Italy, on August 14, 1850. His great uncle was Pope Gregory XVI, who had served as pope from 1831 to 1846. Both of Tornielli's aristocratic parents died before he reached adulthood.

He entered the Society of Jesus in Monaco in March 1873 and became a priest in France five years later. Less than a month after his ordination, he was in San Francisco and had changed his name to Philibert Turnell. After learning English, Father Turnell served at a number of Jesuit missions in Washington, Idaho, Montana, and Wyoming. Finally, in March 1898, he achieved his twenty-year long goal of working in Alaska. By that fall, he was spending most of his time in Skagway. While he served throughout southeast Alaska, he lived in Skagway most of the time from that fall until 1918.[22]

When Father Turnell left Skagway at the age of 68, his congregation must have been saddened. He seems to have been well loved. In 1905, a parishioner had written of him as a "faithful servant of God," who had earned the "respect and good will of every citizen of the town." Another Skagway priest portrayed him as bearing "the reputation of a saintly man; of a guileless man, as pure and innocent as a child." The local newspaper, when he left town, noted that "his friends are legion," and that "by his faithful service and kindly ways [he] had won the esteem and affection of not only his own parishioners but of the whole community." Fellow priests described him as "a jovial companion," and upon his death, "people recalled with love the tall, thin, saintly old man of jovial disposition."[23]

Turnell's stance on Prohibition is difficult to judge. Two days before the November 7, 1916, election, Father Turnell signed a WCTU petition urging the arrest of people found to be intoxicated in public. This action suggests he supported the women in their views on temperance. However, archaeological investigations of the privy pit that he used as a trash pit between 1914 and 1918 indicate that his personal habits differed from his public stance. More than seventy-two liquor bottles and forty-five nonalcoholic beverage containers were recovered from a test excavation that retrieved only about a third of the trash in the pit. A comparison with other family trash deposits of the same period indicates that Father Turnell did not drink any more than the average family that consumed liquor at home; however, he did consume a great deal more nonalcoholic beverages, primarily grape juice. It appears that the aristocratic Catholic priest, accustomed to drinking wine with his meals, began to substitute grape juice as temperance became a political issue in the community. The temperance movement did not stop him from consuming other liquors, however, such as rum, whiskey, gin, and brandy, probably when alone or with people who did not subscribe to temperance.[24]

Turnell had also been forgiving of the prostitutes. In October 1901, prostitute Dora Clifford died of consumption after she had been in Skagway for about eight months. John Troy, with a tone of disapproval, announced that the priest had administered last rites for Clifford. Father Turnell editorialized the next day that she had repented of her life fully two weeks before her death and had resolved to lead "a pure Christian life." He defended himself by asserting that he had no choice but to administer the sacraments of the Catholic Church, "from which she had strayed in childhood."[25] The Catholics seemed to view their God as more forgiving of past sins than many of their Protestant brethren did.

Not that the Protestant male clergy of Skagway had been actively involved in the reform movement. While ministers' names were used in association with petitions to move the districts, it was clear that the WCTU was behind each drive. The young Methodist minister Rev. John Wesley Glenk presented a petition to the city council in May 1907, one that requested the movement of Seventh Avenue to a less public location. He left Skagway only a few months later, before the WCTU had reinvented itself. Each minister of each church stayed only two to four years before moving on; only Father Turnell remained long enough to have a lasting impact, and he refrained from taking a leading position on reform.

Not to be put off by their failure to shut down Tuck Flaharty's Board of Trade Saloon, the women of the WCTU took advantage of their newly won right to vote and went to the polls. In the 1914 city election, Skagway pioneer, hotel owner, and local historian Harriet Pullen ordered her hostler to drive her team of matched horses and her luxurious, rubber-tired Pullen House Bus around the town and pick up the ladies who wanted a ride to the polls. The assistant superintendent of the railroad responded by taking a hand car and pumping it up to the shops to remind the men working there to vote after hours. At the end of the day, Taxpayers Party candidate Si Tanner lost his long-held council seat by four votes.[26]

Harriet Pullen and the Pullen House Bus, which she used to take women to the polls in 1914. Alaska State Library, John Zug Album, UAF-1980-68-146.

Tanner was the man who, as U.S. deputy marshal, had rounded up Soapy Smith's gang in the aftermath of the con man's killing, had collected quarterly fines from the prostitutes from 1903 through 1909 as magistrate, then served faithfully as councilman in 1909, mayor from 1910 through 1912, and councilman again in 1913. He was now a senator representing Skagway and much of southeast Alaska in the first territorial legislature. "For the past ten years, 'Old Si' has had control of the affairs of the town as absolutely as though he owned it in fee simple," accused Sam Wall on the day after the 1914 election. "But thanks to the women voters of Skagway, who yesterday for the first time were accorded the privilege of the ballot in a municipal election, the burden of oppressive bossism has been lifted with every prospect of vast improvement in the conducting of civic affairs from an economic as well as a moral standpoint."[27] There was no denying that the women of Skagway had overthrown the last of Skagway's old guard.

Harriet Pullen was a grand dame of Skagway. She had come to the boomtown in September of 1897 and shared a cabin with John Troy's wife, Minerva, while cooking for mill workers and early stampeders. She quickly put her entrepreneurial talents to work and convinced the town's founder, William Moore, to lease one of his grand houses to her so she could run it as a hotel. In 1904, she purchased the building from him, and turned it into a comfortable tourist destination. She told fantastic stories about the gold rush days to all who would listen, often insisting that other Skagway pioneers keep their mouths shut or get off her porch so as not to interfere with her version of events. She built and maintained one of the first collections of historical artifacts in the town; she and other tourism promoters would maintain bitter rivalries over whose version of history was correct and who knew the most about the town's past.[28]

Tanner took this defeat in April 1914 philosophically. He ran for his old senate seat in November 1916, but the women voters in Skagway again defeated him, and he lost to his Republican challenger. The loss did leave him free of the obligations of public service so that when U.S. Marshal Harry Bishop resigned on April 14, 1917, the Democrat Tanner was ready to step in and accept an immediate appointment to a job he had long desired.[29] Skagway had not seen the last of this irascible old symbol of law and order.

The defeat of the Taxpayers' city council candidate, J. M. Tanner, in 1914 did not, however, signal a change in class politics in Skagway. Of the councilmen who were elected, all but one was a middle-class merchant. The exception was Howard Ashley, who would eventually become the mayor. Ashley was a skilled craftsman, the master mechanic at the railroad shops. All of the councilmen, including Ashley, were married, had families, and had adopted middle-class values.[30]

With the last representative of the Taxpayers Party gone from City Hall, there seemed little left to stop the reform community from making its desired changes. On June 5, 1916, in a special election dictated by the Alaska "Bone Dry" Law, the city voted not to renew the liquor licenses of the town's saloons. Many voters were brought to the polls in Harriet

Pullen's horse-drawn "vehicle of conveyance," which carried the sign "Vote Dry and Protect Your Home." The *Daily Alaskan* announced that "the Woman's Christian Temperance Union, after a closely followed campaign, systematically carried out, have won the election" in a vote of 193 to 153.[31] In 1910 there had been 527 eligible voters, counting all native-born and naturalized citizens over the age of twenty-one, except for the Native Alaskans, who were not considered citizens, and women, who could not vote. By 1920, there were only 264 eligible voters, including the women. (Native Alaskans did not obtain the vote until the Indian Citizenship Act made them citizens in 1924.)[32] It is likely that the 346 votes cast in 1916 included most of the eligible voters, indicating that many people cared deeply about the issue. The majority of citizens, male and female, had spoken, spelling the doom of Skagway's remaining saloons.

On June 6, 1916, Skagway became the second town in Alaska to vote not to issue liquor licenses to the saloon owners. To allow the town's four saloons (Tuck Flaharty's Board of Trade, Albert Reinhart's Mascot Saloon, Herman Grimm's Pack Train Saloon, and John Anderson's Pantheon Saloon) time to dispose of their stock, the licenses were extended until August 21. In similar elections that same year, Haines, Juneau, Petersburg, and Ketchikan voted to renew their liquor licenses.[33]

Reinert quickly disposed of the Mascot Saloon, not even waiting for further blows to Alaska liquor sales. At the end of September 1916, he sold the building and business to William Childs and John Bender.[34] Childs had been Reinert's bartender in 1908. Childs and Bender did not let a little thing like the lack of a liquor license stand in their way of operating the saloon. They and J. F. Anderson, the owner of the Pantheon Saloon, were arrested for selling liquor without a license on November 25, 1916. Anderson had operated the Hot Scotch Saloon in 1898 and 1899, and the Pantheon since 1903. The court decided he should have known better, so he was fined $800. The court was more lenient with Childs and Bender, as they had never owned a business before (although both had been bartenders for years) and thought a business license came with the saloon when they bought it. They were let off on a guilty plea for a $100 fine and an extra $100 for a business license. The court did not address the fact they had been selling liquor.[35]

It seems extraordinary that the court allowed Bender and Childs to purchase a business license when the community had just voted not to issue any liquor licenses. The license may well have been for sales of other items than liquor or for liquor to be used for medicinal purposes only. A label for whiskey to be used for medicinal purposes only found at the Mascot Saloon suggests that some legal liquor sales may have continued in Skagway after August 21, 1916. Perhaps Bender and Childs advertised the Mascot as a pharmacy. Indeed, the next occupant of the Mascot building, Perry Hern, opened a drugstore at that site in January 1918.[36]

In November 1916, Alaska participated in a territory-wide referendum on temperance. Skagway reiterated its stance and voted 168 to 118 for a dry territory. Juneau voted 839 to 499 for dry; Douglas 246 to 195; Treadwell, where the miners lived, voted 155 to 46. Wrangel voted 197 to 73, and Ketchikan, the home of fishermen, voted 311 to 222. Three days after the November 7 election, the vote in southeast Alaska was 2,587 for the "Drys" against 1,532 for the "Wets." In the territory as a whole, the Prohibition measure passed 9,052 to 4,815.[37]

Skagway, having already refused to grant liquor licenses, may not have had the sort of court trouble that Juneau and other communities did in the wake of the territorial referendum on Alaskan prohibition. On December 9, 1916, Judge Robert W. Jennings dismissed a motion of the Juneau Liquor Company asking for an extension of all Juneau liquor licenses until January 1, 1918, to allow them to dispose of their stock of liquor. The judge refused to take action pending a response from the U.S. Congress to the November election that had voted Alaska dry.[38] That action was taken on January 23, 1917, when Alaska Delegate James Wickersham arranged to introduce a congressional bill to implement the provision of the November 1916 ballot to prohibit the sale of liquor in Alaska. In what seems like remarkably rapid fashion to political watchers today, the bill was signed on February 14, 1917, by President Woodrow Wilson.[39]

Called the Alaska "Bone Dry" Law, this bill made it unlawful "to manufacture, sell, give or otherwise dispose of any intoxicating liquor or alcohol of any kind in the Territory of Alaska, or to have in his or its possession or to transport any intoxicating liquor," with only a few narrowly defined exceptions. This measure was much stricter than the upcoming national Prohibition Act, which did not outlaw the possession of intoxicating beverages. The Alaska "Bone Dry" Law went into effect on January 1, 1918. It is unclear whether the territorial legislature made any provisions for disposal of liquor stocks between the signing of the law and the time it went into effect. Because Skagway's saloons had supposedly been shut down since August 1916, there would have been no need for this grace period there. In fact, in November 1917, U.S. deputy marshal N. O. Hardy arrested ten people for selling liquor without a license, indicating that the duly appointed officer of the law, at the very least, was taking Prohibition seriously.[40]

Having closed down the saloons in southeast Alaska, the moral reform community of this region now turned its attention back to the last den of iniquity and vice: the restricted districts. Earlier, it had found that direct attacks on the restricted districts failed to shut them down. Until 1910, shuttling the prostitutes off to less visible parts of town and hoping for enforcement of local ordinances seemed the best the reformers could do. With the reinforcement of the woman's vote, the reformers began to rely on the stiffer federal laws to bring about the end of the districts of sin: the Mann Act of 1910, also known as the White Slavery Act, and the laws against the sale of liquor. To ensure the enforcement of these laws, they enlisted the aid of federal officials, taking prosecution out of the hands of the local police.

Among its many duties, the Office of Immigration and Naturalization was charged with controlling "white slavery" in Alaska. Indeed, the immigration office seemed far more concerned about prostitution than were the territory's municipalities or the Department of Commerce, which controlled the liquor traffic. In 1909, Alaska's immigration inspector in charge Kazis Krauczunas traveled from his headquarters in Ketchikan to Fairbanks, the so-called "Pimp and Prostitute Capital of Alaska," to arrest foreign procurers and their unfortunate victims with the intent of having them deported. Despite a complete lack of cooperation from local authorities, he was able to arrest twelve prostitutes and five pimps, and transfer them all to Seattle for trial.[41]

In addition to the coziness among the authorities, the prostitutes, and the average men on the streets, the immigration official also had to contend with the savvy prostitutes themselves. As soon as the foreign women heard what was happening, many of them promptly decided to marry. Krauczunas decried this action as subversive and dishonest. He accused a Fairbanks woman of paying a naturalized American citizen $1,000 to marry her, prompting a rush on husbands for pay. Men came to his jail cells asking to marry the women he had incarcerated. One man asked if he might get $5,000 to marry any of them, "he was not particular which one."[42] A French woman paid $1,500 to a man in return for his marrying her. The *Valdez Prospector* reported that "Men were at a premium for the first time in Alaska and some fancy prices were paid for a number of god-forsaken specimens who were never able to support themselves before."[43]

Krauczunas also investigated the women in Skagway. His usual mode was to buy cigars for men and drinks for prostitutes when soliciting information. He submitted an invoice for sixteen drinks at 25 cents apiece between April 27 and April 30, 1909, in Skagway, then went on to Dawson, where he purchased twenty cigars and eleven more drinks in his quest to find out information about Skagway prostitutes. His bribery was unsuccessful. On that trip, he was unable to gather enough evidence to deport any of Skagway's women.[44]

Immigration officer Albert H. Joy was more successful five years later. In October 1914, he arrested Essie Miller and three other women and quickly shipped them out of town to Seattle. It is likely that Miller's employees were illegal aliens and she, as the madam, was arrested for trafficking in "white slavery." It is probably no coincidence that "Mrs. F. C. Flaharty" appeared in the 1915 Seattle, Washington, city directory. A quick marriage to Tuck probably helped thwart further harassment from immigration officials.[45]

It is possible—and this is pure speculation—that saloon keeper Flaharty foresaw increasingly difficult times ahead as women obtained the vote and Prohibition forces grew stronger. He probably felt genuine affection for Miller, but he may also have realized she had vast experience in dealing with the illicit sales of liquor. Where the prostitutes and saloon men had been in competition for many years—the latter resenting the fact that the former got away without paying the $1,000 a year liquor licenses—they would all be in the same situation in a few short years. If Flaharty wanted to stay in his lucrative business, teaming up with Miller might not have seemed such a bad idea.

Flaharty had long before voiced the opinion that he did not really need a wife, at least for those purposes most men of the time required them. He and his brother Harry had learned to take care of themselves during the gold rush days. They were liberated men. As he claimed in 1899, "We can cook, wash, mend our clothes, &c., and the only thing we need wives for is to talk to. All they need do is to be at home at meal time."[46] Whether he and Miller married in October 1914, to keep the madam from being deported, or later, after both left Skagway, is immaterial. As he had stated, what Tuck really wanted from a wife was companionship. The arrangement between Tuck and Essie must have suited them both.

Another event that affected the Alaska Street District was the departure from town of Kitty Faith. She, too, may have foreseen the end to vice in Skagway.

Skagway's prostitutes had weathered the high fines and unpredictable arrests by federal prosecutors between 1901and 1903, periodic harassment when they did not obey the rules between 1903 and 1909, a wholesale move of their district in 1910, and an attempt at prosecution under the Mann Act in 1914. Although both Kitty Faith and Essie Miller registered to vote in 1914 (each stating that her occupation was "landlady"), as madams, they were a definite minority in the community. While their views probably coincided with those of their male customers in matters regarding vice, they knew they could not overcome the votes of the other women in town, who had already proved that for them moral reform was an important political issue. It hardly seems coincidental that Faith began to dispose of her Skagway property in March 1915, a few short months after Skagway's women voted for the first time. She started with the old Stinebaugh lot on Seventh Avenue, getting $100 where she had once paid $1,500.[47] She had probably moved the three cribs it contained to Alaska Street shortly after 1910, but the fact that she got any money at all was astounding, considering what would happen to the other madams' investments.

Then—quite surprisingly to anyone who had watched her coolly outlast every other madam in Skagway—sometime between March 25 and July 14, 1916, Kitty got married. Her husband, Chris Wandsted, and she moved to Visitación, a small village in San Mateo County, California, just outside the San Francisco City limits.[48]

In 1916, Wandsted was forty-five years old, five years younger than
Faith. He was Danish but had been in the United States since 1902 and
had papers to become naturalized. In 1920, he was a self-employed
carpenter. With only these few and poor facts available, it is impossible
to know what Kitty Faith, Skagway's longest-lasting madam, found so
attractive about this man to cause her to abruptly abandon all her real
estate and business in the North. When the couple was enumerated in
Visitación in 1920, Kitty claimed to be a housewife working at home.
And while the home belonged to the couple, it was mortgaged. This
snapshot of Kitty's later life hardly seems to be a depiction of the same
astute businesswoman and landlady that Skagway had known.[49] Was
Wandsted handsome and dashing, a charismatic rogue who swept Kitty
off her feet? Or was he a savior to her Magdalene, a man who converted her in later years? Probably no one will ever know.

Over the next few years, Kitty Faith Wandsted continued to sell her
Skagway real estate, all of it for a pittance. In 1916, she sold one of her
brothels to Burmah Belle, who also went by the name Stella Sterling.
Belle had probably been renting the small Alaska Street brothel from
Wandsted (dwelling number 29 on map 3).[50] Wandsted disposed of
her other Alaska Street properties for back taxes in the 1920s and 1940s,
long after the restricted district was shut down.[51]

Kitty Faith, unlike Belle Schooler long before her, was not driven
from Skagway by abrupt changes in rules or policies. She was not hounded
out of town because of her ostentatious and noisy ways, like Frankie
Belmont. Faith chose to leave before circumstances drove her to that
decision, and she apparently left of her own free will. It seems likely
that when women obtained the vote and Si Tanner was voted out of
city office, she understood that the reformers had finally won, and she
wished to cut her losses while she was still able. There seems to be no
other logical reason for a comfortably placed madam to marry a self-
employed carpenter with a mortgage on his back. Faith, at fifty years of
age, may have simply been ready to retire and lead a "normal, respectable middle-class life."

Kitty Faith's story arguably epitomizes the successful madam's career.
She was a solid entrepreneur, investing in real estate and gradually building up her portfolio of business properties. She owned property throughout the town, making sure that all her investments did not rest on the

politics and whims of the community. When she finally did invest in the restricted district, she purchased prime real estate in choice locations. She was careful to keep her name out of the newspapers and to avoid trouble with the law. She was the only madam who successfully fought the effort to oust her from her property in September 1909, when the city shut down the Seventh Avenue restricted district. Faith became one of three owners of the new district on Alaska Street. She married and retired from the prostitution business in Skagway in the spring of 1916, when she was about fifty years old. While she sold all her Skagway businesses for a pittance, it is likely that she had made a great deal of money during the eighteen years she had worked in the sex industry in Skagway. The ending to her story does not sound like an entirely unhappy one. And if the women of the WCTU drove her out of town, she went willingly, with no cloud over her name. Her story is a classic one of middle-class business success. She ended her career as an entrepreneur in Skagway by becoming a middle-class housewife.

By the summer of 1916, only Essie Miller remained as a substantial property owner in the district. Faith may have rented her remaining brothels to madams, and Burmah Belle, aka Stella Sterling, owned a one-woman crib on a small lot once owned by Faith. The district was beginning to die.

———

In retrospect, it seems obvious that the members of the reform community stood poised for a renewed attack on the restricted vice district in 1917. Fresh from the success of their territory-wide vote for Prohibition in November 1916, the reformers jumped on new evidence of the depredations of the demimonde: the violent murder of a prostitute in Douglas on December 18, 1916. The crime triggered the end of the restricted districts in southeast Alaska.

The editor of the *Daily Alaskan* billed the murder as "one of the worst crimes committed in the history of Douglas Island." He proceeded to simultaneously horrify and fascinate Skagway readers with a scene that would have done justice to any R-rated movie in the twenty-first century. The restricted district near Douglas, across the channel from Juneau, boasted forty "regular" women and "several male leeches who make that district their hang-out." "Babe Brown," a recent arrival to that portion of the mining town, was found in her three-room cabin with both sides of her head bashed in, her throat cut, various cuts and slashes all over her body, and a vicious stab in her forehead. Blood saturated her bed and splattered her cabin. A blood-covered hammer stashed behind her dresser surely must have been one of the murder weapons. The newspapers leapt to the immediate conclusion that the crime had been premeditated and that vengeance was the motive. The story ran in the newspapers for several weeks. Unable to find a murderer, the federal courts eventually charged the woman's husband (named a pimp, macque, and several other things) with six counts of violation of the White Slavery Act for having transported his wife from Anchorage for the purposes of debauchery and prostitution.[52]

As happened so many times before in Alaska, newspaper attention to an issue related to a restricted district precipitated law enforcement activity. The Douglas police threatened to shut down their restricted district. The Juneau city council sent their police force into the Juneau restricted district. The constables went round to "every crib, house and cabin," with a message for "the women in residence." In response to a threat from the federal courts, a special agent came from Washington to investigate the matter of illegal liquors funneling into Juneau through the restricted district. In response, the city began to enforce its ordinance against delivering whiskey or beer to a house of ill fame. Any woman within the boundaries of the restricted district who was found with a bottle of beer or whiskey on her premises would be arrested for operating a bawdy house.[53] Of course, the penalty would net considerably less than the minimum $50 fine the federal courts would impose for operating a house of ill fame, or the $100 fine they would impose for selling liquor without a license, but the reformers did not need to know that. The warning was sufficient.

The territorial legislature began its session in March 1917, confident it had addressed the concerns of the temperance forces in its previous sessions. However, the WCTU, principally in the body of Mrs. Cornelia T. Hatcher, president of Alaska's chapter, spent the entire session lobbying her senators and representatives to pass an antiliquor advertising measure to last until the "Bone Dry" Law went into effect on December 31, 1917, in those communities that were not yet dry.[54]

In early May 1917, after the legislative session ended, the Skagway WCTU hosted Hatcher for several days of lectures and inspirational

Cornelia T. Hatcher in 1909. Courtesy Cornelia Templeton Jewett Hatcher Papers, Anchorage Museum, Gift of Robin Rustad, B2008.15.1.14.2.

talks, including slide shows and messages about her recent work with the legislature. Then, on the day before she left town to visit Seward and Valdez with similar messages, the Skagway city council met. It had been brought to their attention that the liquor law was being violated in a "certain section of the city." The council ordered the police "to exercise more vigilance" and asked the city clerk to get a copy of an ordinance that Juneau had in effect so that they might frame a similar one for Skagway.[55] The WCTU had decided to take on Essie Miller.

Who knows what kind of behind-the-scenes turbulence occurred over the next six months. However, by early November 1917, the reform forces won out. The *Daily Alaskan* began printing more and more articles about bootlegging and vice. A woman acting in league with the Juneau Woman's Club tried to remove that city's U.S. commissioner along with the U.S. deputy marshal at Tenakee, near Juneau. She claimed that "Blind pigs,[56] gambling and prostitution are so openly carried on at Tenakee as to become a stench before the respectable people of that community." Her most odious charge was that people were renting land from the forestry agents, then re-renting it to prostitutes, who openly defied the laws controlling gambling and bootlegging. And because the Juneau newspaper published ads for liquor, that publication could not be delivered to Skagway or Sitka, where prohibition was already law. Two prostitutes were driven out of Skagway's neighboring town of Haines and three others "promised to lead a respectable life if allowed to remain." They rented a building and said they would open a restaurant. The Haines city council promised to take a poll to see if anyone would patronize their business.[57]

On November 10, the *Daily Alaskan*'s editor wrote that Skagway had begun to clean itself up in the same manner as Seattle, Tacoma, Juneau, and Douglas. He noted that the real offenders were the "higher-ups" that supplied the liquor to the women in the restricted district. "It is a strange fact in human nature," he argued, "that the unfortunates are usually the ones made to suffer; they must do the dirty work for the 'higher-ups' and they are the first to be arrested for crimes that make the 'higher-ups' wealthy."[58]

Just when the reader thought that Sam Wall had obtained some sympathy for the prostitutes, he disabused them of the notion. He suggested it might "be better for the women themselves for Skagway to

abolish the whole district and do away with it entirely." For the first time, he appealed to a new sort of economic interest that appealed to the middle class. "Skagway is a tourist spot, visited by thousands of tourists yearly who judge all Alaska by what they see here. Let's show them that we can have a city than which there is no cleaner on earth."[59]

The *Daily Alaskan*'s stories on vice in early November 1917 were simply prelude to more sensational events in Skagway. On November 12, Essie Miller, Olive Hazel Crosby, and Nora "Billy" Moore, all madams, were arrested and convicted, not for keeping houses of ill fame but for selling liquor without a license. Miller's fine was highest at $200, and the two others had to pay $100 apiece. Birdie Ash, a fourth prostitute—not a madam—pleaded not guilty. She had been arrested with L. F. Greene in a room at the Dewey Hotel. She had accepted two bottles of beer from Greene for the price of $2.00. Both were found guilty of bootlegging. Ash was fined only $25 for her crime.[60]

More important than their fines, perhaps, was the condition set by U.S. Commissioner Edward A. Rasmusen that all four women leave town. The one remaining madam in the district who was not caught in the sting (Burmah Belle?) would also have to leave. The commissioner's sentence ended the Skagway red light district.

Federal authorities had not arrested a Skagway prostitute for selling liquor without a license since Essie Miller, Helen Storey, and Gypsy Moore had been fined $100 each on December 9, 1903, as the parting volley in the battle between the federal and municipal courts over who had authority in the prosecution of the morality crimes in Skagway.[61] With the arrest of Skagway's madams in November 1917, the federal courts were jumping in once again and making it clear they were there to end legalized prostitution in Skagway once and for all. It is ironic that Si Tanner, the man who had sentenced more than two hundred prostitutes in the years between 1903 and 1909 when he was city magistrate, was now U.S. marshal in the First District, and probably was the man who gave Deputy Marshal Hardy his orders.

It does seem odd that these five women should have given up quite so easily. Possible reasons for their rapid abdication will be explored in greater depth in the next chapter. But for now, it is sufficient to point out that all of them had been around Skagway for some time. Olive Hazel Crosby may have been Nellie Crosby, who was fined on a regular basis between May 1904 and August 1908. Nora "Billy" Moore could well have been Gypsy Moore, who besides being fined with Miller for selling liquor without a license in December 1903, was in Skagway in November 1903 and January 1906. Birdie Ash was in and out of Skagway between July 1904 and August 1909.[62] They were all probably getting on in years and getting tired of Skagway. There certainly were other thriving cities in Alaska, such as Seward, Anchorage, and Fairbanks, along the newly funded Alaska Railroad. They could go there. Skagway, no longer a boomtown, had nothing left to offer them.

Despite this slew of arrests, the federal officials were not quite done with their cleanup of the Gateway to the North. The *Daily Alaskan*'s editor had made it clear that the madams were not entirely responsible for the presence of liquor in Skagway; the "higher-ups" should go as well. Two days after telling Miller and the other madams they had to leave town, U.S. Deputy Marshal Hardy arrested Tuck Flaharty for selling liquor without a license in Skagway. Flaharty had opened a saloon in Juneau when Skagway went dry in 1916, but he frequently visited his former haunts (and his wife, Essie). He wired for his Juneau lawyer, but the Skagway commissioner brooked no delays. The saloon keeper was able to obtain a jury trial. All the details of the case were described in the *Daily Alaskan* because Flaharty was an old-timer in town and fondly remembered.[63] It was shocking: good ol' Tuck could not be one of those villainous "higher-ups"!

Several witnesses reluctantly came forward to admit that they had indeed purchased one or more gallons of whiskey from Flaharty while he was in town during this visit or on previous ones. Nonetheless, the twelve men on the jury brought in a verdict of not guilty on an undefined "point of law." Despite rigorous clarifications from both the defense and the prosecution during a retrial, the verdict of not guilty was once again pronounced. The all-male jury could not be convinced that Flaharty was guilty. After all, Tuck was well known, well liked, and could not possibly be one of those undesirable bootleggers.

Flaharty returned to Juneau to operate his saloon, called simply Tuck's Place, until it was closed down by the Alaska "Bone Dry" Law on December 31, 1917. The last mention of him in a Skagway newspaper appeared on January 16, 1918, when he was bound for Seattle, where he expected to start a new business.[64]

Within the next few months, Miller and Flaharty began to sell off their Skagway properties for almost nothing, apparently simply to get rid of them and to avoid having to pay city taxes. In September 1918, F. C. and Essie Flaharty née Miller sold their combined Seventh Avenue lots to John Wood, once a gambler for Lee Guthrie. When the Flahartys signed the deeds, their signatures were notarized in Seattle, Washington. They had left Skagway for good.[65]

Essie was finally able to sell her Alaska Street properties in 1920 and 1921 for far less than the back taxes, which meant the sales cost her more than she made. Again, the Flahartys' signatures were notarized in Seattle. Tuck Flaharty's new business was a speakeasy at First and Yesler, in the heart of Seattle's tenderloin.[66] He and Essie were not about to give up their old way of life. But no more fortunes were to be made in Skagway—at least not for the likes of Tuck Flaharty and Essie Miller, the last saloon owner and landlady in town.

And who had caused the closing of the district, that one last straw that gave not city hall, but the federal courts their reason to lock up the madams? Having finally won over enough male supporters of their mission to strip a town of its saloons, then a whole territory, the moral reform movement of southeast Alaska had finally convinced the federal courts that they should pay attention to other morality issues. With a dry town followed the specter of bootlegging, and, finally, the muscle needed to remove the prostitutes from the restricted districts. Seizing upon the brutal murder of "Babe Brown," in Douglas, Alaska, the WCTU and the temperance forces enlisted the support of the federal courts of the First District to arrest the madams for selling liquor without a license.

It seemed that the middle-class reformers had "captured" Alaska's "Bone Dry" Law in a way they had not been able to do with the White Slavery Act. They had not been able to drive the prostitutes and madams from the restricted district by running them out of their homes. Instead, the reformers drove the prostitutes away by depriving them of their most important tool of business—liquor. It was the final blow. Essie Miller and her lesser known sisters gave it all up and left. Legalized vice had died in Skagway.

CHAPTER TEN

Retrospect, 1918

I t had taken the middle-class women of Skagway sixteen years to persuade the men of their town to abolish saloonism and vice. To do so, they organized themselves first through the WCTU and then politically. They were not entirely successful until they obtained the vote and had enlisted the assistance of the middle-class business-men, even while these men were concerned about other issues besides moral reforms. In eliminating threats posed to them by labor parties and the working class, the businessmen also voted out the political leaders that had protected the institutions of prostitution, gambling, and saloonism.

When the moral reform community of southeast Alaska appealed to federal authorities to plug the trickle of illicit alcohol that had been flowing into the restricted districts in 1917, they also asked the federal courts to do something that local officials had been unwilling to do since the gold rush days of 1897–1901: enforce the prostitution laws. Imposing large fines on the madams and proving that they would be re-arrested continually until the sporting women left Skagway sent a powerful message. Prostitution would be prosecuted; it would no longer be tolerated. Skagway had no more use for the sanctioned busi-ness of sex.

What made it possible for the U.S. marshals to march into Skagway in November 1917 and simply shut down Skagway's restricted district? While lip service had been paid to those who wanted to shut down the district entirely in 1901, 1907, and 1909, each time the issue came up, the city council had met the suggestion with stunned silence. What was different this time and why did women like Essie Miller, the only remaining person with any real vested interest in the district, simply acquiesce and leave?

The reasons are multiple, and have as much to do with the town's pride as they do with its economy. Its demography, social attitudes, and declining economy, and the rise of the middle class, fear of labor, and the emerging political power of women all played a role.

It is abundantly clear that the blow struck by federal authorities in November 1917 put a stake through the heart of regulated vice in Skagway, one that lasted until World War II and the sudden inundation of hundreds of U.S. Army troops into the small community. The action of the federal courts would not have been successful had the city not condoned it. On November 9, 1917, when four of the five madams still working in Skagway were arrested for bootlegging, only three women owned property in the district: Burmah Belle, Essie Miller, and Kitty Faith. Belle, a woman who operated one small business, was not among the madams arrested. Faith had moved to a San Francisco suburb and had leased her brothels to the other madams. Miller paid the highest fine assessed the madams and promptly left Skagway.

The landladies had a very difficult time selling their properties. Essie Miller Flaharty was not able to dispose of her Alaska Street brothels until the early 1920s, when she and her husband Tuck sold her lots for less than the taxes owed. Ida Freidinger's smaller brothels, which now belonged to Essie Flaharty née Miller, were still standing in the late 1970s. Kitty Faith sold her Alaska Street brothels in the 1920s for less than the amount of back taxes. Burmah Belle stopped paying her taxes in 1920. The city tried unsuccessfully to sell her property well until the present era.[1] The lot remains undeveloped to this day.

It is fairly obvious that by 1918, Skagway's restricted district had indeed been shut down, the madams had fled town, and there was little likelihood the district would ever revive. The property had no value, probably in part due to the reputation of the block and in part to its proximity to the Skagway River, where flooding and erosion could endanger any buildings. Possibly the poor economy of the community in general also played a role in its economic demise.

The declining economy did not only affect the landladies on Alaska Street. All landlords were affected, particularly those with political power.

Although the city's real boom was in 1898 and 1899 during the height of the Klondike gold rush, the community was still doing well in 1901 when the Seventh Avenue restricted district was created. Property held its 1900 appraised value, although prices would soon start to decline. Man landladies who bought lots, then constructed cribs and two-room brothels on Seventh Avenue, supplemented the fortunes they were earning in other businesses by catering to the bachelor subculture.

However, as the Klondike gold rush ran its course and the miners moved on to other northern rushes, Skagway's economic health began to suffer. Its adult population fell from 2,383 in 1900 to 1,400 in 1903, and declined to 1,085 in 1905. On Seventh Avenue, the assessed value of a full lot without improvements dropped from $400 in 1901, to $225 in 1903, and to $200 in 1905. Improvements lost value on a yearly basis unless an owner added buildings to his or her property.[2] The risk-takers, the fly-by-nighters, and the transients moved on. The depressed economy weeded out all but the sturdiest, the most conservative, and the wisest investors.

Surprisingly, the declining economy in the first years of the new century also allowed some of Skagway's most enduring madams to begin investing in its restricted district. Kitty Faith did not purchase her brothel until 1903 and her cribs until 1906. Ida Freidinger's two purchases took place during the same years. Both Faith and Frei-dinger bought their properties from landlords. Absentee landlady Grace Mulroney bought madam Belle Schooler's small brothel in 1904. The weak economy appeared to be favoring the landladies over the man landladies.

As the decade passed, though, Skagway's economy continued to decline, and the man landladies became disenchanted with their invest-ments in Skagway. Lee Guthrie, owner of the Board of Trade Saloon and perhaps Skagway's biggest real estate investor, deserted town by 1910, going to California, where he bought a chicken farm. J. D. Stine-baugh sold his Seventh Avenue real estate in 1906 and left town in October 1910. He returned to Grants Pass, Oregon, where he opened a barbershop. In 1911, Phil Snyder left for Oregon, where he took up ranching.[3] These men had become disillusioned with their investments in vice, so they turned to other pursuits. Other men did not take their place. The downswing in Skagway's economy translated to opportunity for the women entrepreneurs who bought up the Alaska Street district.

Skagway's pioneer citizens had understood the vested interests in vice. John Troy was an unfailingly staunch champion of the respectable saloon man, as well as of the quiet landlady. He understood the economics of a municipality, how to keep the taxes low and the wages of sin high. Let the bachelors who drank and gambled and visited the brothels pay for the schools, streets, sidewalks, night watchman, and other expenses of a city.

But the mood of the town was changing. In 1900, Frank Keelar, Lee Guthrie, and Frank Clancy, saloon owners and known members of the sporting world, could still rank as respectable, powerful city councilmen, just as Mark Twain had predicted for their kind clear back in the 1860s. And yet, in 1909, Chris Shea, one-time owner of the Pack Train Saloon, left town in exasperation at the publicity he received when he was caught eavesdropping on the conversation between potential landlord Lyle Speer and landladies Kitty Faith and Ida Freidinger in Miss Faith's brothel. The prostitutes lost their powerful defenders in City Hall, in the form of the saloon owners who were also city council members.

Relevant to the declining economy was the overall waning health of the White Pass and Yukon Route railroad, both as a business and as an employer. After 1905, gold seekers used other gates to the interior— Valdez, Seward, and the newly hatched Anchorage—all of which vied for the title once claimed by Skagway, "Gateway to the North." The loss in business resulted in the WP&YR paying out its last dividends to investors in 1913. These payments were not resumed until well after the Great Depression. As the Alaska Central Railroad was being built out of Seward, much of Skagway's working-class population moved to that city. It hardly seems surprising that Seward's official restricted district was designated in 1914 just as Skagway's began to wane.[4]

With the decline of the railroad may well have gone the political muscle that perpetuated the institution of prostitution within the community. From 1898 and well into the middle of the first decade of the twentieth century, the WP&YR often suffered from a shortage of steady labor. One of its biggest problems was keeping trained employees. Men would only work long enough to earn the money they needed

to go on to the goldfields. Providing a comfortable, well-accommo-
dated community, in the minds of middle-class railroad management,
may have seemed a "necessity" in order to minimize turnover and retain
a contented workforce. When the WP&YR could no longer generate
revenues for its investors, the necessity of attracting a new work force
disappeared as well. The tendency to tolerate vice so that a labor
force would stay in Skagway was to the advantage of the WP&YR, as
long as its management retained control of city hall through the voice
of John Troy.

This powerful male leadership began to crumble, however, with
the end of the gold rush and the decline of the WP&YR. In 1909, the
likes of Frank Keelar, Lee Guthrie, Phil Snyder, and John Troy were
gone or going. While these men were leaving the city, the WCTU was
experiencing a rebirth: not under the leadership of feminist Sarah
Shorthill but rather of housewife Grace Zinkan. When the WCTU reformulated itself in Skagway, it did so not as a temperance organization
but as a benevolent society whose sole purpose was to uplift the morality
of the youth, which was only fitting and proper for middle-class wives
and mothers to do. The fact that within a year of the newly formed
organization's first meeting the Seventh Avenue restricted district was
shut down hardly seems coincidental. The city council had tabled a
petition to move the district in both 1907 and 1908. In 1909, with only
two members of the Taxpayers Party left, it did not ignore the plea.
The only thing that seems to have changed was the emergence of this
important reform organization and a concomitant loss of political power
by a city council only temporarily dominated by working-class citizens.

A further answer to the question of why vice died in Skagway has to
do with its changing demography. The detailed statistical analysis of
Skagway's three U.S. censuses provided in appendix A indicates that
during Skagway's gold rush, men dominated Skagway's population,
by a ratio of almost four to one. The number of bachelor men exceeded
that of men living with their wives two to one among the middle class
and four to one among the working class. Once the boom was over,
this ratio gradually decreased to two married men to each bachelor
among the middle class and one married man to every two bachelors
among the working class in 1920. Whichever way the data are examined,
it is clear that the middle class in Skagway married more frequently

than did the working class. The town changed from a four-to-one male-to-female sex ratio in 1900, to a two-to-one ratio in 1920, transitioning from a place filled with strangers to a community of neighbors, most of whom knew one another. The Necessary Evil no longer was necessary.

These statistics betray a simple fact: the boundaries of the middle class shifted in the 1910s as working-class men married and moved into homes with their wives. These men aspired to more skilled jobs and their social values became more typically middle class. For all intents and purposes, they became middle class and voted that way. In fact, by 1920, the definition of "working class" as used in this book, which includes skilled craftsmen, is probably no longer appropriate. This group of individuals had shifted value systems, as well as economic status, to mirror those of the middle class.

In the context of this discussion, it is, of course, overly simplistic to assume that the wives of working-class railroad workers voted to sustain the saloons and restricted district and that all the businessmen, clerks, and office workers voted to shut them down. Of course that did not happen. The reality was far more complicated than that. But a change in values among a sector of the working class does suggest a reason why Skagway's vices died out when the same sorts of activities continued almost unabated in other Alaska communities throughout the Prohibition Era, the Depression, World War II, and into the 1950s.

Another shift in demography may explain the success of the middle-class women in shutting down the restricted district. In the early days at Skagway, the "miners" laying over for the winter, and the working-class laborers employed by the railroad and steamship companies, were exactly the sort of population the middle-class businessmen feared would prey on their wives and daughters. The gender ratio had fallen from seven bachelors to each unmarried woman in 1900 to only three bachelors to each unmarried woman in 1910. By 1920, after the restricted district no longer existed, there were still two bachelor men for every unmarried woman in town.[5] Apparently there may still have been a "need" for bachelors to find sexual release, but by the late 1910s, these men were no longer strangers to their neighbors. The businessman and his wife and daughters did not fear the advances of the young men who grew up next door and who were well known to them.

In contrast, young and vigorous Seward, Alaska, with its two-to-one gender ratio in 1920 (483 males and 219 females),[6] had an excess male population of single men building the railroad—young men who were strangers, not ones who had grown up in the community as such laboring men had in Skagway. In that other town "the Row" survived and even thrived during Prohibition.[7] The rapacious stranger was alive and well in Seward, where the wives asked that the restricted district be kept open so that the strangers in their midst would have a place to go to relieve their sexual impulses.[8]

So by the end of Skagway's first decade, it appears that changing demography, value systems, and economic decline created a climate that was ripe for reform in Skagway. In May 1909, when the male voters rejected the Taxpayers Party and voted them out of power, the ladies of the WCTU, who had gently pushed reform by "sitting on their husbands' laps" and "whispering sweet pleas in their ears," had suddenly discovered that their husbands were of an inclination to listen to them. It was only two months later that the middle class men shut down the Seventh Avenue restricted district.

Over the next few years, the ladies of the WCTU changed its purpose from lifting up the morals of their fellow citizens by loving, prayerful, and peaceful methods to bringing about a temperate community as articulated in their May 1915 convention. At that time the WCTU publicly stated that "purity of life is equally binding on men and women."[9] Fueled by such fervent beliefs from the reform community and without the resistance of the man landladies, the women's vote ousted "old guard" Si Tanner from his long regime, and as a result the prostitutes lost the last of their protectors in City Hall.

Another factor in the death of Skagway's vice was, ironically, the working-class rebellion. Middle-class businessmen had dominated Skagway's politics since 1897, with the creation of Committee of 101 and the first city council. Beginning in 1901, John W. Troy, the editor of the city's only daily newspaper, the *Daily Alaskan*, served as the head of the nominating committee for the Citizens Party (the outgrowth of the Committee of 101), which elected the winning ticket each year after ousting man landladies Frank Keelar and Lee Guthrie from office in 1901. Not until 1907, when saloon keeper Chris Shea organized a Labor Party and led the working-class bachelors in a rebellion against the middle-class businessmen, who had shut down gambling and talked of restructuring the way taxes were paid, did the Citizens begin to rethink their political power structure.

Thinking to oust Shea on an antigambling platform, his attackers discovered that he was managing to dance around the issue. Instead, the working class's champion proceeded to chop real estate taxes as he raised taxes on personal property, thereby hurting the businessman as he cut costs for the small property owner. He made a favorable deal for a publicly owned power company—in which a number of his friends had invested heavily—and the low utility rates drove the White Pass and Yukon Route out of the power company business. Both the working man and city hall benefited with lower utility bills, but Skagway's biggest employer, WP&YR, had fewer profits to send to corporate headquarters.

Businessmen who understood trickle-down economics were not happy with the situation. The businessman's champion at the *Daily Alaskan,* John Troy, left Skagway three months after Shea's Labor Party took office. Shea united with the Taxpayers Party and instituted tax reforms that hurt the wealthier businesses. As he began to attack the railroad's pick for the town-site trustee, the ladies of the WCTU found sympathetic ears when they spoke to their middle-class husbands about the need to move the restricted district away from the business area of town. The male voters were ready to get rid of their saloon keeper mayor.

Another factor that brought about the demise of regulated vice in Skagway was a switch in the tactics of the WCTU. During its effort to shut down four saloons in September 1900, the temperance women had learned not to take on the male politicians by themselves. When they began their next reform effort in April 1901, to remove the prostitutes from the alleys in the business district, they enlisted the help of Skagway's male clergymen: the Methodist, Presbyterian, and Baptist ministers. They let their male spokesmen present their petitions to the city council. Future reform efforts, until after John Troy left town, would involve both the middle-class businessmen and clergy. The WCTU itself stopped meeting and women's organizations appeared to be solely domestic in nature to hide their political activities. When a more sympathetic editor came to the daily newspaper, they curried his favor by engaging in the domestic care of the community before doing any temperance or vice reform. As the city's housewives and housekeepers, the reformulated WCTU was a much-loved institution, one that could influence its members' husbands' votes.

After Troy left Skagway, the days when the newspaper editor could or would intimidate the WCTU came to an end. Troy's replacement as owner of the newspaper, dentist Louis S. Keller, hired editor Sam Wall, who took a much more neutral position toward all issues except home rule. While the new editor's suggestions about misbehavior on the part of Chris Shea ended up driving him out of town just in time for the crucial vote on whether to maintain the restricted district on Seventh Avenue, Wall never criticized the reformers as Troy had done. Most important, the *Daily Alaskan's* continuing indulgence toward the WCTU allowed the ladies to build support in the community, garnering much good will, donations of funds, and even buildings in which to carry out their charitable works. By the time it began the serious work of legislating temperance, the WCTU was a well-established, integral part of the community. Wall could not find anything negative to say about its members, should he even have wished to do so.

Beyond their increasingly tolerant view of the WCTU, the newspapers of southeast Alaska paid another influential role. Due to the press's long-term fixation on the single issue of home rule, middle-class male voters were anxious for the opportunity to double their votes at the polls. The new territorial legislature, composed of middle-class men, convened in 1913—and promptly passed a Woman Suffrage Act. Most commentators at the time did not think women's votes would affect the liquor licenses or other reform measures. But they were wrong. In Skagway, and in other Alaskan communities, "old guard" councilmen like Si Tanner were voted out of office and replaced by younger, more progressive members.

Then with the increased political power of the WCTU and other women's organizations in Skagway, on June 6, 1916, the community refused to grant liquor licenses to its four remaining saloons. Shortly thereafter, Alaska passed a "Bone Dry" law that was more stringent than the local measure; it outlawed even the personal possession of alcohol, which was not illegal under the Eighteenth Amendment. Alaska's law went into effect on January 1, 1918, a year before National Prohibition.

The emphasis on temperance would be used in the First District to close down the restricted districts as an avenue for smuggling liquor.

This sequence of events did not occur in other parts of Alaska. For instance, in the Third Judicial District of Alaska—which included Anchorage, Valdez, and Seward—the U.S. district attorney ordered the immediate shutdown of the restricted districts as part of an overall attempt to stop the flow of liquor. But his order was largely ignored. The measure may have dampened spirits in Seward for a short period, but old-timers still have fond memories from the Prohibition Era of Homebrew Alley and of how the women on "The Line" provided them with needed alcoholic sustenance.[10] Seward, after all, had become the principal port of entry for Alaska. The rapacious stranger was common in this town, both as the transient on his way north and as the worker on the railroad. In 1918, Seward's four-year-old restricted district was young and hearty.

On the other hand, Skagway's restricted district, like its madams, was old, weary, and nearly retired. In the wake of the brutal murder of Babe Brown in Douglas in December 1916, the First Judicial District began to shut down each of the restricted districts of southeast Alaska. Finally, in November 1917, the U.S. commissioner fined all of Skagway's madams for selling liquor without a license. All three landladies had left town by the time the Alaska "Bone Dry" Law went into force on January 1, 1918.

Skagway's declining economy, its changing demographics, and the increased political involvement of women all contributed to the demise of regulated vice. One of the remaining questions posed in the introduction of this book is whether class and religion corresponded in some way. In other words, was there a connection between religious affiliation and class in the shaping of political views on reform?

Given the lack of any hard statistical data on church membership and the casting of votes, this is a difficult question to answer. It is true that one of the first people to argue for reform in Skagway was the Presbyterian minister John A. Sinclair, but like most Protestant ministers in the town, he stayed for too short a time to make any lasting contribution to the cause. Only the Catholic priest, Father Philibert Turnell, stayed longer than four or five years. All other reformers appear to have been women associated with the WCTU.

Protestant churches in Skagway supported temperance movements and provided space for WCTU conventions, temperance-promoting guests, and white slavery lecturers; otherwise, their ministers were only marginally involved in the political activities associated with reforms. They preferred to preach to their congregations rather than run for political office. At the most, their political activities took the form of presenting petitions to the male city council. The Catholic priest, however, would go no farther than signing a petition; while he did make an effort to serve non-alcoholic beverages to his guests, privately he continued to drink his wine, whiskey, rum, and gin. In his role as priest, he forgave prostitutes who came to him for redemption. He was not in the business of societal reform.

On the other hand, Judge Melville Brown did not feel any remorse for mixing his Protestant ethics with his judgments on the bench of the First District: the Juneau newspaper called his interpretive style of law "Judicial Christianity." But the other judges and law enforcement officials of southeast Alaska did not espouse a particular denomination or openly support any given church. They seemed to understand the principle of the separation of church and state.

The women of the WCTU did appear to rely heavily on their churches for meeting and convention spaces. Membership of the organization in Skagway came from the Presbyterian and Methodist churches. But it was the individual women, supported by the territorial and national organization, that effected political change, not the churches.

Did the prostitutes and saloon men avoid the churches? That, too, is an almost impossible question to answer. Chris Shea was a Catholic; his wife had been the daughter of a minister, and she was active in the Catholic Ladies Society. Phil Abrahams was Jewish, but he sent his daughter to a Catholic school. He appeared not to be too serious about his own religion, and perhaps he only wanted a good education for his daughter in the absence of his divorced wife. But no other agents of vice were named in the newspapers as members of a specific religious denomination. Perhaps, as Paul E. Johnson suggests in his study of Rochester, New York, in the 1820s and 1830s, the absence of a church affiliation had more to do with a willingness to profit from vice than membership in a church had to do with class.

On April 8, 1914, the day after the women of Skagway went to the polls for the first time, the *Daily Alaskan* announced the end of Si Tanner's regime. It took the women en masse to oust one powerful old man. Some of the other men of Skagway were no doubt in a state of shock, but Tanner took the defeat with equanimity and went on to pursue his long-sought dream of becoming U.S. marshal. The opponents to suffrage had forecast a number of bugaboos related to the women's vote, but none of them materialized. H. B. LeFevre, once Skagway's U.S. commissioner, wrote a letter to the newspaper editor pointing out the success of Election Day, 1914: "The frightful picture that men have drawn of cold dinners and male baby tending was not exhibited. Women waited at home till after dinner, and fond mothers pulled their babies to the polls. No man insulted them, and women knew they wouldn't. Women understand men better than men understand each other."[11]

LeFevre went on to point out that women had to pay taxes and live under the same laws as men. They should be allowed to vote for the city's councilmen as well and to be tried by a jury of a woman's peers, namely other women. It appeared that the men, who, after all, believed ladies to be superior judges of morality, had come to accept that the women had a claim in such issues as saloon licenses and prostitution.

As a result of these women's votes, there was no restricted district remaining in Skagway, Alaska, in 1918. Despite the fact that there were still twice as many unmarried men as unmarried women in the community, Skagwayans had finally decided to enforce their own law.[12] The ladies of Skagway had the ultimate say on how the laws of prostitution would be enforced in their community—in a round-about way, through prohibition, if not by means of the prostitution laws.

Did the people who engaged in vice and reform continue their activities after there was no longer any reason to do so in Skagway?

Tuck Flaharty went to Seattle to run a saloon at First and Yesler "before and during prohibition."[13] Yesler was known in the city as "Skid Road," and was infamous for its saloons, gambling dens, and houses of prostitution. In December 1923, Tuck was arrested for running liquor when the city of Seattle rounded up at least seventy-seven men in an effort to enforce the Prohibition Act. As he continued to bootleg liquor, he also ran a cigar store, and worked as a mechanic, a clerk, and a watchman.[14]

In Seattle, Tuck and Essie took on their real names. In the Seattle city directories, Essie was listed as either Augusta or Jane (her middle name) and Tuck as Frederick. In the 1920s, the couple lived near Squire Park, within a mile of downtown Seattle. Augusta established contact with her daughter, Ruby Margaret Perdue Cadill, and went to visit her in Akron, Ohio, where she bought the young woman a dress. Her grandchildren came to know her as "Grandma Gussie," and the story was passed down through the family that Essie had married a sea captain and lived in a mansion in Seattle. While Tuck continued to bootleg liquor, he eventually secured a position with the Grand Northern Railroad, where he acted as a special officer. In this job, he would "give the bum's rush" to free-loaders on the trains. Tuck died on July 20, 1930, of a heart attack, at the age of fifty-six. Essie followed him on June 15, 1932, at the age of fifty-two, dying of a stroke. Her cousin, John H. Miller, whom she knew as a brother, was living with her at the time of her death.[15]

Kitty Faith, on the other hand, gave up her life of vice. She and her carpenter husband moved to a suburb of San Francisco and lived in a mortgaged house. In 1929, after Kitty's mother, brother, and twin sister had died, the couple moved to Hildebrand, Oregon, in Klamath County, and took over the Faith family farm. In 1929, Kitty died in Hillside Hospital, Klamath Falls, on January 21, 1937, four days short of her seventy-first birthday, still married to carpenter-turned-farmer Chris Wandsted. She is buried in Bonanza Memorial Park, in Klamath County.[16]

The politicians had greater success. When Frank Clancy left Skagway in March 1900, he went immediately to Seattle and re-engaged in political battles alongside his uncle Tom and brother John, while operating their Mascot Saloon. The Clancys backed Mayor Thomas D. Humes in the 1902 election, and then successfully bargained with influential gamblers in the First Ward to siphon off portions of their proceeds in exchange for the funds they had expended to finance Humes's campaign. Frank sponsored major prize fights until Seattle outlawed them. The Clancys continued to make money by staying active in First Ward politics, prize-fighting, and horse-racing but never were as active as they had been in the 1902–1904 period, when they played Seattle city officials against those from the county. In 1904, the railroad and wharf developers took over First Ward politics and removed the gamblers and vice controllers from the area near the waterfront. By the time of Prohibition, Frank Clancy had taken over management of the Detroit Hotel and was managing prize fights in Idaho. He died of pneumonia in Wallace, Idaho, on April 16, 1917, while promoting a prize fight in that city.[17]

Frank Keelar gave up his career in vice and politics, and went on to live to a ripe old age. In November 1905, Frank and wife Mattie turned their jewelry store and pawnshop over to their Japanese foster son, Jinjero Ikuta, and moved back to their home in Oakland, California. Sometime between October 1908 and September 1911, the Keelars abandoned chilly, foggy Oakland for the warmer climate of Los Angeles County. During the 1920 census, they were living in Santa Monica with a manservant. Mattie Keelar lived until February 9, 1927, when she died at the age of eighty. Frank survived another year, dying at the age of eighty-two on March 5, 1928.[18]

Robert Lee Guthrie was not so successful. He left Skagway in 1910 for Santa Rosa, California, still in his prime at the age of forty-seven. There he invested in a chicken farm. Lee and his wife Abby moved to San Francisco by 1930, after the start of the Depression, but were forced to live in a lodging house. In his sixties, Lee was fortunate to find work as a night watchman at a bank. The couple moved once more to Stockton, California, where Lee sold off Abby's jewelry to earn some cash. On September 20, 1934, he died at the age of sixty-nine.[19] Guthrie, once the richest man in Skagway, had fallen upon bad times.

Chris Shea did well when he left Skagway. He continued his work in politics but as an appointee rather than an elected official. He arrived in Seward in July 1909, where he threw himself into his new job as game warden of the Kenai Peninsula. Meeting with the hunters and other local people of the area, he listened to their complaints and worked to revise the game laws, leaving the community generally satisfied with their new warden. He joined with a number of other

community-spirited individuals and helped to found the Seward Hunting Club and the Seward Commercial Club, becoming its first secretary.
The *Seward Weekly Gateway* praised him, proclaiming "C. C. is alright,
alright."[20] He seemed to have found his home.

Then, rather suddenly in August 1912, Shea resigned as game
warden. He stayed on in Seward through the fall of 1912 to face a
number of petty charges of corruption from the son of Sarah Shorthill, William Shorthill, the secretary to Governor Walter C. Clark. Shea
caught a bad cold while on a hunting excursion in November, and he
failed to recover. Although exonerated of wrongdoing by the governor,
he left Seward in January 1913 to take in the healing waters of Soap
Lake, Washington. He died en route of advanced tuberculosis, near
Ketchikan, Alaska, on January 17, 1913, at the age of forty.[21] The temperate Shorthill had succeeded in driving the saloon-owner-turned-
politician from Alaska permanently.

Shea's nemesis, John W. Troy, fared much better in later life than
most of the people connected to Skagway's story of vice and reform.
The great promoter of Skagway, and a power behind all the middle-
class merchants during Skagway's first decade, moved to Juneau when
he sold out his share of the *Daily Alaskan* in 1907. He returned to his
home state of Washington, settling in Seattle for five years, where he
was the secretary and publicity director for the Alaska Club, an organization formed to encourage investment in Alaska. He edited the
Alaska-Yukon Magazine in Seattle in 1911 and 1912. He then returned
to Alaska to become the editor of the *Daily Alaskan Empire*, a Juneau
newspaper. He remained in that capacity for twenty years, becoming
the owner in 1914. He also served as the U.S. collector of customs from
1919 to 1922. In 1933, President Franklin D. Roosevelt appointed him
governor of Alaska, in which capacity he served until 1939. He died
in Juneau on May 2, 1942. He was mourned as one of Alaska's most
beloved citizens.[22]

In contrast to the individuals described above, Josias M. "Si" Tanner
never really left Skagway. He was appointed his long-desired post of
U.S. marshal in mid-April 1917, a position that required him to move
to Juneau for a few years. He served faithfully until 1921, at which time
he returned to Skagway, where he continued to help his son, Fred,
with the family hardware business. He died in his sleep of a heart

attack at age seventy-eight in Skagway on September 20, 1927. Hundreds of people attended his funeral to mourn one of Alaska's most stalwart citizens.[23]

Unlike the investors in vice, who left their careers behind upon leaving Alaska, the reformers continued their efforts elsewhere. Rev. John Wesley Glenk, upon leaving his Methodist ministry of Skagway in 1907, spent the rest of his career in the Bellingham, Washington, and Portland, Oregon, areas ministering to small Methodist and Congregational churches and supplementing his income as a draftsman and statistician. Even while her husband went to work for the State of Washington as a statistician during the Great Depression and afterward, Phydelia Glenk continued her social work with women's organizations in the Methodist Church, the WCTU, and the Daughters of the American Revolution. Rev. Glenk died on June 8, 1956, in Portland, Oregon at the age of eighty-two. Phydelia died two years later, also in Portland, on December 28, 1958, at the age of eighty-five.[24]

The Shorthills, too, stayed involved in reform efforts. Sarah and Thomas Shorthill moved to Tacoma, Washington, after leaving Alaska in 1903, although Sarah still sold dresses from her daughter Elizabeth Harrison's shop in Skagway as late as 1911. The couple returned to Skagway for the 1915 WCTU Convention, where both were accorded much honor, as much for the deeds of their children, Elizabeth Harrison and William W. Shorthill, who was then secretary to the governor of Alaska, as for their own accomplishments in the early history of the town. Thomas died in Spokane on May 28, 1918. Sarah lived with Elizabeth in Skagway for a while after Thomas's death, and then returned to Tacoma to live with her granddaughter, Nora M. Harrison. She died there on May 11, 1928, at the age of eighty-one. She attended meetings of the local chapter of the WCTU just days before her death.[25]

The Shorthills' son, William Werner Shorthill, left Skagway in 1903 for Douglas, where he became a secretary to the Treadwell Mining Corporation. He used his proximity to Juneau to good advantage. There he continued the family's work for temperance and lobbied for prohibition. He could not disassociate his temperance activities from his profession, and always signed himself as a representative of the company for which he worked when he wrote anti-drinking messages to newspapers and other public venues. In January 1911, he became a stenographer for the U.S. attorney at the district court in Juneau; two months later, Republican Governor Clark hired him as his personal secretary, a position that functioned as a lieutenant governor. When the governor traveled out of the territory for most of 1912, he left the bulk of the routine territorial business in the hands of Shorthill. It was in that way that a temperance leader was able to fire Chris Shea, Seward's game warden, who had once owned a saloon in Skagway.[26]

Clark's successor, J. A. F. Strong, a Democrat, retained William Shorthill as his personal secretary, much to the dismay of his political party. Shorthill remained in office throughout the scandal that resulted from Strong's insistence on keeping a Republican in such a powerful position. Shorthill did not return to Tacoma until 1920, at which time he became secretary to the Pacific Steamship Company. He transferred to the company's office in Seattle in 1926. By 1931 he was the secretary for the Olympic Corporation, Ltd. (an oil producer and shipper) and later Calimexico Petroleum Corporation, both owned by Hubbard F. Alexander. He continued with the latter firm until 1935. He then moved to Los Angeles, where he and his wife were enumerated in 1940; there he continued to work as the private secretary for an oil investment company. He passed away at the age of seventy-seven on July 26, 1948, in Glendale, California.[27]

In spite of the efforts of those people interested in reforming Skagway, neither prostitution nor the sale of liquor completely disappeared with the closing of the restricted district and the imposition of prohibition. A rich folklore, supported by some physical evidence, indicates that the Pantheon Saloon became a favorite speakeasy, and what was once the Red Onion Saloon (then the Senate, then the Seattle, then the Totem) was moved to the northeast corner of Second and Broadway and became a speakeasy with rooms upstairs for prostitutes. In fact, the latter business, now a thriving bar, advertises a tour of the "red light district," with a focus on its upstairs rooms, which are decorated with World War II "girly" posters, a sequined "flapper" dress from the 1920s, and stories of the women using dolls to indicate when they were available for customers. The latter custom was common in the second and third decades of the twentieth century, not during the gold rush days when women worked for percentages without the intermediary of a madam. Skagway folklore also indicates that prostitution was

The only remaining authentic saloon from 1898, the Red Onion Saloon, in 1980. Photograph by Robert L. Spude.

openly and widely tolerated during the World War II years when the U.S. Army was stationed in town.

National Prohibition was repealed in 1933, but the institution of the working-class saloon never returned to Skagway. Today, the town, even with its upwards of three-quarters of a million tourists each summer, supports only three or four bars and a handful of restaurants that serve alcoholic beverages with meals. Men and women intermingle in bars and lounges, smoking is not allowed, the proprietor charges for food, and both the state and federal governments excise heavy taxes on each drink. The Red Onion Saloon is a "saloon" in architecture and furnishings only. The women who dress in costume to serve drinks wear something that might have been seen in Paris or on San Francisco's Barbary Coast, not the respectable clothing that even Skagway's prostitutes would have worn in earlier days. They live the dream of Martin Itjen, who, in the 1920s and 1930s, took tourists on a jaunt around Skagway in his homemade tour bus and regaled them with tales of the town's scandals, including its gamblers and dancehall girls. Harriet Pullen, who told her own versions of Skagway's history, focused instead on the struggles of the pioneers, herself included. As a temperance leader, she would did not countenance the glorification of drinking and harlotry in the way Martin Itjen did.[28] In her silence about Skagway's vices, Pullen committed an injustice toward her own reform work and that of Sarah Shorthill, Anna Stinebaugh, and Grace Zinkan. When she told her stories and opened a museum honoring Skagway's history, she left out the saloons, prostitutes, gamblers, and reformers like herself. Itjen, who was not in Skagway during the gold rush days, told tourists—and ultimately the next generation of Skagway storytellers— tales that helped foster an emerging mythology of the "good-time girl" in the saloon. Instead of picturing a woman in a shapeless muslin gown outside her crib or the well-dressed percentage woman dancing with men in the dance halls, the modern tourist now believes the Klondike- era sporting woman served drinks in a Barbary Coast costume in a saloon. Somewhere along the line, Stroller White's Diamond Li'l van- quished any memory there might have been of Pop Corn Kate, Dutch Rosie, Belle Schooler, Frankie Belmont, Ida Freidinger, Kitty Faith, or Essie Miller. It really is too bad. These women's stories speak of rich lives that are object lessons for their failures and inspirational for their successes—like any range of women trying to succeed in business.

The image of the "good-time girl" has grown out of the depiction of prostitutes in popular culture, especially in film. This image emerged from the publication of pulp paperbacks about prostitutes described in the introduction to this book, in which old miners waxed eloquent about visiting golden-hearted madams simply for the conversation. The 1936 film *Klondike Annie*, starring Mae West, contributed much to the misinformation and false image of the northern prostitute in its depiction of Rose Carlton, a dance hall entertainer who assumes the role of a missionary on the way to the Klondike and, in the process, reforms herself. As in her portrayal of Ruby Carter in the 1934 film *Belle of the 'Nineties*, West portrays in *Klondike Annie* a sultry woman with no morals but a heart full of kindness. It was a character that set the mold for all madams that followed in popular culture, simply because the real madams had been cast into oblivion by the middle-class women of the Progressive Era. In Skagway, the image would become set in stone when the town's king of tourism, Martin Itjen, traveled to Hollywood and had his picture taken with Mae West. He then promoted his tour bus by displaying this photograph.[29] Skagway would forever think of its own prostitutes as women who looked like West's characters.

Building on the popular myths perpetuated by West's films, movies about prostitutes spanned the twentieth century, from John Ford's *Stagecoach* in 1939 to Clint Eastwood's *The Unforgiven* in 1992. None proved to be insightful treatments of prostitution in the American West, but were, instead, interesting treatments of their respective eras' attitudes about prostitution.

When matched against a culture predisposed to favor the continuation of the institution of the Social Evil, the story of the middle-class women in Skagway and their struggle to destroy vice becomes even more fascinating—because it is more complex. To understand the actual story of reform and vice, and to do it justice, requires changing the image of the "good-time girl" to that of a middle-class business woman fulfilling a role until the moral reform people convinced the rest of the town that the community no longer had a place for that particular Necessary Evil.

Skagway's story of vice and reform is marked by clashes between class, gender, and economic forces during the Progressive Era. The city's exaggerated male-to-female ratio and a clear distinction between its business sector and the working-class population explain the conflict between its reform community and the group espousing the sins of drinking, gambling and prostitution. As the middle-class women steadily gained more political power, the working-class men espoused middle-class ideals and gave up their favored vices. The town citizens eliminated Soapy Smith and his gang in 1898, restricted the prostitutes in 1901, prohibited gambling in 1906, moved the restricted district away from the center of town in 1909, gave women the vote in 1913, shut down the saloons in 1916, and then let the U.S. marshal's office close down the restricted district for the last time in 1917. The most politically active woman's club, the WCTU, evolved from a feminist organization to one more "domesticated," occupied with "cleaning house" and ridding the town of dirt in the form of shacks, saloons, and vice. Men, on the other hand, relinquished their long-cherished ideal of a masculinity that could not control its animal urges and instead embraced one that mandated restraint and focused on the family.

The progressive reforms that took place in Skagway also occurred in thousands of similar communities across America in the early twentieth century. They presaged the modernization of America by changing societal concepts of what it meant to be male, female, middle class, and working class. Changes in attitudes about race and ethnicity would not occur until decades later; intolerance for Chinese, Japanese, African Americans, and Native Alaskans would not begin to lessen in Alaska until after World War II.

And so it was that legalized vice disappeared from Alaska's southeast port of entry. The change that occurred in Skagway, Alaska, can only be attributed to a morally minded middle class and the strong influence of the women's movement.

Appendix A

Statistical Analyses

Federal censuses taken in Skagway during the years 1900, 1910, and 1920 recorded the age, marital status, occupation, place called "home," and birthplace (among other data) of each enumerated citizen. This body of information was crucial in my construction of the demographic profiles of Skagway's residents that are central to this book.

To arrive at these profiles, I conducted three specific analyses. The first looked at age and gender in order to determine how closely the community corresponded to the American mode. The second studied race and place of birth to determine the degree of ethnic diversity in the city. The third correlated class with marital status or "bachelorhood" (the status of living without a woman to take on household duties). I repeated all three analyses for each of the censuses.

As part of my PhD dissertation research for the University of Colorado–Boulder, conducted during the mid-1980s, I entered raw data from the 1900 manuscript census of Skagway, Alaska, into a Dbase-IV program and analyzed that data. In the 1990s, Skagway archaeologist Doreen Cooper and I collaborated in entering data from the 1910 and 1920 censuses into Excel databases and analyzing that data.[1]

Age and Gender

In the year 1900, the United States census taker recorded 2,383 people in the city of Skagway. The official enumeration was 3,113, but that statistic included people on board the ships in the harbor, men on the work gangs along the White Pass railroad, and a small group of people living over a western ridge in what was known as Smuggler's Cove. The 730 people living outside the city limits were not included in my demographic analysis.

There were almost three men for every woman in 1900 (1,396:523); five single men for every single woman (874:166); and almost twice as many married men as married women (529:339). Children were almost evenly divided in gender ratio: there were 188 boys to 172 girls. Children comprised 19 percent of Skagway's population; in the rest of the United States in 1900, they comprised on average 36 percent.[2] These statistics indicate that Skagway was largely a community of adult, unmarried males.

Skagway's population dropped to 870 people in 1910; the children, however, had increased to 26 percent of the population. While the ratio of boys to girls was still rather evenly divided (127:97), the man-to-woman ratio was still skewed, with two men for every woman (406:241). Like ten years before, more middle-class men had families living with them (56 percent) than working class men (31 percent).

By 1920, Skagway's population had dropped to 510 people, and 30 percent were now under eighteen years of age. This statistic approached the national average of 37 percent, indicating that Skagway was becoming more like the rest of the United States, at least from the standpoint of gender and age demographics.[3] The boy-to-girl ratio was almost even at 82:73, and the adult ratio was also approaching equity at 208 men to 147 women. This statistic meant that there were only 61 excess men in the population, a number that was declining rapidly.

Race and Place of Birth

In 1900, 96 percent of Skagwayans were Caucasian. The 108 Tlingit Indians, fourteen Japanese, two African Americans, and four people of mixed race comprised the remaining 4 percent of the population, indicating that the town was not racially diverse. Three-quarters of the residents in 1900 were born in the United States (77 percent), less than an eighth in Western Europe (12 percent), and a sixteenth in Canada (5 percent). That left only a sixteenth of Skagway's population that could be considered ethnically underprivileged at the time, including 129 Scandinavians, 18 Japanese (counting men working on ships), 16 Russians, a dozen people from the Mediterranean region, and less than a handful each of people from Latin America, Central Europe, the South Pacific, India, and the West Indies. The city's ethnic mix would remain about the same as time passed.

By 1920, 93 percent of Skagwayans were "white" (the term used in the censuses to refer to Euro-Americans) with only 3 percent Tlingit and 3 percent of mixed race. One Chinese, one Japanese, one Filipino, and one African American lived in the town. The only "ethnic" group that changed significantly during that time was the Canadian population, which rose to about 10 percent. This was no doubt due to the presence of the Canadian-owned White Pass and Yukon Route railroad, the town's major employer.

Class

For the purposes of this study, as discussed in the introduction of this book, I define class more in terms of education and values than of economics. I categorize working- and middle-class occupations in much the same way as does Paul E. Johnson in his landmark study of Rochester, New York.[4] Johnson constructed his portrayal of classes using tax records and city directories, matching names of individuals, the amount of money they made, whether they owned property, and whether they employed others. He then ranked each group of occupation type by percentiles (deciles, he called them) and decided whether they fell into the category of middle class or working class.

While the categories of occupations in this study are more intuitive than those used by Johnson, they do mirror his more rigorous precedent, with one group's exception. He classified a group he termed "clerical employee" as working class: this category includes all nonmanual wage earners (clerks, teachers, government officials, bank tellers, and accountants) who were without property or who ranked in the bottom 70 percent of taxpayers.[5] All these types of workers are classified in my study as middle class. I assumed that most of these individuals required some advanced education to do their jobs and that by 1900, they were receiving a better income than those of similar age in a working-class occupation.

The criteria used for this study, therefore, had more to do with the education, training, and skill required for the job, than with property ownership and wealth. It was also apparent that middle-class occupations, more often than not, kept the employee or manager indoors, protected from weather conditions; working-class occupations did not.

That was an important consideration in a place like Alaska, given the length and harshness of its winters and its cool, rainy summers.

The occupations listed in the 1900, 1910, and 1920 censuses did not have systematic nomenclature. Over five hundred occupations were listed in the three censuses. Middle-class jobs included those of accountant, barber, capitalist, dentist, engineer, freight agent, grocer, hotel keeper, immigration inspector, lawyer, minister, nurse, optician, police chief, railroad clerk, saloon keeper, ticket agent, upholsterer, and wood merchant. Working-class occupations included apprentice, bartender, carpenter, drayman, expressman, fireman, gold miner, housekeeper, laborer, machinist, night watchman, porter, railroad baggage man, seaman, teamster, and waiter. A few other "occupations" could not be classified, and these included "at school" (student), boarders, and "none." These latter "occupations" were not included in the analyses.

In 1900, there were almost three men (defined as males over fifteen years of age) for every woman (defined as a female over fifteen) (1,407:505). About one-quarter of all women worked outside the home. This proportion was about the average for women born in the United States (27%), but in Skagway, Alaskan Native (30%), Irish (28%), Scottish (50%), and German (29%) women had paying jobs at a much greater rate than the national average. While the Japanese women said they worked "at home," all eight of them were known to be prostitutes. Canadian women, more than 95 percent of whom worked at home, appeared to be the only women that enjoyed a greater-than-average ability to stay at home.[6]

About 15 percent of the women born in the United States worked in middle-class jobs, more than twice those in working-class jobs, at 6 percent. British women who worked outside the home had almost four times as many middle-class jobs as working-class jobs (28 percent to 8 percent); only the Scandinavian women, who tended to work as housekeepers and servants, were employed in more working-class occupations than middle-class ones. It appears, therefore, that when women whose native language was English worked outside the home, they took middle-class jobs, but women who were not native English speakers were restricted to working-class jobs.

In 1900, most men in Skagway worked outside the home. The only men who were perceived by the census taker to be unemployed were

Alaskan Natives. Those men who were born in the United States outside Alaska and who were still at home all attended school. Sixty-four percent of the men in Skagway in 1900 were employed in working-class jobs; 31 percent were in middle-class occupations. Those figures are only slightly below the 60:35 ratio for Skagway men born in the United States, which indicates that the town had more working-class men than the average American community. Alaskan Native men tended to have working-class jobs (65%), as did all foreign-born men except Germans and Russians. Only Mediterraneans approached the U.S. average (36%). The most likely nationalities to be excluded from middle-class jobs were Japanese, Alaskan Natives, and people from "Other Countries," such as Latin America.

Gender and Marital Status

No question about it. While men flocked to the Klondike gold rush, most women stayed home until their men decided whether they were going to stay. By the time Skagway's boom had peaked and it was on its way to getting settled in 1900, 26.4 percent of its adult population was female, and only about a third (32.9%) of that group was single, widowed, or divorced. The statistic was almost reversed for adult men. Almost two-thirds (62.1%) of the adult men in Skagway in 1900 were single, widowed, or divorced, indicating that a single man was more likely to go to the gold rush than a married one.

Class and Residency with a Wife

Due to the double moral standard in turn-of-the-century Skagway, as discussed earlier in this study, it was not only marital status but also residency with wives that could make a difference in the perceived "need" and use of prostitutes. Indeed, when I examined the census to determine whether husbands were living with their wives, taking class taken into consideration, I observed certain correlations that helped to explain the eventual success of the middle-class wives in shutting down the restricted district.

In 1900, about 38 percent of all men were married in Skagway: 34 percent of middle-class men were married and living with their wives, but only 19 percent of working-class men were doing so (see table 1 in the introduction of this book). In other words, married, working-class men were less likely to have brought their wives north with them during the gold rush years than middle-class men.

By 1910, the frequency of married, middle-class men living with their wives had increased to just a little more than half, and by 1920, it was a little more than two-thirds. Amongst the working class, however, the frequency leveled out at just under one-third.

These statistics indicate that working-class men were less likely to marry, and when they did, they were less likely to have their wives with them in Skagway. During the boom years in Skagway, both working- and middle-class men were unlikely to have their wives with them. Both working- and middle-class men brought their wives north as the town settled into its permanent, transportation-hub status, but middle-class men were much more likely to be married and to be living with their wives.

Conclusion

During Skagway's boom years, men dominated Skagway's population, by a ratio of almost four to one. Bachelor men exceeded men living with their wives two to one among the middle class and four to one among the working class. Once the boom was over, by 1920, this ratio gradually had decreased to two married men to one bachelor among the middle class and one married man to every two bachelors among the working class. This analysis suggests that while the middle class married more frequently than the working class, the frequency of married working-class men increased over time.

Overall, these analyses indicate that during the first two decades of the twentieth century—a period synonymous with the Progressive Era—Skagway had more men than women, a larger working class than middle class, and that it was the middle-class men who tended to bring their families north with them. The analyses also indicate that the population was largely Euro-American with very little racial or ethnic diversity.

Appendix B

Summary of *United States v. Gius and Penglas*

In December 1902, the U.S. First District court charged Sam Gius and J. J. Penglas, proprietors of the Douglas Opera House, with keeping a house of ill fame. After losing the case, they appealed to the Nineteenth District Court in San Francisco, on the basis that the Alaska judicial system provided only six jurors. Because of this expected appeal, which the defense had warned it would file, all testimony was recorded during the original 1902 trial in Juneau. The typed transcript provides a fascinating glimpse into the inner workings of a dance hall in Alaska in 1902. What follows is a summary of this testimony. The full, 130-page transcript is on file at the National Archives, Pacific Alaska Region (Anchorage; now removed to Seattle), Record Group 21, U.S. District Courts, First Division, Juneau Criminal Case Files, 1900–1911, Box 9, File 340 "B (1)," *United States v. Gius and Penglas.* All quotations and references, except when otherwise specified, are from that document.

Alaska stipulated that common fame was sufficient to establish that a given business was a house of ill repute. Therefore, the district attorney called a number of witnesses in this case and asked them to describe the physical layout of the opera house and the activities observed in the house. They were also asked to indicate what they knew of the reputation of the place. These descriptions constitute the bulk of the deposition.

The witnesses described the Douglas Opera House as a two-story frame building measuring about 45 by 130 feet, very similar in size to Clancy's Music Hall in Skagway. "In entering the building on the lower floor," George Hill, U.S. deputy marshal at Douglas testified, "you enter the saloon part. In the saloon there is a bar and fixtures, a roulette wheel, and a black-jack table; and from there you go past the bar into the dance hall." The saloon was about sixty feet deep. Two swinging doors separated the dance hall from the saloon. "At the rear end of the [dance] hall is a stage; and back of the stage there is a number of rooms, I don't know how many."

The marshal then described the second floor: "Well, in going up stairs from the dance hall, you reach the second floor and there is an open space as in most dance halls or theaters with a row of boxes; these are all closed with doors and then curtains in front. Going around these boxes on the north side of the house you pass to the rear, and in the rear end of the house there is rooms [sic] there." Under careful questioning, the marshal acknowledged he had seen the insides of some of these rooms and that they were furnished as bedrooms. Other witnesses made it clear that there were rooms above both the saloon and stage areas, not just at the rear of the dance hall. Penglas, during his defense, admitted to a total of fourteen bedrooms, with a dozen women occupying them at the present time. He said that he furnished them the same way that he did in another enterprise he owned—the Northern Hotel in Douglas.

The upstairs bedrooms in the opera house were of the greatest interest to the prosecution. In addition, there were living rooms behind the stage, which a witness described as "good sized," covering the entire width of the opera house. One of the rooms behind the stage included a kitchen for the use of the people living in the opera house. The total of fourteen rooms probably included the five rooms behind the stage.

There were two methods people used to get from the first to the second floor: either by a stairway in the dance hall or by an outside stairway on the north side of the building. The prosecuting attorney was careful to establish that the marshal had often seen drunken women who would permit men to hold their waists and utter profanity in their presence as they accompanied the women up these stairs. The implication was that any woman who allowed a man to swear without apologizing for doing so could be considered a prostitute.

Besides the drinking and gambling that took place in the saloon area, the primary attraction of the Opera House was the dance hall. Every night a show was performed on the stage, at which time chairs were brought out on to the dance floor so that the audience could sit and watch the show. Men and their consorts could also watch from the boxes on the second floor. The chairs were removed from the dance floor between the acts so that the men and women could dance.

Once or twice a month the opera house presented shows that were open to the "reputable people of Douglas and their families." On those nights there was no dancing, an entrance fee was charged, and the chairs were set up on the dance floor all throughout the show. The "reputable people, men and women" could be seen upstairs, in the vicinity of the boxes. It was commonly understood that by attending only on Family Nights, "reputable women" could enter the opera house and still maintain their reputation. Men on those nights behaved like gentlemen, removed their hats in the presence of ladies, restrained their language, and confined their drinking to the saloon area.

On "regular nights," no entrance fee was charged, and the atmosphere was entirely different. When asked what activities he observed in the dance hall, the Douglas marshal replied, "Well, I have seen men and women dancing, and after they would get through with the dance they would go in and have a drink at the bar." The prosecutor wanted to make sure that he, the judge, and the jury all understood that the women who were present at the opera house on these regular nights were drinking and getting drunk. He asked, "With reference to the conduct of the men and women assembling there, with reference to their general deportment?" The marshal answered, "They would get full[1] and have a good time generally." The district attorney returned, "Have you seen women drunk in there?" to which the marshal replied, "Have seen them pretty well intoxicated, yes sir." The prosecutor proceeded in the same vein to establish that both men and women used obscene language, that men used profanity in the presence of women, and that the marshal had heard the word "bitch" in particular. He also established that the marshal had seen men with their arms around women's waists. Throughout his questioning of both the marshal and later witnesses, the prosecutor made sure that the jury understood that the women who frequented the Douglas Opera House on regular nights were no "ladies." The men danced while wearing their hats, used loud and coarse language, and smoked, and the women did nothing to discourage such behavior.

One witness intimated that women with "immoral" reputations would frequent the Opera House, although they were not specifically connected with the house. The defense attorney at one point tried to introduce testimony that stipulated that women in Alaska often frequented saloons and establishments such as the opera house owned by Gius and Penglas. However, as was pointed out, "women of respectability" were never seen at that place except on the family nights. Much of the testimony by both the prosecutor and the defense revolved around whether the women in the dance halls could be regarded as women with good "reputations" or not. The male witnesses either claimed they did not know their reputations or stated that some of the women were indeed known to be prostitutes. Witnesses, prosecution, defense, and jury all seemed to understand exactly what "reputation" meant in this context, for it was not defined in the court documents.

It became fairly clear during the trial that all the women in the opera house on regular nights were either actresses or women of less than stellar reputation. It was never firmly established whether all the women commonly seen in the downstairs part of the house were conducting side businesses or not, but both Gius and Penglas, when placed on the stand, did admit that many of the women were not there simply to have a good time.

Penglas testified that some of the women that worked for the house did not work on the stage but instead worked for percentages. Their job was to dance with the customers, get them to buy drinks, and in return they received a percentage of earnings from the bartender for each drink that was sold. They were also reimbursed for drinks they bought themselves. Ordinarily, the men paid to dance, then would buy drinks for both themselves and their partners. The men paid from 25 to 50 cents for drinks. Unfortunately, the court documents do not specify how much of a percentage the women earned. One source states that in Skagway during the winter of 1897–1898 their earning was 25 percent.[2]

Penglas further testified that the rooms upstairs were rented to the "ladies that works [sic] on the stage," and that he had no knowledge of what went on behind the closed doors. He charged $5.00 a week for room rent. This rent covered only the room and fuel. Food was not furnished. The women had to purchase and prepare their own food or make other arrangements. Under questioning, he admitted that not just the actresses but also some of the women earning percentages rented these upstairs rooms. The $5.00-per-week rent was withdrawn from their percentages or salaries. And while he and Gius provided housing for these women, not all of the women who were earning percentages lived at the opera house. Women who lived elsewhere would also come in and dance. Even the outsiders received percentages (see photograph in chapter 5 of the Douglas Opera House adjacent to several cribs).

Because they had to furnish their own food, some of the women, it appears, did not care to make use of the kitchen provided behind the stage. Two witnesses had worked as waiters at nearby restaurants. They had each been called to the opera house several times to take orders and deliver meals to the women who occupied the rooms. One waiter guessed that there were anywhere from twelve to fifteen women living in the house at any one time, always one to a room. The women would ask for meals at all times of the day. The other waiter stated that some of the women would stay for only a week or so and then move on, so he rarely got to know any of them, although he brought meals to them often. Despite the prosecution's attempt to get him to say he had heard men's voices in the rooms, he said he had only seen the women alone or visiting with other women. He also stated that the women he served in the rooms were the same women with whom he had personally danced on the floors below.

It seems likely that even the actresses would have needed to supplement their income. When asked about the salaries for the performers, Sam Gius stated they ranged "anywhere from sixty to eighty-five dollars a week [for the men]; ladies from $25.00 to $30.00 and as a rule $35.00; and there are ladies at $40.00 a week." One witness was an actress who was working at the opera house. She had her two children living with her at the opera house: a three-month-old baby and a four-year-old. She testified she was paid $25 a week and performed every day. This means after accounting for rent and food for herself and her children, she might have cleared $15, worth the equivalent of $400 a week in today's currency.[3]

It defies credibility to imagine that the women earning percentages could have afforded to pay $5.00 a week for rent solely by getting men drunk. And apparently the grand jury found this questionable, too. Gius and Penglas were each found guilty of operating a house of ill fame and each drew a six-month sentence in federal prison.[4] While their sentences were eventually overturned on the basis that the six-man jury system used in their trial was unconstitutional, the merits of the case against them were never questioned.

Notes

Abbreviations

ASA	Alaska State Archives
KLGO	Klondike Gold Rush National Historical Park
RG	Record Group
NA	National Archives
SBD	*Skagway Business Directory*
SHR	Skagway Historical Records (in ASA, RG 202)
SMD	Skagway Magistrate Docket (in SHR)
USCR	U.S. Commissioner's Records (in ASA, RG 506, Series 57, U.S. District Court First Division, 1897–1910)

General Note

All business directories were accessed through the online database of Ancestry.com, except for those indicated with the abbreviation SBD (see above list). The Skagway business directories have not been digitized or put online. They are cited by date and listed in the bibliography according to publisher under the general heading "Skagway Business Directories." The directories accessed through Ancestry.com are cited by city, state, date, and page number, where appropriate.

All international, U.S., state, and territorial censuses were likewise accessed through Ancestry.com. They are cited by date, state, county, town, and, if appropriate, page, or other finding number. Censuses are U.S. federal censuses unless otherwise indicated.

Preface

1. Rhodes, *Archeological Investigations*, vol. 3, *The Mill Creek Dump and the Peniel Mission*; Ray DePuydt et al., *Archaeological Investigations in Skagway, Alaska*, vol. 5: *Additional Investigations at the Mill Creek Dump and the Peniel Mission*.

2. Blee, *Sorting Functionally-Mixed Artifact Assemblages*.

3. Spude, "Red Light District Cribs."

4. Spude, *Mascot Saloon.*

5. Spude et al., *Eldorado!*, 55.

Introduction

1. *Daily Alaskan* (Skagway, Alaska), November 6, 1901.

2. USCR, Criminal Cases, Vol. III (OS549), November 5, 1901, 6–7.

3. *Daily Alaskan*, November 6, 1901.

4. Anzer, *Klondike Gold Rush*, 138–39. It is difficult to determine whether Anzer's memoirs are the genuine memories of a true Klondiker or a mish-mash of tales taken from old-timers. If authentic, Anzer must have been in his eighties when the tales were finally written down.

5. For example, see Bordin, *Woman and Temperance;* Butler, *Daughters of Joy;* Goldman, *Gold Diggers;* McGerr, *Fierce Discontent;* Morone, *Hellfire Nation;* Murphy, *Mining Cultures;* Petrik; *No Step Backward;* Porsild, *Gamblers and Dreamers;* Putman, *Class and Gender Politics;* Rosen, *Lost Sisterhood.*

6. Johnson, *Shopkeeper's Millennium*, 6–8.

7. McGerr, *Fierce Discontent*, 1–58.

8. Ibid.; Morone, *Hellfire Nation;* Powers, *Faces along the Bar.*

9. Morone, *Hellfire Nation;* Powers, *Faces along the Bar.*

10. Beyreis, "Middle Class Masculinity," 11.

11. Ibid., 75.

12. Beyreis's primary resources include Bederman, *Manliness and Civilization;* Carnes and Griffen, eds., *Meanings for Manhood;* Chudacoff, *Age of the Bachelor;* Frank, *Life with Father;* Griswold, *Fatherhood in America;* Kann, *On the Man Question;* Kimmel, *Manhood in America;* and Rotundon, *American Manhood.*

13. Putman, *Class and Gender Politics*, 99.

14. Ibid.

15. Ibid., 172.

16. Ibid., 145–96.

17. Johnson, *Shopkeeper's Millennium*, 135.

18. Butler, *Daughters of Joy;* Goldman, *Gold Diggers and Silver Miners;* Rosen, *Lost Sisterhood;* Hobson, *Uneasy Virtue.*

19. Ryley, *Gold Diggers of the Klondike;* Porsild, *Gamblers and Dreamers;* Naske, "Red Lights of Fairbanks"; Morgan, *Good Time Girls.*

20. Murphy, *Mining Cultures.*

21. Petrik, *No Step Backward.*

22. Blaire, *Madeline;* Rosen and Davidson, eds., *Maimie Papers;* Washburn, *Underworld Sewer.*

23. Simmons, *Red Light Ladies.*

24. Bird, *Bordellos of Blair Street.*

25. Seifert, "Sin City"; Spude, "Saloons and Brothels."

26. Furnas, *Life and Times;* Lender and Martin, *Drinking in America;* Gray, *Booze;* Anderson, *Alaska Hooch.*

27. Blocker, *American Temperance Movements*; Clark, *Deliver Us from Evil*; Timberlake, *Prohibition and Progressive Movement*; Johnson, *Shopkeeper's Millennium*.

28. Duis, *The Saloon*; Noel, *City and Saloon*; Dixon, *Boomtown Saloons*; Johnson, *Shopkeeper's Millennium*, 82.

29. Powers, *Faces along the Bar*; Kingsdale, "'Poor Man's Club.'"

30. Morone, *Hellfire Nation*; Jenkins, *Gambler's Wife*; Fabian, *Card Sharps*; Smith, *Alias Soapy Smith*; Spude, *"That Fiend"*; Porsild, *Gamblers and Dreamers*.

31. See in particular Stelzle, *Liquor and Labor*, 33–34.

32. Bordin, *Woman and Temperance*; Ward and Maveety, *Pacific Northwest Women*; Movius, *Place of Belonging*; Haarsager, *Organized Womanhood*; Morone, *Hellfire Nation*.

33. Cole, "Jim Crow in Alaska."

34. Kirke E. Johnson letter to Mrs. P. A. Johnson, Fon-du-Lac, Wisconsin, from Skagway, Alaska, March 17, 1898, KLGO, manuscript on file. The conversion of nineteenth- and early-twentieth-century dollars to their equivalents in 2013 (defined throughout this book as today's currency) was made with "The Inflation Calculator," http://www.westegg.com/inflation/.

35. *Seattle Post-Intelligencer*, March 5, 1898.

36. The author analyzed raw data from the 1900, 1910, and 1920 manuscript censuses of Skagway, Alaska, and entered that data during the mid-1980s into a computerized database program as a part of her doctoral research for the University of Colorado–Boulder. In addition to appendix A in this book, see also Blee, *Sorting Assemblages*, and Spude, "Bachelor Miners." Analysis of the 1910 and 1920 censuses was conducted on data entered into Excel databases by Doreen Cooper and the author in the 1990s. All three databases are on file at Klondike Gold Rush National Historical Park.

37. *Century of Population Growth*, 208.

1. Hell on Earth, 1897–1898

1. Spude, "Bachelor Miners," 24–26; Porsild, *Gamblers and Dreamers*.

2. Steele, *Forty Years*, 296.

3. Berton, *Klondike*, 43.

4. Thanks to Karl Gurcke for setting this story straight. He referred me to the following quote: "They always mix it up when they talk about how those boys found gold: they say Tagish Charlie was with them, but he wasn't. The one who found gold with Skookum Jim is Skookum Jim's own nephew, Dawson Charlie, brother of Billy Smith and Patsy Henderson" (Sidney, et al., *Life Lived Like a Story*, 38). Actually, the name Tagish Charley was used in a document listing the people who had staked claims on Rabbit Creek early on during the rush. Gurcke suspects that after the rush, the First Nation's peoples wanted to make a distinction between the two men from Tagish with the same Euro-American name, so they renamed one of the "Charlies." After all, the name "Dawson" probably would not have been in existence until the rush.

5. Ducker, "Gold Rushers North." By 1900, one out of every twenty non-Native people in Alaska was female. 1900 Census, Alaska, as indexed by Generations Archives, Heritage Quest, Sierra On-Line, 2001, on CD-ROM.

6. Thornton, *Ethnographic Overview*, 53–54; Robert Spude, *Skagway*, 6.

7. Adney, *Klondike Stampede*, 41–42.

8. *Chicago Daily Tribune*, August 19, 1897; *San Francisco Examiner*, August 21, 1897; Adney, *Klondike Stampede*, 54.

9. Adney, *Klondike Stampede*, 54.

10. NA-RG 21, Sitka Criminal Files, 1885–1900, Boxes 11–13; SBD, 1898; USCR, Vol. I (OS569), April 22, 1898, 238–84; NA-RG 21, 1885–1900, Sitka Criminal Cases, Boxes 14 and 15.

11. DeArmond, *"Stroller" White*, SBD, 1899.

12. NA-RG 21, Sitka Criminal Cases, 1885–1900, Boxes 16, 17, 19.

13. See data in Noel, *City and the Saloon*.

14. *Skaguay (Alaska) News*, December 31, 1897.

15. Anderson, *Alaska Hooch*, 144, 205, and 206.

16. SBD, 1899, 79; *Skaguay News*, December 31, 1897.

17. "Smith the 'Con' King of the West," *Denver Times*, August 7, 1898; USCR, Vol. I (OS569), March 9, 1898, 143–55. It should be noted that Frank Clancy was not one of those charged with gambling on March 9.

18. Haigh, *Political Power*.

19. Spude, *"That Fiend,"* 5, 6, 22–23; Smith, *Alias Soapy*, 104, 107–108; Haigh, "Political Power," 317.

20. Spude, *"That Fiend,"* 24–34.

21. Haigh, *King Con*, 75; *Dyea (Alaska) Trail*, March 11, 1898; Spude, *"That Fiend,"* 35–48.

22. Haigh, *King Con*, 75; *Seattle Post-Intelligencer*, March 16, 1898; *Dyea (Alaska) Trail*, March 11, 1898.

23. See, in particular, Brown, *Strain of Violence*; Brown, *No Duty to Retreat*; Abrahams, *Vigilant Citizens*; and McGrath, *Gunfighters, Highwaymen and Vigilantes*.

24. Spude, *"That Fiend,"* 35–48.

25. In the decades that followed, the word "boss" would evolve into the word "king," and Soapy would become, in legend, the "King of Skagway," due to this newspaper debate. Spude, *"That Fiend,"* 33.

26. *Seattle Post-Intelligencer*, February 12, 1898; *Dyea (Alaska) Trail*, February 25, 1898; *San Francisco Examiner*, March 16, 1898; Spude, *"That Fiend,"* 42–43.

27. *Skaguay News*, May 13, 1898; SHR, Lot Locations, 1897–1898; SHR, Deed Records, Vol. 1, 1897–1898; National Park Service, *Jeff. Smiths Parlor*, 3.

28. The story has been told hundreds of times. The original version was in the *Skaguay News*, July 9, 1898; recent versions include Spude, *"That Fiend,"* 71–86, and Smith, *Alias Soapy*, 524–42.

29. *Daily Alaskan*, July 15, 1898.

30. See, for example, *Toronto Globe,* July 19, 1898. For detailed analysis regarding these events, see Spude, *"That Fiend,"* 87–109.

31. NA-RG 21, Sitka Criminal Files, 1884–1900, Box 16, File 1022, *United States v. Mrs. M. J. Torpey.*

32. USCR, Vol. I (OS569), April 9, 1898, 192–213.

33. Ibid., April 22, 1898, 238–84; NA-RG 21, Sitka Criminal Cases, 1885–1900, Boxes 11–17 for December 1898.

34. *Daily Alaskan,* January 1, 1900.

35. USCR, Vol. II (OS568), February 10, 1900, 157–58.

36. USCR, Vol. I (OS569) and Vol. II (OS568).

37. Sinclair, *Mission: Klondike.*

38. John A. Sinclair Papers (in total), British Columbia Archives; Sermon, *Daily Alaskan,* July 11, 1898.

39. Sinclair, *Mission,* 70–71, 181, 253, 255; John A. Sinclair Papers; John C. Sinclair, "Rev. John A Sinclair."

40. DeArmond, *"Stroller" White.*

41. Ibid., 36, 42, 51, 60; Berton, *Klondike,* 148.

42. DeArmond, *"Stroller" White,* 21, 29, 66.

43. Simmons, *Red Light Ladies,* 139.

44. For example, the 1900 Skagway census lists 24 bartenders, gamblers, and clerks living at the Board of Trade Saloon and 5 gamblers and a bartender living at a hotel that was probably the Grotto Hotel and Saloon on Fifth Avenue.

45. A photograph dating to spring 1898 shows a sign on the building at the northeast corner of Sixth and State declaring the Red Onion Saloon. This building had only one story and does not appear to resemble the first story of the building that is now known as the Red Onion. Whether this Red Onion is the one mentioned by Stroller White or a previous business is not yet known. There was no Red Onion Saloon in Skagway in April 1898, when customs officials arrested 75 owners of saloons in Dyea and 30 in Skagway for allegedly smuggling liquor into Alaska. A Mr. Matthews owned a business of the same name in Dyea at the time. Dyea's population was beginning to decline as the Brackett Road over the White Pass was completed and the White Pass and Yukon Route railroad began construction. Skagway, on the other hand, was thriving. It seems likely that the business that was in Dyea closed down and moved to Skagway (USCR, Vol. I [OS569], 363). The Red Onion is a listing of the establishment in the 1899 business directory for the community, owned at the time by Peter C. Lawson and O. Frick (SBD, 1899, 143). The information for this directory was collected in the fall of 1898, and Stroller White remembered the saloon's presence in the community during the summer of that year.

46. A madam would not appear in the Red Onion Saloon until after the building was moved to its current location at the northwest corner of Second

and Broadway in 1914, after the restricted district was closed on Alaska Street. See the discussion in chapter 9 and in appendix B.

47. *Daily Alaskan*, August 2, 31, 1901.

48. Ibid., January 1, August 2, 1901.

49. Ibid., August 31, 1901.

50. Grimm's successor at the southeast corner of Sixth and State was the Totem Saloon, whose proprietor rented from owner Fred Ronkendorf. It began operation in August 1903 and closed in September 1905. The saloon sat empty until it was moved in 1916. *Daily Alaskan*, August 8, 27, September 5, 6, 1903, July 19, September 1, 1905; Robert L. S. Spude, *Skagway, District of Alaska*, 134.

51. *Skaguay News,* June 17, 1898. Emery Valentine, a jeweler, was an investor in both Dyea and Juneau. He is best known as the owner and builder of the handsome Valentine Building (1913) in Juneau. Valentine was the brother-in-law of J. M. "Si" Tanner, a prominent Skagway citizen, the man who rousted out the Soapy Smith gang in early July 1898 and went on to become one of the town's leading citizens for the next thirty years. Valentine became a Juneau city councilman and mayor. Atwood and DeArmond, *Who's Who*, 101; DeArmond, *Old Gold*, 64.

52. DeArmond, *"Stroller" White*, 18.

53. Ibid.

54. *Daily Alaskan*, February 1, 1900.

55. 1870 Census, East Machias, Maine, 211A; 1880 Census, East Machias, Maine, 308C; 1880 Census, Seattle, Washington, 257B; 1885 Washington Territorial Census, Seattle.

56. Quoted in *Seattle (Wash.) Daily Times*, December 14, 1915; 1885, 1887, Washington Territorial Censuses, Seattle; "Great Seattle Fire."

57. *Tacoma (Wash.) Daily News*, March 2, 8–10, October 17, 27, November 5, 1892; *Seattle Daily Times*, January 4, 1903, May 5, 1904. A fanciful poem by William Devere published in the *Tacoma (Wash.) Daily News*, April 8, 1892, about the Orleans Club in Jimtown, Colorado, lists a number of infamous gamblers at the betting tables. They include Big Ed Burns, Soapy Smith, and Pete Burns. Jeff Smith uses this poem as evidence that the older Pete Burns was a member of "Soapy Smith's gang" (Smith, *Alias Soapy*, 211). I disagree with Smith on this point, as the poet calls this a heterogeneous gang. While Smith believes the poem describes a real event, I interpret it as a fanciful allegory. The Seattle newspapers indicate that Burns was in Seattle during the time the event Devere describes, and I believe Devere was simply making a statement about gamblers in general, not documenting a historical event.

58. *Tacoma (Wash.) Daily News*, March 2, 1892.

59. Putman, *Class and Gender Politics*, 96.

60. Ibid., 61–62.

61. *Morning Oregonian* (Portland), June 29, 1897.

62. SHR, Lot Locations, Vol. 19, 1897–1989, 8.

63. *Skaguay News*, November 25, 1897, February 11, June 17, December 9, 1898, September 7, 9, 1899; March 24, 28, 1900; April 20, 1901; March 9, 1902; USCR, Vol. I (OS569), April 22, 1898.

64. *Daily Alaskan*, January 9, 1900.

65. *Daily Alaskan*, March 1, 1900.

66. Frank Norris compiled a listing of advertisements from the *Dyea (Alaska) Trail.* Jeff Smith claims that "Clancy & Co. included Soapy Smith as an investor" (Smith, *Alias Soapy*, 523), but he provides no evidence supporting this interpretation, other than speculation that Soapy may have housed his roulette table in the establishment. Written documentation indicates only that Smith leased his "parlor" from Frank Clancy. See Spude, *"That Fiend,"* 53; *Skaguay News*, May 13, 1898; *Daily Alaskan*, May 16, 1898.

67. *Skaguay News*, October 14, November 25, 1898. Perhaps this roulette wheel is the same as the one that has become known as Soapy's. See Soapy Smith's Soap Box, http://soapysmiths.blogspot.com/2014/01/soapy-smiths-roulette-wheel-as-it.html (accessed May 7, 2014).

68. *Daily Alaskan*, April 20, 1900.

69. NA-RG 21, Juneau Criminal Case Files, U.S. District Courts, First Division, 1900–1911, Box 9, File 340 "B (1)," *United States v. Sam Guis and J. J. Penglas*; Steele, *Forty Years*, 296.

70. NA-RG 21, Juneau Criminal Case Files, U.S. District Courts, First Division, 1900–1911, Box 9, File 340 "B (1)," *United States v. Sam Guis and J. J. Penglas*.

71. Spude, *"That Fiend,"* 18–21.

72. Quoted in *Skaguay News*, December 31, 1897; NA-RG 49, Brief for Moore, 11.

73. Twain, *Roughing It*, 318.

74. *Skaguay News*, November 5, December 31, 1897; August 26, 1898.

75. *Daily Alaskan*, July 11, 1898; August 3, 1898; *Skaguay News*, July 15, 1898.

76. SBD, 1898, 79; *Skaguay News*, June 16, 1898; *Daily Alaskan*, August 3, 1898.

77. Smith, *Alias Soapy*, 523; *Tacoma (Wash.) Daily News*, September 16, 1898.

78. *Daily Alaskan*, March 24, 1900.

79. Rev. R. M. Dickey letter to Mrs. J. A. Sinclair, June 20, 1944, Sinclair Papers.

80. *Daily Alaskan*, January 1, 1901, May 13, 1915.

81. *New York Tribune* (New York City), August 18, 1897; *Morning Oregonian*, December 16, 1897; OMH, September 12, 1898; Boyd, *History of Synod of Washington*, 277–82.

82. Quoted in Hittson, *History of the Peniel Missions*, 37. See also Cox, *Lady Pioneer*, 7, 19, 42–44; Blee et al., *Historic Structures Reports for Ten Buildings*, 430; Rhodes, *Archeological Investigations*, vol. 3, *The Mill Creek Dump and the Peniel Mission*, 80, 83; Blee, *Sorting Functionally-Mixed Artifact Assemblages*, 135.

83. Cox, *Lady Pioneer*, 36.

84. Ibid., 47–48.

85. Ibid.

2. Saloon Reform, 1899–1901

1. Anderson, *Alaska Hooch*, 144, 205, 206.

2. NA-RG 21, Sitka Criminal Files, Boxes 11–13, 1897, cases 681–849. Skagway's cases are numbered 733–800.

3. DeLorme, "Liquor Smuggling," 151; Hunt, *Distant Justice*, 31.

4. USCR, Vol. I (OS569), March 3, 1898, 143–55, and April 9, 1898, 192–13.

5. USCR, Vol. I (OS569), March 22, 1898, 238–84, and April 22, 1898, 299, 346–57, 360–69.

6. Inflation Calculator (accessed January 3, 2014).

7. *Daily Alaskan*, January 16, 1899, 1; NA-RG 21, Sitka Criminal Cases, 1898, Boxes 16–17, cases 1061–1148.

8. Gruening, *State of Alaska*, 108.

9. *Daily Alaskan*, January 16, March 3, 1899; "Inflation Calculator" (accessed January 16, 2012).

10. *Daily Alaskan*, March 3, 1899.

11. Quoted in Anderson, *Alaska Hooch*, 223.

12. *Daily Alaskan*, May 26, May 30, 1899.

13. Ibid., May 30, 1899; New Year's Edition, January 9, 1900.

14. The *Daily Alaskan* reprinted the election register for the first licensing election in twenty-five issues of the newspaper, under a heading entitled "Looking Backward." The names, place of birth, place of residence, occupation, and date of arrival were given for each registered voter in the following issues: February 13–16, 25–28, March 1, 4–9, 13–16, 21, 25, 26, 28, and April 26, 1918.

15. SBD, 1899, 143.

16. Snow and Spude, *Historic Structure Report, Mascot Saloon Group*, 7.

17. Spude, *Skagway, District of Alaska*, 11.

18. For instance, see Noel, *City and Saloon*, 116. Noel uses per capita figures when discussing saloons in relation to population. When his statistics are adjusted for potential (male) customers only, the Denver saloons consistently served an average of eighty men apiece, similar to other population centers.

19. 1900 Census, Skagway, Alaska. This figure is for adult males eighteen years of age and older, and includes all the men in Skagway proper: the men on the railroad line camps, those in Smuggler's Cove, and those enumerated on the ships in port. The last group may well represent most of the transients typically passing through in spring or fall.

20. *Daily Alaskan*, June 12, 21, 1900.

21. Ibid., July 8, 1900.

22. Ibid., July 14, 1900.

23. Ibid., May 13, 23, June 4, August 30, 1902.

24. State of California, Department of Public Health, Vital Statistic, Standard Certificate of Death, No. 34–050987; 1880 Census, Rock Roe, Arkansas, 7; 1900 Census, Skagway, Alaska, 100; 1910 Census, Skagway, Alaska, family no. 324; Voter Registration, SHR, 1908–1914.

25. USCR, Vol. I (OS569), April 22, 1898, 238–84.

26. DeArmond, "*Stroller*" *White*, 35.

27. 1900 Census, Skagway, Alaska, 100, household no. 990.

28. USCR, Vol. II (OS568), July 11, 1901, 558–59.

29. SHR, Deed Records, Vol. 4, 1906, 90–91.

30. SBD, 1899, 79.

31. Ibid., 105.

32. *Daily Alaskan*, January 9, 1900.

33. Ibid., April 5, 1900; January 1, 1901.

34. *Biographical Directory of the United States Congress*, "Hearst, George 1820–1891."

35. *Daily Alaskan*, October 13, 19, 1900.

36. Ibid., May 5, 1901. It has not been possible to verify whether Abbie Atkins and the "niece" of George Hearst were one and the same person. However, some of Hearst's father's family went to Texas in the 1850s, so it is possible that the two were distant cousins.

37. *Daily Alaskan*, November 1, 3, December 12, 1901, January 31, May 20, 1902.

38. *Daily Alaskan*, May 25, August 16, 1902, December 6, 1903, July 7, 1904.

39. USCR, Vol. I (OS569), March 9, 1898, 143–55; NA-RG 21, Sitka Criminal Files, case 1333, *United States v. Lee Guthrie*; 1900 Census, Skagway, Alaska, 100; NA-RG 21, Juneau Criminal Files, 1900–1960, Box 3, cases S-145, 146, 148, 149, 151–55.

40. *Daily Alaskan*, September 6, 1900.

41. Ward and Maveety, *Pacific Northwest Women*; Haarsager, *Organized Womanhood*; Movius, *Place of Belonging*.

42. *Daily Alaskan*, May 22, 1900, January 1, 1901, March 27, 1901.

43. Ancestry.com, Shorthill Family Tree (accessed January 9, 2014).

44. Washington State and Territorial Censuses, 1850–90; 1880 Census, Trego, Kansas, 305A; Tacoma, Washington, business directories, 1889–1891.

45. 1900 Census, Skagway, Alaska, 27; SBD, 1899, 133, 134, 139; 1901, 850, 856; 1903, 247–48; 1905, 362, 368; Tacoma business directories, 1893, 1895, 1897; William Werner Photographic Collection, Alaska State Library, Juneau, Alaska.

46. *Tacoma (Wash.) Daily News*, August 22, 25, 1892; March 22, 1893, February 7, 1895; *Morning Oregonian*, October 23, 27–31, November 3, 6, 1896; *Evansville (Ind.) Courier and Press*, November 4, 1896; Shorthill, "Memories," 103–105, 121–22.

47. *Daily Alaskan*, March 27, 1901, September 23, 1900.

48. Ibid., March 27, 1901.

49. Ibid., September 23, 1900.

50. Ibid., September 23, 26, 1900.

51. Ibid., October 12, 1900.

52. Ibid., September 27, 1900.

53. Ibid., October 14, 1900.

54. ASA, RG 506, Series 66, Book 1363, 1900–1902. This source gives Ronkendorf and Chisholm's last names only. While there is substantial newspaper, deed, and tax record evidence to tie Fred Ronkendorf to the Senate Saloon, less is known about the man named Chisholm and his connection to this property. "A. Chisholm" is listed in the 1900 census of Skagway. Alexander or Alex Chisholm appears several times in various Polk and Co. business directories for Alaska and the Yukon. Between 1909 and 1912, Chisholm was listed as a bartender in Dawson, and between 1901 and 1907, he was listed as either a miner or a hardware store owner. It seems likely that Alexander was the Chisholm that partnered with Ronkendorf at the Senate Saloon. Ronkendorf was actually better known as a baker with a bakery on Sixth Avenue, and probably left the day-to-day operations to Alexander Chisholm.

55. Ibid., Book 1284, 1902–1903.

56. *Daily Alaskan*, January 1, 1901.

57. Ibid., February 16, March 2, 1901.

58. Ibid., March 15, 1901.

59. Ibid., March 19, 1901.

60. ASA, RG 506, Series 060.

61. *Daily Alaskan*, November 6, 1901.

62. NA-RG 21, 1900–1911,Skagway Criminal Files, Business Licenses, October 1901, cases S-72–95, 97–13, and 115–16; *Daily Alaskan*, November 6, 1901.

63. Beyreis, "Middle Class Masculinity."

3. A Restricted District, 1901

1. SHR, Deed Records, Vols. 6, 10, and 22; Spude, *Mascot Saloon*, 19–31; SBD, 1900–1902; ASA, RG 506, Series 060, 1899–1902.

2. *Skaguay News*, September 16, 1898.

3. See Washburn, *Underworld Sewer*, 45–52, for a scathing portrayal of the men who built and rented cribs in a large Nebraska city in the early twentieth century.

4. Simmons, *Red Light Ladies*, 31.

5. USCR, Vol. I (OS569), April 9, 1898, 192–213, Vol. II (OS568), February 10, 1900, 157–58.

6. *Daily Alaskan*, November 15, 1900, 1; USCR, Vol. II (OS568), November 14, 1900, 363–72.

7. Morgan, *Good Time Girls*, 40; *Daily Alaskan*, May 7, 1902.

8. *Daily Alaskan*, July 1, 17, 1902; USCR, Vol. IV (OS551), July 16, 1902, 4, July 17, 1902, 9–10, August 19, 1902, 19–20.

9. SHR, Ordinances, 1900–1908, Article 5, Sections 1, 8.

10. See Gusfield, *Symbolic Crusade,* for a lengthy discussion of token law enforcement.

11. USCR, Vol. II (OS568), November 14, 1900.

12. Porsild, *Gamblers and Dreamers,* 117.

13. Morone, *Hellfire Nation,* 302–308; Powers, *Faces along the Bar,* 55–64.

14. *Skaguay News,* January 13, 1899.

15. Putman, *Class and Gender Politics,* 58–61.

16. *Skaguay News,* January 13, 1899.

17. Ibid., March 17, 1899.

18. *Daily Alaskan,* May 10, 1903, September 13, 1906.

19. Ichioka, "Ameyuki-san," 1–21; Yamazaki, *Story of Yamada Waka.*

20. Ichioka, "Ameyuki-san,"4; *Daily Alaskan,* July 25, 1898.

21. Morgan, *Good Time Girls,* 273–74; Yamazaki, *Story of Yamada Waka.*

22. 1900 Census, Skagway, Alaska, 101–102.

23. Ibid.

24. USCR, Vol. I (OS569), May 9, 1898, 192–93.

25. USCR, Vol. II (OS568), July 6, 1900, 247–48, 250.

26. *Daily Alaskan,* November 16, 1900.

27. Washburn, *Underworld Sewer,* 45–52.

28. Ibid.

29. Ibid., vi.

30. Ibid., 52.

31. San Francisco, California, business directory, 1880, 496; 1885, 662; 1886, 677; 1889, 743; 1892, 790; Oakland, California, business directory, 1890, 465; 1891, 482; 1892–93, 296, 303; 1894, 255; 1896, 254; 1895, 252; 1897, 280.

32. 1900 Census, Skagway, Alaska, 114; *Daily Alaskan,* January 9, 1900.

33. *Daily Alaskan,* January 1, 1901.

34. SHR, Deed Records, Vols. 1, 2, 5, 6, and Book 3.

35. *Daily Alaskan,* January 1, 1901.

36. SHR, Deed Records, Vols. 1, 2, 5, 6, and Book 3.

37. *Skaguay News,* October 14, 1898.

38. Ibid.

39. Ibid., January 27, 1899.

40. *Daily Alaskan,* August 19, 1900.

41. 1900 Census, Skagway, Alaska, 114.

42. SBD, 1903, 238; 1910 Census, Skagway, Alaska; SHR, Marriage Book 1, Certificate 210, 163; SHR, Birth Book 1, Certificate 14; SHR, Birth Book 2, Certificates 43 and 104; SHR, Deed Records, Vol. 9, 1916, 53–54, 276, 277; SHR, Deed Records, Vol. 8, 1908, 531; *Daily Alaskan,* January 5, 1918.

43. *Daily Alaskan,* September 7, 9, 1899; SBD, 1899, 79.

44. Ibid., February 27, May 25, 26, 1901.

45. Ibid., April 3, 1901.

46. USCR, Vol. II (OS568), April 1, 1901, 449–50.

47. USCR, Vol. II (OS568), April 2, 1901, 451–52; *Daily Alaskan*, April 4, 1901.

48. *Daily Alaskan*, April 10, 11, 1901.

49. Ibid., April 11, 1901.

50. Ichioka, "Ameyuki-san"; U.S. Congress, Public Law 68–139, 43 Statute 153.

51. SHR, Deed Records, Vol. 5, 218–19, and 416–20.

52. A derogatory term for an African American.

53. *Daily Alaskan*, April 10, 1901.

54. Ibid.

55. SHR, Minutes of the First Common Council, Vol. 2, 1900–1903, 212–16.

56. *Daily Alaskan*, April 11, 1901.

57. Ibid.

58. Ibid.

59. Ibid., April 23, 1901.

60. Ibid.

61. Ibid.; SHR, Minutes of the First Common Council, Vol. 2, 1900–1903, 212.

62. Atwood and DeArmond, *Who's Who*, 100.

63. *Daily Alaskan*, October 12, 1900, March 19, 1901.

64. Ibid., August 21, 1901.

65. Ibid., February 5, 1903.

66. Ibid., April 23, 1915.

67. Haarsager, *Organized Womanhood*, 60, 69.

68. SBD, 1901–1912.

69. Morone, *Hellfire Nation*.

70. SHR, Tax Records, 1901.

71. *Daily Alaskan*, April 10, 1900.

72. Ibid., January 29, 1901.

73. Ibid., April 4, 1901.

74. Beyreis, "Middle Class Masculinity."

4. Behind Red Curtains, 1901–1906

1. Prostitutes of the time were notorious for frequently changing their names, taking on new identities whenever the old life became wearisome, no longer lucrative, or their legal troubles caught up with them. Searches of Pueblo, Colorado, newspapers and historical documents, including an 1895 Colorado State Census, yielded no Maggie Marshall, which was no surprise. Pop Corn Kate seems to have been a sobriquet acquired by Marshall in the far north. There was a Maggie Marshall in New York City in 1900, but she was probably not Pop Corn Kate. Dodds, *What's a Nice Girl*; Joanne Dodds letter to Catherine Spude, December 8, 1999; Noreen Rife, special collections

librarian, Pueblo Library District, Pueblo, Colorado, letter to Catherine Spude, February 8, 2000. It was common to title prostitutes "Mrs.," regardless of their marital status. Apparently a woman's chastity was implicit in her title, more so than in her actual marital status.

2. 1900 Census, Skagway, Alaska, 127.

3. Anzer, *Klondike Gold Rush*, 138–39.

4. Ibid., 167–69.

5. Quoted in Anzer, *Klondike Gold Rush*, 168–69; Porsild, *Gamblers and Dreamers*, 102–106; Starr, *My Adventures*, 28–29.

6. Anzer, *Klondike Gold Rush*, 168–69, 188.

7. *Daily Alaskan*, May 13, 1900. Maggie Marshall was arraigned on charges of being drunk and disorderly on May 10, 1900. After she pled guilty, she was fined $5.00 plus court costs of $4.70, which were paid. C. A. Sehlbrede was the presiding officer. USCR, Vol. II (OS568), May 10, 1900, 223; USCR, Vol. III (OS549), November 5, 1901, 6–7; *Daily Alaskan*, November 6, 1901.

8. *Daily Alaskan*, November 19, 1901; USCR, Vol. III (OS549), November 18, 1901, 378.

9. SHR, Deed Records, Vol. 5, 508–509.

10. *Daily Alaska Dispatch* (Juneau, Alaska), December 5, 6, 1914.

11. Find-A-Grave.Com, Margaret J. "Maggie" Murphy Marshall, Timothy Murphy, Catharine B. Eustace Murphy; 1892 Census, Washington State, Pierce County, Tacoma, Line 39; 1900 Census, Washington State, Pierce County, Tacoma Ward 1, Enumeration District 0161, 6B, and Enumeration District 0162, 9A; 1910 Census, Washington State, Pierce County, Tacoma Ward 1, Enumeration District 0213, 6A; Washington Death Register for T. Granville Marshall, Pierce County, Gig Harbor.

12. *Tacoma (Wash.) Daily News*, March 5, 1897; *Daily Alaska Dispatch*, December 5, 6, 1914; Tacoma business directories, 1892–1950; Find-A-Grave.Com, Margaret J "Maggie" Murphy Marshall, Nicholas J. Marshall.

13. *Anaconda (Mont.) Standard*, February 10, 1900; 1900 Census, Washington State, Pierce County, Tacoma Ward 1, Enumeration District 0161, 6B; 1900 Census, Skagway, Alaska, 127.

14. Isenberg, *Wyatt Earp*, 80–82; Kirschner, *Lady*, 36–37, 42; Monahan, *Mrs. Earp*, 128–30; Tefertiller, *Wyatt Earp*, 12.

15. *Daily Alaskan*, July 19, 1902; USCR, Vol. IV (OS551), July 2, 1902, 11–12.

16. USCR, Vol. IV (OS551), September 5, 1902, 39–42; *Daily Alaskan* September 8–10, 1902.

17. *Daily Alaskan*, January 7, 1902.

18. Porsild, *Gamblers and Dreamers*, 131–33, discusses the role and relationships of prostitutes and their "macques" in Dawson, as does Ryley, *Gold Diggers*, 42–46, and Morgan, *Good Time Girls*, 92–96. All these references equate macques with pimps. With Skagway's strong connections to the Klondike, there is little wonder that the Klondike terminology would have been adopted in the early years.

19. Zanjani, *Goldfield*, 203.

20. *Daily Alaskan*, June 3, 1901.

21. USCR, Vol. II (OS568), July 11, 1901, 558–59.

22. Hunt, *Distant Justice*, 60–61; *Skaguay News*, June 3, 1898.

23. University of Alaska, Alaska and Polar Regions Collections, Skagway, Alaska Inquest Records, 1898-1959 (USUAFV6-432).

24. Ryley, *Gold Diggers*, 42–46.

25. *Daily Alaskan*, October 7, 16, 17, 1902.

26. Ibid., November 12, 1906.

27. 1910 Census, Skagway, Alaska, family #45; *Daily Alaskan*, November 12, 1906.

28. SBD, 1907, 458; 1909, 444; 1915:1, 486; 1917, 563.

29. Mazzulla and Mazzulla, *Brass Checks and Red Lights*, 49.

30. Mayer, *Klondike Women*, 151–52.

31. Ibid., 152.

32. NA-RG 21, Sitka Criminal Files, 1885–1900, Box 19, case 1272; SBD, 1899, 136, 143; USCR, Vol. I (OS569), December 9, 1898, 192–213; Mayer, *Klondike Women*, 244.

33. SHR, Deed Records, Vol. 2, 1899, 537 (lot 12, block 127); SHR, Deed Records, Vol. 5, 1903, 96–97 (most of lot 11 on block 59); SHR, Deed Records, Vol. 4, 1904, 233 (lot 1 on block 129); State of Washington, County of Skagit, marriage certificate no. 311, Beryl Schooler to James Rowan, July 27, 1895. The marriage certificate and the 1899 deed are the only times Sarah Belle Schooler used her full name. All other documents specify Belle Schooler.

34. SHR, Taxes, 1900, 47, and 1901, 56.

35. *Daily Alaskan*, March 21, 1902.

36. *Daily Alaskan*, June 9, 10, 1903; USCR, Vol. IV (OS551), June 8, 1903, 219–20.

37. SMD, Vol. 8, 1903–1907, 4–15.

38. *Daily Alaskan*, April 5, 1903, September 25, 1903; NA-RG 21, 1901–1909, Box 4, case S-166.

39. SMD, Vol. 8, 1903–1907, 6, 100, 153, 204, 232, 264, 271, 287.

40. SHR, Deed Records, Vol. 6, 1905, 196–97.

41. Ibid., 292.

42. Petrik, *No Step Backward*, 61.

43. SHR, Deed Records, Vol. 1, 1899.

44. Ibid., Vol. 4, 1906, 224–25.

45. *Daily Alaskan*, August 2, 1901.

46. Ibid.

47. Ibid.

48. Ibid., November 6, 1901.

49. USCR, Vol. IV (OS551), September 9, 1902, 51–52.

50. NA-RG 21, Skagway Criminal Files, 1901–1909, Box 3, case S-127, Journal A, 477.

51. *Daily Alaskan,* October 14, 1902.

52. Ibid., October 16, 1902.

53. NA-RG 21, Skagway Criminal Files, 1901–1909, Box 3, case S-127, Journal A, 477; *Daily Alaskan,* October 15–17, 1902.

54. SHR, Deed Records, Vol. 5, 1903, 366–67; Inflation Calculator (accessed May 10, 2014).

55. *Daily Alaskan,* November 4, 1902; Inflation Calculator (accessed May 10, 2014).

56. *Daily Alaskan,* April 11, 1903.

57. SMD, Vol. 8, 1903–1907, 4–15; USCR, Vol. IV (OS551), September 24, 1903, 272–84; *Daily Alaskan,* September 25, 1903.

58. SMD, Vol. 8, 1903–1907, 4, 58, 103, 137, 179.

59. SHR, Tax Records, Vol. 40, 1904, 33.

60. SHR, Tax Records, Vols. 40–43 and 45, 1904–1907, 1912.

61. SHR, Minutes of the City Council, Vol. 4, 1907–1910, November 1, 1909, 336.

62. SHR, Taxes, Vols. 36–43, and Vol. 45, 1900–1907, 1912.

63. Certificate of Death, Oregon State Board of Health, State Registered No. 25, Klamath County, Klamath Falls, Local Registered No. 18; 1870 Census, Lyon, Missouri, 827–28; 1880 Census, Jackson, Oregon 59B; *Evening Herald* (Klamath Falls, Oreg.), October 13, 1921.

64. 1900 Census, Skagway, Alaska, household no. 474; 1910 Census, Wrangell, Alaska, 233; 1920 Census, Visitación, California, 1A; SHR, Voter Registration, 1914.

65. SHR, Deed Records, Vol. 4, 1904, 116–18.

66. 1900 Census, Skagway, Alaska, household no. 474.

67. SMD, Vol. 8, 1903–1907, 29, 30, 32, 35, 36, 38, 39, 45, 46, 71–78, 81, 82, 114–21.

68. SHR, Deed Records, Vol. 5, 1901–1903, 2.

69. SHR, Deed Records, Vol. 5, 1901–1903, 508–509.

70. *Daily Alaskan,* September 12, 1902; SBD 1903, 234.

71. SHR, Deed Records, Vol. 5, 1901–1903, 509–10.

72. KLGO Research Library, S059/1,107.

73. SHR, Deed Records, Vol. 7, 1908, 190–91.

74. *Daily Alaskan,* January 25–27, 30, 31, February 1, 16, 1905; SMD, Vol. 8, 1903–1907, 218, 220, 228–29.

75. SHR, Marriage Certificate of John Powers and Fannie Kiger, signed March 17, 1908, by H. B. LeFevre, U.S. commissioner and ex officio Justice of the Peace; SHR, Deed Records, Vol. 8, 1912, 202–203.

76. SMD, Vol. 8, 1903–1907, 398, 476, and Vol. 9, 1907–1911, 52, 89, 132.

77. Ida's last name was spelled many different ways in the historic record. In this study, I have used "Freidinger," as that was the way she signed her name as a witness to a criminal case and that was the spelling used most often in the magistrate's docket. Other versions commonly encountered were Freidenger, Friedinger, Fredinger, and even Fredenberger. SHR, Vol. 30, Probate Register—Vol. III, 1916, 99; 1910 Census, Skagway, Alaska, family no. 43; *Daily Alaskan*, February 10, 1912; ASA, Probates, Ida Freidinger, 99.

78. *Daily Alaskan*, September 12, 1902; SBD 1903, 235. The address of 617 Broadway sounds very close to where the Skagway Inn is today, no doubt contributing to the local folklore that the inn was a brothel. However, I can find no evidence that a brothel ever existed south of the north half of the lot. At this point, Freidinger was probably leasing a small house that fronted on Broadway, on the south twenty feet of the north half of lot 1, which in October 1904 was purchased by Minnie Wallace (SBD, 1903, 235; NA-RG 21, Skagway Criminal Cases, *United States v. E. Maher*; SHR, Deed Records, Vol. 5, 1903, 519).

79. SMD, Vol. 8, 1903–1907, 261, 298, 331, 368, 399, 426, 474, 494; SMD, Vol. 9, 1907–1911, 52, 84, 94, 115, 133, 161.

5. Nurturing Vice, 1902–1905

1. Sanger, *History of Prostitution*, 35.

2. *Daily Alaskan*, February 19, 1909.

3. Ibid.

4. Ibid., April 10, 1901.

5. Haller and Haller, *Physician and Sexuality*, 191–234; Royden, *Sex and Common Sense*; Kinsey et al, *Sexual Behavior*; Lindsey, *Companionate Marriage*; Walling, *Sexology*.

6. Chudacoff, *Age of the Bachelor*.

7. Ibid.

8. *Daily Alaskan*, April 3, 1903.

9. Bateman, *Regulated Vice*, 16–17.

10. Powers, *Faces along the Bar*, 29–31.

11. McGerr, *Fierce Discontent*, 1–58.

12. Beyreis, *Middle Class Masculinity*.

13. Atwood and DeArmond, *Who's Who*, 11.

14. *Daily Alaskan*, December 2, 1902; *Daily Alaska Dispatch*, December 1, 1902.

15. *Daily Alaskan*, October 7, 1902.

16. Ibid., October 11, 1902.

17. Ibid., October 12, 1902.

18. *Daily Alaska Dispatch*, December 1, 1902.

19. Morone, *Hellfire Nation*, 192–93, 227–28, 240, 245, 285; Powers, *Faces along the Bar*, 48–61.

20. *Daily Alaskan,* October 28, December 4, 6, 17, 1902; *Daily Alaska Dispatch,* December 4, 1902.

21. *Daily Record-Miner* (Juneau, Alaska), December 17, 1902, 1; NA-RG 21, Juneau Criminal Cases, 1900–1960, Box 3, cases S-145–49, 151–55.

22. *Daily Alaskan,* January 17, 1903.

23. Ibid., February 21, 1903.

24. *Daily Record-Miner,* February 17, 1903.

25. *Douglas (Alaska) Island News,* January 7, 1903.

26. *Daily Record-Miner,* January 28, 1903.

27. Ibid., December 13, 1902.

28. *Daily Alaskan,* January 28, 1903; *Daily Alaska Dispatch,* January 26, 1903; NA-RG 21, Juneau Criminal Case Files, 1900–1911, Box 10, File *United States v. Fred Rasmussen.*

29. *Daily Alaskan,* January 28, 1903; *Daily Alaska Dispatch,* January 27, 1903; NA-RG 21, Juneau Criminal Case Files, 1900–1911, Box 9, File 340 "B (1)," *United States v. Sam Gius and J. J. Penglas.*

30. *Daily Alaskan,* January 3, 1903. Both Rasmussen and the Douglas Opera House owners appealed all the way to the Supreme Court. Their judgments were overturned in April 1905. *Daily Alaskan,* April 11, 1905, 1; NA-RG 21, Juneau Criminal Case Files, 1900–1911, Box 10, File *United States v. Fred Rasmussen*; NA-RG 21, Juneau Criminal Case Files, 1900–1911, Box 9, File 340 "B (1)," *United States v. Sam Gius and J. J. Penglas.* Naske and Slotnick in their text on Alaska history, *Alaska,* incorrectly state (p. 85) that it was a Fairbanks prostitute whose case, when taken to the Supreme Court and then overturned, resulted in the constitutional convention of a twelve-man jury in Alaska. Morgan, *Good Time Girls,* 265–66, indicates that Rasmussen's wife was involved with the business as a madam, but none of these authors define a "madam." Mrs. Rasmussen does not appear in the U.S. court documents. The objective of the reformers, of course, was to make the business owners responsible.

31. *Daily Record-Miner,* January 21, 1903.

32. *Daily Alaskan,* January 17, 1903.

33. Ibid., January 28, 1903.

34. *Daily Record-Miner,* December 18, 1902.

35. See Spude, *Mascot Saloon,* 19–44, for a detailed discussion of the changing landscape of the saloons in Skagway.

36. *Daily Alaska Dispatch,* December 20, 1902.

37. NA-RG 21, Juneau Criminal Case Files, 1900–1911, Box 9 and Box 13, File 465, *United States v. Louis Harris.*

38. NA-RG 21, Juneau Criminal Case Files, 1900–1911, Box 21, File 633B, *United States v. E. M. Barnes.*

39. *Daily Alaskan,* August 9, 1903, August 21, 1903.

40. Ibid., April 5, 1903.

41. Ibid., September 25, 1903; USCR, Vol. IV (OS551), September 24, 1903, 272–84.

42. *Daily Alaskan*, September 25, 27, 1903.

43. SHR, Register of U.S. Prisoners in County Jails, Skagway Jail Log, September 12, 1900–April 12, 1951; SMD, Vols. 8 and 9, 1903–1909, in entirety.

44. *Daily Alaskan*, November 29, 1903, 1; SMD, Vol. 8, 1903-1907, 48–51, 58–68.

45. USCR, Vol. V (OS550), December 9, 1903, 16–19.

46. *Daily Alaskan*, June 18, 19, 1901, June 13, 18, 1902, June 11, 12, 16, 17, 1903, June 16, 21, 22, 1904, April 5, 17, 18, 1905.

47. Spude, "Josiah M. 'Si' Tanner"; Spude, "*That Fiend*," 78–100.

48. SMD, Vol. 8, 1903–1907, 217–18, 220, 227–32, 234.

49. Ibid., 164, 184.

50. *Daily Alaskan*, January 25–27, 30, 31, February 1, 16, 1905; SMD, Vol. 8, 1903–1907, 218, 220, 228–29.

51. *Daily Alaskan*, January 25–27, 30, 31, February 1, 16, 1905; SMD, Vol. 8, 1903–1907, 218, 220, 228–29.

52. *Daily Alaskan*, August 30, 1904.

53. Porsild, *Gamblers and Dreamers*, 65, 122, 131.

54. Welch et al., "African American Military."

55. Ibid.

56. *Daily Alaskan*, February 1, 1905.

57. Welch et al., "African American Military."

58. 1910 Census, Skagway, Alaska, 13, household no. 164.

59. Hittson, *History of the Peniel Missions*; Cox, *Lady Pioneer*.

60. *Daily Alaskan*, February 6, March 6, 1905.

61. Ibid., October 1, 1905.

6. Saloons and the Working Class, 1902–1908

1. Powers, *Faces along the Bar*, 207–26.

2. *Daily Alaskan*, May 2, 1902.

3. Ibid., January 31, 1903.

4. Ibid., May 12, 1903.

5. Ibid., May 13, 1903.

6. Ibid., May 24, 28, 1903.

7. Ibid., July 15, 1903.

8. Ibid., July 19, 1903.

9. Ibid.

10. Ibid., July 19, August 9, 1903.

11. Ibid., August 8, 13, 1903.

12. ASA, RG 506, Series 66, Book 1284, 1903, License no. 132.

13. *Daily Alaskan*, August 2, 4, 8, 18, September 3, 1903.

14. Photograph no. B1–36–148, KLGO Research Library. Original photograph from the Alaska State Library, PCA-01–1703.

15. For instance, see *Daily Alaskan*, December 4, 1908.

16. *Daily Alaskan,* June 27, July 3, August 8, September 6, 1903.

17. Advertisements in *Daily Alaskan,* late 1904.

18. *Daily Alaskan,* June 7, 11, 1904; SBD, 1905, 355.

19. Ibid., November 17, 19, 26, December 3, 1904.

20. Ibid., December 12, 1904; quoted in *Daily Alaskan,* January 6, 1905, and *Daily Alaska Dispatch,* January 4, 1905.

21. *Daily Alaskan,* March 31, April 4, 1906.

22. San Francisco, California, business directories, 1889–1900; 1910 Census, Seward, Alaska, 92A; 1920 Census, San Francisco, California, 5A.

23. Skagway City Museum, Hotel Mondamin Register; SHR, Voter Registration, 1908–1914; *Daily Alaskan,* September 12, 1902, January 6, February 24, 1903; *Daily Alaska Dispatch,* January 18, 1913; SBD, 1903, 233, 235, 247.

24. Skagway City Museum, Skagway City Death Records.

25. *Daily Alaskan,* July 23, August 5, 8, 1904, June 22–24, 26, 28, 1905, May 31, June 1, 4, 5, 22, 23, 1906.

26. Ibid., July 3, 1903, December 24, 1904; *Alaska Club's 1905 Almanac,* 66; SBD, 1905, 367; 1907, 456, 467.

27. NA-RG 21, Juneau Criminal Files, 1900–1960, Box 4, cases 172, 175; SMD, Vol. 8, 1903–1907, cases 340, 350, 380, 381, 390, 391.

28. SBD, 1905, 367.

29. Barry, *Seward, Alaska,* 121; 1900 Census, Skagway, Alaska; *Daily Alaskan,* June 5, 1906; *Interloper* (Skagway, Alaska), May 5, 1908; SHR, Deed Records, Vol. 8, 1912, 97–107.

30. *Daily Alaskan,* October 23, 1906.

31. Ibid., October 30, November 7, 1906.

32. Ibid., November 6, 9, 1906.

33. Ibid., March 22, 1907.

34. Ibid., March 25, 27, 30, 1907.

35. Ibid., March 27, 1907.

36. Ibid., April 3, 1907.

37. Ibid., March 15, April 4, 1907.

38. Ibid., May 21, 24, 27, 28, 31, June 1, 5, 1907.

39. Ibid., July 1, 1907.

40. Ibid., May 4, 7, 1907.

41. Ibid., July 14, 1905.

42. Ibid., May 7, 1907.

43. *General Alumni Catalogue of New York University, 1906,* 126; 1916, 163; *Violet, Yearbook for New York University,* 50; *Alumni of Drew, New York Tribune,* April 15, 1896; 1900 Census, Grays River, Wahkiakum County, Washington, 8B; Washington Marriage Records, Lewis County, Reference No. SW-321-2-1-001753; *Seattle Daily Times,* November 8, 9, September 20, 1902.

44. *General Alumni Catalogue of New York University, 1906,* 163; *Seattle Daily Times,* December 1, 1907; *Bellingham (Wash.) Herald,* September 10, 13, 22,

1908, October 14, 1909, January 2, July 16, October 31, 1910; 1910 Census, Whatcom, Ward 2, Bellingham County, Washington, 7B; Bellingham, Washington, business directories, 1910–1917; *Daily Record-Miner*, July 16, 1904.

45. *Morning Oregonian*, July 14, 1901; *General Alumni Catalogue of New York University, 1906*, 126.

46. *Bellingham (Wash.) Herald*, September 10, 1909, October 31, 1910, May 13, 1911, March 11, 1915, April 25, December 6, 1916; *Olympic Daily Recorder* (Olympia, Wash.), May 19, 1920, July 26, 28, November 9, 10, December 28, 1921, January 18, June 3, August 29, October 30, 1922; *Morning Oregonian*, May 20, 1920, July 27, 1921, January 19, June 4, 1922, January 3, 1924.

47. *Seattle Daily Times*, December 1, 1907.

48. *Daily Alaskan*, February 28, 1901; September 4, 1902; December 7, 1908.

49. SHR, Deed Records, Book 3, p. 79, and Book 4, p. 182.

50. Census Returns of England and Wales, 1861, Kew, Surrey, England, 7; 1880 Census, Dallas, Texas, Enumeration District 057, 83C; 1900 Census, Kansas City, Missouri, 11A.

51. SHR, Deed Records, Vol. 2, 1898–99, 725, Vol. 3, 1900, 36, 79, 224, 469, 476–77, Vol. 4, 1904, 70–71, 157, 182, 195, 507, Vol. 7, 1908, 39–40.

52. Census Returns of England and Wales, 1861, Kew, Surrey, England, 7; New York passenger lists, 1820–1957: 1860, list 721, line 16, 1870, list 446, line 11; 1880 Census, Brooklyn, Kings County, New York, 1A; 1892 New York State Census; 1900 Census, Brooklyn, New York, 13A; 1870 Census, Brenham, Texas, 61B; 1880 Census, Austin, Travis County, Texas, 188C; 1880 Census, New Braunfels, Comal, Texas, 6D; *Texas Siftings* (Austin), November 4, 1882; *Fort Worth (Tex.) Daily Gazette*, July 2, 1883, May 20, 1887; *Dallas (Tex.) Morning News*, July 23, 1887.

53. *Morning Oregonian*, September 5, 1897, OMH, September 6, 1897; *Idaho Statesman* (Boise), September 6, 1897; *Dallas (Tex.) Morning News*, September 6, 1897.

54. *Skaguay News*, June 17, 1898; *Daily Alaskan*, January 1, 1900; SHR, Skagway Lot Locations, 228, 387; 1900 Census, Skagway, Alaska, 20, 413; SBD, 1901, 1903, 1905, 1907, 1923.

55. *Alaska Record-Miner* (Juneau), November 8, 1899; *Daily Record-Miner*, May 16, 1908, February 11, 1910.

56. *Daily Alaskan*, January 1, 1901; *Daily Alaska Dispatch*, May 25, 1900, May 11, 26, 1904, December 14, 1900, February 16, April 3, 1912, January 13, 1913, April 6, 1916; *Seattle Daily Times*, June 2, 1900; *Seattle Star*, May 27, 1904; *Jersey City (N.J.) Journal*, January 24, 1917; *New York Tribune*, March 23, 1918; *Daily Alaska Dispatch*, December 2, 1917.

57. 1910 Census, Skagway, Alaska, family no. 173; 1920 Census, Skagway, Alaska, 10; *Daily Record-Miner*, September 1, 1908.

58. SMD, Vol. 8, 1903–1907, Vol. 9, 1907–1911.

59. *Daily Alaskan*, July 20, 1905.

60. Ibid., April 4, 6–7, 1908; Spude, "Christopher C. Shea," 21, 22.
61. Ibid., April 24, 1908.
62. Ibid., June 2, 1908.

7. The Closing of the Seventh Avenue District, 1909–1910

1. *Daily Alaskan,* October 8, 9, 1908.
2. Stinebaugh Family Tree; *Daily Alaskan,* June 15, 1907.
3. *Daily Alaskan,* March 31, 1904.
4. Ibid., June 17, 1904.
5. Stinebaugh Family Tree; 1900 Census, Skagway, Alaska, 17; SHR, Voter Registration, 1908–1914; *Skaguay News,* July 1, 1898; SBD 1899, 129.
6. SBD 1899, 856, 1903, 249, 1905, 369, 1907, 468; 1910 Census, Skagway, Alaska, family no. 138.
7. *Daily Alaskan,* June 17, 1907, 4.
8. Ibid., April 23, 1901.
9. SHR, Deed Records, Vol. 7, 1908, 146–47; SHR, Taxes, Vols. 36–41, 1900–1905; KLGO Research Library, photograph no. SO 98/2007; Skagway City Museum, photograph no. A01–70.
10. McGerr, *Fierce Discontent,* 42.
11. SHR, Deed Records, Vol. 7, 1908, 147.
12. *Daily Alaskan,* July 18, 1908.
13. SBD, 1907, 463; 1900 Census, Skagway, 140; *Daily Alaskan,* December 2, 1907; Atwood and Williams, *Bent Pins to Chains,* 297.
14. *Daily Alaskan,* September 11, 17, 1908; Furnas, *Demon Rum,* 135.
15. *Daily Alaskan,* September 11, October 3, 21, 28, November 4, 1908.
16. Ibid., March 20, 1909.
17. Ibid., May 28, June 1, 1901, December 5, 1908, February 6, 1909.
18. Ibid., July 21, September 9, 1909.
19. Ibid., November 7, December 31, 1908, June 24, 26, 28, July 22, 31, 1909.
20. Riley, *Inventing,* 296–99; Blair, *Clubwoman;* quoted in *Daily Alaskan,* April 2, 1909.
21. *Daily Alaskan,* June 8, 1909.
22. NA-RG 49, Files 74–76.
23. *Daily Alaskan,* March 16, 1909.
24. Ibid., April 30, 1909.
25. *Skagway (Alaska) Police Gazette,* April 5, 1909.
26. *Daily Alaskan,* April 6, 7, 1909.
27. Ibid., May 5, 1909.
28. Ibid., May 22, 1909; SMD, Vol. 9, 1908–1911, 213.
29. *Daily Alaskan,* July 9, October 29, 1903; NA-RG 21, Skagway Criminal Files, 1901–1909, Box 4, case S-166.
30. *Daily Alaskan,* June 8, 1909.
31. Ibid.

32. Ibid., June 8, 1909.

33. Ibid., July 1, 6, 16, 17, September 10, 1909.

34. Spude, "Christopher C. Shea," 25.

35. Spude, "Josiah M. 'Si' Tanner"; KLGO, "Skagway City Councils" database; Atwood and DeArmond, *Who's Who*, 98.

36. *Daily Alaskan,* June 11, 12, 16, 17, 1903, April 5, 18, June 16, 21, 22, 1905, March 31, April 2, 4, 1906, March 30, April 4, 1907, April 4, 1908.

37. Ibid., April 10, 1910; SHR, Minutes of the City Council, Vol. 4, 1907–1910, 306.

38. *Daily Alaskan,* June 22, 1909; SHR, Minutes of the City Council, Vol. 4, 1907–1910, 300, 304.

39. SHR, letter to the mayor of Pasco, Washington, March 27, 1915.

40. SHR, Minutes of the City Council, Vol. 4, 1907–1910, 309–10.

41. SMD, Vol. 9, 1907–1911, 222, 223, 225–28, 232–43, 246; *Daily Alaskan,* September 20, 21, 1909.

42. Morone, *Hellfire Nation,* 265–67.

43. Ibid., 271–72.

44. 1900 Census, Skagway, Alaska, 69; SBD, 1903, 249; SBD, 1905, 368.

45. *Daily Alaskan,* May 28, 1903, August 30, October 13, 1904.

46. SHR, Deed Records, Vol. 7, 1908, 97, 337–338, Vol. 8, 1912, 53–55, 290; SHR, Tax Records, Vol. 45, 1912, 21–22.

47. *Daily Alaskan,* June 30, 1909.

48. SHR, Minutes of the City Council, Vol. 4, 1907–1910, August 2, 1909, 313–14, August 16, 1909, 318–19, November 1, 1909, 336.

49. SHR, Deed Records, Vol. 4, 1907–1910, November 1, 1909, 336–37.

50. SHR, Voter Registration, 1908–1914.

8. The Alaska Street District, 1910–1914

1. 1910 Census, Skagway, Alaska, family nos. 42–45, 253.

2. Ibid., family nos. 42 and 43; SBD 1903, 231.

3. 1910 Census, Skagway, Alaska, family nos. 42–45; SMD, Vol. 9, 1907–1911, 233, 235; Freidinger Probate, 99.

4. SMD, Vol. 8 and 9, 1903–1911; 1900 Census, Seattle, King County, Washington, Ward 7, enumeration district 0111, 13A; Seattle, Ward 5, enumeration district 0099, 38A.

5. 1910 Census, Petersburg, Alaska, 233.

6. SHR, Minutes of the City Council, Vol. 4, 1907–1910, 381 and 395.

7. SHR, Deed Records, Vol. 8, 1912, 388–89; SHR, Townsite Trustee Deeds, Moore Lawsuit, Roll 1, 236.

8. SHR, Assessment Tax Roll, Vol. 43, 1907, 9, Vol. 45, 1912, 9, Vol. 46, 1913, 9, Vol. 47, 1914, 9. The tax records are missing for 1908–1911.

9. SHR, Townsite Trustee Deeds, 310; SHR, Deed Records, Vol. 8, 1912, 533; *Daily Alaskan,* September 8, 1909.

10. SHR, Deeds, Vol. 8, 1912, 468–69.

11. SHR, letter to the mayor of Pasco, Washington, March 27, 1915.

12. *Daily Alaskan*, February 10, 1912.

13. Freidinger Probate, 99–104.

14. Ibid., 113–14.

15. Gove, ed., *Webster's Third New International Dictionary*, 1768.

16. Ibid., 2325.

17. Ibid., 388.

18. Emmet, *Montgomery Ward and Company Catalogue . . . 1897*, 604–605.

19. Kirby, "Brief History of Wayne County, West Virginia."

20. Washington State, King County, Death Record no. 2090, Augusta Flaharty; Censuses, Ceredo, Wayne County, West Virginia: 1870, 31A, 1880, 317A, 1900, 27A, 1910 2B.

21. Roma "Ruby" Margaret Miller Caudell's death certificate names Augusta Miller Flaharty as her mother and Clinton Perdue as her father. Obviously the birth father was not known, and Dewitt Clinton Perdue adopted Augusta Miller's daughter when she was born. Ohio State, Death Certificate for Ruby Margaret Caudill, March 20, 1957; 1910 Census, Ceredo, Wayne County, West Virginia, 2B; SHR, Voter Registration, 1908–1914.

22. USCR, Vol. V (OS550), December 9, 1903, 16–17; *Daily Alaskan*, December 10, 1903.

23. SMD, Vol. 8, 1903–1907, 404, Vol. 9, 1907–1911, 8.

24. SMD, Vol. 8, 1903–1907.

25. Ibid., Vol. 9, 1907–1909.

26. *Daily Alaskan*, February 10, 1912; SHR, Deed Records, Vol. 8, 1912, 468–69, Vol. 9, 1916, 60–61; SHR, Taxes, Vol. 45, 1912, 9; 1914 Sanborn Insurance Map, Skagway, Alaska.

27. Evans, *Madam Millie*.

28. Spude, "*That Fiend*," 153–55; Norris, "Showing Off Alaska."

9. Women's Suffrage and the End of Vice, 1910–1917

1. Spude, *Mascot Saloon*, 24–44.

2. Kingsdale, "'Poor Man's Club,'" 472; Powers, *Faces along the Bar*; Spude, *Mascot Saloon*, 36–44.

3. Morone, *Hellfire Nation*, 281–317; Haarsager, *Organized Womanhood*; Soden, "Woman's Christian Temperance Union"; Bordin, "Temperance Crusade."

4. *Daily Alaskan*, February 1, April 27, May 1, July 14, 1908.

5. Ibid., February 1, 1908.

6. Ibid., June 24, 1909.

7. 1910 Census, Skagway, Alaska.

8. For more detailed dates, owners, and lengths of operation of Skagway's saloons, see Spude, *Mascot Saloon*, 76–77.

9. Beyreis, *Middle Class Masculinity*; Frank, *Life with Father*, 126, 130; Marsh, Margaret. "Suburban Men and Masculine Domesticity"; see also, Carnes and Griffen, eds., *Meanings for Masculinity*, 122.

10. Harper, *History*, 713–14; Mead, *How the Vote Was Won*, 2.

11. Catt and Shuler, *Woman Suffrage*, 189; Harper, *History*, 713–14; *Daily Alaska Dispatch*, March 1, 13, 14, 1913; Territory of Alaska, *Session Laws, 1913*, 3–4.

12. *Daily Alaska Dispatch*, August 31, 1912.

13. Ibid., July 29, December 7, 1911, July 22, 1912.

14. Ibid., March 13, 1913.

15. Catt and Shuler, *Woman Suffrage*, 189; *Daily Alaska Dispatch*, February 14, 1911.

16. *Daily Alaskan*, April 9–11, 1914.

17. 1910 Census, Skagway, Alaska, family no. 93; SHR, Voter Registration 1908–1914; Washington State, King County, Death Record No. 485, Fred C. Flaharty; Roehr, ed., *Klondike Gold Rush Letters*.

18. SBD, 1903, 235; *Daily Alaskan*, October 7, 1904.

19. SBD, 1907, 460.

20. *Daily Alaskan*, September 23, 1907, February 6, 15, 18, 1908.

21. SHR, Deed Records, Vol. 10, 1922, 165–66.

22. *Daily Alaskan*, April 9–11, 1914; Spude et al., *Archaeological Investigations*, vol. 4, *Father Turnell's Trash Pit* (hereafter cited as *Father Turnell*), 75.

23. Spude et al., *Father Turnell*, 80; *Daily Alaskan*, June 14, 1905, August 2, 1918.

24. Spude et al., *Father Turnell*, 80–106; SHR, Petition, WCTU, 1916.

25. *Daily Alaskan*, October 16, 17, 1901.

26. Ibid., April 8, 1914.

27. Ibid.

28. Norris, "Showing Off Alaska"; Spude, "*That Fiend,*" 155–60; Willoughby, *Alaskans All*, 165–75; *Daily Alaskan*, December 10, 1897.

29. *Daily Alaskan*, November 6, 1912, December 5, 1916, April 14, 1917.

30. Ibid., April 6, 1914.

31. Ibid., June 7, 1916; Spude et al., *Father Turnell*, 93.

32. 1920 Census, Skagway, Alaska; 1910 Census, Skagway, Alaska. The lower number is for native-born and naturalized citizens eighteen years old and above in 1920 but does not include Native Alaskans, who were not considered citizens. The higher number is for the same group in 1910. The voting age was twenty-one. Alaskan women were allowed to vote in the 1916 election.

33. *Daily Alaskan*, June 7, 1916, August 22, 1916; Spude et al., *Father Turnell*, 93; Snow and Spude, *Historic Structure Report, Mascot Saloon Group*, 12.

34. *Daily Alaskan*, September 30, 1916.

35. Ibid., November 27, 1916, December 4–6, 1916.

36. SHR, Deed Records, Book 10, 190. The bottle is in the KLGO museum collection.

37. *Daily Alaska Dispatch*, November 19, 1916; Conn, "No Need of Gold," 24; Smith, "Prohibition," 178.

38. *Daily Alaskan*, December 11, 1916.

39. Spude et al., *Father Turnell*, 91–92.

40. Ibid., 91–92, 95.

41. Kazis Krauczunas, inspector in charge, Immigration Service, Department of Immigration, Ketchikan, Alaska, letter to the commissioner-general of Immigration, Washington, D.C., NA-RG 85, August 22, 1909; Naske, "Red Lights," 27–32.

42. Kazis Krauczunas, letter, NA-RG 85, August 22, 1909.

43. *Daily Alaskan*, September 15, 1909.

44. Kazis Krauczunas letter, NA-RG 85, August 22, 1909.

45. SHR, U.S. Jail Register, 38–39; Seattle, Washington, business directory, 1905, 682.

46. Roehr, ed., *Klondike Gold Rush Letters*, 32.

47. SHR, Deed Records, Vol. 9, 1916, 329.

48. Visitación is now part of Bisbane, California. San Mateo, California, business directory 1920, 10; SHR, Deed Records, Vol. 10, 1922, 34.

49. 1920 Census, Visitación, California, sheet 1A.

50. SHR, Taxes, Vol. 49, 1916, 16.

51. SHR, Deed Records, Vol. 10, 1922, 349, 390; SHR, Taxes, Vols. 39–75, 1903–1907, 1912–1943. The tax records are missing for 1908–1911.

52. *Daily Alaskan*, December 19, 1916, February 2, 1917.

53. Ibid., January 3, 1917.

54. Ibid., March 8, April 4, 21, 1917.

55. Ibid., April 21, May 7, 8, 1917.

56. A blind pig was a place that sold intoxicants illegally, such as a speakeasy. Gove, ed., *Webster's Third New International Dictionary*, 234.

57. *Daily Alaskan*, November 8, 9, 10, 1917.

58. Ibid., November 10, 1917.

59. Ibid.

60. Ibid., November 12–14, 1917.

61. USCR, Vol. V (OS550), December 9, 1903, 16–19.

62. SMD, Vol. 8, 1903–1907, Vol. 9, 1907–1909, Vol. 10, 1909–1913.

63. *Daily Alaskan*, November 16, 19, 20, 1917.

64. *Daily Alaskan*, January 16, 1918, 4; Juneau telephone directory 1915, 23.

65. SHR, Deed Records, Vol. 10, 1922, 165–66; SMD, Vol. 8, 1903–1907; SBD 1917, 574.

66. SHR, Deed Records, 1922, Vol. 10, 310, 402–403; Roehr, ed., *Gold Rush Letters*, 52; Meier and Meier, *Naughty Ladies*.

10. Retrospect, 1918

1. SHR, Taxes, Vols. 52–85, 1916–1962.

2. 1900 Census, Skagway, Alaska; SBD 1903, 223; 1905, 355; SHR Taxes, Vols. 37–41, 1901–1905, pp. 3, 4 (in each volume).

3. SHR, Election Register, 1908–1914; SHR, Deed Records, Vol. 9, 1916, 281; SHR, Taxes, Vol. 48, 1915, 4; 1920 Census, Santa Rosa, California, 136B; Stinebaugh Family Tree; 1920 Federal Census, Oregon State, Josephine County, Grants Pass, Enumeration District 212, 14A; *Daily Alaskan*, December 4, 1917.

4. Bateman, *Regulated Vice*.

5. 1900 Census, Skagway, Alaska, 1–150; 1900 Census, Alaska, Company L, 215–17; 1910 and 1920 Censuses, Skagway Alaska.

6. 1920 Census, Seward, Alaska, 2–15.

7. Bateman, *Regulated Vice*, 15, 21, 63.

8. Ibid., 16–17.

9. *Daily Alaskan*, March 20, 1909, May 18, 1915.

10. Bateman, *Regulated Vice*, 25; *Seward (Alaska) Daily Gateway*, June 27, 1918; July 1, 1918.

11. *Daily Alaskan*, June 24, 1914.

12. There were 86 unmarried men and 39 unmarried women in the 1920 manuscript census of Skagway.

13. Roehr, ed., *Gold Rush Letters*, 52.

14. *Seattle Daily Times*, December 23, 1923; 1920 Census, Seattle, King County, Washington, Enumeration District 265, 8A, and 1930 Census, Enumeration District 149, 18A; Seattle business directories, 1919–1930.

15. State of Washington, King County, Death Certificates, Fred C. Flaharty and Augusta Flaharty; Rathbun Family Tree, Augusta Miller.

16. 1930 Census, Hildebrand, Oregon, 60; Oregon State Death Index, Certificate nos. 55, 2336; Klamath Falls, Oregon State, Certificate of Death, Local Registered No. 18; *Morning Oregonian*, January 24, 1937; Find A Grave, Henriette "Kittie" Faith Wandsted.

17. *Seattle Daily Times*, May 5, 1904, December 14, 1915, April 17, 1917; Idaho State Death Index, 1890–1962.

18. California State Death Index, 1905–1929, Vol. IV, I–L.

19. SHR, Deed Records, Vol. 9, 1916, 281; SHR, Taxes, Vol. 48, 1915, 4; 1920 Census, Santa Rosa, California, 136B; 1930 Census, San Francisco, California, 263; California Death Index, 1930–1939, Vol. III, F-H, State File no. 50987, 2743.

20. Quoted in Barry, *Seward, Alaska*, 120, 133; *Seward Weekly Gateway*, January 29, 1910.

21. Barry, *Seward, Alaska*, 120; *Seward Weekly Gateway*, January 18, 1913; NA-RG 348, June 1912–January 1913.

22. Atwood and DeArmond, *Who's Who*, 100; Gruening, *State of Alaska*, 292.

23. Atwood and DeArmond, *Who's Who*, 98; Spude, "Josiah M. 'Si' Tanner."

24. *Bellingham (Wash.) Herald,* September 22, 1908, September 10, 13, October 14, 1909, January 2, July 16, September 11, October 16, 31, 1910, May 13, 1911, March 11, 1915, April 25, December 6, 1916, May 28, 1917; *Olympic Daily Recorder,* May 19, 1920, July 26, 28, November 9, 10, December 28, 1921, January 18, June 3, August 29, October 30, 1922; *Morning Oregonian,* June 16, 1918, May 20, 1920, July 27, 1921, January 19, June 4, 1922, April 22, 1923, January 3, 1924, April 11, 1925, June 12, 1956; 1910 Census, Bellingham Ward 2, Whatcom County, Washington, Enumeration District 0326, 7B; 1920 Census, Olympia Ward 6, Thurston County, Washington, Enumeration District 387, 2A; 1930 Census, Tumwater, Thurston County, Washington, Enumeration District 49, 3A; Bellingham, Washington, business directories, 1910–1913, 1916, 1917; Olympia, Washington, business directories, 1923, 1925; Portland, Oregon, business directories, 1953, 1955–1957; World War I Draft Registration Cards, Thurston County, Washington State, Roll 1992175; Oregon State Death Indexes, certificates 7199 and 15012.

25. *Daily Alaskan,* May 13, 1915, June 4, July 27, 1918; 1920 Census, Tacoma, Washington, 4B; Washington State Death Records, 1883–1960; *Morning Oregonian,* October 9, 1926; *Seattle Daily Times,* June 5, 1927.

26. *Daily Record-Miner* (Juneau, Alaska), November 1, 1903; *Daily Alaska Dispatch,* January 10, March 29, April 20, 1911, January 4, 1912; Spude, "Christopher C. Shea," 26–27.

27. Tacoma business directories, 1920–1924; Seattle, Washington, business directories, 1925–1935; 1940 Census, Los Angeles County, Los Angeles, California, Enumeration District 60–254, 1; California Death Index, 1940–1997; Find A Grave, William Shorthill (accessed January 24, 2013).

28. For published versions of Itjen's and Pullen's stories of Skagway, see Itjen, *Story of the Tour,* and Pullen, *Soapy Smith.*

29. Skagway City Museum, photograph, PC 93.02.091.

Appendix A

1. Data were initially published in Blee, *Sorting Functionally-Mixed Artifact Assemblages,* and in Spude, "Bachelor Miners." All three databases are on file at Klondike Gold Rush National Historical Park.

2. *Century of Population Growth,* 208.

3. *Historical Statistics of the United States,* 10.

4. Johnson, *Shopkeeper's Millennium.*

5. Ibid., 149.

6. *Historical Statistics of the United States,* 133–36.

Appendix B

1. "Full" was a common slang word for being drunk.

2. Steele, *Forty Years,* 296.

3. Inflation Calculator (accessed May 14, 2014).

4. *Daily Alaskan,* January 28, 1903.

Bibliography

Archival Collections and Manuscripts

Alaska State Archives (ASA), Juneau, Alaska
  Probates, Ida Freidinger, March 12, 1912.
  Record Group (RG) 202, City of Skagway Historical Records (SHR)
    Assessment Tax Roll, Vols. 36–79, 1900–1962.
    Birth Books 1 and 2.
    City of Skagway Ordinances, 1900–1908, Article 5, Section 1.
    Deed Records, 1897–1922; Volumes 1–15, Microfilm Rolls 2C–8C.
    Docket of the Municipal Magistrate of Skagway (SMD), 1903–1909,
      Volumes 8 and 9.
    Letters and Memoranda File.
    Marriage Records, Microfilm Roll 17A.
    Minutes of the City Council Meetings, Vol. 4, 1907–1910.
    Minutes of the First Common Council, 1900–1903.
    Ordinances, 1900–1908.
    Petition, WCTU, Phase II, file 4–6, November 6, 1916.
    Probate Register Volume 30–Vol. III, 1916.
    Register of U.S. Prisoners in County Jails, Skagway Jail Log,
      September 12, 1900 to April 12, 1951, Volumes 12 and 13.
    Skagway Lot Locations.
    Townsite Trustee Deeds, Moore Lawsuit, Roll 1.
    Voter Registration, 1908–1914.
  Record Group 506, U.S. District Court, First Division,
      Territorial Court Systems, 1897–1910.
    Series 57, United States District Court, District of Alaska,
      First Division, U.S. Commissioner's Records (USCR), Criminal
      Cases, Division No. 1.
    Series 60, U.S. District Court, First District, Clerk of the Court,
      Liquor Licenses, Petitions and Election, 1900–1917, Tom Murton
      Collection, folder 451.
    Series 66, Business License Register, 1900–1902, Book 1363.

Alaska State Library, Historical Collections, William Werner Shorthill,
    "Memories," unpublished memoir, 1943.
British Columbia Archives, John A. Sinclair Papers, MS-1061.
Klondike Gold Rush National Historical Park, Skagway, Alaska (KLGO)
    Historic Letter file.
    Photograph Collection.
    "Skagway City Councils," database on file.
Library of Congress, Geography and Map Division, Sanborn Fire
    Insurance Maps, Skagway, Alaska, 1914.
National Archives, Seattle, Washington (previously Anchorage, Alaska)
    Record Group (RG) 21, Records of the U.S. District Courts,
        District of Alaska, First Division, Criminal Case Files, Juneau
        and Sitka Divisions, 1885–1960.
    Record Group (RG) 348, M939, General Correspondence of the
        Governor of Alaska 1909–1958, file 4, Game Warden Matters, Roll 3.
National Archives, Washington, D.C.
    Record Group (RG) 49, Division K, Townsite Files, Selected
        Documents Related to the Skagway Townsite.
    Record Group (RG) 85, Records of the Immigration Department,
        Box 113, file 52484/28.
Norris, Frank. Compiled listing of advertisements from the
    Dyea Trail, 1897–1898. Manuscript on file, n.d., Klondike
    Gold Rush National Historical Park.
Sinclair, John C. "Rev. John A Sinclair 1863–1905." Copy of
    manuscript, n.d., in author's collection.
Skagway City Museum, Alaska
    Hotel Mondamin Register, 1898–1899, Vol. 10, FOE Aerie No. 25.
    Skagway City Death Records.
Spude, Robert L. S. "Red Light District Cribs." Manuscript on file,
    n.d., Klondike Gold Rush National Historical Park.
United States Congress, Public Law 68–139, 43 Statute 153.
University of Alaska, Fairbanks, Alaska and Polar Regions Collections
    Skagway Inquests, 1898–1959 (USUAFV6-432).
Welch, Deborah, Catherine Holder Spude, and Roderick Sprague.
    "The African American Military in Skagway." Draft manuscript,
    ca. 2011, in author's collection.

Books and Articles

Abrahams, Ray. *Vigilant Citizens: Vigilantism and the State.* Cambridge, U.K.:
    Polity Press, 1998.
Adney, Tappan. *The Klondike Stampede.* Vancouver: University of British
    Columbia Press, 1994. First published 1900 by Harper and Brothers.

Alumni of Drew Theological Seminary, 1902. Madison, N.J.: Drew Theological Seminary Alumni Association, 1902.

Anderson, Thayne J. *Alaska Hooch: The History of Alcohol in Early Alaska.* Fairbanks: Hoo-Che-Noo, 1988.

Anzer, Richard "Dixie." *Klondike Gold Rush As Recalled by a Participant.* New York: Pageant Press, 1959.

Atwood, Evangeline, and Robert N. DeArmond. *Who's Who in Alaskan Politics: A Biographical Dictionary of Alaskan Personalities, 1884–1974.* Portland, Oreg.: Binford and Mort, 1977.

Atwood, Evangeline, and Lew Williams, Jr. *Bent Pins to Chains: Alaska and Its Newspapers.* N.p.: Xlibris, 2006.

Barry, Mary. *Seward, Alaska: A History of the Gateway City.* Vol. 1, *Prehistory to 1914.* Anchorage: M. J. Barry, 1986.

Bateman, Annaliese Jacobs. *Regulated Vice: A History of Seward's Red Light District, 1914–1954.* Anchorage: National Park Service, 2002.

Bearss, Edwin C. *Proposed Klondike Gold Rush National Historical Park Historic Resource Study.* Washington, D.C.: U.S. Department of the Interior, 1970.

Bederman, Gail. *Manliness and Civilization: A Cultural History of Gender and Race in the United States, 1880–1917.* Chicago: University of Chicago Press, 1995.

Berton, Pierre, *Klondike: The Last Great Gold Rush, 1896–1899.* Toronto: McClelland and Stewart, 1972.

Beyreis, David Charles. "Middle Class Masculinity and the Klondike Gold Rush."Master of Arts thesis, Oklahoma State University, http://dc.library .okstate.edu/utils/getfile/collection/theses/id/3353/filename/3354. pdf (accessed March 9, 2013).

Bird, Allan. *The Bordellos of Blair Street: The Story of Silverton, Colorado's Notorious Red Light District.* Rev. Ed. Grand Rapids, Mich.: The Other Shop, 1992.

Blaire, Madeline. *Madeline: An Autobiography.* 1919. Reprint, New York: Persea Books, 1986.

Blair, Karen J. *The Clubwoman as Feminist: True Womanhood Redefined, 1868–1914.* New York: Holmes and Meier, 1980.

Blee, Catherine Holder. *Sorting Functionally-Mixed Artifact Assemblages with Multiple Regression: A Comparative Study in Historical Archeology.* Boulder, Colo.: PhD dissertation, University of Colorado, 1991.

Blee, Catherine Holder, Robert L. Spude, and Paul C. Cloyd. *Historic Structures Reports for Ten Buildings: Administrative, Physical History and Analysis Sections, Klondike Gold Rush National Historical Park, Skagway, Alaska.* Denver: United States Government Printing Office, 1984.

Blocker, Jack S. *American Temperance Movements: Cycles of Reform.* Boston: Twayne, 1989.

Bordin, Ruth. "The Temperance Crusade as a Feminist Movement." In *Major Problems in American Women's History,* edited by Mary Beth Norton, 215–24. Lexington, Mass.: D.C. Heath, 1989.

————. *Woman and Temperance: The Quest for Power and Liberty, 1873–1900.* Newark, N.J.: Rutgers University Press, 1990.

Boyd, Rev. Robert. *History of the Synod of Washington of the Presbyterian Church in the United States of America.* Seattle: Synod of Washington, 1909.

Brown, Richard Maxwell. *No Duty to Retreat: Violence and Values in American History and Society.* Norman: University of Oklahoma Press, 1991.

————. *Strain of Violence: Historical Studies of American Violence and Vigilantism.* New York: Oxford University Press, 1975.

Butler, Anne M. *Daughters of Joy, Sisters of Misery: Prostitutes in the American West, 1865–90.* Urbana: University of Illinois Press, 1986.

Carnes, Mark C., and Clyde Griffen, eds. *Meanings for Manhood: Constructions of Masculinity in Victorian America.* Chicago: University of Chicago Press, 1990.

Catt, Carrie Chapman, and Nettie Rogers Shuler. *Woman Suffrage and Politics: The Inner Story of the Suffrage Movement.* New York: C. Scribner's Sons, 1926.

A Century of Population Growth from the First Census of the United States to the Twelfth, 1790-1900. Washington, D.C.: U.S. Government Printing Office, 1909.

Chudacoff, Howard P. *The Age of the Bachelor: Creating an American Subculture.* Princeton, N.J.: Princeton University Press, 1999.

Clark, Norman H. *Deliver Us from Evil: An Interpretation of American Prohibition.* New York: W. W. Norton, 1976.

Cole, Terrance. "Jim Crow in Alaska: The Passage of the Alaska Equal Rights Act of 1945." *Western Historical Quarterly* 23, no. 4 (November 1992), 428–49.

The Compiled Laws of the Territory of Alaska, 1908. Washington, D.C.: U.S. Congress, 1908.

Conn, Stephen. *No Need of Gold—Alcohol Control Laws and the Alaska Native Population: From the Russians through the Early Years of Statehood.* Edited by Antonia Moras. Alaska Historical Commission Studies in History, no. 226. Anchorage: School of Justice, University of Alaska, 1971.

Cox, Mabel Holmes. *The Lady Pioneer: Pioneer Missionary Work in Alaska and the Northwest.* Roseburg, Oreg.: printed by author, 1968.

DeArmond, Robert N., ed. *Old Gold: Historical Vignettes of Juneau, Alaska.* Juneau, Alaska: Gastineau Channel Historical Society, 1998.

————, ed. *"Stroller" White: Klondike Newsman,* Skagway, Alaska: Lynn Canal, 1990.

DeLorme, Roland L. "Liquor Smuggling in Alaska, 1867–1899." *Pacific Northwest Quarterly* 66, no. 4 (Spring 1975): 145–52.

DePuydt, Ray, Gwen Hurst, Stephanie Ludwig, and Alfred Cammisa. *Archaeological Investigations in Skagway, Alaska.* Vol. 5, *Additional Investigations at the Mill Creek Dump and the Peniel Mission.* Anchorage, Alaska: U. S. Department of the Interior, National Park Service, 1997.

Dixon, Kelly J. *Boomtown Saloons: Archaeology and History in Virginia City.* Reno: University of Nevada Press, 2005.

Dodds, Joanne West. *What's a Nice Girl Like You Doing in a Place Like This? Prostitution in Southern Colorado 1860–1911.* Pueblo, Colo.: Focal Plain, 1996.

Ducker, James H. "Gold Rushers North: A Census Study of the Yukon and Alaskan Gold Rushes, 1896–1900." *Pacific Northwest Quarterly* 85, no. 3 (July 1994): 82–92.

Duis, Perry R. *The Saloon: Public Drinking in Chicago and Boston, 1880–1920.* Urbana: University of Illinois Press, 1983.

Emmet, Boris. *Montgomery Ward and Company Catalogue and Buyer's Guide No. 57, Spring and Summer 1897.* Reprint, New York: Dover Publications, 1969).

Evans, Max. *Madam Millie: Bordellos from Silver City to Ketchikan.* Albuquerque: University of New Mexico Press, 2002.

Fabian, Ann. *Card Sharps and Bucket Shops: Gambling in Nineteenth-Century America.* New York: Routledge, 1999.

Frank, Stephen. *Life with Father: Parenthood and Masculinity in the Nineteenth-Century American North.* Baltimore: John Hopkins University Press, 1998.

Furnas, J. C. *The Life and Times of the Late Demon Rum.* New York: F.P. Putnam, 1965.

General Alumni Catalogue of New York University, 1833–1906. New York: General Alumni Society, 1906.

Goldman, Marion S. *Gold Diggers and Silver Miners: Prostitution and Social Life on the Comstock Lode.* Ann Arbor: University of Michigan Press, 1981.

Gove, Philip Babcock, ed. *Webster's Third New International Dictionary of the English Language Unabridged.* Springfield, Mass.: Merriam-Webster: 1986.

Gray, James H. *Booze: The Impact of Whisky on the Prairie West.* Toronto: MacMillan of Canada, 1972.

"The Great Seattle Fire," http://content.lib.washington.edu/extras/seattle-fire.html (accessed January 14, 2012).

Griswold, Robert L. *Fatherhood in America: A History.* New York: Basic Books, 1993.

Gruening, Ernest. *The State of Alaska: A Definitive History of America's Northernmost Frontier.* New York: Random House, 1954.

Gusfield, Joseph R. *Symbolic Crusade: Status Politics and the American Temperance Movement.* Urbana: University of Illinois Press, 1986.

Haarsager, Sandra. *Organized Womanhood: Cultural Politics in the Pacific Northwest, 1840–1920.* Norman: University of Oklahoma Press, 1997.

Haigh, Jane G. *King Con: The Story of Soapy Smith,* Whitehorse, Yukon: Friday 501, 2006.

———. "Political Power, Patronage, and Protection Rackets: Con Men and Political Corruption in Denver, 1889–1894." PhD diss., University of Arizona, 2009.

Haller, John S., Jr., and Robin M. Haller. *The Physician and Sexuality in Victorian America.* Urbana: University of Illinois Press, 1974.

Harper, Ida Husted, ed. *The History of Woman Suffrage.* Vol. 6. New York: Fowler and Wells, 1922.

Historical Statistics of the United States, Colonial Times to 1970. Part 1. Washington, D.C.: U.S. Department of Commerce, 1975.

Hittson, Paul A. *History of the Peniel Missions.* Homeland, Calif.: printed by author, 1975.

Hobson, Barbara Meil. *Uneasy Virtue: The Politics of Prostitution and the American Reform Tradition.* New York: Basic Books, 1986.

Hunt, William. *Distant Justice: Policing the Alaskan Frontier.* Norman: University of Oklahoma Press, 1987.

Ichioka, Yuji. "Ameyuki-san: Japanese Prostitutes in Nineteenth-Century America." *Amerasia* 4, no. 1 (Spring 1977): 1–21.

Isenberg, Andrew. *Wyatt Earp: A Vigilante Life.* New York: Hill and Wang, 2013.

Itjen, Martin. *The Story of the Tour on the Skagway, Alaska Street Car.* N.p.: printed by author, 1934.

Jenkins, Malinda, as told to Jess Lilienthal. *Gambler's Wife: The Life of Malinda Jenkins.* Lincoln: University of Nebraska Press, 1998.

Johnson, Paul E. *A Shopkeeper's Millennium: Society and Revivals in Rochester, New York, 1815–1837.* New York: Hill and Wang, 1978.

Kann, Mark E. *On the Man Question: Gender and Civic Virtue in America.* Philadelphia: Temple University Press, 1991.

Kimmel, Michael. *Manhood in America: A Cultural History.* New York: Free Press, 1996.

Kingsdale, John M. "The 'Poor Man's Club': Social Functions of the Urban Working-Class Saloon." *American Quarterly* 25, no. 4 (October, 1973): 472–89.

Kinsey, Alfred C., Wardell B. Pomeroy, and Clyde E. Martin. *Sexual Behavior in the Human Male.* Philadelphia: W.B. Saunders, 1948.

Kirby, Wesley D. "A Brief History of Wayne County, West Virginia," 1926, http://www.wvculture.org/history/agrext/wayne.html (accessed January 8, 2013).

Kirschner, Ann. *Lady at the O.K. Corral: The True Story of Josephine Marcus Earp.* New York: Harper Collins, 2013.

Lender, Mark Edward, and James Kirby Martin. *Drinking in America: A History.* New York: Free Press, 1987.

Lindsey, Ben B. *The Companionate Marriage.* New York: Boni and Liverwright, 1927.

Marsh, Margaret. "Suburban Men and Masculine Domesticity, 1870–1915." *American Quarterly* 40, no. 2 (June 1988), 165–86.

Mayer, Melanie J. *Klondike Women: True Stories of the 1897–1898 Gold Rush.* Athens, Ohio: Swallow Press/Ohio University Press, 1989.

Mazzulla, Fred, and Jo Mazzulla. *Brass Checks and Red Lights.* Denver: printed by authors, 1966.

McGerr, Michael. *A Fierce Discontent: The Rise and Fall of the Progressive Movement in America*. New York: Oxford University Press, 2003.

McGrath, Roger D. *Gunfighters, Highwaymen and Vigilantes: Violence on the Frontier*. Berkeley: University of California Press, 1984.

Mead, Rebecca J. *How the Vote Was Won: Suffrage in the Western United States, 1868–1914*. New York: New York University Press, 2004.

Meier, Gary, and Gloria Meier. *Those Naughty Ladies of the Old Northwest*. Bend, Oreg.: Maverick, 1990.

Monahan, Sherry. *Mrs. Earp: The Wives and Lovers of the Earp Brothers*. Helena, Mont.: Twodot, 2013.

Morgan, Lael. *Good Time Girls of the Alaska-Yukon Gold Rush*. Fairbanks, Alaska: Epicenter Press, 1997.

Morone, James. *Hellfire Nation: The Politics of Sin in American History*. New Haven: Yale University Press, 2003.

Movius, Phyllis Demuth. *A Place of Belonging: Five Founding Women of Fairbanks, Alaska*. Fairbanks: University of Alaska, 2009.

Murphy, Mary. *Mining Cultures: Men, Women and Leisure in Butte, 1914–41*. Urbana: University of Illinois Press, 1997.

Naske, Claus M. "The Red Lights of Fairbanks." *The Alaska Journal* 14, no. 2 (Spring 1984): 27–32.

Naske, Claus M., and Herman E. Slotnick, *Alaska: A History of the 49th State*. Grand Rapids, Mich.: William B. Eerdmans, 1979.

National Park Service. *Jeff. Smiths Parlor Museum Historic Structure Report, Skagway and White Pass District National Historic Landmark, Klondike Gold Rush National Historical Park, Skagway, Alaska*. Anchorage: U.S. Department of the Interior.

Noel, Thomas J. *The City and the Saloon: Denver 1858–1916*. Lincoln: University of Nebraska Press, 1982.

Norris, Frank. "Showing Off Alaska: The Northern Tourist Trade, 1878-1941." *Alaska History* 2, no. 2 (Fall 1987): 1–18.

Petrik, Paula. *No Step Backward: Women and Family on the Rocky Mountain Mining Frontier, Helena, Montana, 1865–1900*. Helena: Montana Historical Society Press, 1987.

Porsild, Charlene. *Gamblers and Dreamers: Women, Men and Community in the Klondike*. Vancouver: University of British Columbia Press, 1998.

Powers, Madelon. *Faces along the Bar: Lore and Order in the Workingman's Saloon, 1870–1920*. Chicago: University of Chicago Press, 1998.

Pullen, Harriet S. *Soapy Smith, Bandit of Skagway, How He Lived; How He Died*. Reprint. Seattle: Sourdough Press, 1973. First published by Skagway Tourist Agency, ca. 1929.

Putman, John C. *Class and Gender Politics in Progressive-Era Seattle*. Reno: University of Nevada Press, 2008.

Rhodes, Dianne Lee. *Archeological Investigations in Skagway, Alaska.* Vol. 3, *The Mill Creek Dump and the Peniel Mission, Klondike Gold Rush National Historical Park.* Denver: U.S. Government Printing Office, 1988.

Riley, Glenda. *Inventing the American Woman: An Inclusive History.* Vol. 2. 3rd ed. Wheeling, Ill.: Harlan Davidson, 2001.

Roehr, Charles, ed. *Klondike Gold Rush Letters along the Trail of '98 from Dyea, Alaksa, to Dawson, Yukon Territory.* New York: Vantage Press, 1976.

Rosen, Ruth. *The Lost Sisterhood: Prostitution in American, 1900–1918.* Baltimore: Johns Hopkins University Press, 1986.

Rosen, Ruth, and Sue Davidson, eds. *The Maimie Papers.* New York: Feminist Press and Indiana University Press, 1977.

Rotundon, E. Anthony. *American Manhood: Transformations in Masculinity from the Revolution to the Modern Era.* New York: Basic Books, 1993.

Royden, Maude. *Sex and Common Sense.* New York: G.P. Putnam, 1922.

Ryley, Bay. *Gold Diggers of the Klondike: Prostitution in Dawson City, Yukon, 1898–1908.* Winnepeg: Watson and Dwyer, 1997.

Sanger, William W. *The History of Prostitution: Its Extent, Causes and Effects throughout the World.* New York: Eugenics, 1897.

Sidney, Angela, Kitty Smith, and Annie Ned. *Life Lived Like a Story: Life Stories of Three Yukon Elders.* Lincoln: University of Nebraska Press, 1990.

Seifert, Donna, ed. "Sin City." *Historical Archaeology* 39, no. 1 (January 2005): 1–141.

Simmons, Alexy. *Red Light Ladies: Settlement Patterns and Material Culture on the Mining Frontier.* Anthropology Northwest, no. 4. Corvallis: Oregon State University Press, 1987.

Sinclair, James M. *Mission: Klondike.* Vancouver: Mitchell Press, 1978.

Smith, Becky. "Prohibition in Alaska—When Alaskans Voted 'Dry.'" *The Alaska Journal* 3, no. 3 (Summer 1973): 170–79.

Smith, Jeff. *Alias Soapy Smith: The Life and Death of a Scoundrel. The Biography of Jefferson Randolph Smith II.* Juneau, Alaska: Klondike Research, 2009.

Smith, Kitty, and Annie Ned. *Life Lived Like a Story: Life Stories of Three Yukon Elders.* Lincoln: University of Nebraska Press, 1990.

Snow, David E., and Robert L. Spude. *Historic Structure Report, the Mascot Saloon Group, Historical and Architectural Data Sections, Klondike Gold Rush National Historical Park, Skagway, Alaska.* Denver: U.S. Department of the Interior, 1981.

"Soapy Smith's Soap Box," January 20, 2014, http://soapysmiths.blogspot .com/2014/01/soapy-smiths-roulette-wheel-as-it.html (accessed May 7, 2014).

Soden, Dale E. "The Woman's Christian Temperance Union in the Pacific Northwest: The Battle for Cultural Control." *Pacific Northwest Quarterly* 94, no. 4 (Fall 2003): 197–207.

Spude, Catherine Holder. "Bachelor Miners and Barbers' Wives: The Common People of Skagway in 1900." *Alaska History* 6, no. 2 (Fall 1991): 16–29.

————. "Christopher C. Shea, 'King of Skagway': Progressive Era Mayor and Game Warden in Alaska." *Pacific Northwest Quarterly* 99, no. 1 (Winter 2007/ 2008): 16–29.

————. "Josiah M. 'Si' Tanner: Southeast Alaska's Favorite Lawman." *National Outlaw and Lawmen Association Quarterly* 40, no. 1 (January 2006): 29–37.

————. *The Mascot Saloon: Archaeological Investigations in Skagway, Alaska, Volume 10.* Anchorage: U.S. Department of the Interior, 2006.

————. "Saloons and Brothels: An Archaeology of Gender in the American West." *Historical Archaeology* 39, no. 1 (January 2005): 89–106.

————. *"That Fiend in Hell": Soapy Smith in Legend.* Norman: University of Oklahoma, 2012.

Spude, Catherine Holder, Robin O. Mills, Karl Gurcke, and Roderick Sprague, eds. *Eldorado! The Historical Archaeology of Gold Mining in the Far North.* Lincoln: University of Nebraska Press, 2011.

Spude, Catherine Holder, Douglas D. Scott, and Frank Norris. *Archeological Investigations in Skagway, Alaska.* Vol. 4, *Father Turnell's Trash Pit.* Denver: U.S. Government Printing Office, 1993.

Spude, Robert L. S. *Skagway, District of Alaska, 1884–1912: Building the Gateway to the Klondike.* Occasional Paper No. 36, Anthropology and Historic Preservation, Cooperative Park Studies Unit. Fairbanks: University of Alaska, 1983.

Starr, Walter A. *My Adventures in the Klondike and Alaska, 1898–1900.* N.p.: Walter A. Starr, 1960.

Steele, Samuel B. *Forty Years in Canada.* Toronto: Prospero Books, 2000. (First published 1915 by Dodd, Mead.)

Stelzle, Charles. *Liquor and Labor: A Survey of the Industrial Aspects of the Liquor Problem in New Jersey.* Newark, N.J.: Anti-Saloon League of New Jersey, 1917.

Tefertiller, Casey. *Wyatt Earp: The Life behind the Legend.* New York: John Wiley and Sons, 1997.

Territory of Alaska. *Session Laws, Resolutions and Memorials, 1913.* Juneau: Daily Empire, 1913.

Timberlake, James H. *Prohibition and the Progressive Movement, 1900–1920.* Cambridge, Mass.: Harvard University Press, 1966.

Thornton, Thomas F. *Ethnographic Overview and Assessment.* Klondike Gold Rush National Historical Park. Anchorage: United States Department of Interior, 2004.

Twain, Mark. *Roughing It.* Hartford, Conn.: American Publishing, 1888. Reprint, Berkeley: University of California Press, 1993.

The Violet, Yearbook for New York University, 1896. New York: New York University, 1896.

Walling, William H. *Sexology.* Philadelphia: Puritan Publishing, 1904.

Ward, Jean M., and Elaine A. Maveety. *Pacific Northwest Women, 1815–1925: Lives, Memories and Writings.* Corvallis: Oregon State University Press, 1995.

Washburn, Josie. *The Underworld Sewer: A Prostitute Reflects on Life in the Trade, 1871–1909*. Lincoln: University of Nebraska Press, 1997.

Willoughby, Florence Barrett. *Alaskans All*. Boston: Houghton Mifflin, 1933.

Yamazaki, Tomoko. *The Story of Yamada Waka: From Prostitute to Feminist Pioneer*. San Francisco: Kodansha International, 1977.

Zanjani, Sally. *Goldfield: The Last Gold Rush on the Western Frontier*. Athens, Ohio: Swallow Press, 1992.

Online Sources and Other References

Alaska-Yukon Goldrush Participants. Database for *The Only Yukon-Alaska Directory for 1901*, as compiled by M. L. Fergusen, Barnes & Baber, http://www.familychronicle.com/klondike.htm (accessed May 17, 2014).

Ancestry.com, Provo, Utah, Ancestry.com Operations, Inc.

Census Returns of England and Wales, National Archives of the United Kingdom, Public Record Office, RG9.

Idaho Death Index, 1890–1962. Bureau of Health Policy and Vital Statistics, Idaho Department of Health and Welfare, Boise, Idaho.

New York Passenger Lists, 1820–1957, Microfilm Roll M237_203.

Ohio State, Department of Health, Division of Vital Statistics, Death Records.

Oregon State, Board of Health, Certificates of Death; Death Index, 1903–1998.

Rathbun Family Tree, http://trees.ancestry.com/tree/19004823/family (accessed January 9, 2014).

Shorthill Family Tree, http://trees.ancestry.com/tree/63990373/family (accessed January 9, 2014).

State of California, Department of Public Health, Bureau of Vital Statistics and Data Processing, California Death Index, 1905–1929 and 1930–1939.

Stinebaugh Family Tree, http://trees.ancestry.com/tree/64789457/family (accessed January 9, 2014).

United States Census databases. Original data: United States of America, Bureau of the Census, National Archives and Records Administration, Washington, D.C.

Washington State and Territorial Censuses, 1850–1895.

Washington State, Bureau of Vital Statistics, Board of Health, Birth, Marriage, and Death Records.

World War I Selective Service System Draft Registration Cards, 1917–1918, United States Selective Service System, National Archives and Records Administration. Washington, D.C., M1509.

Biographical Directory of the United States Congress, 1774–Present. http://bioguide.congress.gov/biosearch/biosearch.asp (accessed January 9, 2014).

Find A Grave, http://www.findagrave.com/cgi-bin/fg.cgi.

"The Inflation Calculator," http://www.westegg.com/inflation/ (for conversions to 2013 currency) (accessed May 2014).

Skagway, Alaska, Business Directories (SBD)

The Alaska Club's 1905 Almanac, The Alaska Club, Seattle, 1905.

Baird, Morgan. "Directory of Skagway Advertisers in 1898." Klondike Gold Rush National Historical Park, Skagway, Alaska, manuscript on file.

Directory and Guide, Skagway, 1899. C. Clinton: Skagway, Alaska, 1899.

Polk's Alaska-Yukon Gazetteer and Business Directory, 1903. R. L. Polk: Seattle, 1903. Also published in 1905, 1907, 1909, 1915–16, 1917–18.

Index